PATRIOT GANGSTER

PATRIOT GANGSTER

Volume 1, Evolution of an Outlaw

JEFF "TWITCH" BURNS

Mountain House Media

DISCLAIMER

I have tried to recreate events, locales, and conversations from my memories of them. To maintain their anonymity in some instances I have changed the names of individuals and places, I may have changed some identifying characteristics and details such as dates, physical properties, occupations, places of residence, etc. The conversations in this book all come from my recollections, though they are not written to represent verbatim transcripts. Rather, I have retold them in a way that evokes the feeling and meaning of what was said, and in all instances the essence of the dialogue is accurate.

FAIR USE NOTICE

This book contains copyrighted material the use of which has not always been specifically authorized by the copyright owner. I am making such material available in my effort to advance understanding of Outlaw Motorcycle Club culture, criminal justice, political, human rights, democracy, law enforcement corruption, scientific, and social justice issues, etc. I believe this constitutes a fair use of any such copyrighted material as provided for in section 107 of the US Copyright Law. In accordance with Title 17 U.S.C. Section 107, the material in this book is distributed for the purposes of providing commentary on and criticizing the copyrighted work, to support my arguments, enrichment of society, news reporting, and teaching about the realities of Outlaw Motorcycle Club culture and Undercover Operations.

Cover Illustration Copyright © 2021 by Cali Graphics Inc.
Cover design by Cali Graphics Inc.

SECOND EDITION
ISBN: 978-0-578-95350-2
Library of Congress Control Number: 2019907409

First Printing, 2021

To my beautiful daughter. If I could do it over again, I would do it differently.

ACKNOWLEDGMENTS

If you want to achieve greatness, you must surround yourself with great people and I have been fortunate enough to have surrounded myself with some of the greatest people on earth. The people on this list have touched my life in ways I can never explain, and their influence has made me a better man and American. I am truly honored to have had you in my life and can never thank you enough for being part of it. I extend my sincerest love, loyalty, honor, and respect to; my inspiration my daughter, Candace Burns, Stephanie Burns, Josh Binder, Irish McKinney, Dr. William L. Dulaney, Lucky Les (Bandidos MC), Gimme Jimmy (Bandidos MC), Boar (Sons of Silence MC), Paul Landers (Escondidos MC), Tack and Chalupa (Pagans MC) Sarge (Vagos MC, retired), Jason (Hells Angels MC), Colt (Legion MC), Big John and Diamond Dave (Warlocks MC), RoadBlock (Outlaws MC), Lil Dave, Benji Leyva and the rest of the Mongols MC, PigPen (Outsiders MC), Dr. Bart De Gols, Charles Tate, Congressman Jamie Raskin, and all the righteous motorcycle club members from Washington state and across America who helped change history with me and gave me something great to fight for and write about.

CONTENTS

DEDICATION   v
ACKNOWLEDGMENTS   vii

1   THE REUNION   1

2   EVOLUTION OF AN OUTLAW   10

3   THE BASICS   25

4   OUTLAW MOTORCYCLE GANG (OMG)
    INVESTIGATIONS: THE REAL CRIMINAL
    ENTERPRISE   41

5   IF THE TARGET OF YOUR INVESTIGATION IS
    NOT COMMITTING CRIMES, COMMIT CRIMES
    FOR THEM: THE BIRTH OF ATF'S ENHANCED
    UNDERCOVER PROGRAM   55

6   DIRTY DEEDS DONE DIRT CHEAP: ATF
    UNLEASHES THEIR RATSNAKES.   66

7   RUNNING WITH THE DEVIL   82

8   THE 2002 LAUGHLIN RIVER RUN RIOT   104

9   OPERATION BLACK BISCUIT   118

10 THE IN-BETWEEN YEARS   134

11 OUTLAW MOTORCYCLE GANG (OMG)
    TRAINING   168

12 PAPA IS KILLED AND STONEY CATCHES A RICO
    FOR IT.   178

13 PRAHHH-SPECT!   185

14 THE CONFEDERATION OF CLUBS   258

15 OPERATION BLACK RAIN   284

16 THE BEGINNING OF A REVOLUTION   288

17 UNITED WE STAND   317

18 OUTLAW MOTORCYCLE CLUB FUNERALS   330

19 NEVER LETTING OFF   338

20 TWITCH GOES GATOR HUNTIN'   343

21 MOTORCYCLE CLUBS AND RACING   367

22 THE SWISS   377

23 STEPPING UP OUR GAME   384

24 PULLING PATCHES   388

25 I KNEW I WAS GOING TO TAKE SOME HEAT   407

26 MOTORCYCLE CLUB TATTOOS   413

27 OUTSIDERS AND ALOHA   433

28 VICTORY IN WASHINGTON   446

ABOUT THE AUTHOR   475

THE REUNION

So why the hell would I write a book if I was an honorable 1%er, it violates the 1% code? The answer is simple, and it is because after thinking about it for a year and a half, I concluded that there is no reason for me to be honorable to men who failed to show me one-tenth of the loyalty, honor, respect, and brotherhood that I showed them for all those years. More importantly, I wrote this book to give the world a real and accurate look inside outlaw motorcycle club culture from a perspective unlike anyone else has ever been able to share, and to bring awareness to a culture that is being destroyed by a criminal enterprise comprised of members of law enforcement whose motive is careerism, profit, and fame. I wrote this book so that good men like me, men who seek adventure and want to commit to a culture founded on loyalty, honor, respect, and brotherhood will hopefully rethink their ideas and not waste twenty-two years of their own lives, destroy their relationship with their family, and go to prison or end up dead, for what in the end is all an illusion. I made it out the other side and I did it in "Good Standing" which I am sure will change as soon as my old club reads this book, but honestly, I do not give a damn what they say about me in an effort to save face for one of their best members quitting, so fuck them. America needs to know this story because our Constitution is being attacked, our freedom threatened, innocent people are being framed and murdered, and the outlaw motorcycle club culture is on the verge of extinction. I wrote this book because it is time to tell the truth about the culture, and my unique experience makes me the best person to do that. The truth is, we are not the gangster's law enforcement and the media make us out to be, but we are also not the choir boys we portray ourselves as. As with most things the truth is somewhere in the middle and hopefully my story gives you a much better understanding of this mysterious culture. It is important to mention that some of the names and details have been changed because I do not want anyone getting in any trouble, however it is very important to me that I don't shiny up my story any more than I absolutely have to. With that said, I hope you enjoy.

The last time I saw Josh was December 19th, 2007, when he gave me a smile and a wink after addressing the court just prior to being sentenced to fifteen years in prison for his role in racketeering crimes ranging from robbery to murder, and which he committed during his time as a well-known and respected enforcer for the Hells Angels Motorcycle Club. Shortly after his trial, the Angels changed his status to "Out Bad, No Contact" and since there is a practice amongst the 1% clubs of honoring the out-bad status of other 1% clubs, that meant I could not have any contact with Josh for as long as I was a member of a 1% outlaw motorcycle club. I could not even write him in prison. That said, I kept an eye on his wife Lisa and daughter Hannah because I loved them like my own family, and he had no brothers left to look out for them while he did his time. Eventually due to unfortunate circumstances Lisa and I lost contact and she ended up moving to Texas and hooked up with another guy at which point I quit feeling responsible for her.

Josh, Hells Angels MC Nomads Washington

During his time in the Hells Angels, Josh was hands-down one of the most loyal and hardcore Hells Angels and 1%er's I have ever known. He always impressed me as exactly what an HA Sergeant at Arms and enforcer should be. He was dedicated to living his life by the 1% code of loyalty, honor, respect, and brotherhood, and he was committed to being the very best Hells Angel he could be. With his hulking size, club tattoos covering both arms and the Hells Angels death-head tattooed on both sides on his head, he was visually intimidating but his charisma, intelligence, tactical mindset, and ability to charm any crowd from the clubhouse to my parents' dinner table was what really made me understand just how dangerous Josh could be. Not to mention what I had experienced first-hand when I was on the wrong side of Josh's take care of business side the first time we met. When Josh was roped up in his RICO case and was facing the death penalty, he never cooperated, never provided any information, and rather than take a plea deal, he faced trial alongside men that had betrayed him.

At that time, his wife Lisa was a petite ex-stripper who was battling a meth addiction and trying to make ends meet by working at Taco Time while raising their young daughter Hannah, standing by Josh's side during his RICO trial and facing the fact that her husband was going to at least spend an exceptionally long time in federal prison. Then there was sweet little Hannah, Josh's "Baby Girl", a little blonde angel who could take that tattooed giant and melt him anytime she wanted to with nothing more than a smile. The last time I saw Hannah she was about three and half years old and trying to act as tough as she could by telling their German Shepherd mix "Shut up Frankie!" in the kitchen of Lisa's apartment in North Bend, while Lisa and I tried to talk on the phone with Josh who was in federal lockup at FDC SeaTac.

Man, how things have changed since then. In May 2018, I got a friend request on Facebook from Lisa and that weekend I went to visit her and Hannah. As soon as we were together it was like no time had passed between us. I had my sister Lisa and little Hannah back in my life, but the circumstances of our lives were completely different in really good ways. After we lost contact, Lisa fell deeper into addiction, moved around the southern U.S., then eventually cleaned up and was now over ten years clean, working as a preschool teacher and living in a quiet community in Western Washington. She has gained some weight, has a few new tattoos and I am pretty sure those are gray hairs but I'm not going to fuckin say anything to her because she's feisty and I don't need a black eye. What impresses me most about Lisa is her loyalty. No matter what happened, how dark the future looked or how long she had to wait, she was there for Josh.

Hannah has a special place in my heart. The love Josh showed that little girl made me want to protect her as much as I would my own daughter. When he was arrested on Valentine's Day in 2006, the things ATF deliberately did to terrorize Lisa and Hannah when they served the warrant on their apartment and after they had already taken Josh into custody down the street when he had gone to get Lisa gas, ate at me and I felt like my family had been attacked by a bunch of terrorists who happened to be cops. I understand that the service of a high-risk warrant is a violent, scary event but it is what the agents did after Josh was in custody that I took offense to. As I saw it and see it, when you choose to get involved in the outlaw motorcycle club world you voluntarily accept the consequences of the lifestyle, one of which is law enforcement harassment and abuse. I am not saying it is right or that you have to tolerate it, but it's going to happen to you, and if you fight back it has to be done professionally which is what I tried to do via my involvement in the American Motorcycle Profiling Movement, and my primary motivations were my daughter, Hannah, and protecting America and the Constitution. The last time I saw Hannah she was almost four years old with long blonde hair, beautiful blue eyes, and her mom's feisty attitude. She was always a little ray of sunshine and just the cutest little girl, so I understandably experienced a brief mental disconnect when this beautiful young blonde with curves came walking into the room the first time after a fourteen-year gap. Hannah is doing great. She is involved in ROTC and has a boyfriend who she's been dating for a few years and appears to be treating her just as Josh and I would expect him to treat her. Plus, it is really freaking cute how after three years together she still blushes, gets all mushy lookin' and puts her hand on her chest when she talks about him and the nice things he does for her.

Calling a convicted violent organized crime member and a recovered meth addict your closest family might seem sad to some, but you must understand, with me the most important thing I can have in my life is loyalty, honor, respect, and brotherhood. With my unconventional outlaw family, I have that, and it has been forged and tested with a level of adversity that most can never understand. All motorcycle club members will say "I can depend on my brothers no matter what." Well, I can tell you from having done the motorcycle club world at a level unlike anyone before me or that anyone ever will again, it is all bullshit, and I will let this book serve as my argument. That said, I can truly depend on my brother Josh, Lisa, and Hannah, the four of us will always be there to face the wolves together and I am truly blessed for and proud of my outlaw family.

Lisa, Hannah & Josh Binder Shortly after they were married in 2003.
Photo courtesy of Josh & Lisa Binder

It was warm the afternoon I went to see Josh for the first time when he got out of prison. I had just come from training dogs and my Multi-Purpose Canine Harvey was getting some much-needed rest after his workout with the decoy during his protection training and had been snoring away in the back seat until he felt the car slow as I approached the gated community. I laughed out loud as I thought about how high society Josh and Lisa were that I was coming to visit them in a gated community. Lisa met me at the front gate to let me in and escort me back to her house. She lives in a peaceful little rural community with its own lake and the last time I was out there I saw a few deer running through the neighborhood. A far cry from the place they had when they lived in the hood in Tacoma.

I threw the car in park, jumped out, ran up the steps of the house and into the kitchen expecting to see Josh but he was nowhere to be seen. I could hear him deliberately repeating a long string of numbers and I knew that he must be doing his check-in call with Bureau of Prisons (BOP). After thirteen years in the federal prison system, Josh had just been released from FCI Sandstone in Minnesota to a halfway house in Tacoma a few days earlier and this was the first time I was getting to see my brother face to face in over fourteen years. I wanted to run in there and give him a big bear hug, but I was not sure what fourteen years in federal prison had done to harden him, and what no contact had done to distance us. Lisa had told me that he was a model prisoner, found God, gotten into powerlifting, and obtained certification as a CNC operator while he was in prison, which is exactly what I was hoping for. I had faith in my brother, but fourteen years in the federal system with some of America's most notorious gangsters is a long fucking time. Lisa went into the bedroom, and I heard her tell him I was there, and then she returned to the kitchen and offered me a drink. A few seconds later Josh came striding out of the bedroom. His heavily tattooed muscular arms and barrel chest were products of over a decade in the federal prison system and made him look even more intimidating than ever. He had added about 80lbs of muscle while he was in, his trademark Fu Manchu had greyed, and the wire rimmed glasses and large silver cross that hung around his neck made him appear wise like a wild west outlaw who gave up the life and found Christ.

The floor shook as he crossed the room and his smile got bigger and bigger until he broke out in his familiar belly laugh and in one sweeping motion swept me up in a giant bear hug. As I hung there, feet off the ground, I grabbed both sides of his head and planted a big kiss on the side of his head and then we both went back and forth with a few I love you brothers, before sitting down at the kitchen table to catch up. It was just like it had been with Lisa and seemed like Josh and I had not missed any time together. Not a lot went on in prison in fourteen years that was worth talking about, so Josh did not have a lot to fill me in on but my life over that period had been one wild adventure that I had started with him almost twenty years ago, and as a result the conversation naturally came to the subject of the motorcycle club world. Ironically, even though Josh had spent fourteen years in prison, and I had spent those fourteen years running around the motorcycle club world, we had both come to the same conclusion about the motorcycle club world, and that was that it does not matter what club you're in, the loyalty, honor, respect and brotherhood is all a big hoax.

Josh told me how he had spent time with members of other 1% motorcycle clubs, the American Mafia, Mexican Mafia, Nortenos, Gangster Disciples, etc., and it does not matter what organization you belong to, the brotherhood is all a big lie, and in the end the most committed and loyal members are used and thrown away or forgotten by their organizations. Josh impressed me with his accountability for his crimes, how committed he was to turn his life around, and he explained to me that he wanted to try and use his experiences in the outlaw motorcycle club world and his time in prison to have a positive impact on society. He told me that he wanted to start teaching classes for law enforcement and academics on outlaw motorcycle club and prison life. I told him that I felt the same way and the next thing you know we are developing the most comprehensive and unique training course on outlaw motorcycle club (OMC's) ever, collaborating on this book and trying to rebuild our lives together as good men and brothers.

**Josh Binder & Jeff Burns at their reunion in
May 2018**

2

EVOLUTION OF AN
OUTLAW

With outlaw motorcycle club culture being over seventy years old, one of the interesting facts about the culture that no one ever discusses is the fact that there are very few second-generation patch-holders. For clarification, when I use the term second generation patch-holders, I am referring outlaw motorcycle club members whose fathers are or were long-term members of an outlaw motorcycle club. Additionally, when I say outlaw motorcycle club, I am referring to any motorcycle club that has existed since at least the Viet-Nam era and is respected as an outlaw motorcycle club by the traditional outlaw motorcycle club community, they hold a cultural influence in the areas they operate and includes clubs that may or may not self-identify with a one-percent patch. During my twenty-two years in the club world, I had friends in every major outlaw motorcycle club in the United States, I can only recall meeting less than a dozen second generation patch-holders, and I was fortunate enough to have had two of them in my own chapter. The fact that there are so few second-generation patch-holders is dramatic evidence that the brotherhood of motorcycle clubs is a lie, because if there was true brotherhood in MC's, there would be numerous second and now third generation patch-holders. With the number of second-generation guys being so small, where does the average outlaw motorcycle member come from? My response is you never know.

Mainstream culture tends to stereotype members of outlaw motorcycle clubs as being uneducated and having blue collar jobs if they work at all which is consistent with law enforcements portrayal of the culture, but the reality is strikingly different. With clubhouse fees, membership dues, travel costs, motorcycle maintenance, etc. it is awfully expensive to be a prospect or member of an outlaw motorcycle club and as a result you must have a reliable source of income to at least support your membership and personal lifestyle, and in many cases your family as well. Some one percent clubs require members to have a legitimate source of income as a requirement of membership and while law enforcement claims this is done by the clubs to help conceal and facilitate criminal activity, the truth is this done to help discourage and prevent the membership from engaging in criminal activity that could later come back and be falsely attributed to the motorcycle club by law enforcement, or used by law enforcement to coerce the criminal member to make false statements against the club or its members, when in fact it was a members individual criminal activity that caused their contact with law enforcement and had nothing to do with the motorcycle club. I have known one-percenters who were/are doctors, lawyers, private military contractors, executive protection agents, bodyguards, investigators, actors/entertainers, ER nurses, anesthesiologists, railroad engineers, firefighters, social workers, substance abuse professionals, teachers & college professors, mechanics, special operators, youth counselors, pastors, and even former police officers. You name it and at some point, there is or was a one-percenter who was involved in that profession, so there is no average one-percenter, and I would say I was definitely not your average one percenter.

I was born and raised in the greater Seattle, Washington area. My dad is an attorney who specialized in first amendment law that was born and raised in Seattle, and my mom was a stay-at-home mom who was born and raised in a small town in southern Utah. At a young age I was deemed "gifted" which led to me spending the part of summers in gifted children's programs and attending the most exclusive private schools before completing high school at one of the best public schools in an afflu-ent suburb of Seattle. I was never an academic and did not like school, but I have always been an athlete and excelled in football, ski racing and bodybuilding at various levels over the years. Ski racing and skiing af-forded me the opportunity to begin to travel internationally at a young age and helped me identify my passion for international travel and ad-venture. My parents led me to believe that the only path to success was to graduate high school, go to a good college, get married, raise a family, and accumulate fancy stuff to show off how successful you are. My de-finition of success is quite different and without a doubt it is the result of the impact my maternal grandfather Tulley Harvey played in shaping me as a man.

Some of my favorite experiences were my summers I spent with my grandpa on his ranch in southern Utah, and it is where I learned some of the most important lessons on life from my Grandpa Harvey. One of those lessons in particular is that you don't define success by hav-ing a fancy house or car, your success as a man is defined by the stories other people tell, about you. I got to see this firsthand with the people who surrounded my grandpa, whether they be his own family or the people we would see around town who knew him, they all would treat him with the utmost respect, and they still talk about him long after his death. The things I saw and did with my grandpa and the lessons he taught me whether they were intentional or not, led me to believe that my Grandpa Harvey was a true success and the real-life incarnation of all of John Wayne's coolest characters rolled into one man. Most impor-tantly, he taught me about loyalty, honor, respect, and brotherhood. I will share a little of his backstory and one of my favorite stories about him with you, so you can understand a little about the man that shaped me to be the man I am.

As I mentioned, my grandpa's name was Tulley Harvey, and he was my hero. He was a big man standing over six feet tall with a sturdy frame and physique that reflected his prior athletic careers. He was a product of a dying culture, of true wild west tough guys with giant hearts who adhered to a lifestyle of loyalty, honor, respect, and brotherhood, and who looked out for their families and their communities no matter what the personal cost may be to them. Growing up, he and his brothers were remarkably successful in catching, breaking, and selling wild horses in Arizona, this is how he developed a passion for horses, and he dreamed of raising and selling high quality saddle horses. He graduated from Gila Bend High School near Mesa Arizona and went to Arizona Teachers College which is now known as Arizona State University on a football scholarship. During his early twenties he had become a very accomplished amateur boxer, having defeated opponents all over the country and he was considering a professional career, but shortly after moving to Utah he met who would become my grandma Laveda Rhodes, at a local dance and as his relationship with her developed, she and his mother would convince him to abandon his boxing career and he and my grandmother were ultimately married in the Temple of the Church of Jesus Christ of Latter Day Saints, on July 26th, 1934.

He and my grandmother would settle in southeast Utah in the town of Monticello, where they would raise their six children. During his lifetime he would be professionally involved in gold, copper and uranium mining, farming, welding, a breeder of award-winning quarter horses, a rancher, owner and operator of a water drilling rig, owner and operator of a grocery store, volunteer firefighter, worked on the state roads, he was involved in the development of a shrimp processing plant in Mexico, and while his career plans never included law enforcement, he even served as Sheriff of San Juan County Utah from 1951-1954. That is right, the outlaw biker just told you that the most influential person in his life had been a cop at one point. Oh yeah, while we are on the subject, the idea that one-percenters hate all cops is a myth as well. Respect gets respect and I know of several current and former one-percenters whose immediate family members were or are law enforcement and even one-percenters themselves who are former law enforcement.

My grandpa's introduction to law enforcement was completely un-expected and resulted from the prior sheriff being forced to resign due to health issues. My grandpa was persuaded to finish what remained of that sheriff's term, however when elections came my grandpa was the popular choice and elected for the next term. During his time as sheriff, he was required to furnish his own vehicle, red light, uniforms, gun, etc. and his salary never exceeded $145.82 per month. The county refused to provide a two–way radio for his vehicle and when the State of Utah offered to provide a radio for his vehicle on the condition the county paid installation costs, the county still refused. There was no academy in those days and his only training came in the form of advice from other law enforcement officers and the information shared at the occasional meetings of the Peace Officers Association headquartered in Salt Lake City. As a result, my grandpa could take his own unorthodox approach towards law enforcement, and he did.

He always loved young people and kids and he made a deliberate ef-fort to cultivate the respect of the youth of the community, with the idea that he could use his relationships and respect to reduce juvenile delinquency if he could interact with them as their friend and not just the sheriff. With first time juvenile offenders even if he was certain of their guilt, he would sit them down and explain the legal consequences of their offense if he allowed things to be handled by the courts, but told them that he was willing to help them avoid these consequences if they would agree to cooperate with the following:

- Drive together to the offender's parents' house where he would sit in silence as the offender explained their offense to their parents.
- Agree to make full restitution to the victim and my grandfather would work closely with the victim to ensure compliance.
- Agree to not re-offend with the understanding that if they did, he would make sure the offender was given a recommendation for the harshest sentence allowed.

My grandfather's approach to juvenile criminal justice appears to have worked for his community as there were very few repeat offenders. The only hiccup to this approach my grandfather experienced was from offenders with prominent wealthy families who would often insist that he was mistaken and, in some cases, accuse him of framing their child or forcing them to confess to a crime they did not commit.

During his time as sheriff most people never even knew he carried a gun, since he believed that guns make people nervous, and it was easier to reason with people if his pistol was concealed from view. That said, even as a small-town sheriff he had multiple chances to look down the wrong end of the barrel of a loaded gun and in those incidents his calm demeanor and quick hands allowed him to distract and disarm the suspect. One of my memories of his ranch house in Monticello from when I was a kid is of the large pile of rifles he kept in the corner just outside the kitchen on the way out the back door, several of which I was told my grandpa took from various suspects he disarmed as sheriff.

One story I remember from his time as sheriff took place after members of the local Navajo tribe had announced they were going to expand the reservation boundaries to include the communities of Bluff and Blanding which were within my grandpa's jurisdiction, and they were driving their sheep north. While there was no indication of how many people were involved this had to be addressed, so my grandpa and one other deputy loaded a couple of horses on the back of a large truck and drove out to Montezuma Canyon where despite being at the tactical disadvantage of being able to be easily shot by anyone hiding in the steep rocky walls, they rode deep into the canyon until they encountered a large number of Navajo men and women, and after a brief scuffle in which the deputies finger was broken, they arrested the ringleader and eighteen associates. That incident and several other Navajo disturbances over the following weeks brought the attention of the national news media on the county.

My grandpa ultimately left law enforcement but over the course of subsequent decades he would be approached by several men who would shake his hand and thank him for helping them turn their lives around by giving them a second chance and it was encounters like these which I was fortunate enough to personally observe that would engrain this mentality of finding the good in people and the importance of protecting your community with integrity.

Tulley R. Harvey

My grandpa was as unorthodox a grandpa as he was a sheriff. As soon as I could walk, he gave me a Shetland pony I named Lisa and he started teaching me to ride. As soon as I was potty-trained, he started taking me to work in the fields with him and teaching me to drive the tractors and combines. At age six, we started to get into "Meanness", and you never knew what that could lead to. After breakfast, my grandpa would look at me and ask, "Are you ready to go get into meanness?", after which we would start the day by exploring the Anasazi ruins in the canyons, hunting for rattlesnakes, and honing my shooting skills by hunting jackrabbits and prairie dogs, followed by some farm chores and more time in the canyons or desert. Meanness to my Grandpa Harvey included teaching me to stand up for what I believe, not quit because of discomfort or pain, expect others to treat you the way you treat them, and it gave me valuable skills like; firearms safety, marksmanship, gunsmithing, survival skills, how to break horses, how to drive a pickup, tractor and combine, how to castrate a colt with a five dollar hardware store pocket knife, to kill things that are tough to kill, and to keep secrets that need to be kept.

One of those tough incidents occurred when I was about eight years old. After breakfast grandpa told me it was time to go feed the horses and get into meanness. Now, even though I was only eight years old, I already had two summers of driving experience. My Grandpa had built some wooden blocks with Velcro straps that he would strap to the pedals of his farm truck so that I could reach the pedals and drive. When we would leave the house, as soon as he was sure my grandma and mom were not watching he would pull the blocks out from under the seat of his pickup, strap them on the pedals, hop into the passenger seat and off we would go. This morning was the same and just like every morning I secured my Winchester .22 semi-automatic rifle in the rifle rack of his pickup, hopped in and away we went to the field where he kept his horses.

When we got there, we added water to the trough and loaded a couple bales of hay into the back of the pick-up. Like I mentioned, I have been shooting since I was about five years old and grandpa had me refine my shooting skills by shooting dynamic targets like prairie dogs and jackrabbits, so I was a particularly good shot with a rifle by this time. Grandpa Harvey loved to challenge me, so he told me to hop into the back of the truck and shoot any prairie dogs or jackrabbits I saw while we were driving out to find the horses. As we were driving across the dusty southern Utah prairie, we crested the top of a small hill and on the other side saw a couple of dogs chasing the horses in a wide circle at a full run. "God damn it!" my grandpa yelled as he accelerated towards the horses. "They're going to injure one of those horses and we're going to have to kill the horse. Shoot the dog's son!" he said as we continued towards the chaos. "What?" I asked. It was clear to me that these were someone's pet dogs, and they were just getting into their own "meanness". "You heard me, shoot the damn dogs!" my grandpa said. With my orders clear, I took aim at the lead dog who was about one hundred yards from us and squeezed the trigger. The report of the shot cracked, and the lead dog immediately tumbled, its lifeless body flopping against the red dirt until it came to rest in a sage bush. Undeterred the second dog continued to chase the horses who had broken their circle and now made a run for it across the field. We continued after them and I took aim on the second dog, the horses turned back toward us and then made another direction change away, and when they turned, I got a brief head-on view of the second dog and squeezed a shot off which struck the dog in the center of its chest causing it to drop and roll like the first one, but it did not die immediately.

My mission successfully completed, my heart fell, and as the chaos began to slow, I watched the life drain out of that dog, the city boy not understanding that what I had done was perfectly fine by the rancher code. You see, in my grandpa's mind, those dogs were somebody's pets, but they had failed to properly care for and control their dogs, and now their dogs were going to potentially cause damage to one of my grandpa's horses that were worth thousands of dollars. Either way, those dogs were going to cost him a lot of money if we allowed them to continue what they were doing, so lethal intervention was the best and safest remedy possible, and it was fair under the rancher code. Once he explained that, I felt better about what I had done but that feeling would not last. You see, several hours later when we were back home at his house sitting in the living room watching T.V. together with my grandma and mom in the kitchen cooking, there was a knock on the door. I answered the door and standing there with a concerned look on his face was a young boy about my age. Can I help you? I asked. He explained that his dogs have not come home, and he was wondering if we had seen them. It was a total kick in the nuts, here was a kid who looked like a nice kid that I would get along with if I had met him six hours earlier but now, he was looking into the eyes of the young boy who killed his dogs. I paused long enough that my grandpa who was still sitting in his chair intervened and made small talk before telling the boy we had not seen his dogs and wishing him luck in finding them. When the door was shut my grandpa told me to never say anything to my mom or grandma about what we did. I kept that secret until after both he and my grandma had passed away, and I was in my thirties.

Most importantly, my Grandpa Harvey taught me that a man of respect is a man of character, and the foundation of his character is loyalty, honor, respect, and brotherhood, which you will see in the man's actions, and being an outlaw does not mean being a criminal, good men are outlaws, and the world needs outlaws. Unfortunately, my grandpa died when I was just barely into my early teens, and I did not have the benefit of his guidance into my adult years.

Jeff (riding Lisa) with Grandpa Harvey

Jeff with one of the many jackrabbits.

After my grandpa's death I continued to focus on my ski racing but ultimately sustained a devastating knee injury that ended my ski racing career and led to me finding the sport of bodybuilding. I qualified for my first national bodybuilding championship at the age of seventeen in 1992.

Having followed my parents plan, I attended college at the University of Idaho where I majored in Criminal Justice. Being a police officer did not interest me at all but being an investigator or being on the SWAT team did. My plan would take a detour after I met a VIP who I began providing bodyguard services for. That would lead to real international executive protection (E.P.) and eventually high-threat protection and covert operations contracts which combined all of those professional skillsets plus the international travel and adventure that I loved, and over twenty years later I've had a ton of adventures and become an internationally recognized subject matter expert on the fields of high-threat dignitary and executive protection, as well as counterterrorism.

Like a lot of outlaw bikers from the west coast, my first memories of outlaw motorcycle clubs were when I saw a pack of Hells Angels as a kid while on vacation in California, and ever since then I have been fascinated by outlaw motorcycle clubs. I have read every article, book, and watched every documentary and movie on the subject that I can get my hands on over the years. I continued to study the culture from the perspective of an academic throughout my involvement as an outlaw motorcycle club member, and I have published several articles and produced a documentary on the outlaw motorcycle club culture.

1996 was a pivotal year for me because it was the year my daughter was born, and it was also the year that I decided I was going to begin my journey to become a Hells Angel. In retrospect, I am not sure what made me think that was a good time to start working on becoming a one-percenter but that is the kind of decisions I made at twenty-one. I did not get involved in the outlaw motorcycle club world to feel powerful or become a member of an organized crime group, and I believed I could be a one-percenter without being involved in criminal activity. I got involved in the outlaw motorcycle club world looking to commit to a culture based on loyalty, honor, respect, and brotherhood, and seeking the truth, believing that the government and law enforcement had it wrong and that outlaw motorcycle clubs are not criminal organizations, but in fact they are misunderstood brotherhoods, that from time to time have members who are involved in criminal activity for which the club is often unfairly associated with.

The Hells Angels Motorcycle Club (HAMC) is an international one percent outlaw motorcycle club that started in San Bernardino California in 1948, is arguably the largest and most well-known outlaw motorcycle club in the world and is designated a criminal organization by the United States Department of Justice. I wanted to be a Hells Angel and while the Norsemen MC had just patched over to become the Hells Angels Nomads Washington charter, they were a bunch of guys involved in what appeared to me to be a lot of methamphetamine induced tweeker drama that I didn't want to part of. I knew I needed to know more about the culture before I would be ready to be a one-percenter and I decided the best way to learn what I needed to know would be to attend various public events hosted by the Hells Angels in California. Why California? Because I knew enough to know Canadian Hells Angels were nothing like American HA and since I wanted no part of Canadian motorcycle club culture, my closest HA charters were in California, and since that is where the HA started, that is where I went to learn how to be a Hells Angel.

How do you join a 1% outlaw motorcycle club? If you are me, you hop on your Harley Davidson motorcycle and ride down to Oakland California, knock on the red steel door at 4010 Foothills Blvd, the Oakland Hells Angels clubhouse, introduce yourself and tell them you want to prospect for the Hells Angels. The move was ballsy as fuck and almost got me a good beat down, but it all worked out and that was how I met a man who I would come to look up to, a man who would teach me how to be a one percenter, legendary Oakland Hells Angel Mouldy Marvin Gilbert.

Over the next couple of years, I would attend several runs and events hosted by the Oakland, San Fernando Valley, Daily City, and San Francisco charters of the Hells Angels. I paid attention to how they dressed, walked, spoke, their mannerisms and slang. I did not try and jump right in; I knew I was not ready for that, and I knew I would only get one shot to try and become a Hells Angel, so I wanted to make sure I was ready to succeed and just paid attention and learned. My conversations with members were meaningful and I took care to learn the history of the club, the conflicts, and the individuals who helped shape the culture. I reveled in the chance to get to hear stories firsthand from men who had obtained legendary status in outlaw motorcycle club culture. Over time I began to learn outlaw motorcycle club history to the point I could recite it better than American history. I did not just dress like them and hangout with them, I walked the way they walked, spoke like they spoke, and I had learned to ride my motorcycle the way they rode. The viral memetic infection of loyalty, honor, respect and brotherhood, the club comes first, this is about America and freedom, brainwashed my young mind. I began to believe what they believed, and I committed myself to living by the one-percenter code of honor, and to becoming a Hells Angel. As I "got with the program", I began to get small bits of validation from these men I looked to as legends and it further fueled my mission, but it also gave me confidence and with confidence can come ego, and as I would soon find out, ego can get you killed in the outlaw motorcycle club world.

3

THE BASICS

I want to go over some of the basics on the history of the American motorcycle club culture and motorcycle club protocol. I deliberately use the term American motorcycle club culture because motorcycle club culture is quite different internationally, even when you are talking about clubs that originated from the United States. However, motorcycle club culture is vastly different depending on where you are at within the U.S., even when you are dealing with the same national clubs. In this chapter, I will give you an overview on the history of motorcycle club culture. We will discuss the history of the three-piece patch and the one-percent diamond, motorcycle club protocol, evolution of the motorcycle club world, and major incidents of violence that impacted club relations. The information that I share with you in this chapter is nothing secret, it is the information that I knew when I decided to become part of the outlaw motorcycle club world, and it is what I learned from first reading and watching everything I could on outlaw motorcycle clubs and then being around motorcycle clubs prior to making my decision to get serious about joining. I use it to establish a baseline of knowledge for you so that you can understand the significance of the incidents I describe throughout the course of the book and why they happened, and so that you can recognize the changes that occurred in the culture over the course of my twenty plus years in the life, as well as understand how they impacted American motorcycle club culture. Now, before some of you jump all over some of what I will say over the next few paragraphs and say it is incorrect, remember this is what I knew as a green pea getting into the culture and not what I would come to know to be reality over the course of my twenty-two years involvement in American outlaw motorcycle club culture.

It is generally accepted that outlaw motorcycle clubs are a product of World War II, when groups of returning veterans formed motorcycle clubs in search of adventure and to build a brotherhood based around their love of riding and racing motorcycles. These clubs began hosting their own racing events which were not sanctioned by the American Motorcycle Association (A.M.A.), and as a result these events were called "outlaw" events and the hosting clubs were subsequently kicked out of the A.M.A. In protest, several of the offending clubs cut their traditional one-piece back patches that identified their club into three pieces to make it appear larger on the back of their vest in a show of pride for their club and to set them apart from the traditional one-piece patch of A.M.A. member clubs and they embraced the outlaw moniker. The three-piece patch consists of a top rocker which identifies the name of the club, a center patch which is the emblem of the club, and a bottom rocker which identifies the country, state, or city where the chapter the member belongs to is from. Until recent years the three-piece patch was only worn by outlaw motorcycle clubs and was an easy way to identify an outlaw club, regardless of whether the club chose to wear a one-percent diamond or not.

War and drugs have had a major influence on outlaw motorcycle club culture and with the Viet Nam war, American combatants saw a level of extreme close quarter's violence that had never been experienced which resulted in severe P.T.S.D. that was not being addressed, and a society that did not support them or the war. In addition, motorcycle clubs were beginning to experiment with hard drugs like opium, P.C.P. and methamphetamine, and during this period there was not only a huge surge in membership in outlaw motorcycle clubs due to disenfranchised veterans returning from the war, but there was a dramatic increase in violence as the clubs became very territorial. The territorial violence continued throughout the 70's, 80's and 90's as clubs expanded or bumped heads over respect issues that were generally the result of substance over-indulgence, disputes over women, or expansion into foreign areas. Some of these led to long-term disputes or "war's" which lasted decades, such as with the Hells Angels MC and the Outlaws MC, or the Hells Angels and the Mongols MC. At the time I decided to get involved in the club world the HA had on-going conflicts with the Bandidos, Outlaws, Pagans, things were really starting to heat up in California with the Mongols MC, and relations with the Vagos MC were very tense.

Back then, there was a process to starting a new club which included getting the blessing of the dominant club or clubs in your state. However, in the case of an outlaw motorcycle club, you announce your intentions and back your play no matter what when you get tested, and you could expect to be tested by the major clubs. If you wanted to be a new club, you had to earn your respect. Clubs that failed to follow the process were routinely subject to beatings and having their patches taken by force, a custom known as patch pulling. In some cases, their motorcycles and valuables may be taken from the vanquished club members as well. The motorcycle club world back then consisted of outlaw motorcycle clubs, traditional motorcycle clubs, support clubs, veteran's clubs, religious motorcycle clubs, one women's motorcycle club out of Florida called Leather & Lace MC, which was started by murdered Warlocks MC President Bear Chaffin's wife, Jennifer, and a few cop clubs. There were not all the special interest clubs that you see today, and there certainly were none of these bullshit "law abiding" motorcycle clubs like the Iron Order MC, etc. The outlaw motorcycle clubs violent enforcement of how new clubs were established prevented bullshit motorcycle clubs like the Iron Order from existing and it was not until the outlaw clubs adopted a policy of no longer pulling patches due to the legal consequences, that these bullshit problem-causing law-abiding motorcycle clubs came into existence.

Violence was a big part of the culture and lifestyle at the time and something you accepted when you got involved. If you chose to join a club that was at war, you accepted that you would be hunted and may be murdered for your choice. If you lied, cheated, stole from your brothers, or fucked around with their ol' lady, you would likely be beaten and have your colors and motorcycle taken. Failing to stand-up for yourself, your brothers, or your club was unacceptable and warranted a beating and expulsion from the club. Your patch was your flag and you do not disrespect it or give it up for any reason. No intravenous drug use is tolerated. Snitching on the club is an offense that can lead to death, and any offense that got you kicked out of the club resulted in your club tattoos being removed with a hot iron, belt-sander, knife, etc. Those were the rules and consequences as I understood them, and I was fine with it. The way I saw it, just like joining a boxing club or mixed martial arts club, violence was an accepted part of being in the club, it was necessary for the accountability that was part of the culture, and it is what led to the high level of respect that I had seen members showing each other. I was joining a culture based on loyalty, honor, respect and brotherhood and I understood the consequences, so I was fine with being held accountable if I fucked up, no matter what those consequences were.

Outlaw motorcycle clubs' range in size from small clubs with only a couple of chapters. To large international outlaw motorcycle clubs like the Hells Angels MC and Outlaws MC. For clubs with numerous chapters, there will usually be National and Regional officers whose roles are consistent with the roles of chapter officers, but with a regional and national responsibility. The authority of National and Regional officers varies from club to club and is established by the by-laws of each club. Chapter officers include a President, Vice-President, Secretary, Treasurer, Sargent at Arms, and in some clubs, there may be an Enforcer and or Road Captain. The authority and responsibilities for each position is established in the club's by-laws, but they are generally consistent with the roles of officers as established in Robert's Rules of Order, as this is the format that most clubs use when they conduct their meetings or what is called "church."

The requirements for joining an outlaw motorcycle club may vary slightly from one club to another but for the most part the criteria include:

- Must be male.
- Must be over 21 years of age.
- Must own an American made motorcycle.
- No cops or snitches.
- Must undergo a hang-around period to get to know the club and then prospect to learn how to be a good member and prove yourself to the club.

While there were a few clubs that have or had membership policies banning minorities and law enforcement likes to portray outlaw motorcycle clubs as notoriously racist and forbidding minorities, that simply is not the case for most of the major one-percent motorcycle clubs and I have personally met minority members including African American members from every major one-percent outlaw motorcycle club.

Left – Right, Top to Bottom: Bandidos MC, Pagans MC, Outlaws MC,
Hells Angels

In terms of identification, outlaw motorcycle clubs will identify themselves with a patch which often is a three-piece patch consisting of a top rocker that identifies the name of the club, a center patch which will be the logo of the club, and a bottom rocker identifying the city, state, region, or country the member's chapter is from. Some clubs will identify their national officers with a "National" bottom rocker instead of a location bottom rocker. The patch almost always remains the property of the motorcycle club and the member is simply allowed to wear the patch and items bearing the center patch so long as they remain in good standing with the club.

Outsiders MC colors

That said, there are one percent outlaw motorcycle clubs like the Vagos MC, Sons of Silence MC, and the Pagans MC who historically wore a two-piece patch since the club was founded but the with the Pagans recent expansion they have begun wearing East Coast, South West, and West Coast bottom rockers. There are even a couple of one percent outlaw motorcycle clubs such as the Galloping Goose who wear a one-piece patch.

Regardless of what style patch the motorcycle club wears they will always have the letters M.C. (Motorcycle Club) incorporated somewhere in their back-patch whether it be as separate letters, a cube, or incorporated into the center-patch. For some clubs, the placement of the M.C. may have some significance as well. For example, in the Outsiders MC the placement of the M.C.'s allows you to read the linage of the member and you can tell what charter members line they and their sponsor are from. The same is generally true of the placement in Outsider MC member tattoos. The American version of the Gypsy Joker MC are another one percent club with which the placement of the members MC's on their back patch have significance.

Not all outlaw motorcycle clubs will identify with the use of a one percent diamond and some of the new "one percent" clubs who use the diamond have not earned the respect of the community to make it mean anything. Basically, the man makes the patch, the patch does not make the man, so these new or internet transplant clubs that throw on bottom rockers and one percent diamonds have not earned the respect of the community and thus are excommunicated from it. Just as with the placement of M.C.'s, the placement of the one percent diamond may have significance as well and it may appear on the front of the members vest, the back, or both. For example, if a Pagan is wearing a one percent diamond on the back of his vest above his top rocker it identifies him as a President or "Diamond Back."

Pagans MC President or "Diamond Back's" colors (old style
two-piece patch)

Another patch with significant history in outlaw motorcycle club culture is a patch bearing the number thirteen. The patch may be square, circular, diamond shaped, etc. and worn on either the front or the back of a member's vest. Law enforcement claims that the number 13 stands for the thirteenth letter in the alphabet M which stands for methamphetamine and signifies the wearer of the patch is a methamphetamine dealer. This is false, and while there may have been some tweaked-out junkie club member who told a cop that at some point in the 1970's, it sounds like made up law enforcement bullshit to me because you have to be a dumbass drug dealer to identify yourself as such for all the world to see with a patch. Based on my experience it is true that the 13 on the patch stands for the letter M. However, the wearer is not signaling the world that he is a meth dealer or even user, rather they are showing their love for and dedication to "Motorcycling" or "Motorcyclisim", the act of committing every aspect of your life to the motorcycle culture. For the Pagans Motorcycle Club, a member with a thirteen patch on the back of their vest signifies that the wearer is a member of the Pagans "Mother Chapter", a governing body of the club consisting of members from various chapters.

Pagans MC Mother Chapter member, post
2017 with the addition of the East Coast
bottom

Once again, law enforcements definition that they stand behind in court, the media and documentaries does not pass the logic test when compared to my definition. It makes no sense that if outlaw motorcycle clubs are sophisticated criminal organizations as law enforcement alleges, that the members would go around advertising they are a meth dealer with a thirteen patch. There is nothing sophisticated about that.

Front patches vary from club to club and may include a one percent diamond, chapter name/location, officer position, memorial patches, club sayings, side rockers representing the member's chapter or a chapter they are close to, etc. Non club sanctioned club patches may be worn as well and might include a Confederation of Clubs patch or Confederation of Clubs ribbon if the wearer has been involved in the C.O.C. since the early days, name tags, and novelty patches.

Then there is what federal law enforcement has termed "Murder Patches" and knowingly and falsely claims to mean that the member has killed for the club, such as the Hells Angels Filthy Few, Outlaws S.S. bolts, Mongols Black Hearts patch. etc. While those patches may have originally been made by a small group of individual club members to commemorate a violent confrontation in defense of their brothers and their club, they were not a club sanctioned patch and because they were not club sanctioned with their issuance controlled by the bylaws of the club, over the years other members who had not gone to such extremes began wearing those patches and the meaning of the patch was diluted to the point of legend. Simple logic tells us that if those patches were truly earned by committing murders on behalf of the club that the American motorcycle club community would be responsible for thousands of unreported, uninvestigated, unprosecuted homicides, and if they were that smooth why would they advertise they were killers, and why would the most common form of club violence be spontaneous fights on video in casinos? It makes no sense right now but hopefully it will by the end of the book, because what law enforcement says is total bullshit.

You will learn from the photos in the book and my story that over the years some of the major outlaw motorcycle clubs have changed their patch design. The Outlaws have made slight changes to their patch design multiple times over the years. The Hells Angels moved from their "Bumble Bee" version of the deaths head to the larger version pushed by Sonny Barger and the Oakland charter, then several years later added stitches to the death head's mouth. In 2011 the Bandidos changed the design of their center patch and their font, but we will get into that in a later chapter. The Mongols center patch design has changed multiple times over the years, and most recently the Pagans MC began wearing bottom rockers when before they had traditionally never worn a bottom rocker. I have included photos in no particular order of the most recent version of colors for the one percent motorcycle clubs who along with the Outsiders MC make up the most respected and influential outlaw motorcycle clubs in America.

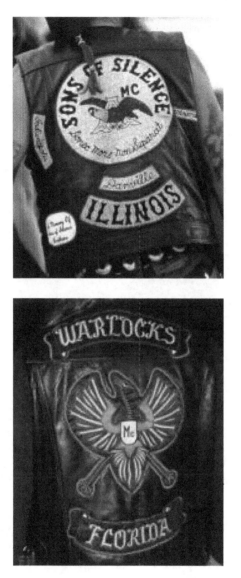

Before I got involved in the club world, I did my best to learn the history of the major clubs in the U.S. and their histories with each other. At the time I got into the club world law enforcement had what they called the "Big Three", meaning Hells Angels, Bandidos and Outlaws. Then they changed that to "The Big Four" to add the Pagans MC to the list. I quit keeping track of their nicknames for the clubs, but the list would grow to include the Vagos, Sons of Silence, Warlocks, Outsiders, and numerous other outlaw motorcycle clubs, support clubs and even veterans and Christian motorcycle clubs have been labeled outlaw motorcycle gangs.

It is basic but that is what I knew at the time I decided I wanted to become an outlaw motorcycle club member.

4

OUTLAW MOTORCYCLE GANG (OMG) INVESTIGATIONS: THE REAL CRIMINAL ENTERPRISE

It is irrefutable that one of the most negative influences on American outlaw motorcycle club culture is law enforcement, specifically the undercover operations that target OMC's, and when you set aside what you think you know about American outlaw motorcycle club culture and conduct an examination of the evolution of the undercover operations targeting outlaw motorcycle clubs, their tactics, and apply the Constitution, what emerges is an undeniable pattern of entrapment, manipulation, and murder, that is shrouded in secrecy and demands Congressional oversight and intervention.

To truly understand outlaw motorcycle club culture, you must understand what law enforcement calls Outlaw Motorcycle Gang (OMG) investigations and their evolution, so I will delve into the origin of what law enforcement calls "Outlaw Motorcycle Gang (OMG)" investigations which prejudicially implies the organization is operating as a criminal enterprise.

Academics, journalists, attorneys, and investigators understand the value of the Freedom of Information Act (FOIA) and public records requests when evidencing their conclusions surrounding law enforcement investigations and misconduct, however when it comes to using those tools to obtain any law enforcement records related to outlaw motorcycle clubs, whether it be simple dash cam video of a traffic stop to evidence motorcycle profiling, or the training and personnel records related to the undercover agents and informants who conduct the investigations, in almost all cases FOIA and public records requests for any records related to outlaw motorcycle clubs are denied using various law enforcement sensitive information exclusion policies, and this has created a situation where OMG enhanced undercover operations and the law enforcement agencies involved are able to hide all evidence of misconduct, entrapment and corruption, thus they are able to operate without any legitimate oversight or accountability. Additionally, the motorcycle club members who find themselves victims of these enhanced undercover operations (EUO's) are in most cases forced to trade their integrity and silence for their freedom, and admit under penalty of perjury to a set of facts and committing a serious felony racketeering offense for a crime that was manufactured by an undercover operation with the specific intent of proving a false narrative about the targeted motorcycle club, and which the agencies behind the operation knew to be false when they targeted the organization(s). The use of sensitive information exclusions by law enforcement to conceal evidence of everything from motorcycle profiling to undercover agent misconduct and even exculpatory evidence, appears to have begun with records related to operations conducted by agents from the ATF's Enhanced Undercover Program (EUP) and the 2002 Laughlin River Run Riot, and it has become systemic in response to me teaching the motorcycle club community on a national level to use FOIA's and public records requests to evidence incidents of motorcycle profiling and harassment by law enforcement in support of motorcycle profiling legislation. In fact, I testified about the problem of law enforcement using sensitive information exclusions to conceal this type of evidence in front of both the Maryland House of Representatives and Senate in 2015, and during my testimony I was able to use public records requests related to a mass motorcycle profiling stop from the annual Blessing of Bikes event to evidence a specific incident where the records had been denied when requested by an individual associated with a motorcycle club, but were provided when requested months prior by a civilian and before any public attention was brought to the mass profiling incident.

You see OMG investigations are not about the pursuit of justice or public safety, they are about careerism, ego and most importantly profit, and it is the information exclusion policies used to deny public records requests and defense subpoenas, plea agreements forever silencing defendants, and law enforcement's ability to arbitrarily classify outlaw motorcycle clubs as gangs, Military Trained Gang Members (MTGM), and a domestic terrorist threat, that has allowed the ATF Enhanced Undercover Program and their associated operations targeting outlaw motorcycle clubs to be able to trample on the Constitution, falsely define an American subculture, and they very well may deal a death blow to the First Amendment and wrongfully make it illegal to belong to an American outlaw motorcycle club, unless there is immediate oversight and transparency.

According to the U.S. Department of Justice, outlaw motorcycle gangs (OMG's), are organizations whose members use their motorcycle clubs as conduits for criminal enterprises. That definition was almost certainly developed from a highly inflammatory March 1965 report by then California Attorney General Thomas C. Lynch which detailed a six-month investigation of outlaw motorcycle clubs in the state. The investigation was prompted by reports of a gang rape at a Monterey, CA beach on Labor Day the previous year involving the Hells Angels Motorcycle Club. The specific incident occurred when over three-hundred

Hells Angels members and associates had gathered to raise money to send the body of a club member who was killed in an accident back to his mother in North Carolina. Several club members were arrested in connection with the case and law enforcement escorted the Hells Angels from town. Almost immediately the front pages of newspapers all over California were running headlines advertising the heinous gang rape in the quiet seaside town and stories that told of two young girls, aged 14 and 15 that were allegedly violently taken from their dates by a gang of filthy, frenzied, booze-addled motorcycle hoodlums, and dragged off to be repeatedly assaulted. Such an incident should definitely warrant concern and even public attention but in coming weeks the investigation would raise concern as to whether any forcible rape had even been committed, if the identifications made by the alleged victims were even correct, a doctor had examined the girls and found no evidence to support the charges, one girl refused to testify while the other failed a lie detector test and was found to be wholly unreliable, and by September 25th of that year the charges against the arrested Hells Angels had been quietly dismissed leaving law enforcement with their first black eye related to outlaw motorcycle clubs and their allegations of organized criminal activity. Seizing on the sensationalism and using it as a political opportunity, Senator Fred Far demanded an investigation of the Hells Angels and several other motorcycle clubs.

Bent on reaffirming law enforcement's false definition vilifying outlaw motorcycle clubs as gangs and violent criminal organizations, Attorney General Lynch sent questionnaires to 100 sheriff's, district attorneys and police chiefs, asking for any information they had on motorcycle clubs and calling for suggestions as to how law enforcement should deal with them. After six months, Lynch compiled the responses he received into a heavily biased 15-page report containing numerous provably false findings that generated headlines across the nation intended to instill fear of outlaw motorcycle clubs in the public, such as a March 16th, 1965, article in the New York times titled *California Takes Steps to Curb Terrorism of Ruffian Cyclists.: Attorney General*

Gives Plan, Drawn Up After a Six-Month Study of Gangs, to Coordinate Efforts of Police. The article appears to be the first ever to reference motorcycle clubs and terrorism. Lynch's plan was to centralize information on outlaw motorcycle clubs, it urged more vigorous prosecution, and advised law enforcement to put outlaw motorcycle club members under surveillance whenever possible.

In May 1965, Hunter S. Thompson published an article titled *The Motorcycle Gangs: A Portrait of an Outsider Underground*, which called out Lynch's report and described the realities of the Hells Angels and outlaw motorcycle clubs based on his interviews and experiences with the Hells Angels. Thompson's article was not the story of murder and mayhem described in the Lynch report and promoted by Senator Far, and it failed to do anything to bring attention to the sensationalized false narrative that was being promoted by an element of law enforcement in the interest of careerism. The Lynch report's impact on the publicly accepted narrative regarding outlaw motorcycle clubs was dramatic and as a result, law enforcement agencies in California totally revamped their approach to policing and investigating outlaw motorcycle clubs, becoming the model for law enforcement across the nation to follow, and the false narrative regarding outlaw motorcycle clubs being violent criminal gangs was set and new career specialty emerged for law enforcement.

With the public and law enforcement accepting the narrative that outlaw motorcycle clubs were really sophisticated criminal enterprises, in the early 1970's, federal investigators and prosecutors began to take interest in outlaw motorcycle club investigations and started to incorporate the tactics and techniques they had been using against the mafia. Specifically, they began using a method in which they would offer a plea deal to a member to excuse him from crimes he committed in exchange for his testimony against members of the club that fit law enforcement's narrative, even if they knew it was false. The first significant incident of this type occurred in 1972 and started when a Hells Angel who had been implicated in insurance fraud and drug dealing cut a deal to save himself and told police about two bodies that were buried on former Hells Angel George Wethern's ranch. When police raided Wethern's ranch that he shared with his wife and children they found a substantial amount of marijuana and when they threatened to lock him and his wife up for the rest of their lives and send their kids to foster homes, Wethern cut a deal and told them where to find the bodies, then named other Hells Angels as the killers in exchange for total immunity for him and his wife. Keeping consistent with the narrative established by his predecessor, California Attorney General Evelle Younger described the scene as a "Hells Angels burying ground." and declared to legislators that the Hells Angels "are no longer merely a gang of loosely organized bikers but are rapidly becoming large-scale organized crime operators." In the November 1972 report on organized crime issued by California Justice Department it states, "The most active gang appears to be the Hell's Angels followed by the Hessians (a southern California outlaw biker club), "The Hell's Angels are no longer merely a gang of loosely organized bikers but are rapidly becoming large-scale organized-crime operators. Motorcycle gang members are active in the purchase of land. They make investments in legitimate businesses, and motorcycle gangs now possess sophisticated electronic devices to intercept police communications. They are extremely mobile, thus benefiting from a basic law enforcement weakness, jurisdictional fragmentation. Members of outlaw motorcycle gangs have frequently been associated with major organized-crime figures in the state." While the case did result in the convictions of three members of the Hells Angels, it failed to establish the crimes were committed as part of a criminal enterprise and it took providing immunity to two serious criminals motivated by saving themselves, to gain those convictions. The solution to jurisdictional fragmentation was the next area we saw evolve in outlaw motorcycle club investigations.

During the 1970's undercover operations targeting criminal organizations went through a notable transformational period because of the formation of the Bureau of Alcohol, Tobacco and Firearms in 1972, and their subsequent creation in 1974 of the first undercover operations academy intended to deliver a specialized program that would increase the safety and effectiveness of undercover agents. The curriculum was developed by a couple of former IRS investigators with organized crime experience, and covered techniques and protocols for cover stories or what is called backstopping, dealing with invitations to indulge in drug use, side stepping entrapment, agent misconduct, handling sexual advances, and use of technology. The first training academy was held in Virginia Beach, and on the Thursday afternoon of the first week of the first academy in 1974, the ATF Director of Internal Affairs was scheduled to teach for several hours. As he was beginning his presentation a student asked the director if he or any of his staff had ever conducted any real undercover work buying drugs, guns, or explosives, and when the Director admitted that none of them had, all the students and staff turned their chairs facing their backs to the Director, thus ending his presentation, and launching a troubled and storied relationship between ATF Internal Affairs and the undercover agents.

Additionally influencing the transformation of outlaw motorcycle club investigations was the formation of the International Outlaw Motorcycle Gang Investigator's Conference which would later become known as the International Outlaw Motorcycle Gang Investigators Association (IOMGIA), a professional training organization made up of federal, state, local law enforcement, and prosecutors that was formed in San Diego, California in 1974, for the purpose of creating an educational organization that would improve the investigative skills and information exchange among its members, and resulted in centralized specialized Outlaw Motorcycle Gang investigation training. The men who formed the IOMGIA were some of the same men who had provided false information for and supported the Lynch report, and who were considered the recognized "experts" on outlaw motorcycle clubs at the time, which created a funnel of top-down misinformation and propaganda from the IOMGIA that was received by all law enforcement and the media as credible, it infected and prejudiced the masses, and reinforced the false narrative that outlaw motorcycle clubs were really criminal organizations.

The first organized crime prosecution of an outlaw motorcycle club under the Racketeer Influenced and Corrupt Organization Act (RICO) occurred in 1979, when a task force investigation involving the DEA, FBI, and the recently formed Bureau of Alcohol, Tobacco and Firearms (ATF) resulted in indictments of members of the Hells Angels, alleging they were a criminal enterprise that conducted a pattern of racketeering crimes that violated state and federal laws in furtherance of the enterprise. Under the Racketeer Influenced and Corrupt Organization Act (RICO), prosecutors can combine individual crimes to show a pattern of racketeering activity and use past crimes even if adjudicated to establish a conspiracy for the group. The case titled *United States v. Barger*, centered around the prosecution's allegations that as an organization the Hells Angels illegally trafficked in guns and narcotics. The jury acquitted Barger on the RICO charges and hung on the predicate acts, proving to be another incredibly expensive and embarrassing failure in law enforcement's national war on outlaw motorcycle clubs and the Hells Angels that was being spearheaded by law enforcement in California. This investigation was launched in response to the Hells Angels being declared an organized crime organization by the California state Department of Justice, and a task force was established to investigate each, and every crime committed by members of the Hells Angels, including misdemeanor crimes.

While some ATF agents cite this case as the first successful infiltration undercover operation against an outlaw motorcycle club, the two ATF undercover agents Les Robinson and Douglas Gray were only in play for two months and used an ATF budget of $300 and their own personal money to fund the operation that consisted of them hanging out at a motorcycle shop, drinking beer, working on motorcycles, and making the occasional small purchases of stolen motorcycle parts, firearms and narcotics. ATF's undercover operation was closed after just two months and without the agents even becoming prospects, so that ATF could focus the manpower and funding on higher priorities.

While the ATF undercover agents involved had previously been pushing for approval to launch an infiltration attempt against an outlaw motorcycle club for months, they had been told no until rumors started to circulate that the fledgling agency would be shut down, at which point their ATF Regional Director approved the undercover operation against the Hells Angels in an apparent bid to generate a high profile case using the Hells Angels reputation to justify his agency/office existence and save his career. This appears to be the birth of the culture of ATF careerism from outlaw motorcycle gang investigations. Additionally, because the Regional Director and the agents supervisor had to be aware that the two undercover agents were using their own personal funds, not authorized ATF funds to buy the contraband used to generate the indictments, it could easily be argued that those were not ATF authorized purchases of contraband in their official capacity, and were in fact illegal purchases made by the undercover agents in their personal capacity and as part of a criminal conspiracy with their supervisor and Regional Director, thus this appears to be the first time ATF employees engaged in a criminal conspiracy for the purposes of framing members of an outlaw motorcycle club for RICO offenses to further the agents and supervisors own careers, and in the process those ATF undercover agents intentionally and illegally possessed and trafficked in firearms, narcotics and stolen property.

Clearly, the OMG investigations at the time were being conducted using the Lynch model involving a task force, and now they were being prosecuted at the federal level, they were utilizing centralized training and intelligence sharing related to outlaw motorcycle clubs, which was starting at the federal level and working its way to local line level officers via superiors and specialized units. This top-down flow of information from highly specialized units is received by line officers as factual and accurate, but when the information is false it poisons the well and creates extreme prejudice amongst law enforcement officers from the federal level to the local police officer. Additionally, in the book *Ratsnakes: Cheating Death by Living a Lie...Inside the Explosive World of ATF's Undercover Agents and How We Changed the Game* by former ATF agent Vincent Cefalu, he describes this failed undercover investigation as a success because it drained the Hells Angels legal defense fund and "put the Hells Angels on notice: The Hells Angels weren't the boogeymen, ATF was." Cefalu goes on to discuss the organizational structure of ATF and how its lack of oversight allowed agents to use unethical and illegal behavior to build cases, and because of this ATF became the go-to for other agencies when it came to undercover work. Specifically, agent Cefalu discusses one incident from this period in which an undercover ATF agent he identifies as "Gene" was approached by the DEA to accompany one of their informants to purchase five pounds of marijuana from a dealer. Gene and the CI went and made the buy from the dealer but when they turned in the evidence to DEA, it was discovered what they had bought was not marijuana and the DEA wanted their buy money back from the ATF. According to Cefalu, undercover ATF agent "Gene" then kidnapped the CI, the dealer, conducted two armed robberies, a breaking and entering, and made the dealer take him to the sources home at which point he was informed by the sources father that the source had died the night before, so Gene decided that the DEA would only get part of their buy money back. It is critical that we recognize the importance of Cefalu's admission that not only do ATF undercover agents have a history of committing serious felonies including kidnapping and armed robbery against their targets and informants, but also because it establishes that ATF's undercover program's lack of oversight was recognized and exploited by the other law enforcement agencies when those agencies deemed an operation too controversial to conduct themselves because of their direct Department of Justice oversight, so they outsourced these operations to ATF who had almost no oversight which insulated the agency and offered those agencies plausible deniability should the operation go bad. As you will see this pattern of behavior will develop into a culture within the agency that would be refined over time to further their enterprise, and result in ATF atrocities like Waco, Ruby Ridge, and Operation Fast and Furious.

By the late 1970's, the false narrative surrounding outlaw motorcycle clubs had gotten so sensationalized and publicly accepted despite there being no incidents of provable organized criminal activity by outlaw motorcycle clubs, certain corrupt elements of law enforcement across the nation began to exploit the outlaw motorcycle club culture's code of silence and the publicly accepted narrative that OMC's are really violent gangs, and in the interest of making headline generating busts, law enforcement began raiding outlaw motorcycle club clubhouses dressed as bikers to try and instigate a violent confrontation with the targeted clubhouse, and worse they were planting contraband and then charging the outlaw motorcycle club members with serious crimes. The first prominent case of this type occurred in October 1976, when 13 armed, bearded men wearing biker attire spilled out of a van, began breaking windows and assaulted the Outlaws MC clubhouse in Tampa, FL. An Outlaws MC member named Harry "Harpo 1%er" Ruby was sleeping inside the clubhouse with his girlfriend when he was suddenly awakened by the armed bearded men assaulting the house, he responded with gunfire. In reality it was 13 plain-clothes police officers disguised as bikers raiding the clubhouse on a narcotics warrant, and when Ruby fired, law enforcement responded by firing over two dozen rounds into the clubhouse, one of which struck Ruby in the head. Ruby survived his injuries but was left with severe brain damage and while he was still in a coma, Ruby was charged with three counts of first-degree murder, possession of a short-barreled shotgun, and possession of marijuana. The charges brought by the state of Florida were eventually dismissed because Ruby had severe brain damage from the gunshot to the head and he was unable to communicate adequately enough to assist with his own defense. A civil suit filed by the wounded officers was also dismissed for the same reason. The raid failed to recover any evidence of organized criminal activity and the small amount of moldy marijuana that was recovered under the floorboards appears to either have been planted by officers or left behind by a prior resident. In December 1982, Ruby was indicted for the incident, this time as part of a federal Racketeer Influence and Corrupt Organizations (RICO) case involving the Jacksonville and Tampa chapters of the Outlaws MC. Somehow the government found him fit for trial, and he would become the first outlaw motorcycle club member ever convicted under the RICO act.

This modus operandi would reemerge across the country on December 12th, 1979, at the Outsiders MC clubhouse in Portland Oregon, when members of the Portland Police Bureau Narcotics Task Force executed a search warrant that was obtained using false information and with the intent of planting drugs at the Outsiders MC clubhouse to manufacture arrests and charges against members of the motorcycle club. Just like with the raid on the Tampa Outlaws MC clubhouse, the Portland officers were dressed like bikers and failed to identify themselves or announce their purpose, and simply assaulted the house. As the unknown bikers attempted to beat in the front door, Outsiders MC member Robert "PigPen" Christopher armed himself with a shotgun and took a defensive position on the stairs while the other members and their girlfriends sought refuge in an upstairs bedroom and attempted to call emergency services. Christopher warned the unknown attackers that he was armed and would shoot if they entered, and when the door broke open and one of the bikers took aim at him with a revolver, Christopher fired in self-defense and the man was struck in the face. Portland Polie responded to PigPen's one shot by firing over 142 rounds into the Outsiders Clubhouse. Emergency Services informed the group that the men outside were police officers serving a warrant and they were advised to surrender, which the Outsiders did, and they were all beaten severely by officers upon surrender, including the pregnant woman with the group. Christopher was charged and convicted with the officers murder but the conviction would later be overturned when one of the undercover officers was arrested in a sting investigation, became a witness against the other officers in the unit, he testified that the officers cited an informant who did not exist in order to get the warrant on the Outsiders MC clubhouse, and the officers came with drugs they intended to and did plant at the clubhouse. The information the officer would provide related to similar incidents involving the task force would lead to over 82 convictions being overturned and what has been the largest police corruption scandal in Oregon history.

These two incidents are critical to understanding the evolution of outlaw motorcycle club investigations and how easily the mystique created by the false narrative lends itself to corruption by those seeking to exploit it for personal gain. They also evidence an escalating trend of law enforcement undercover operatives manufacturing indictable offenses against motorcycle clubs that prove the false narrative that outlaw motorcycle clubs are violent drug dealing gangs. Additionally, the consistency between the tactics used in two incidents which occurred on opposite sides of the U.S., evidences the centralization of outlaw motorcycle club investigations training and that the IOMGIA was training law enforcement across the country to use consistent illegal tactics in their outlaw motorcycle club investigations, and these tactics included law enforcement deliberately trying to instigate violent confrontations with outlaw motorcycle clubs and planting drugs. Since March of 1965, with the release of the Lynch report and law enforcement beginning to aggressively surveil and target outlaw motorcycle clubs, an element of law enforcement have alleged outlaw motorcycle clubs are really organized criminal gangs, but they were unable to prove it for almost two decades of trying. While individually some motorcycle club members had been convicted of crimes related to drugs, firearms and even murder, these were crimes committed by the individual(s), for the sole benefit of the individual, and the members who committed them had done it without the knowledge or consent of the club. It was not until 1982 with the Outlaws MC that law enforcement got their first RICO success and even that case involved only a handful of members from just two chapters, a little bit of moldy weed, prosecutors had to go back and somehow get Harry "Harpo 1%er" Ruby deemed competent for trial, and then use his incident and other questionable incidents to gain those convictions.

There is much more to the evolution and corruption of "OMG" investigations, but now you have an accurate understanding of how they began, the roots of the corruption, and most importantly you understand how the big lie that outlaw motorcycle clubs are really sophisticated organized crime groups was started. In reality OMG investigations are a criminal conspiracy that was started by some dirty politicians and cops who were looking to save and further their careers, and they have continued to operate, insulate, and refine the criminal enterprise using their implied credibility as law enforcement and abuse of power.

5

IF THE TARGET OF YOUR INVESTIGATION IS NOT COMMITTING CRIMES, COMMIT CRIMES FOR THEM: THE BIRTH OF ATF'S ENHANCED UNDERCOVER PROGRAM

With the success of Operation Sun Apple that ran between September 1976 and July 1981 and used FBI undercover agent Joe Pistone to infiltrate the Bonano crime family, it was only natural the FBI try to run an operation to infiltrate an outlaw motorcycle club. The FBI would make the first successful infiltration of an outlaw motorcycle club using a paid Confidential Source of Information named Anthony Tait to infiltrate the Hells Angels in 1982.

Tait was a bouncer at a bar in Anchorage, Alaska which put him in a position to make friends with several members of a local outlaw motorcycle club who would later patch-over to become the first Hells Angels charter in Alaska. With outlaw motorcycle clubs all over the news and law enforcement warning the public that the Hells Angels were in town, Tait saw an opportunity to use his relationships with the new Hells Angels as an exciting new career opportunity for himself and he approached law enforcement and offered to infiltrate the Hells Angels. For three years Tait worked as a paid confidential source of information and was handled by FBI special agent Ted McKinley out of the San Francisco office. Hells Angels members would later describe Tait as acting and dressing like a drug dealer, wearing lots of gold rings and chains, ivory, cowboy boots, and spending excess amounts of cash with no apparent source of income. By the mid 1980's, Tait had worked his way into the West Coast representative position. In August 1986 when an Alaskan Hells Angel and former Outlaws MC member named J.C. Webb was shot and killed in a bar fight in Kentucky, the FBI spread the word of an impending war between the Hells Angels and Outlaws, while Tait did the same within the HA, and he began to travel the country to various Hells Angels charters attempting to buy explosives, firearms, narcotics, and incite retaliation towards the Outlaws. Webb had been killed by the Outlaws but when the Angels conducted their investigation of the incident, not only did they learn that Webb had previously been an Outlaws member, but they learned that Webb had pulled a gun on the Outlaw that shot him first and was killed in an act that was essentially self-defense and far from one that warranted a war between the clubs.

None the less, Tait's investigation of the Hells Angels which lasted more than three years resulted in indictments of 41 Hells Angels members and associates, but it was far from a success, mired in allegations of entrapment by Tait, and ultimately of the 20 Hells Angels members who stood trial, 18 were acquitted and only Irish O'Farrell and Sonny Barger were convicted of conspiracy to commit murder for supporting Tait's fictitious plan to bomb the Outlaws. For his three years of undercover work against the Hells Angels, Tait received over $63,000 and became a subject matter expert on outlaw motorcycle club infiltrations, worked with an author to publish a book about his experience, and began traveling the world and getting paid to preach law enforcement's false narrative as an "OMG Expert". What the FBI's infiltration of the Hells Angels taught them and is reinforced by the resulting indictments and convictions, is that outlaw motorcycle clubs are not sophisticated criminal enterprises, and while some individual members may be involved in serious criminal activities the organizations as a whole are not, and OMC's are a waste of time and money to infiltrate, investigate and prosecute.

The FBI was still receiving praise for their undercover operations targeting the mafia and having learned that outlaw motorcycle clubs are not organized crime groups that warrant the time and expense of deep cover operations, the FBI abandoned outlaw motorcycle club undercover operations and downgraded their responsibility to the non-violent gangs unit, which created a vacuum in outlaw motorcycle club investigations that the Bureau of Alcohol, Tobacco and Firearms was quick to fill, with ATF agent Ted Baltas who had been involved in the Tait investigation coordinating all ATF outlaw motorcycle club investigations from Washington D.C. Despite the fact that a deep cover infiltration of the Hells Angels conducted by the FBI and involving ATF had confirmed the HA were not a criminal enterprise, the FBI abandoning OMG investigations and downgrading them to the non-violent gang's unit, ATF ignored this and instead doubled-down, intent on proving the lie to be true.

Between 1987 and 1990, there were several new aggressive undercover agents hired by ATF including Steve Martin, John Ciccone, Jay Dobyns, Vince Cefalu, Darren Kozlowski, John Carr, Eric Harden, and Carlos Canino. There was also a change in instructors and curriculum at the ATF Undercover Academy, and this resulted in a change in the tactics used to investigate outlaw motorcycle clubs which included the birth of the use of "street theater", undercover operations that involve

the undercover agent enticing a target to be present while the undercover agent commits a serious criminal act with "criminals" played by
other undercover agents, in front of the target, who is then indicted for
the crimes the undercover agents committed in their presence.

In 1990, ATF first successfully had an undercover agent infiltrate an
outlaw motorcycle club during an investigation of the Warlocks Motorcycle Club in Florida that ran for almost two years before the operation was terminated for safety concerns after the murder of Warlocks
President Raymond "Bear" Chaffin. This landmark undercover operation utilized a blend of conventional undercover tactics and aggressive
new techniques and resulted in the arrest of forty-one members and associates of the Warlocks MC, but once again most ultimately had their
charges significantly reduced or totally dismissed. This operation taught
ATF just how easy and relatively safe it is to infiltrate outlaw motorcycle
clubs and then build big flashy cases against their members.

In their operation against the Warlocks, ATF agent Steve Martin approached and befriended Warlocks National President. John "Spike"
Ingrao at the gym where Spike worked out at. Spike was a very person-
able guy, and it was easy for the ATF agent with long hair, a beard, and
a Harley Davidson motorcycle to find common ground with Spike and
gain his trust. Martin's cover story was that he dealt in surplus military
equipment and made money protecting Columbian cocaine dealers and
their shipments in South Florida. Martin and Ingrao worked out daily
together and ate lunch together several days a week. Ingrao was eager to
expand the Warlocks MC and after about six months Martin began to
ask about going probate/prospect for the Warlocks MC. When agent
Martin learned that he could avoid the traditional probate period by
becoming a Probationary Member and starting his own Warlock MC
chapter, Martin jumped at the opportunity and patched-in three more
undercover ATF agents and a task force officer to start the Warlocks
MC, Fort Lauderdale chapter.

Once patched-in the agents used their access and influence to build cases against a handful of Warlocks members and several associates. To demonstrate that he was a criminal, agent Martin asked Ingrao to accompany him as he delivered a shipment of weapons to his Columbian drug bosses in South Florida. At the meeting, Ingrao was introduced to Martin's drug bosses, one of whom paid Ingrao for providing security and making the trip. Ingrao was later charged for his participation in a crime that was totally manufactured by the ATF undercover operation. Spike Ingrao pleaded guilty to trying to arrange a 525-pound marijuana deal that never was made, the illegal transfer of 21 machine guns, and the sale of 84 homemade bombs to undercover agents from the U.S. Bureau of Alcohol, Tobacco and Firearms. In exchange for his plea, 19 other charges were dropped.

Undercover ATF agent Steve Martin with Warlock MC president
Spike Ingrao.

Not only was Spike's case the first successful infiltration of an outlaw motorcycle club by ATF, but it was also the first case where the ATF would have to solicit the members of the targeted club to commit criminal activity, even manufacture the criminal activity, and the club members would be charged for crimes that never actually happened and would have never existed but for ATF's infiltration and their undercovers influence. The case was so tainted by allegations of misconduct and unethical behavior by the agents involved that the bulk of the charges were dismissed. Retired ATF Agent and ATF Whistleblower Vincent Cefalu reveals some of the corruption in his book *Ratsnakes Cheating Death By Living A Lie... Inside the Explosive World of ATF's Undercover Agents and How We Changed the Game*, that during the infiltration of the Warlocks MC agent Martin filed complaints about other UC's drinking, yet Martin drank excessively himself, he regularly set up his own UC deals without the knowledge of the rest of the team to make himself look like the hero, he alludes to agent Martin purchasing a motorcycle Martin knew was stolen for his own personal property, Martin was involved in a romantic relationship with one of the targets of the investigations sisters, and at the close of the investigation he was caught apologizing to Ingrao for his work on the operation, an act the agents of the ATF undercover program would ostracize him from the program for.

Even with the corruption, because the investigation had resulted in plea deals and the technique of using street theater in OMG investigations had achieved a highly publicized federal indictment that praised the ATF infiltration capabilities, and it had a huge impact on the Warlocks MC financially, so as far as the ATF undercover program was concerned this operation was a huge victory. Variations of the undercover role agent Martin used of the over-the-top gunrunning; drug trafficking criminal would become the model used by every male ATF undercover agent that has infiltrated an outlaw motorcycle club to this day. In reality, this is one of the worst covers you could have when trying to conduct a deep-cover infiltration of an outlaw motorcycle club, but it would take too longs to explain here, and you'll understand why it's a bad cover by the end of this book.

In the outlaw motorcycle club world, Florida is one of the top tier states. It has got a dangerous and violent history and is one of those places that as a motorcycle club member you better be on top of your game and understand where you are or there could be severe consequences for a breach in protocol. Additionally, because of the high activity, exposure to, and interaction with the big national clubs due to events like the annual Bike Week in Daytona Beach and Biketoberfest, the infiltration of the Warlocks MC made ATF experts on outlaw motorcycle clubs in general, not just the Warlocks. If you are starting a chapter of an outlaw motorcycle club in a prominent location like Fort Lauderdale, the club you represent is going to make sure you have sufficient knowledge of the protocol, community, politics, and relationships, to do that. Without those basics the chapter will surely violate protocol and likely fail which brings dishonor to the motorcycle club as a whole and creates problems in the community.

Thus, what we know is that at least the Warlocks MC including their National President believed that agent Martin knew enough about all the different types of motorcycle clubs operating in Florida and the national clubs that come through Florida, that the Warlocks MC felt comfortable letting agent Martin start a chapter and represent the Warlocks MC in a high-profile and likely contested location like Fort Lauderdale. It is fair to say that since the Warlocks are undeniably experts on outlaw motorcycle clubs because they have been one of the most respected outlaw motorcycle clubs in the United States since 1967, and they deemed ATF agent Steve Martin to be an expert on outlaw motorcycle clubs and allowed him to start the Warlocks Fort Lauderdale chapter during an undercover operation that ran for almost two years, the ATF as an agency has been an expert on outlaw motorcycle clubs since at least 1990 when Martin made member in the Warlocks, and based on ATF's tactics and techniques used during this operation and the resulting allegations of misconduct by undercover agents, it is clear that ATF has been aware that as organizations outlaw motorcycle clubs are not criminal organizations, forcing ATF to use street theater and exploit the one percent code of loyalty, honor, and brotherhood, as a tool to influence the member's behavior in order to get them to be present for "crimes" manufactured and committed by undercover ATF agents.

Additionally, ATF targeted the President of the club to create an organizational link, as well as targeting the members who were the most vulnerable to influence or were involved in criminal activity to build some legitimate predicate charges to support the major criminal activity conducted in the street theater incident, all of which would support law enforcements narrative that OMC's are criminal enterprises, when in fact it was a crime committed by the individual member(s), who but for the encouragement and access of the ATF, wouldn't have committed the offense. During the course of the investigation when one of the undercover ATF agents was tasked with driving one of the "crash trucks" (truck used to haul gear and bikes that break down) to a run and ATF tried to use an undercover vehicle with expired tabs, a Warlocks officer noticed the vehicle had expired tabs and told the undercovers they would need to get tabs or they would not be allowed to drive the vehicle with the club. When the agents found out that it was going to take too long to get new tabs for the undercover vehicle, they counterfeited a tab and used that, however on the way to the run the counterfeit tab led to the undercover agent being pulled over by the police.

Once again, because the outlaw bikers who were the targets of the investigation did not want the agents committing any crimes, we see a group of undercover ATF agents conspiring together and committing crimes for the purpose of furthering their undercover operation, and I believe that at the point undercover agents conspire to and commit actual crimes that were not authorized by ATF, they are clearly acting outside their scope of authority, and that undercover operation then becomes a criminal enterprise of its own and the ATF the offenders. Additionally, what this incident illustrates is that outlaw motorcycle clubs understand that law enforcement is constantly looking for any reason to target the club and as a result outlaw motorcycle clubs will go to great lengths to avoid any violation that exposes the club to trouble with law enforcement, including something as minor as an expired tab violation. It should be noted that in comparison to later operations, even though agent Martin and the undercovers started their own chapter and were authorized to open a clubhouse by the Warlocks, they never actually did because of ATF funding, they only rented a warehouse on one occasion to host a party, and because he only borrowed an undercover apartment that led to a conflict with the real landlord that compromised the operation, and those elements would be addressed and refined for use in future operations.

The response of the outlaw motorcycle club community across the nation to the operation was to slow or even freeze any plans for expansion when it was learned Ingrao's desire to expand had allowed an entire chapter of undercovers and their street theater to wreak havoc on the Warlocks. In fact, numerous news articles published in 1991 quoted agent Martin noting that the Warlocks biggest vulnerability was Ingrao's desire to expand so quickly, and it was how he was able to infiltrate the club. The membership and expansion freeze by the motorcycle club community made it very difficult for ATF to make another direct approach on an outlaw motorcycle club and with ATF agent John Ciccone having focused his attention on outlaw motorcycle clubs while working out of the L.A. office during the mid-nineties, the ATF's approaches changed and they conducted a series of operations in which they used Confidential Informants to make introductions for the undercover agents to various outlaw motorcycle clubs including; Kozlowski in Wisconsin to target the Outlaws MC, then Queen and Kozlowski targeted the Hells Angels in southern California, while Carr was making attempts against the North Hollywood Devils Diciples and Sun Downers, and Cefalu was working the bay area.

In 1997, agent Kozlowski conducted a failed operation against the Vagos MC that was run by John Ciccone and was the first undercover operation the two ran together against outlaw motorcycle clubs. Kozlowski was running a CI against the Vagos who ATF had provided with a motorcycle so that he could prospect for the club. Thirty days into the operation the CI was killed in a traffic accident while riding the motorcycle. As is common with undercover vehicles, the motorcycles license plate came back to the CI, but the VIN was registered to ATF, and when Vagos members received a copy of the accident report it identified ATF as the legal owner of the motorcycle. Kozlowski continued the operation and after being interrogated by Vagos members about the prospects connections and the motorcycle belonging to the ATF, he was allowed to hang-around and prospected for the club. The operation was shut down in early 1998 when the former girlfriend of the dead CI provided Vagos members with one of Kozlowski's business cards that he had given the CI, outing Kozlowski. This operation taught Ciccone and the undercover agents involved that public records could compromise undercover operations and they needed to be able to restrict access to any records related to these investigations and be able to get better backstopping on their cover identities than what was currently legally available to their undercover agents.

Details surrounding the formation and operations of the ATF's Enhanced Undercover Program (EUP) are shrouded in secrecy, but it appears that the EUP started around this time with ATF undercover agents Carlos Canino, Jay Dobyns, Vincent Cefalu, Darren Kozlowski, Billy Queen, Eric Harden, John Carr, Chris Bayless, Joe Slatalla, Paul D'Angelo, Greg Gaioni, Jenna McGuire, Erin Zapata, Holley Longacre, April Howell, and others serving as founding members and instructors for all new EUP agents recruited into the program. What we do know from court testimony by members of the EUP is that it consists of a team of 23 agents from across the United States who receive more extensive training and backstopping to allow them to infiltrate criminal organizations and are used when agents will be vetted by the target organization. The EUP infiltration operations work almost identical to the covert intelligence operations conducted by our various intelligence agencies including the CIA. For example, part of the additional training EUP agents receive includes how to pass a polygraph exam and their backstopping includes cover residences and businesses wired with sophisticated audio and video surveillance equipment, cover identities that include lengthy criminal histories, credit histories, identification documents and credit cards under their cover identities, and even backstopped cover educational and tax histories. In addition, to prevent compromising their undercover identities and their operations, it was at this point that the law enforcement agencies began using various sensitive information exclusions to make public records related to outlaw motorcycle club investigations largely exempt from FOIA and public records requests, regardless of if the investigation has been closed and the cases adjudicated. All these enhanced techniques were justified as necessary for officer safety because according to ATF and IOMGIA, outlaw motorcycle clubs are so sophisticated and dangerous to infiltrate that they warranted extreme measures not available to traditional undercover agents.

This triggered another transformational period in outlaw motorcycle club investigations, and now the operations that were being conducted by the ATF's Enhanced Undercover Program became incredibly elaborate and began to mimic the tactics and techniques used by our covert intelligence operations conducted overseas against terrorist organizations and hostile foreign governments. The infiltration and street theater technique used during the Warlocks operation were expanded on and the operations became well-funded, well backstopped, targeted infiltrations that used undercover agents to manufacture street theater crimes that would result in criminal indictments and supported the false narrative ATF wanted to prove about the targeted outlaw motorcycle club.

6

DIRTY DEEDS DONE DIRT CHEAP: ATF UNLEASHES THEIR RATSNAKES.

A pivotal evolution in the tactics and techniques the ATF Enhanced Undercover Program (EUP) uses in what they call Outlaw Motorcycle Gang investigations occurred during an operation ATF ran against the Sons of Silence M.C. between 1998 and the fall of 1999, in which two ATF agents named Blake "Bo" Boetler and Cole Edwards hung around, prospected for, and subsequently patched into the Sons of Silence MC in Colorado.

ATF agent Blake "Bo" Boetler during his infiltration of the Sons of Silence MC.

The Sons had never had any club related convictions or even any members arrested prior to the operation, but at the culmination of the operation thirty-seven people were arrested in dramatic televised raids on October 8th, 1999, that took place in Denver, Colorado Springs, and Fort Collins, Colorado, and touted the dismantling of the Sons of Silence Outlaw Motorcycle Gang (OMG). In fact, over half of the people indicted were not even members of the Sons of Silence, and it was established that during the raids ATF agents vandalized and stole the targets private property, and ultimately most of the charges were dismissed or reduced, once again tainted by allegations of misconduct by the ATF undercover agents and them soliciting, inducing, and even inciting many of the criminal charges outlined in the indictments.

One particular criminal charge in the indictment against the Sons involved a bar fight in Colorado Springs. An undercover ATF agent with the Enhanced Undercover Program (EUP) named Jay Dobyns gives us a look at EUP tactics and takes credit for starting the fight and inciting the crime in his New York Times best-selling book *No Angel*. As we now know, ATF has been an expert on outlaw motorcycle clubs since at least 1990, which means they definitely know what will start a fight with an outlaw motorcycle club and what wont. In his book *No Angel*, Dobyns details the incident on pages 83 and 84 stating, "The Sons were a minor biker gang in Colorado Springs. We were running around as a made-up club called the Unforgiven and we wanted to demonstrate that the Sons used intimidation and the threat of violence to maintain their turf. If we could do this, we could roll it into a RICO case being built against them. We wanted to do it that night by putting the screws to them, by hanging out in their place and showing them up. They were small-time and my confidence was high." Dobyns goes on to describe how he disrespects a Sons of Silence officer until the Sons member was honor-bound by the one percent code and likely his clubs' bylaws to defend his and the club's honor, and he punched Dobyns, setting off a bar fight that resulted in the charges Dobyns went into the bar with the intentions of manufacturing and leaving with. Again, it is important to remember that the charges from this incident were dismissed because ATF started the fight, but now you understand the tactics that agents in ATF's Enhanced Undercover Program are allowed to use when it comes to investigating outlaw motorcycle clubs and other groups. Furthermore, this is another incident in which ATF undercover agents conspired together to incite a crime in order to entrap members of an outlaw motorcycle club on federal RICO charges because the targeted club was not committing the crimes ATF wanted them to, and fortunately for the Sons of Silence members indicted, the judge agreed and threw out the charges.

In terms of the transformational impact this operation had on outlaw motorcycle club investigations it was a milestone operation because it marked the very first time that when the traditional undercover tactics and techniques used by Beotler and Edwards were failing to produce any significant charges let alone organized crime charges, the EUP agents including Dobyns stepped-in to manufacture indictable offenses consistent with ATF's investigation theory. Additionally, with this operation ATF began using an undercover technique I like to call to call "Dynamiting the pond.", in which they establish a motorcycle club consisting of law enforcement officers in an area of the country where the existing outlaw clubs are known to be very territorial, with the hopes of getting the undercover agents beat up and their patches pulled (taken), and then charge the offending outlaw motorcycle club members with R.I.C.O. crimes, alleging they did it to enforce their territory and further the criminal enterprise.

Patch pulling was a tradition of the motorcycle club culture that was used by the motorcycle club community to enforce the protocols related to how new clubs were established in that area, as well as respond to major violations of a club's honor. This operation also marks the point where the ATF and outlaw motorcycle club investigations began using the tactic of adopting the identities of existing respected outlaw motorcycle clubs for their fake clubs made up of undercover agents, and they do this in an attempt to instigate violent conflicts between real outlaw motorcycle clubs which would generate indictable offenses. At the time of this operation, the real one percent outlaw motorcycle club named the Unforgiven MC had multiple chapters in Washington State and a few Nomads running around elsewhere.

The next operation of this type would be conducted by Detective Steve Cook and other undercovers as part of a task force operation out of Missouri that stole the identity of the Outsiders MC from the Pacific Northwest, arguably one of the most influential one percent outlaw motorcycle clubs in American history.

The tactics of intentionally instigating conflict between two groups to generate a desired political outcome is one that has been used successfully in American covert human intelligence (HUMINT) operations in the interest of our national security since the very beginning, but their use was restricted by law to the C.I.A. Under U.S. law, the Central Intelligence Agency (CIA) must lead covert operations unless the president finds that another agency should do so and properly informs the Congress. The CIA's authority to conduct covert action comes from the National Security Act of 1947. President Ronald Reagan issued Executive Order 12333 titled *United States Intelligence Activities* in 1984. This order defined covert action as "special activities", both political and military, that the US Government could legally deny. The CIA was also designated as the sole authority under the 1991 Intelligence Authorization Act and in Title 50 of the United States Code Section 413(e). The CIA must have a "Presidential Finding" issued by the President of the United States in order to conduct these activities under the Hughes-Ryan amendment to the 1991 Intelligence Authorization Act. These findings are then monitored by the oversight committees in both the U.S. Senate and the House of Representatives and as a result of this structure, the CIA receives more oversight from the Congress than any other agency in the federal government. The Special Activities Center (SAC) is a division of the CIA's Directorate of Operations, responsible for Covert Action and "Special Activities". These special activities include covert political influence and paramilitary operations. Covert operations are employed in situations where openly operating against a target would be disadvantageous. Operations may be directed at or conducted in association with allies and friends to secure their support for controversial components of foreign policy throughout the world. Covert operations may include sabotage, assassinations, support for coups d'état, or support for subversion, and the tactics typically include the use of a false flag or front group. The activity of organizations engaged in covert operations is in some instances similar to, or overlaps with, the activity of front organizations. The new aggressive outlaw motorcycle club investigation tactics being used by the ATF's Enhanced Undercover Program were more consistent with the tactics of the CIA's Special Activities Center and less consistent with the tactics used by mainstream American law enforcement undercover operations, and they are undoubtedly the result of the large number of EUP instructors and agents who had been members of U.S. military special operations prior to their employment with ATF and had direct experience participating in these types of operations. That said, the tactics were clearly at odds with the law at the time and the Constitution.

The Sons of Silence MC started in Colorado in 1967, eventually spread throughout multiple states and are a nationally respected one percent outlaw motorcycle club. The Sons are big, tough men who are known for standing up for themselves and being the original outlaw motorcycle club to call Colorado home. They were at the top of the political food chain of the motorcycle clubs in the state and known to pull patches if a club came into their state or a new club tried to form without following established motorcycle club protocol. ATF had been running their operation against the Sons for quite some time and it was not productive, so to bolster a flimsy case against the Sons the ATF decided to call in the EUP and dynamite the pond. ATF established a motorcycle club called the Unforgiven MC that consisted entirely of undercover law enforcement officers, with the intent of getting their patches pulled in order to demonstrate the Sons of Silence used intimidation and threats of violence to maintain their territory, and then indict the Sons under R.I.C.O. This wasn't a case where the ATF started a club of undercovers and waited to see what happened, this was a case where ATF started a club of undercovers with the intent of exploiting existing motorcycle club culture protocols and picking a fight with the Sons of Silence to elicit an honor-bound response of violence, and then indict the Sons for a crime that wouldn't have occurred but for the ATF and their fake Unforgiven MC chapter. As Dobyns himself describes it in his book *No Angel*, he and agents John Carr and Chris Bayless, all wearing their new Unforgiven colors, went into a bar the Sons of Silence were known to regularly hangout in and the agents began drinking. When a member of the Sons of Silence approached agent Dobyns and asked him who he was, Dobyns responded with deliberately disrespectful and antagonistic comments. Honor bound; the Sons member punched Dobyns tipping off a bar brawl. As intended, the ATF rolled the charges from the brawl into the R.I.C.O. case and hailed the case as a victory, claiming they had totally dismantled and destroyed the Sons of Silence MC.

However, of the forty-two people arrested in the R.I.C.O. case, twenty-one turned out not be members of the Sons of Silence, eight motorcycles had been illegally seized without warrants, one had "ATF" scratched into the custom paint job and the ATF had vandalized some of the houses, for which they were eventually held financially accountable for by the courts. Most of the defendants had their cases dismissed, at trial evidence was suppressed because it had been improperly obtained or was fabricated, and many of the members who chose to take their cases to trial were acquitted. Larry Pozner, a former head of the American Criminal Defense Bar was quoted in the media saying the case epitomized taking, "relatively minor offenses and trumpeting them as the crime of the century. This is garden variety stuff made to sound like a major law enforcement coup."

When Doc Cavazos joined the Mongols MC in the mid-nineties the club had less than thirty members and Doc was easily able to gain influence and control over the club by recruiting members of Los Angeles street gangs to become Mongols. While the name of the club and the patch may have been the same, Doc's influence on the Mongols dramatically changed their identity as a motorcycle club, prospective members were no longer required to prospect or even own a motorcycle and he quickly built the Mongols to over three hundred members in the Los Angeles area alone. Additionally, because Doc was recruiting street gang members and not bikers, the new Mongols behaved like street gang members and law enforcement had noticed a dramatic increase in the number of assaults, stabbings and shootings involving Mongols members at night clubs and hip hop parties that were not places traditionally frequented by bikers, which made the Mongols a target for agent John Ciccone.

Once again, a motorcycle clubs desire for rapid expansion and re-laxed membership standards had created the opportunity for ATF to easily infiltrate an outlaw motorcycle club, and along with ATF under-cover agents John Carr and Eric Harden, they planned the infiltration of the Mongols that would become known as Operation Ivan. ATF un-dercover agent Darren Kozlowski was brought in on the case to advise and in early February 1998, ATF undercover agent William "Billy Slow brain" Queen was recruited to serve as the undercover operative, and Operation Ivan was launched. Queen and Ciccone had worked together on ATF's SRT team from 1992-1998, and Queen was selected for his ex-perience with ATF, his ability to ride a motorcycle, and the fact that he already had extensive backstopping in place for his undercover identity that included an undercover apartment which reduced the chance the Mongols would become suspicious about an applicant who just moved into their residence prior to applying for membership in the club. A confidential informant who was an associate of the Mongols had ob-tained a copy of the Mongols membership application, so ATF knew what personal information the Mongols would want on a prospective member, and they used that information to backstop Queen's identity even further. Using an ATF front business, Queen was provided with six years of W-2 forms and since the application asked for phone num-bers of family members, an undercover phone was installed in Queen's brother's home, and he was provided with scripted responses should he receive a call. ATF even went so far as to plant yearbook photos in the yearbooks at the school Queen allegedly attended per his cover identity. Just like we saw with agent Steve Martin and his infiltration of the War-locks MC, Queen's cover identity was that of a gunrunning enforcer and was so over the top that it immediately drew concerns from the Mongols that Queen was an undercover agent. In the book *Angels of Death* by Julian Sher and William Marsden, John Ciccone is quoted as saying that the Mongols were always messing with Queen saying, "Hey undercover." and making other references to their suspicions Queen was an undercover law enforcement officer.

While Operation Ivan did result in indictments against several Mongols members, the case failed to establish that the Mongols Motorcycle Club was operating as a criminal enterprise, and it was hardly the success that ATF represented it to be. Ciccone goes on to state in the book that the operation taught them several things, most importantly that they needed more staff for these operations and more administrative support. In the book Ciccone is quoted as saying "We had constant headaches from management: we're spending too much money; where are the results?" Ciccone's rational is that it takes time to infiltrate an OMC and gain the trust of members before an undercover will be invited to commit crimes, and it can take at least a year to see any search warrants or indictments. In reality, the lengthy infiltration's with no warrants or indictments are clear evidence that outlaw motorcycle are in fact not criminal enterprises, but just like law enforcement, the Catholic church, schoolteachers, politicians, judges, professional athletes, military members, etc., there are criminals in every social group, and it is those lone bad-actors' crimes that law enforcement uses to evidence and reinforce their false narrative regarding outlaw motorcycle clubs. Law enforcement preaches this false narrative because OMC investigations equal fun, fame, and fortune for those who conduct them. Ciccone continues: "All management was seeing was tens of thousands of dollars being spent on repairs to the bikes, the undercover apartment, utilities, phones, this and that, and no arrests and no search warrants were happening. They were so hung up on that, they wanted to shut the case down every other month." Ciccone and many of the EUP undercover agents had built their careers on outlaw motorcycle club investigations and they were at risk of losing those careers due to their lack of results and failure to prove that outlaw motorcycle clubs were really the criminal enterprises that Attorney General Lynch had falsely labeled them as in 1965, and ATF had been pursuing them as so aggressively to justify their existence since the rumored shut down of the agency in 1974. Ciccone and the EUP agents had a vested interest in producing results, even if those results came at the expense of innocent Americans.

Evidencing the link between the ATF and the International Outlaw Motorcycle Gang Investigators Association, in 2001, the Jackson County Drug Task Force including Independence Missouri police detective Steve Cook used the Dynamiting the Pond technique again against the Galloping Goose MC, when Cook and others formed a club made up of undercover law enforcement officers, that they named the Outsiders MC. Just like with the prior operation in Colorado involving agent Dobyns and the fake Unforgiven MC, Cook's operation stole the name of a real and respected outlaw motorcycle club that had been in existence since 1968 and had multiple chapters in Washington and Oregon. The Galloping Goose are one of the oldest outlaw motorcycle clubs in the United States, having started in Sylmar California in 1943. By 1948, they had spread to the Midwest, establishing a base in Kansas City and by the late 1960's, they began enforcing a "fifty-mile rule", which meant no new motorcycle clubs were allowed to form within fifty miles of Kansas City. The goal of the operation was to use the fake club's sudden appearance and 50-mile rule to incite a violent confrontation between the Galloping Goose MC and the fake Outsiders MC. For 18 months Cook and his fake "Outsiders" ran around Kansas City trying to antagonize the Galloping Goose. However, times had changed, and the Galloping Goose did not respond with violence, rather they simply told Cook and the rest of his fake Outsiders that there was already an Outsiders MC and he and his friends should join an existing motorcycle club that was more their speed so that they could learn the protocol of the culture and work their way up to an outlaw motorcycle club. The Galloping Goose made arrangements for the undercovers to start riding with a Bandidos support club called the Hermanos MC, but according to multiple news interviews Cook has given, he and the other undercovers stopped hanging out with the Hermanos or returning their calls because it didn't allow them to focus on the "gangs" they wanted to.

Cook achieved nothing with his attempt to dynamite the pond but he refused to stop targeting the Galloping Goose, and in 2006 he used a confidential informant to make several drug buys from four members of the Galloping Goose, one of whom, Mike "Joe Poke" Hensley flipped when he was indicted in 2008 for conspiracy to distribute methamphetamine, cocaine and marijuana, and then provided information that led to convictions against three members of the Galloping Goose and their brother club El Forstero MC. The case failed to prove that the Galloping Goose was a criminal enterprise and in fact the Outsiders MC debacle and referral to the Hermanos proved the Galloping Goose were not using violence and intimidation to control territory as law enforcement alleged, as well as showed how prejudice law enforcement is when it comes to outlaw motorcycle clubs. It did not matter that the behavior of the Galloping Goose indicated they were not a criminal enterprise as Steve Cook and law enforcement alleged, they continued targeting the club until they could arrest a member for their own criminal activity, indict them, and then get them to lie and make statements that supported law enforcements false narratives.

The culture amongst some members of law enforcement of careerism from OMG investigations that began in 1965 with the Lynch Report is clearly evidenced by this operation which Cook used to springboard his career as an OMG expert. He won multiple awards for the mediocre investigation which hailed him as a hero, became Director of the Midwest Outlaw Motorcycle Gang Investigators Association, an officer in the IOMGIA, and began getting paid to travel the world teaching OMG investigation courses to other law enforcement officers and prosecutors, as well as paid to do interviews for T.V. and Media and serve as a consultant for various documentaries and television series. Then in 2015, Cook and his former undercover partner and a current training coordinator for the Midwest Outlaw Motorcycle Gang Investigators Association named Edward "Fingers" Jauch premiered a staged reality show about their work called "Outlaw Country", giving him creative control in spreading the false narrative on outlaw motorcycle clubs to an international audience of millions.

Since 1965, when Attorney General Lynch used false information to create the Lynch Report and arbitrarily classify OMC's as organized crime, then law enforcement launched their crusade against OMC's, the undercover operations conducted had been largely unsuccessful and most importantly, the few RICO convictions the federal government had been able to piece together using the broad reach of the RICO Act failed to prove the organizations were operating as criminal enterprises when you look past the convictions and analyzed the criminal activity that resulted in the charges. Law enforcement was taking crimes committed by individual members and then using the broad reach of the RICO act to make the crimes appear as if they were committed with the knowledge of the club and in furtherance of the alleged enterprise.

The failure of ATF's EUP to produce results and the huge costs associated with the tactics of the EUP put tremendous pressure on Ciccone and the rest of the agents to produce a case that would prove the narrative that outlaw motorcycle clubs were really sophisticated criminal enterprises and this combined with the inherent corruption of the new aggressive EUP agents and the program in general that was being developed at ATF's Advanced Undercover School would lead to the most significant and troubling transformation in the tactics of outlaw motorcycle club investigations.

The ATF has always had a reputation for running fast and loose with their undercover operations but because of the lack of oversight that ATF undercover operations receive combined with using senior EUP agents as instructors at the Advanced Undercover School, the EUP has created a self-perpetuating culture of prejudice, corruption, careerism, and substance abuse among their agents that is more disturbing than the behavior of the outlaw motorcycle clubs they investigate and would lead to atrocities committed by the EUP such as Operation Fast & Furious in which ATF undercover agents sold so many guns knowing they were being taken back to Mexican drug cartels, that eventually one of those guns was used to kill a U.S. Customs & Border Protection officer named Brian Terry. There is nothing holding these undercover agents accountable for their actions and with the use of sensitive information classifications related to officer and operational safety, the EUP can cover up their corruption and illegal activity. For those who are sworn to serve and protect, the EUP thumbs its nose at their oaths, laws, and the Constitution, and this attitude is instilled and fostered by the instructors and administrators at the ATF Advanced Undercover School. In his book *Ratsnakes*, former EUP member Vincent Cefalu describes his first experience as an instructor at the school and notes that the first class he taught at the ATF's Advanced Undercover School was known as "The Class From Hell" and he "had it on good authority that in the back of the classroom there were half gallons of Gin, Bourbon, Scotch, and Vodka, and several coolers of beer. There was one rule: Be on time. It didn't matter how you were dressed, or whether or not you were completely sober, but you better be on time. There had to be standards, right?" It is easy to dismiss this behavior as harmless hi-jinks, but all the participants are sworn law enforcement officers who are being paid to attend this school using taxpayer money and the instructors feel it is acceptable for them to show up for class drunk and were allowing students to drink during class. Since advanced undercover school always involves real-world scenario based field training exercises out amongst the general public, what Cefalu minimizes as harmless partying amongst agents, actually outs the students for committing repeated acts of driving under the influence in government owned vehicles, as well as they were allowing intoxicated undercover agents to carry firearms while drunk in public, and most importantly because this is their Advanced Undercover School, they are teaching the "elite" agents of the EUP that this corrupt and illegal behavior is not only acceptable, it is a best practice.

The party lifestyle and substance abuse amongst EUP undercover agents would almost be exposed to the public but for a hearing in 2006 in my brother Josh's case, USA v. Fabel ET. Al, against the Hells Angels Washington Nomads charter and it revolved around ATF's golden boy agent Jay Dobyns. During the hearing, defense attorneys produced a photo of Dobyns wearing a bikini with a banana stuffed in the crotch, that Dobyns had found in a female agent's room when he had broken in during a drunken raid at an ATF training event. This incident would lead to a huge internal scandal when a sexual harassment complaint was filed by the female agent against several undercover agents and additional allegations were made. The photo and associated story were so damning that the government elected not to call Dobyns as an expert witness on the Hells Angels in the most significant Hells Angels R.I.C.O. case to date.

For all the OMC investigations and indictments, we have discussed thus far, there are dozens that garnered little to no results at all. In a criminal justice system where you are innocent until proven guilty the sheer number of failed and fruitless OMC investigations further evidences the reality that outlaw motorcycle clubs are not gangs or criminal enterprises, and that false narrative about OMC's is one established and maintained by members of law enforcement who have used outlaw motorcycle clubs as a tool to advance their careers, enrich themselves, and further the criminal enterprise of the EUP and the IOMGIA. ATF undercover agent Joe Slatalla had worked at least a dozen outlaw motorcycle club investigations over the years and in 2001, he and Tempe Gang Unit officer Chuck Schoville decided to target the Hells Angels in Arizona. The Dirty Dozen MC had patched over to become Hells Angels and there had been no investigations of the HA in the four years since. In the book *Angels of Death*, Schoville is quoted; "Everybody said it was organized crime, the mafia of the new day. Well, my question was, if this is organized crime, what are we doing about it." Schoville's statement further evidence's what prior OMC investigations have proved over and over, and that is OMC's are not criminal enterprises. Additionally, crime statistics based on actual arrests and convictions support they do not warrant the investigative attention that ATF and IOMGIA say they do. If the statistics and evidence proved they were a criminal enterprise the agencies would have no issue allocating the funds and personnel to investigate them, but just like we saw with ATF's initial undercover operation against the HA in 1974, the investigations and facts prove the funds and manpower are needed on higher priorities.

According to interviews Schoville and Slatalla provided for *Angels of Death*, in 2001, Slatalla and Schoville both members and officers of the IOMGIA, launched an investigation of the Hells Angels. Slatella is quoted in the book; "I felt they were pretty ripe to be exposed and to be beaten," he says. Only this time he was going to run a tight ship and not let the bureaucrats screw it up." There are several things important about these quotes, they evidence that there was no predicate criminal activity being committed by the Hells Angels that Slatalla and Schoville based their investigation on, it was simply their own personal prejudice and the idea that the Hells Angels were a criminal enterprise that needed to be exposed and punished. Most importantly, it shows the contempt that some members of the EUP and IOMGIA have for the restraint placed on them, their use of lack of organizational and administrative support as excuse for the lack of success with OMC investigations, and finally, that agent Slatalla deliberately took actions to conceal his activity from administration to further his own personal agenda and not the agenda of the administration and ATF. Slatalla began this investigation from an intelligence standpoint and went back through twenty years of police reports to identify members and associates of the club in an attempt to identify potential human intelligence assets that he might be able to recruit as contract informants, then he began planning for wire taps, tools that can legally only be used once all other methods of investigation have been exhausted. Slatalla's investigative approach and attempts to circumvent the bureaucracy of ATF and the Department of Justice would give birth to a new transformational period in outlaw motorcycle gang investigations, one that would result in outlaw motorcycle gang investigations mirroring the high-threat covert human intelligence operations used by our intelligence agencies and special operations. In the case of OMG investigations, the result is complex covert operations that rather than being conducted based on probable cause, are based on personal prejudice, and planned and conducted in a targeted manner designed to manufacture indictable offenses to "prove" a narrative that law enforcement knows is factually untrue, as well as conceal the operation from oversight. Moreover, their method of investigation became infiltrate, influence, entrap, instigate, and indict.

7

RUNNING WITH THE DEVIL

In early 2001, I was contacted by a biker named Crazy Phil who identified himself as the National President of a one-percenter outlaw motorcycle club called the Aliens MC. Phil had gotten my number from a mutual acquaintance and told me that he and his brother Lefty were two charter members of the Aliens MC out of the Bronx, NY. According to the two brothers the Aliens MC had patched over to become the New York City chapter of the Hells Angels while the brothers were serving time in federal prison, but now that they're off paper the Hells Angels had given them their blessing to start flying the Alien patch again as a support club with the intent on patching them over to Angels when the time was right, and Phil asked me if I would be interested in running Aliens MC operations in Washington state.

I was familiar enough with my biker history to know that in the late 1960's the Aliens MC did in fact patch over to the Hells Angels and it was my understanding that when a club patched over, their prior club colors were burned and the club permanently disbanded, but when I questioned Phil about this he agreed that was traditional protocol but the Angels were making an exception in this case because he and Lefty were respected members of the Aliens MC at the time of the patch-over and would have been Angels but for the fact they were in prison for taking care of club business at the time of the patch-over. This was a way for them to become Hells Angels without having to put on prospect patches. Phil told me that they had an old and close relationship with the Hells Angels and advised that they would be attending a Hells Angels Nomads Washington party in Tacoma Washington in a few weeks, and he asked me to attend with them so that he could introduce me to the Washington Hells Angels and in particular their president Smilin' Rick. Over the next few weeks, we spoke almost daily. The guy talked the talk, knew all the right names and ultimately, I accepted his invite and agreed to meet them at the Hells Angels poker run.

Phil told me that there would be three prospective chapters of the Aliens MC attending the event and the Angels had invited them to party with them at the clubhouse Friday night. He asked me to meet them at the hotel where they were staying in Tacoma on Friday afternoon and then ride with them over to the Angels clubhouse. I think that we have all had those moments in our lives that we distinctly remember. For me, one of these is cutting my daughters umbilical cord when she was born, and another equally vivid moment was when I packed for this trip to Tacoma. I was not nervous about the trip, but I had a feeling in my gut something was wrong.

The afternoon sun shined through my bedroom window onto my saddle bags laying on the bed and had warmed the mildewed leather of my saddle bags enough to remind me of every rainy road trip I had ever taken. It was going to be a short trip and the weather was nice, so I packed light, just a change of clothes, flannel shirt and a digital camera. I strapped the bags on my Harley Davidson FXST and went back in the house, instinctively took my belt off and grabbed my H&K pistol in its custom leather holster. As soon as I grabbed my gun, it was like I got struck with a bolt of lightning and even though I had that "something's wrong" feeling, I had an even more overwhelming feeling that having that gun on me was not a good idea this time. What the fuck? I thought to myself as I wrestled with the constant mantra repeating in my head: "It's better to have a gun and not need it, than need it and not have it."

It was fucking simple and made sense, I'm going to meet with a one per-cent outlaw motorcycle club I've never met and more importantly, I'm going to meet with a charter of the Hells Angels with a reputation for extreme violence. Fuck yeah, I would rather have a gun and not need it, than need it and not have it with those guys. None the less, that over-whelming feeling that a gun would be a bad idea this time won out and I left the gun behind. Despite it being sunny and warm as I left the house, I remember getting chills as I rode away from the house towards Tacoma and thought, "Well, if you regret leaving that gun behind, you won't get a second chance to make that mistake." The closer I got to Tacoma the more serious my mood got and the more I questioned my decision to entrust my protection to a CRKT folding knife and my wits.

When I arrived at the hotel, I did a drive-by to check the lot for bikes and did not see any. I tried to be as security conscious as possible when planning this trip and had deliberately booked my hotel room on the ground floor knowing that the rooms were high enough someone could not climb through or shoot through the window from the outside, but at the same time they were low enough that I could jump from them in the event of a fire. I checked in and made a call to Crazy Phil but no an-swer. I figured they got held up on the road and I decided to take a quick nap.

At about 8:30pm, my phone rang, and Phil tells me they just got in and are waiting for the other chapters to arrive but they wanted me to come upstairs and meet with him and Lefty so they could get to sleep because they were worn out from a long road trip. When I en-tered Phil and Lefty's room, it was hazy with smoke from the Ameri-can Spirit cigarettes that Phil and Lefty smoked. Both Crazy Phil and Lefty were in their 60's. Phil was skinny with long gray hair and a face and physique that told a story of long-term methamphetamine addic-tion, while Lefty's physique told a story of time in prison, hard work and a seriousness that even though Crazy Phil was the ranking officer told me Lefty was the more dangerous of the two. As soon as I walked into the room I saw another red flag, Crazy Phil had an old school Aliens MC tattoo on his upper right arm that had knife marks through it, a large divot of missing flesh, and it was clear someone had tried to cut his Aliens MC tattoo off of his arm. Crazy Phil ran down the story of the Hells Angels blessing them opening the Aliens MC back up as a support club with the intent of patching them over and told me that it would be a fast track to an H.A. patch. He went on and on about how good their relationship with the Angels was and how this was the perfect fit for me. I bought it, hook, line, and sinker, I agreed to be the Aliens MC Washington President and left the room with a brand-new set of red and white Aliens MC colors and one percent diamond. My gut was still telling me something was wrong, so I deliberately did not sew the Aliens colors on and went to bed feeling like there was no turning back, I had no idea where I was headed, and it did not feel good.

I do not remember what time I met Phil or Lefty the next morning or most of that day but here is what I do remember. I met Crazy Phil and Lefty across the street from the hotel at the waffle house for breakfast. When I walked into the restaurant, I was surprised to see two national officers from a one percenter motorcycle club having breakfast by themselves with no security in sight, I told Crazy Phil I was looking forward to meeting the other chapters and asked him when they would be here. Crazy Phil got visibly nervous, paused for several seconds, and then told me that the other chapters had met up and got into an accident while riding together, a member had been hurt and so they turned around and headed home. My mind went blank, no one-percenter club would leave two national officers on their own. Club members would have been sent to provide security for Phil and Lefty but that is not the story, they just turned around and went home and that did not agree with what I knew about the protocol of one percent outlaw motorcycle clubs, and it certainly did not follow the one percenter code. I remember thinking I could bail on these guys and go home but what if the Hells Angels had surveillance on the hotel and had identified me as being with the Aliens and if they had done that and I just ditched these guys and headed for the hills, then I may have the Hells Angels come after me and I wouldn't know they were coming and it may come at my home with my family. Or I could stay and take what I had coming to me and hopefully it all works out, that way at least it will keep any consequences away from my home and my daughter. I decided to stay.

It was when we checked in at the Hells Angels poker run things got really weird. Crazy Phil and Lefty had gone on and on about how close they were with the Angels, but I was the new guy and I noticed that they were deliberately hanging back when we entered the event and left me to break the ice with social interactions, and this raised more red flags. I was not ignoring the red flags and was convinced that some level of bad day was coming my way, but if the devil was coming for me, I wanted to face him here with just me and these two idiots and not have it anywhere near my daughter or fiancé. I tried to justify their behavior to myself thinking they were just testing me to see if I could interact in the motorcycle club community comfortably and follow protocol but that was not working. I got more concerned when I checked in for the run and the Hells Angels hang-around running the check-in took a copy of my driver license. I came to the run with the belief that just because I wanted to be involved in the outlaw motorcycle club world did not mean my family had to, and now the Hells Angels had my home address and that did not make me feel good at all, they now knew too much about me and there was definitely no turning back. We went on the poker run, had a good time and at the end of the run we were invited back to the Angels clubhouse to an after-party.

When we arrived at the Hells Angels clubhouse there was already a long line of Harley's backed to the curb in front of the clubhouse. The white cinderblock clubhouse looks like many HA clubhouses with its red trim and red iron bars over the windows and doors. A heavy black velvet curtain hung over the door on the inside blocking the view from the outside as people entered or exited the clubhouse. Numerous CCTV cameras were perched prominently on the building giving whoever was watching the monitor a view of not only what was going on outside the clubhouse, but the cameras also looked up and down the street giving them the ability to see who was coming. Law enforcement in both marked and unmarked cars had established a perimeter around the clubhouse and were surveilling the event and gathering intelligence on all its attendees which was standard for an HA party. People milled about in front of the clubhouse as a prospect stood guard at the front door and searched everyone entering for weapons. For the first time since I left home, I felt like I might have made the right choice by leaving my pistol at home. There was a no weapons policy for the clubhouse, so I ditched my knife in my saddle bags and took my place in line to get searched with Crazy Phil and Lefty behind me. Another red flag was raised when Lefty stepped up to get searched and they found the small pistol he had hidden in his vest. It was clear from the "No Weapons" signs and the line of people being searched that no weapons were allowed but he had thought somehow, he was going to be able to get that little Saturday night special into the clubhouse. What he did accomplish is bringing even more attention to us than his red on white Aliens rockers had already brought us.

An outlaw motorcycle clubs colors consist of a top rocker that identifies the name of the club, a center patch that consists of the club's logo and in many cases a bottom rocker that identifies the city or state the member's chapter is based out of. While there are a few exceptions to this set-up in most cases outlaw motorcycle clubs self-identify with this three-piece patch scheme. Additionally, the most prominent and respected outlaw motorcycle clubs will identify as one-percenters and wear a small diamond shaped patch with a 1% in the middle on either the front or back of their colors. While law enforcement claims that this indicates they are the one percent who live outside the law and engage in criminal activity, in reality it means we are the most elite in the motorcycle club world. It is no secret that the club world has been at times, particularly in the 70's and 80's, a very territorial and violent place and clubs have been known to kill over things like colors. The Hells Angels colors are red and white, and they have made a point of making sure that they and their support clubs are the only ones who use that color combination. The only exception to this I can think of is the Outsiders MC in the Northwest. The original Aliens MC colors were red on white rockers with a black Maltese cross and skull as their center patch. The colors Crazy Phil and Lefty wore were consistent with what I knew to be the original Aliens MC patch design and colors, and with their story that Smilin' Rick had given them their blessing I tried as best I could to ignore the stares of disbelief from the other clubs in attendance at the clubhouse.

Aliens Motorcycle Club center patch design

The inside of the clubhouse was like any other HA clubhouse that I had been in. Decked out in red and white, there was long bar, pool table, booths, and comfortable seating. The wall across from the main entrance was adorned with a large Hells Angels Nomads Washington mural. A stocky HA prospect in his mid-twenties tended bar as guests from numerous Washington state motorcycle clubs and citizens milled about and mingled inside the clubhouse. In the corner below the TV was a monitor that showed the views from the surveillance cameras. I was impressed with the quality of the image and care that went into determining camera position to get such effective coverage. As I moved between the two main rooms in which guests were allowed, I noticed the front windows on the clubhouse were ballistic glass. Two large barbeques and a temporary bar were set up in the back yard and the clubhouse dog was conducting a methodical search for scraps dropped by the guests. I made my way around the event and introduced myself to the other clubs but Phil and Lefty stayed seated in a booth inside the clubhouse and kept to themselves. This concerned me and I thought enough is enough. I was feeling like I had been played and now I had walked into the lion's den believing a bunch of lies and there was no turning back.

I grabbed myself a burger and a Corona and went and sat down with Crazy Phil and Lefty. "Hey man, I know I'm the new guy but something ain't right here. Why the fuck are you two so shy?" I asked. "We're not shy, you need to understand there is a way things are done and follow our lead." Phil replied. "I've been trying but you guys haven't been doing much leading and that's been concerning me. I'm the new guy and things just aren't making sense." I said. Phil stuttered and his hands shook as he tried to formulate a response and when he finally pulled it together, he gave me his first presidential order and told me to go find the Hells Angels Sergeant at Arms and set up a meeting with Smilin' Rick. It was at this point I knew that we were fucked. If these guys had a great relationship with the H.A.'s and Smilin' Rick, why were they sending me to set up a meeting? That's the process for clubs you have no relationship with, not ones that had blessed you as a support club, and at this point I was not even sure Phil and Lefty knew what Smilin' Rick looked like.

I scanned the room, and my eyes were immediately drawn to a hulking Hells Angel with the Hells Angels death head prominently tattooed on both sides of his bald head, a testament to his commitment to his club, and he wore Filthy Few and Thug Crew patches proudly on his chest which told me that he was as serious a Hells Angel as they come. I studied him as he stood there scanning the room, first looking at the individuals faces and then what their hands were doing. In an instant he assessed them and then moved on to the next individual methodically scanning the crowd for threats as I had done and seen so many professional protection specialists do when we work high threat environments. I knew that he had at least a basic knowledge of professional protection tactics and techniques, and the danger level of the situation I was in just went through the roof in my mind. I rehearsed my introduction and request in my mind so that I would be free to actively listen to him and analyze his responses, then I confidentially walked over to the monster, stuck out my hand and introduced myself. I was shocked when he took my hand and in a friendly and welcoming tone said "How ya doin Jeff? I'm Josh, Sargent at Arms, Hells Angels Nomads Washington." He engaged me in some small talk and asked me about my motorcycle and if I was having a good time. I noticed he was not drinking alcohol but was instead drinking soda which told me that he must be a shooter and carrying a gun. I had learned enough that with the more serious motorcycle clubs if a member is going to carry a firearm for self-defense they will not drink so as to not interfere with their reflexes or judgment and create potential use of force issues if they have to use the firearms in self-defense or in defense of others. When I felt the moment was right, I told Josh that Crazy Phil and Lefty had requested a sit down with Smilin' Rick. Josh advised that it would be tough to do during the party, but they would make some time afterwards to meet with them. I excused myself and went back and informed Crazy Phil and Lefty of what had transpired, and while they seemed pleased, they were still not eager to engage with the rest of the guests. I enjoyed the environment and I enjoyed interacting with the Hells Angels and the members of the other motorcycle clubs, so rather than sit there with Phil and Lefty I continued to mingle but I kept finding myself engaging with Josh.

Josh was exactly what I thought a Hells Angels Sergeant at Arms should be. He was big, intimidating in appearance, carried himself with confidence but deliberately avoided displaying any tough guy attitude and had a charisma and personality that was disarming. You could tell he took his membership and position in the club very seriously, had been trained by other senior Hells Angels for his role in the club, and appreciated the significance and honor of the role he was entrusted with. He had an above average knowledge of Hells Angels history for a Hells Angel, and you could tell he really loved the club, was proud of its history and we spent some time talking about his travels to New York and a legendary former Hells Angel named Big Vinney Girolamo. We discussed my work in security and investigations, my criminal defense experience, and I volunteered to do criminal defense investigation work pro-bono for a member that was facing murder charges at the time. I enjoyed Josh's company and during our conversation, while I could tell we were both very deliberate with our words, I felt like we clicked in a genuine way. After several hours at the clubhouse Phil & Lefty said that they wanted to go back to the hotel. Protocol dictates that one percenter presidents do not go anywhere without security, so to demonstrate good protocol I escorted Phil and Lefty back to the hotel before returning alone to the Hells Angels where I continued to socialize for about three hours before deciding it was time for me to call it a night. I made my way around the clubhouse and respectfully said my good-byes with Josh being the last member I spoke to. He told me that he would get in touch with me as soon as they got done with the party and we would get together then. We exchanged numbers and I went back to the hotel.

When I got back to the hotel I stopped in and saw Phil and Lefty. They both seemed nervous, almost to the point of being scared and this made me nervous. I knew that I had just met these guys and could not trust them. I had a feeling we were about to be in deep shit, I knew I could not run, so I was going to have to face the devil with these two shit-bags in tow. I asked them if they wanted to go out and get dinner and they refused saying they were not hungry, and they just wanted to go to bed. It was like they were trying to shoo me out of their room so they could talk, and they told me to call them when Josh got in touch with me. I went back to my room knowing in my gut that I was about to have a really bad day. I tried to watch TV but my mind kept focusing on the myriad of stories I had heard about how the Hells Angels dealt with motorcycle clubs that started in their territory without permission, and my mind wouldn't let me forget that this was not that situation, this was much worse, this was a one percent motorcycle club with red & white rockers that had patched over to the Hells Angels and was supposed to be dissolved forever, that had started back up without permission in H.A. territory. This was the ultimate disrespect, and I knew that whatever was coming our way was deserved under one percenter code and I could either run like a bitch or stay and face the consequences of my decisions like a man. The memory of the hang-around photocopying my driver license and the thought of bringing violence to my home and little girl because I was not man enough to face the consequences for my decisions immediately suppressed my desire to run, and I decided to grab some beer and order pizza to pass time as I waited on the devil. Just before midnight I got a call from Josh, and he said that they had some guests in from out of town and that they had to stay at the clubhouse, and he asked if we could get together for some breakfast in the morning. I agreed and then called Phil and Lefty to advise them of the change in plans and went to bed.

It was about 5:50am when Josh called that Sunday morning and once again it was more "Hey, we really want to go to breakfast but it will be just a couple of more hours." When I relayed that news to Phil and Lefty, that was the excuse they were looking for and said that they could not wait any longer and needed to hit the road for home. I pointed out that if we waited a couple more hours it would only be 8am and they said that they would wait in their room. Around 8:00am Phil & Lefty made the call that they were done waiting and they were heading home. I did not like not knowing what was coming but decided if they were headed home then so was I, and headed outside to where we had all parked our bikes the night before.

Outside, Crazy Phil was already on his bike with his helmet on, ready to pull out of the parking lot and Lefty was just getting on his bike. It was clear they were way past nervous and full on scared at this point. I started to strap my saddle bags on my bike as we said our goodbye's and all of the sudden up rolls a silver Ford Crown Victoria driven by the prospect that I had seen tending bar at the clubhouse, and Josh was in the passenger seat. I could see three other large men in the back seat who I assumed were Hells Angels but had never seen them before. Suddenly my red flags that I had seen turned to alarms because I knew Hells Angels deliberately never rode motorcycles or wore any clothing or jewelry indicating their membership when they committed acts of violence, and here we were meeting with five H.A's, none of which displayed anything including a tattoo referencing their membership. Even Josh wore a black beanie which could have been explained by the cool morning temperature, but I interpreted to be intentional to conceal his death head tattoos. I knew we were in the shit, it was game time, and the only man I could depend on for any help was me. However, I was the genius who made the wise decision to leave my trusty H&K 9mm back home. I almost laughed out loud at myself as I accepted responsibility for my situation, and the better to have a gun and not need a gun, than need one and not have it mantra kicked me in the balls as I accepted the reality of my situation, then the adrenaline kicked my mind into high gear. The passenger window of the Crown Vic rolled down and Josh greeted me, then Lefty, and Phil who sat on his bike with it still running and pointed towards the exit of the parking lot, an undeniable look of desperation and terror in his eyes. After some quick small talk Josh says, "Hey ahhh, do one of you guys have a room we can go to and talk business in private before we go grab breakfast?" God damn it, that was not what I wanted to hear. There was nothing that we had to talk about that could not have been discussed in hushed voices in that parking lot and it was clear that my day was about to get really bad.

Now let me just say, it's a tremendously overwhelming feeling when you realize that you are in the process of being set-up by the Hells Angels and the Angel calling the shots is a guy you saw wearing Filthy Few and Thug Crew patches just the day before. You see at the time, my understanding of the Filthy Few patch was the same as law enforcement's, and I thought that if a Hells Angel had a Filthy Few patch it meant he had killed for the club. I would later come to learn that is not the true meaning of that patch and that is, yet another myth generated by law enforcement and the patch actually is reference to the first guys to a party who are also the last to leave. None the less, at the time the sight of Josh's Filthy Few patch wouldn't leave my mind and the reality of my situation was terrifying. This is one of those situations as a man where you get to find out if you are a real tough guy or just a guy who likes to pretend that he's tough, and whether you will stand your ground no matter what the odds or run like a coward. I knew the Hells Angels had my driver license information and there was nothing they couldn't find out about me with that information, there was no way I was letting my dumb ass decision bring violence to my little girl, so I immediately volunteered my room knowing that if I'm going to have a bad day with the Hells Angels I wanted it to be in my ground floor room and not in Phil and Lefty's fourth floor room that would be too high to jump from if that needed to be part of my survival plan. Realizing my mind was thinking about the situation from a tactical perspective gave me comfort and allowed me to focus on looking for an opening to survive. Josh and the other Hells Angels exited the vehicle leaving the prospect with the car which at this point had been backed into a parking spot, another bad sign. Lefty got off his bike and Josh turned and asked Crazy Phil if he was going to join us as he motioned us all towards the side door of the hotel. Phil said he would park his bike and join us as we were walking towards the side door of the hotel. Rather than back his bike into one of the open parking spots perpendicular to where he was idling on his bike, he accelerated forward out of view around the building and it was then we learned who was man enough to face the devil, and who was not. Josh played it cool and said let's head inside and Phil can meet us there, and we headed to my room.

Things were friendly enough outside, but I knew what was up and it was just like a scene from a mob movie. The guys they send for you are nice as pie until they get you exactly where they want you and then they make their move and kill you. It was my hotel room which meant I would be the one opening the door and that would give the Angels control of us because they would be the last to enter the room and thinking ahead, I knew I needed to position myself next to the window because I may need to use it as an escape route. As I attempted to get the card key to activate the lock, Josh asked if he could use the bathroom once we got inside and I agreed. Once unlocked, I walked directly into the room and sat myself on the bed next to the window and began scanning for items that I could use to break the window and as improvised weapons. Lefty took a seat in the corner with his back to the wall and facing me directly across from where I was sitting on the bed. I knew he had that pistol in his pocket and I also knew it was not the right weapon to get into a gunfight with five Hells Angels, would only make this fucked up situation even more fucked up if he pulled it, and I hoped to hell he was smart enough not to. The meanest looking Hells Angel I had ever seen took a seat with his back to the wall, putting himself between me and Lefty while the others stood blocking the entrance. Within a second or two of Josh entering the bathroom I see the flash of a chromed Taurus .45 pistol exit the bathroom just before his hulking frame and he pointed the gun at Lefty and tells him "Don't make me turn this into a homicide." There ya go, we are in the shit and oddly enough Josh's statement about making him turn this into a homicide gave me comfort as I took it to mean he was not planning on murdering me unless he had to, and that gave me hope and time. Josh quickly disarmed Lefty of his pistol, stripped him of his Aliens MC colors and explained very clearly that when a club patches over to Hells Angels that club is permanently dissolved, the huge disrespect the Aliens had shown by trying to restart the club and showing up to an HA event with patches on, and he joked that it had saved him a trip to come find them. Then Josh turned his attention to me. He demanded to know where Crazy Phil had gone and questioned me about whether or not he would run out on us or if he'd return. I told him that Phil and Lefty had told me they were twin brothers and old school one-percenters, so I was shocked that he would pull this kind of shit and assumed he would return. He quizzed me about where his room was and eventually, he ordered me to make a call to Phil's room to see if he had gone back to his room. When Josh ordered me to make the call the Hells Angel standing next to me who had been keeping his gun trained on my head told me to hand him the pillow from my bed as I moved towards the phone in the corner. Oh shit, he is going to use the pillow to control the blood splatter from a head shot I thought. My mind immediately decided I would hand him the pillow to occupy at least one of his hands and then smash him in the face with the phone and use it to break the window before diving out and making a run for it, but as soon as I handed him the pillow, he stripped it of its case and used the case to grab the phone and hand it to me. I was momentarily nauseous as I tried to stifle the adrenaline rush caused by my fight drive, and then it was back to thinking because I knew they could not leave an unaccounted-for witness and had to wait for Phil to come back or go find him themselves. I dialed Phil's room and it must have rung thirty times before Josh told me to hang up and sit back down.

As I took my seat on the bed, I decided it was time to arm myself so that I could be ready to fight as effectively as I could. If Phil came back, there would-be no-lose ends and I would have no choice but to fight for my life as soon as he came back. I saw the pizza box on the nightstand and the half drank six pack of Budweiser bottles and knew I needed at least one of those beer bottles. I'd been kidnapped by five armed and pissed-off Hells Angels and still trying to play it cool I tell Josh, "Man, this is not the way I wanted to start my day. Can I have one of those beers and a piece of pizza while we wait?" Josh looked and me with a bit of shock and to my surprise he handed me a beer, then held out the box of half-eaten pizza and I took a piece. I could not believe it, he had given me an improvised weapon, this is great. I silently celebrated by downing the beer making it seem to be a huge stress reliever and then put the bottle down by my feet out of direct view and asked for another beer. To my surprise Josh gave me a second improvised weapon, which I deliberately sipped on to keep the bottle weighted for maximum effectiveness. While I have never asked him why he allowed me to have those beers, I'm sure his logic had to have been who would be dumb enough to bring a beer bottle to a gunfight with five Hells Angels with guns. While it sure was not my preferred weapon, the reality of the situation is those beer bottles were probably the best available weapon for the situation because while I would have taken some of them with me, I would have not likely survived had I had my gun on me that day and pulled it in such a confined space and that dramatically outnumbered. Those beer bottles forced me to use courage, patience, and tactics to survive.

We sat there at gunpoint for what seemed like hours waiting for Phil to come back and he never did. Finally, Josh calmly and very seriously tells Lefty and I that they know who we are, where we live, and where our families live. He tells us that we have twenty-four hours to find Crazy Phil and bring them his patch, or else. That motherfucker Phil had deliberately trick-bagged me with the Hells Angels and now my life was on the line because of him. "Fuck that guy!" I said. "I'll make sure you get his patch." I told Josh, knowing that to retrieve his patch would likely require a multi-state road trip and violence. Lefty agreed and assured Josh that he would get Phil's patch. Josh instructed me to call him as soon as we had Phil's patch. I understood why the Hells Angels had done what they did and because I understood one per-center protocol and the violation, I understood it was just business and I was simply some green dumb ass who was in the wrong place with the wrong people, at the wrong time. Additionally, I was impressed with how smoothly the Angels had handled the incident and how they and Josh took care of business, and oddly it made me want to be a Hells Angel even more. I stood up, looked Josh in the eye and told him, "I understand this wasn't personal and was just business, so I have no hard feelings.", and I reached out my hand to shake his. Josh could not hide the look of surprise on his face but attempted to hide it with a smile as he reached out, gave me a firm handshake, and then turned and they all left the room.

As soon as the door shut, I tore into Lefty for putting me in this situation. He apologized desperately and I told him I did not want to hear it and that he was going to take me to find his brother. With that I made a call home to my fiancé and left her a voicemail letting her know that I loved her and would be home as soon as I could, but if this was the last time that I got to speak to her I wanted her to know that I loved her with all my heart. I hung up the phone and told Lefty how I could not believe his own twin brother would run out on him and leave him hanging like he did. Lefty mother-fucked his brother in what appeared to be an attempt to establish rapport with me, but I could tell he did not have the balls to stand up to even his own coward of a brother and told him it was time to go.

My eyes squinted as they adjusted to the bright sun when we walked out into the crisp morning air, and I remember how great it felt to be outside. Just like it was planned, up rolls Crazy Phil on his motorcycle and he stops in the middle of the access road between the hotel and waffle house. As if it had been no big deal that Phil had run out on us, Lefty exclaimed, "See, I told you he didn't leave us." as he beamed with a smile and walked towards Phil who was sitting on his idling Harley bagger, as if he was going to give him a hug. Rage flashed over me and the adrenaline I was still fighting to manage overwhelmed me. In two strides I overtook Lefty, shoving him aside and walked with purpose directly to Crazy Phil still sitting astride his Harley, and I delivered a solid right hook to his chin which caused him and the bike to topple to the ground, pinning his left leg beneath the bike, trapping him. I walked around the bike which had died and gave him a solid kick to the face and took great satisfaction when his nose and mouth erupted with blood, and he coughed blood and teeth onto the asphalt. His eyes rolled back in his head, and he let out a defeated sigh as he laid back onto the ground in submission. He attempted to regain focus and I could tell he did not understand what was happening to him. I explained to him that he had lied to me, trick bagged me, then run out on us like a bitch, leaving us to be killed by the Hells Angels. Then I told him I was taking his colors and the Aliens MC is permanently shut down. I stripped his colors off him, told him he had one hour to get out of the state of Washington or else, then spit on him before turning and walking away towards the waffle house. Lefty helped Phil out from under his bike and Phil took a minute or two to pull himself together, then got on his bike and left like he was told.

Lefty, then came trotting across the road after me like a little puppy dog, apologized for his brother's actions and asked if he could stay with me and see what the Angels say. I told him I wanted nothing to do with him, but he could stay if he wanted and then called Josh on his cell phone. They clearly hadn't even made it back to the clubhouse yet because within five minutes the silver Crown Vic pulls into the parking lot of the waffle house with Josh in the front seat. His window rolls down and I handed him the rolled-up denim vest with red and white Aliens MC patches identifying the colors as belonging to the National President. Josh unrolled the vest and held it out carefully inspecting it as if it was a piece of fresh fruit that he was considering buying and then turns to me, extends his hand to shake mine and tells me, " Good work." I ask him "Are we all squared away here?", and he tells me our business is done, and they drove away leaving me and Lefty standing in the parking lot of the waffle house. It was going to be a long ride home so we both went inside and ordered breakfast. We did not speak at all. I remember taking two bites of my omelet before deciding fuck this I just wanted to be home. I told Lefty he was buying my breakfast and I walked out of the restaurant and started the long trip home. That would be the last I ever saw of Crazy Phil and Lefty.

As I rode east towards home, I reran the events of the weekend in my head, analyzing every wrong move I had made and every lie I had been told. I thought about how effectively the Angels had set us up and how smoothly they operated as a team. At the first rest area I stopped to take a piss and make sure I did not have any Aliens paraphernalia on me. After a short stop, I headed back out and as I accelerated down the on-ramp from the rest area, I noticed a Harley Davidson approaching from behind and I could see the distinctive red and white front patches of the Hells Angels on the front of the rider's vest. Oh shit, they must have sent a trailer to shoot me off my bike I thought, and at the pace he was going, he was either going to fall in right behind me giving him perfect position to shoot me off my bike, or I could accelerate out in front of him and try and make a run for it. I decided to slow just enough that he would have no choice but for us to merge together with him along side of me, or he'd have to accelerate or brake which would be a tell as to his motive. As the rider drew closer, I was able to positively identify him as a Hells Angel but even more concerning, he was one of the Hells Angels from the hotel room. He must be a trailer and I slowed so that we merged next to each other. The Angel looked over at me, I looked at him and he gave me what appeared to be a nod of approval. We rode side by side for about thirty minutes before I decided he was riding too slow and I wanted to get home bad enough that I was willing to take my chances in front of him, and I accelerated away.

The next day I was home relaxing when my phone rang and whose name should pop up on the caller ID? Josh, Hells Angels Nomads Washington. God damnit, I thought I was done with these guys! Again, thinking it was better to talk to him and try and find out if I had a problem with the Hells Angels rather than ignoring the call and not knowing, I answered my phone. Hello, I said. Pretending not to know who was calling. Hey Jeff, this is Josh, Sergeant at Arms, Hells Angels Nomads Washington. Josh always followed proper outlaw motorcycle club protocol when handling club business. Josh's voice was upbeat, almost jovial and he told me that their President Smilin' Rick had asked him to give me a call and let me know that they thought I handled myself like a man in that hotel room yesterday, they'd like it if I came around the club, and he invited me to the clubhouse for drinks and dinner with Smilin' Rick prior to their meeting that week. I thought about it for a second and while I knew it could be a set-up and I could easily end up dead, the Angels had taken the brand new digital camera that had been given to my wife and I as an early wedding gift, and with our wedding only two weeks away I feared disappointing that gorgeous little 5'2" blonde way more than I feared the HA, and because I still wanted to be a Hells Angel and figured there weren't many guys that got the chance to have a story like mine as the beginning of how they became an H.A., I agreed to meet Josh and Smilin' Rick at the clubhouse as requested. Ultimately, I would go to the table and express my desire to become a Hells Angel prospect.

Jeff Burns in a Hells Angels MC Nomads Washington jacket, circa, 2002.

Over the next few years, Josh would mentor me and teach me everything legendary Hells Angels like Mouldy Marvin, Cisco Valderamma and Bart from New York City had taught him was important to be a good Hells Angel. He taught me the importance of understanding club history, the tactics and techniques of Hells Angels club security, the importance of being a man of action rather than talk, and he instilled in me a fundamental drive to always put the club and your brothers first and adhere to the one percent code.

Josh with Hannah in his front yard. Tacoma, WA circa, 2003.

Just before the Hells Angels USA Run in 2003, Josh asked me to come to his house for dinner with him and another Hells Angel. After dinner, the other Angel left and as we walked back toward the house Josh and I settled into the chairs on his front porch. Over the last few years Josh and I had gotten very close, and I could tell something had been weighing on my brother's mind for quite some time, but officially in terms of the club we weren't brothers, so protocol kept me from even asking him what's wrong. We sat there for several minutes discussing life, motorcycle clubs and just generally bullshitted having a good time and trying to pretend there wasn't something I didn't and couldn't know anything about. Then suddenly Josh spoke. The way he started his sentence caused my stomach to turn. "Heyyy Ahhh" he started, his voice serious and heavy it was the same way he started his sentence that morning outside the hotel. What the fuck was I in for now I thought. "Heyyy Ahhh Bro, you trust me, right?" "Yeah bro, I trust you. What's up?" I responded. Josh continued; "I know you want to be a Hells Angel and I think you'd make a great Hells Angel but there's some shit going on in the club that I can't talk to you about and it would mean a lot to me if you just sat back and watched things play out over the next month before we bring you to the table. If you don't like what you see it's not too late for you to change your mind, and if not, I'll make sure you're a great Hells Angel, but I need you to trust me on this." This totally blindsided me, but his message was clear, there's trouble in paradise and I needed to pay attention and slow down. Josh had taught me well and I agreed to be patient.

Josh came home from the USA Run to find a pipe had burst in his home, his house had flooded and was uninhabitable and he had gone to stay with his parents in Spokane. I was at our property on a small lake in a suburb of Seattle with my wife at the time and my daughter, enjoying a beautiful summer evening, when I get a call from Josh. "Heyyy ahhh brother." he said, his tone and inflection making the use of the term obviously deliberate. "Hey bro, I just wanted you to know that I love you and I wanted you to be the first to know that I quit the club. I showed up at the clubhouse for our meeting and nobody was there, so I walked around the corner and turned all my shit in to Happy Jack. I'm done bro and I just wanted you to know that I love you and I hope this doesn't change things between us." No bro, this does not change anything between us I said, but it changed a lot for me. I remember feeling honored that Josh chose to call me after he quit the club. That is a difficult time for any loyal one percenter who finds themselves knowing it is in their best interest to quit their club. Josh was the ultimate Hells Angel in my eyes and if he had quit after only a little over five years as a member, after everything he had invested and done for the club, I knew I did not want to be a Hells Angel anymore. A week later, I watched another prominent member and enforcer for the charter quit the club and at that point I had no doubt I no longer wanted to be an H.A. and began moving in my own direction.

8

THE 2002 LAUGHLIN
RIVER RUN RIOT

The 2002 Laughlin River Run Riot between the Hells Angels and Mongols was of such political and historical significance to motorcycle club culture that I feel it deserves its own chapter to help you understand it, as well as events involving the Mongols MC and their evolution.

The Mongols Motorcycle Club was formed in Montebello, California in 1969 by a group of Viet Nam veterans and bikers who had allegedly been refused membership in the Hells Angels. In the mid 1970's, the Mongols switched from wearing local bottom rockers (Long Beach, South Bay, So. Cal) and began to wear a California bottom rocker much to the Hells Angels ire, as it was the Hells Angels contention that only the HA could wear a California bottom rocker. The perceived disrespect the Mongols showed the Hells Angels by daring to wear a California bottom rocker led to the most well know bottom rocker war in American motorcycle club history.

The Hells Angels launched their first attack against the Mongols in San Diego, CA on September 5th. 1977, when they machine-gunned Mongols Emerson "Red Beard" Morris, Raymond "Jingles" Smith, and their ol' ladies off their bikes as they rode home from a Mongols run. At the funeral service for the two murdered Mongols, someone parked a 1962 Rambler and placed a bouquet of red and white carnations and then walked away. A few minutes later the Rambler exploded injuring two Mongols members and a couple of guests. A few weeks later a customer dropped a motorcycle wheel and tire off for repair at a motorcycle repair shop called Frame-Up in Highland Park that was owned by a couple of Mongols. The tire exploded and killed two people, one of which was a fifteen-year-old boy. A few weeks later, a van belonging to the President of the San Fernando Valley chapter of the Mongols exploded when he opened the door. In 1982, San Diego Mongols Scott "Junior" Ereckson and Bill "Mike" Munz confronted and killed San Diego Hells Angels President Raymond "Fat Ray' Piltz, who allegedly was one of three Hells Angels involved in the machine-gun murders of Red Beard and Jingles back in 1977. At this point, the two clubs agreed to a cease-fire, the Mongols agreed to restrict their operations to southern California and the two clubs have had a troubled relationship ever since.

By the late 1990's, Mongols MC membership had dwindled to less than thirty mostly aging members, when an egomaniacal former Surenos criminal street gang member and radiologist named Ruben "Doc" Cavazos was allowed to join the club without prospecting. Doc joined the Mongols with the goal of becoming the leader of a powerful organized crime group and within a year of becoming a Mongol, Doc had quickly worked his way into the National Sargent at Arms position and had recruited over two hundred young new Mongols that were more loyal to him than the established club hierarchy. This totally changed the identity of the Mongols since many of the new members were not bikers but Surenos criminal street gang members. Then Doc used his influence to relax membership criteria to accommodate the new Surenos membership, so that not only were prospective Mongols being made members without prospecting, but they were not even required to ride or own a motorcycle for up to eighteen months after making member. Many of Doc's new membership were involved in drug dealing and other criminal activity that was controlled by the Mexican Mafia (EME), and when these Surenos became Mongols and stopped paying their drug dealing taxes and interfered with Mexican Mafia operations, this angered the Mexican Mafia who declared war against the Mongols MC. In addition, these new members' drug use and unpredictability led to an increase in random violent acts committed by Mongols, and their lack of understanding or respect for outlaw motorcycle club protocol and history was creating increased conflict with the Hells Angels in California.

The Laughlin River Run takes place every April in Laughlin, Nevada and is the largest motorcycle event west of the Mississippi, regularly drawing over 50,000 bikers from all over the world to party for four days in the little casino town on the banks of the Colorado River. My brother Josh was the Sargent at Arms of the Hells Angels Nomads Washington charter and was working security at the Hells Angels command post they had established at a hotel directly across the river in Bullhead City, AZ from Harrah's casino and resort in Laughlin, and this was where most of the Hells Angels charters were staying for the Laughlin River Run that year. There were a few H.A. charters staying at the Flamingo in Laughlin and one charter of H.A. was staying at Harrah's in Laughlin where they had traditionally stayed.

Now pay attention because this part of my story will be critical to you understanding my whole story and the big picture when it comes to understanding outlaw motorcycle club culture. It is where I introduce some key players, and it is a point in time where it got incredibly dangerous to be an outlaw motorcycle club member. My account and opinion of Laughlin is derived from my own personal experience, the conversations that I have personally had with men like Josh from both clubs who were involved on the front lines, men that I trust and consider(d) friends, and publicly available law enforcement records, witness statements, and sworn testimony. Regardless of who tells the story, there was undeniably three groups involved in what would come to be known as the Laughlin River Run Riot, and they were the; Hells Angels MC, Mongols MC and Bureau of Alcohol Tobacco, Firearms and Explosives

(ATF) Enhanced Undercover Program. Ironically, only the A.T.F. would go to great lengths to conceal their presence in Laughlin and participation in the riot.

I want to make sure we all agree on the roles of each of the parties present at Laughlin as we know them to be with the understanding we have at this point in my story. While I don't want you to go out and buy his trash book, since I'm going to quote from it I encourage you to use Google or visit your local public library to get access to a free copy of Jay Dobyns book *No Angel* if you have any questions regarding the validity of the quotes I used, because I am having to rely on it and other interviews of ATF personnel and the limited available public records to establish ATF's role and attempt to determine what really happened that night in April 2002.

The Hells Angels and Mongols roles at Laughlin in 2002 were to coexist peacefully, protect their brothers, represent their clubs, and have a good time. They were NOT there to go to war in the middle of a casino full of cameras, innocent bystanders/witnesses, and cops at one of America's largest motorcycle events. I think we can all agree that is not an environment conducive to committing crime and what have been alleged to be sophisticated criminal organizations should understand that and take care of business elsewhere. Representing your club means you defend your club, your brothers and your honor no matter what, and the ATF knew that if either club was disrespected by the other it could potentially kick off a major incident of violence that would all be caught on the casino cameras, providing sensational visual evidence and allowing both clubs to easily be charged with major RICO offenses, manufactured from the start just like the charges against the Sons of Silence, but this time the ATF wouldn't make the mistake of actually throwing the first punch, they would get the clubs to do it for them.

How do we know the clubs were truly there just to have a good time? I have/had lots of friends who are or were members of both clubs, were there and have told me that is what they were there to do. That is what my brother Josh and other Hells Angels have always told was the reason why the club goes to Laughlin every year, that makes sense based on my experience personally being at Laughlin and numerous other major motorcycle events over the years, I have been to numerous events where hundreds of members from all the major one percent clubs were confined to a single hotel for several days and is consistent with the attitude and behavior exhibited by the Mongols and Hells Angels at those events. It was very much a; you do your thing, and we will do ours, and so long as nobody disrespects anyone, we'll all just have a good time. I know the idea of one percent outlaw motorcycle clubs mixing like this sounds crazy but trust me it happens often, and you will see photos of it later in this book and throughout my trilogy that will blow your mind. Respect gets respect and communication is always preferred to war and a RICO indictment.

Supporting the theory that ATF was there to instigate and video record a major incident of violence between the two clubs was testimony from a Harrah's employee during a subsequent civil trial in which he testified he worked with ATF agent John Ciccone extensively to develop surveillance strategies and he provided him access to the casino surveillance system during the Laughlin River Run.

Finally, when we look at the role the ATF played in the 2002 Laughlin incident, you must consider the roles their paid informants may have played in the incident. What would not become known until years later is that at the time of the 2002 Laughlin River Run, ATF was running multiple undercover operations against the Hells Angels that were not generating any valuable intelligence or indictable criminal activity, and they had multiple paid informants in both the Hells Angels and Mongols. One of the paid informants ATF had in place at the time of the 2002 Laughlin River Run was Hells Angel Michael "Mesa Mike"

Kramer. Mesa Mike was a methamphetamine addict and one of the numerous members of the Dirty Dozen MC from Arizona that patched over to the Hells Angels in 1996. Consensus is that on October 25th, 2001, a tweaked-out Mesa Mike was the primary aggressor in the murder and near beheading of Cynthia Garcia, along with Hells Angels Kevin Augustiniak, Paul Eischeid, and witnessed by Hells Angel Richard Hyder.

Garcia's body was found on October 31st, 2001. On November 26th, Kramer contacted ATF outlaw motorcycle gang investigations specialist agent John Ciccone about becoming an informant and he was immediately debriefed by Ciccone. Kramer became a registered ATF Confidential Source of Information and was placed on the ATF's payroll on December 1st, 2001, and in doing so he became a primary ATF asset in Operation Dequaillo which targeted the San Fernando Valley charter of the Hells Angles. Because Kramer was a convicted felon, he could not legally possess firearms, so agent Ciccone contacted Assistant United States Attorney Rod Castro-Silva and arranged for a waiver for Kramer which would allow him to carry a firearm. Kramer then transferred his membership from the Mesa HA charter to the San Fernando Valley charter and began collaborating with ATF undercover agents Darren Kozlowski and John Carr as part of Operation Dequaillo. Kozlowski and Carr were Mesa Mike's ATF controllers which means they were directing his activities and conducting covert physical surveillance of his operations during the Laughlin River Run that fateful weekend in April 2002, and it was in the bar at the Flamingo Hotel where Kramer was introduced to ATF undercover agent Jay Dobyns for the first time.

There was another ATF Contract Source of Information (CSOI) that was part of a penetration and intelligence gathering operation against the Hells Angels out of the ATF Reno, NV office named Dan "Coconut Dan" Horrigan. For over two years the convicted felon had been a paid informant used to gather intelligence on the Hells Angels in an operation that was going nowhere. To get their in, ATF recruited

Horrigan, a recently paroled convicted felon who was doing charity strength demonstrations at local biker events in Reno, because Horrigan had developed a friendship with the local Hells Angles. ATF offered Horrigan a job as a paid CSOI to gather intelligence on the newly formed Nomads charter of the Hells Angels in Reno, Nevada. Horrigan jumped at the chance and although he failed to develop any significant indictable evidence, he was able to provide valuable operational intelligence that would be used by the ATF in future operations.

At the time of the Laughlin incident Horrigan was a Hells Angels prospect who would have been able to provide real-time intelligence on what the Angels were and were not doing, their operations, security at Laughin, even location and movement of the membership, and he would also be able to make introductions, establish credibility for other U.C.'s, and serve as an agent provocateur for ATF. Surprisingly, his work and this operation would not be exposed until 2008, when testimony became public in another case ATF had put together against the Mongols MC. Horrigan's behavior began to raise suspicions within the Hells Angels and a Monterey member of the Hells Angels confirmed Coconut Dan was a law enforcement informant and his prospect period with the Hells Angels was terminated at a meeting in San Francisco at the end of April 2002. Contrary to law enforcements assertions that the Hells Angels and outlaw motorcycle clubs will kill an informant or U.C. if discovered, Dan walked away from that meeting in San Francisco without so much as a black eye. In fact, as you will see from reading my trilogy, there have been numerous times throughout American outlaw motorcycle club history that the Hells Angels and outlaw motorcycle clubs have identified undercover agents and C.I.'s within their ranks and they have never been harmed or threatened, they are simply kicked out.

"Coconut Dan" Horrigan poses in his Hells Angels hang-around
colors.
Photo by Dan Horrigan

According to his book *No Angel*, Jay Dobyns version of ATF's role
in Laughlin is this; "We went to the Flamingo, which was where all of
the Angels were staying. We went to a centrally located bar and took a
couple of stools. Everyone eye-fucked us. There were Hells Angels coming and going all around. JJ, in an observational role (ATF agent Jenna
Maguire), sat at the end of the bar and watched while fighting off offers
for free drinks and motorcycle rides. The situation in the casino was pal-
pably tense. The Angels knew the Mongols were around. They expected
a fight, but they didn't know when or where it would start. The Angels
had sent spies to the Mongols' hotel and were convinced that the Mongols had returned the favor. No one seemed approachable, and I hadn't
yet seen Smitty, the main guy I wanted to meet. After an hour of nurs-
ing beers, Koz (Agent Darren Kozlowski) and I concluded that maybe it
wasn't our night." Alright, now we know ATF's role according to Agent
Dobyns, but I want to inject some of what I know from my experience
and the other folks who were there.

First, not all the H.A. were staying at the Flamingo, most were staying across the river in Bullhead City, AZ, and at least one chapter of Angels was staying in Harrah's casino itself, so the notion of sending spies is ridiculous because the Hells Angels had no need to send spies since they had one H.A. chapter that was openly staying there, just as that chapter and the Mongols had been doing with no problems for several years prior. Second, Josh says that earlier in the day law enforcement had come to the HA and spoke with Sonny Barger, telling him the Mongols were going to attack them which Sonny has maintained since that day as well and been confirmed by law enforcement, but Josh disputes that there was any more tension than normal with the Mongols at the event. He says that immediately prior to the incident in Harrah's, the H.A. security command post in Bullhead City got a call from the guys staying at Harrah's saying that things were getting kind of weird with the Mongols and they may want to send somebody down. He said discussions were had and a group of H.A. from the Flamingo was dispatched to go extract their brothers from the bar in Harrah's.

Dobyns describes it like this is his book *No Angel*, "The Mongols did not want the Angels there—Harrah's was their home turf. The Frisco Angels knew this, so they'd put out a surreptitious distress call, and Smitty answered it. He went to Harrah's as an Angel undercover agent—no HA cut, no flash—just another dude surveying the lay of the land, seeing which table was bathed with the aura of Lady Luck. He stepped to the bar for a drink. A group of Mongols stood next to him. He overheard strands of their conversation. I can only imagine the bullshit insults that wafted from their lips—but it's not hard to do that. The Mongols would have called the Angels "Pinks," "faggots," "losers," "cocksuckers." I'm sure Smitty heard it all, and I'm sure he didn't like it. He forced a broad smile and sipped his beer, wiping the suds from his mustache. He watched the far end of the bar, where his Frisco brothers huddled. A group of Mongols orbited them. Something had to give." Dobyns version is a great story, but it does not make sense with what we know to be true, and that is that an H.A. chapter had been staying there at Harrah's with the Mongols for years prior and ATF knew it from having conducted surveillance on both clubs at Harrah's during the prior River Run's. What Dobyns says here is clearly him attempting to establish a reason for conflict between the clubs based on a false ATF narrative that will make sense to a jury because the jury will have no understanding of outlaw motorcycle club history, culture, or politics, beyond what they have learned from prosecutors, law enforcement, and the media's portrayal and all of which is based solely from information and analysis provided by the International Outlaw Motorcycle Gang Investigators Association.

Additionally, one percenter security is very much based off military and dignitary and executive protection best practices, and the Hells Angels were the best I ever saw at it. To think that their brothers, an entire chapter, called them for help and they had another lone Hells Angel take off his colors and go down as a spy just to confirm that their entire chapter was in-fact needing back-up is laughable, as that wastes several precious minutes to accomplish something that would not even be an issue because you always take your brothers at their word. It is fucking insane to believe that with their brothers on the phone with the ability to describe the threat they were facing, opposition numbers, etc. that the HA security command post would deem their bothers who called them for help incompetent liars and make the decision to send spies for intel, rather than dispatch a Quick Reaction Force (QRF) of HA and prospects to extract them and bring them to safety. Josh's version makes sense and since he was in the command post it is clear he knows more than Dobyns or even Dobyns C.I. Smitty. Josh says the Angels responsible for security had a quick conversation and a group of Angels and prospects were sent from the Flamingo to extract their brothers. In casinos there is nowhere to hide from the cameras but the bathroom, but for some reason there has never been any video evidence produced supporting Dobyns version of events and showing Smitty's alleged spy operation, probably because it doesn't exist or it shows misconduct by the ATF agents which they need to hide, but evidence supporting Josh's version can be seen in some of the surveillance video of the incident which shows leaders from each group having a conversation, joking and laughing, before a Hells Angel not involved in that conversation throws a kick to a Mongols chest. If the Hells Angels were there for war, there would have been no talking beforehand. Additionally, if the HA were there to go to war, they would have brought the majority of their members and certainly their primary enforcers which would have meant Josh and as many of the other enforcers possible would have been there for sure if the HA anticipated violence.

Dobyns version of this incident also makes sense, but only if you apply the tactics we know that the EUP uses and assume ATF was there to manufacture RICO charges against both the Mongols and the Hells Angels for violent crimes, that Dobyns and Koz were there to get close to the H.A. and stir up shit, and Smitty was the Hells Angel they had targeted to use for plausible deniability as an unwitting agent provocateur and a conduit to a RICO charge for the incident, by encouraging him to go visit his brothers down at Harrah's because his beer fueled "I'm not afraid of any Mongols." attitude had started to rear its ugly head and he'd make the perfect match to light the fire without the ATF directly getting their hands dirty like in the Sons of Silence incident.

Finally, is it possible that the ATF had sleeper undercover agents and C.I.'s left over in the Mongols from the Billy Queen investigation, that had infiltrated the Mongols with Billy Queen's help just prior to the close of Operation Ivan with the intent of carrying on a more lucrative investigation against the Mongols who were currently undergoing a massive identity change which included a dynamic increase in criminal activity under the growing influence of Doc Cavazos, and those agents/CI's may have been undercover as Mongols inside that bar in Harrah's, deliberately talking shit about the H.A. in hopes of inciting a fight between the two clubs, so the feds could get their RICO indictments.

Regardless of which version you are choosing to believe so far, we know from their own sworn testimony that the Casino Security Manager had gone to Roger Pinney the National President of the Mongols that night and asked him to have all Mongols members disarm and take their weapons to their rooms because the ATF had informed him that there was going to be a fight between the two clubs, and what happened next is indisputable. The two clubs' officers were talking when the sergeant at arms for the Sonoma County Hells Angels Raymond "Ray Ray" Foakes kicked a Mongol in the chest tipping off the melee. Numerous Hells Angels were charged with racketeering offences including my friend Ron Arnone who can be seen in surveillance video cowering against a wall for the entirety of the incident, but he was charged with Racketeering and Murder for his involvement. More than a hundred members of the two clubs were stabbed, shot, and beaten. About an hour later a Hells Angel member named Christian "Christo" Tate was found dead approximately a hundred miles west of Laughlin. Christo had been riding his motorcycle away from Laughlin toward home in California to get home for his child's birthday at the time he was killed. He was found with his Hells Angels colors and had been shot multiple times in the back and torso. His helmet was found on the seat of his motorcycle with his license and registration placed underneath the helmet. The murder has never been solved and some H.A. and former members have suggested that law enforcement may have seen the Laughlin incident as a free pass that provided enough plausible deniability to murder a Hells Angel, knowing it could easily be blamed on the Mongols. I have to say, after what the Outlaws, Outsiders, and other outlaw motorcycle clubs have been going through since the late seventies and based on the tactics Agent Dobyns outlines that ATF uses, I do not think their theory of law enforcement being responsible for Christo's murder is too far of a reach and is absolutely plausible since they had means, motive, and opportunity.

Hells Angel Raymond "Ray Ray" Foakes (center-right in the white
long sleeved shirt at the top of the slot machines) throws the karate
kick that tips off the 2002 Laughlin River Run Riot.
Harrah's Casino surveillance video.

While he was in the hospital, somebody sent Mongols National President Roger Pinney a bouquet of red and white flowers. Red and white
carnations were delivered to the Mongols funeral for Red Beard and
Jingles just prior to a car bomb detonating, and now someone takes
the time to send flowers to Roger in his secured and confidential hospital room. The feds would have been one of the very few with access
to Rogers hospital information because he was a protected patient/sus-
pect, and for the Angels to get that information just to rub salt in a
wound when two of their own H.A. brothers were dead would leave a
paper trail and would make it difficult for the HA to deny they were
at war with the Mongols and that the Laughlin incident was self-defense like the HA always claim with incidents of violence involving their
members and did with the Laughlin incident. It makes no sense it was
the Angels sending those flowers but does make sense it was the ATF
Enhanced Undercover Programs agents trying to poke the bear when
the clubs were most vulnerable and volatile in hopes of inciting fur-

ther violence which would tip off a full-scale war between the clubs and mean further charges. Of the forty motorcycle club members charged with racketeering related offenses from the Laughlin incident, all but six would have their charges dismissed, and once again there were allegations by both clubs' attorneys that the government agents had acted inappropriately in setting up the melee and then withholding exculpatory evidence as well as evidence of law enforcement misconduct.

The sensationalism of the Laughlin incident by law enforcement and the media proved to be an incredibly effective propaganda tool for law enforcement and ATF exploited Operation Ivan, Black Biscuit, and a case against the Bandidos, by directly assisting in the development of documentaries on the various cases for reputable media sources such as National Geographic, History Channel, and Discovery, and as a result the ATF/IOMGIA propaganda machine was able to terrify mainstream society of American outlaw motorcycle clubs, getting them to believe that they are warring sophisticated criminal enterprises to be feared. The Laughlin incident was so visually powerful that even though the incident never resulted in any significant criminal convictions and the majority of the charges were dismissed, ATF and federal prosecutors would tactically use the video of the Laughlin incident to this day to reinforce their false narrative that outlaw motorcycle clubs are warring criminal enterprises to be feared. This tactic makes it clear that the government understands the false narrative they have created with law enforcement and the public is so powerful that outlaw motorcycle club cases are not about having to prove the charges, they're about scaring a jury that IOMGIA, ATF, and DOJ has been aggressively using the media to prejudice since the 1970's, to the point that juries believe that narrative so strongly they will now overlook evidence or lack thereof and ignore common sense.

9

OPERATION BLACK BISCUIT

The Laughlin incident and all the ATF propaganda surrounding it captured the nation's attention and forced every law enforcement agency in the country to take the myth surrounding outlaw motorcycle clubs seriously, and as a result the ATF EUP was able to get the funding and administrative support, they needed to dramatically increase the level of sophistication and intensity of their operations targeting outlaw motorcycle clubs. They merged the three ongoing undercover operations against the Hells Angels into the one operation that was being planned by Slatalla and Ciccone to become Operation Black Biscuit.

Slatalla's focus was on the Hells Angels in Arizona, but Ciccone's interest started in Arizona and included Nevada, California, and wherever else he could reach with the infiltration, and their two operations intertwined and involved some of the same individuals. Ciccone's case had begun as Operation Dequaillo when he signed Hells Angel Mike Kramer as an informant in December 2001, and debriefed with Ciccone, during which Kramer confessed to participating in the murder of Cynthia Garcia, and according to the book *Angels of Death by Julien Sher*, Ciccone chose the name of the operation because he viewed it as payback for the Angels wearing a small patch saying Dequaillo, that law enforcement alleges means the wearer has assaulted a police officer. I have never been a member of the Hells Angels, so I don't know for sure, but I do know Hells Angels who wear or have worn that patch and do not have criminal histories that include assaulting a police officer and some have no criminal record at all, and the meaning of Dequaillo has no specific reference to law enforcement, so I must conclude that this is either another patch that was started by a click within the club and then its award criteria and meaning was diluted over time, or like most things the ATF and law enforcement allege about outlaw motorcycle clubs, their narrative is total bullshit. What is clear from the name that agent Ciccone chose and the reason behind it, is that agent Ciccone hates Hells Angels and wants to stick it to them and let them know any chance he can get.

Ciccone's goal was to use Hells Angel Mike Kramer to get indictments against as many Hells Angels as possible for gun, drugs, or whatever other criminal charges that they could. With Ciccone being based out of Los Angeles, he could not run Kramer as an informant in Arizona, so they had Kramer put in for a transfer to the Hells Angels San Fernando Valley charter which fell in Ciccone's jurisdiction. Kramer was used to secretly record conversations with Hells Angels Paul Eischeid and Kevin Augustiniak to obtain evidence associated with the Cynthia Garcia murder, and was then sent around the country to different HA charters to have audio recorded incriminating conversations with various targets in the Laughlin incident. Kramer had admitted to participating in Cynthia Garcia's murder, but Ciccone was allowing him to earn a deal by implicating as many Hells Angels as he could in various crimes and was particularly interested in using him to build indictments related to the Laughlin incident. It took Det. Chuck Schoville and two prosecutors' three conferences with Garcia's family to win them over on the idea of giving Hells Angel Mike Kramer a deal on Garcia's murder because the ATF still needed to use him as an informant against the Hells Angels, but eventually they were successful. Additionally, to protect Operation Dequaillo the ATF could not arrest Eischeid or Augustiniak for Garcia's murder which created the risk that they may kill again while left out on the street because ATF needed to protect an undercover operation, and that would mean a black eye and liability for ATF if they did, but it was a risk Ciccone was willing to take.

Operation Black Biscuit was significant because it was the first time that undercover agents had started a chapter of a real motorcycle club with the intentions of instigating a violent dispute over territory with the Hells Angels, and or get on their good side and purchase drugs and guns from members of the club which could be charged as RICO offenses, and it is another example of the use of too elaborate a cover for the U.C. agents by ATF, and extreme criminal activity by the undercovers and their informants. Most importantly, Operation Black Biscuit is the first undercover operation we can prove was the result of what appears to be a criminal conspiracy and racketeering enterprise committed by ATF undercover agents, case agents, and their contract sources of information, and thus Operation Black Biscuit was really a criminal enterprise and not a legitimate undercover law enforcement operation because all the evidence developed that resulted in criminal charges was fruit of the poisonous tree.

Over the years, transitioning accounts of how the undercover chapter came to exist were given to the media and journalists by agent Dobyns, Ciccone, and the other undercovers, with the original version given by Dobyns himself that he simply paid a five hundred dollar fee to the Solo Angeles CM to start a chapter of the club, however the version given by the agents in *Angels of Death* is that contract informant Rudy Kramer was the link to the Solo Angeles which would insulate federal agents from allegations of entrapment should the Hells Angels pull their patches. The undercover chapter included three ATF agents, an ATF Task Force officer from a local police department, and one drug addict and Contract Source of Information named Pops who was the team's credibility drug user. To someone with not much experience in outlaw motorcycle clubs, especially to a case agent managing an undercover operation targeting the Hells Angels, the use of a charter of an existing club as cover, especially a club in Mexico, might sound like a great cover because it has the credibility of a known club but they're from Mexico, so they're hard to contact and the UC's will check out because they're official, and because the mother chapter, the only chapter of the Solos Angeles CM other than the agents' Nomad chapter is located in Tijuana Mexico, that means the mother chapter can't control the U.C.'s schedule or activities, and will have no knowledge of them or their activities other than what they agents choose to expose them to.

In reality, ATF's use of the Solo's Angeles CM should have been a huge tell to the Hells Angels and every other club in Arizona, that the new Solos Angeles CM were most likely undercover cops, and here's why. First, the Solos Angeles CM were founded in 1959 and evolved from the first two motorcycle clubs to start in Tijuana Mexico, one of which was a motorcycle police acrobatic club. Because they have always been a community service-oriented club and allow law enforcement in their membership, they have never been an outlaw club or worn a 1% diamond on their colors. In addition, because they have interacted with American outlaw motorcycle clubs since their inception, they have never worn a 1% diamond to avoid conflict with American clubs over their use of a three-piece patch. They have no U.S. chapters, and restrict their operations to Mexico. While they do have a few members living in San Diego, those members must attend meetings and events in Tijuana. So, to the Hells Angels and the rest of the motorcycle clubs in Arizona, and even me when I heard there were Solo Angeles running around Arizona and they were all Americans and all white guys that was a huge red flag. The lack of connection to Mexico represented by the photos and décor of their undercover house would have been another tell that something was not right about the new Arizona Solos Angeles.

Jay Dobyns Solos Angeles CM colors.
Photo: Nevada Public Radio

Next, like I mentioned, the Solos Angeles have never been an outlaw club and have gone to great lengths to make sure that they are not perceived that way by both other clubs and the public, so Dobyns chapter wearing a 1% diamond on their colors would have been another huge red flag, since it is not consistent with the history or values of the Solos Angles CM and a community service oriented club, and membership in the Solos Angeles CM totally conflicts with Dobyns cover identity as a gun-running debt collector for the American mafia, and would raise further questions that could not easily be explained away. Furthermore, Dobyns chapter wearing 1% diamonds when the Solos as a club have made the decision not to, would have caused conflict with the entire Solos Angeles CM, and likely gotten the U.C. chapter shut down for failing to adhere to the Solos Angeles club values and bylaws. Evidence that Dobyns and the informant were attempting to hide the use of the 1% diamond on their colors can be seen in the credibility photos Dobyns and

Pops took while with the Solos in Mexico and show they were not wearing 1% diamonds on their Solos colors there. I believe the ATF agents intentionally added the 1% diamond patch to their Solos Angeles CM colors as a deliberate disrespect to the Hells Angels in hopes of inciting the Hells Angels to pull their patches, so they could charge the HA with R.I.C.O. charges related to using violence and intimidation to control territory.

Looking way too over the top for the reality of the outlaw motorcycle club world, ATF agent Jay Dobyns does his best gangster pose in his Hells Angels hang around colors.
Photo: Jay Dobyns

The Angels did not take the bait and over the next year and a half the case resulted in minimal evidence against the Angels. In April 2003, the undercover ATF agents were told by the Hells Angels to shut down the Solo Angeles and prospect for a real motorcycle club, the Hells Angels. This created conflict between Dobyns and Slatella, because Slatella knew that if the agents began the prospect process, the ATF would relinquish control of their undercovers and informant to the HA who would be dictating the agents' schedules as prospects, there would be no ability for the agents to avoid drugs, and they lost the tactical advantage the use of the Solo Angeles gave them. Dobyns pressed and eventually Slatella agreed to allow the operation to continue but set a hard closure date of July 8th, 2003.

With permission to prospect for the Hells Angels, a hard close date set for Operation Black Biscuit that was less than three months away, no significant evidence had been developed from the undercover agent's involvement in the operation, agent Dobyns was under a tremendous amount of pressure by the agency to justify the operation which was constantly on the verge of being shut down by ATF for being too expensive and its failure to produce.

Providing additional pressure to perform was agent Dobyns own tremendous ego and his own personal agenda of becoming the first undercover agent to ever become a full patch member of the Hells Angels, which anyone who knows anything about prospecting for the HA knows would never happen in just two and a half months. It appears Dobyns own personal agenda led him to lie about incidents and he manufactured charges against the Hells Angels. For example, in multiple books and interviews Dobyns describes an incident in which as a prospect, he received a call from a Hells Angel officer and was told to "get all your guns, get all your knives, get all your weapons, and come to the clubhouse." In the book *Angels of Death,* Dobyns states; "The Bandidos planned to crash a large coalition meeting of bikers sympathetic to the Angels scheduled for that night at the Eagles Lodge in Las Vegas." Dobyns claims he was told by the Angels; "If they show up, we're taking their asses out." Dobyns further claims that he was ordered by the Hells Angels to shoot any Bandidos they saw before they could even get their kick stands down, and if it were not for his quick thinking and a surreptitious call to Slatella that there would have been a massacre. Dobyns allegations resulted in indictments for Conspiracy to Murder members of the Bandidos MC against the three real Hells Angels who were members of the chapter Dobyns, and the undercovers were prospecting for.

Once again it appears Dobyns is lying about this incident, the Hells Angels intentions, his involvement in the incident, and he did it for his own personal gain. In reality, the incident Dobyns is referring to was a meeting of the Southern Nevada Confederation of Clubs, a motorcycle rights group consisting of all the motorcycle clubs of southern Nevada, including the Hells Angels and Bandidos, both of whom had and continue to operate chapters in Las Vegas. Contrary to agent Dobyns sensational and self-serving narrative that the COC is a group loyal to the Hells Angels, the COC is a collaboration of all the respected motorcycle clubs from that particular state or area, is not loyal to any particular motorcycle club, and there was no feud between the Hells Angels and Bandidos that would have warranted violence at a COC meeting, nor would members of the Hells Angels who are known to be very wary about what they say on the phone due to electronic surveillance, tell a prospect to 'get all your guns, get all your knives, get all your weapons and come to the clubhouse." This is clearly another self-serving statement of Dobyns that he needed to use as the nexus to be able to turn the incident into a criminal act that involved guns, the club, and criminal conspiracy. Furthermore, the Arizona Hells Angels are from Arizona with its own COC and would have no standing in Nevada with the COC, and the Las Vegas and Reno chapters of the HA would handle the political issues with other motorcycle clubs within their own state, including with the Bandidos. Even more curious is the fact that the COC meeting Dobyns was talking about went off as planned without any violence or conflict, and both the Hells Angels and Bandidos participated in the meeting that night which clearly establishes Dobyns committed further racketeering offenses when he lied about the entire incident and made statements under penalty of perjury to manufacture criminal charges against members of the Hells Angels, further the criminal enterprise of Operation Black Biscuit, and he did it to advance his position within ATF, his career, and enrich himself.

Not content with bogus conspiracy to commit murder charges against one chapter and with an unrelenting personal desire to become the first undercover agent to successfully become a Hells Angel, agent Dobyns and the other ATF agents took their entrapment to a new level and staged the murder of a member of the Mongols to manufacture further charges against the Hells Angels. According to Dobyns in *Angels of Death*, the staged murder of the Mongol was of no legal or evidence gathering value, but he planned the staged murder with the goal of showing the Hells Angels were a warring organized crime syndicate who celebrate and reward assassinations, and his secondary objective was to make it harder for ATF management to shut Operation Black Biscuit down. In fact, according to his own statements in *Angels of Death*, Dobyns made a deliberate effort to conceal the staged murder from Slatella. Dobyns made up a story about a Mongol who was running around in Mexico bad-mouthing the Hells Angels and told the HA he was going to kill the Mongol for his disrespect. Dobyns approached Hells Angel Joby Walters, told him the story, and got a gun from Walters which Dobyns would later tell the Hells Angels he used to commit his fabricated Mongol murder.

While the other Black Biscuit undercover agents took a few days off, Dobyns went into the Arizona dessert with other law enforcement officers, and using a seized set of Mongols colors, an undercover officer, and some cow blood, he staged the phony murder scene and took photos. Once back at his undercover house with the rest of the agents and on surveillance, Dobyns would hand the Angels a FedEx box containing the seized Mongols colors and photos of the staged murder. Dobyns claims that the Hells Angels were so impressed that they made him and undercover officer Billy Long Hells Angels members on the spot, however over the years after pushback from the Hells Angels and even their ATF's own confidential source of information from the operation, Dobyns has changed his story to claim that he was offered a patch to wear by a member until he could get his, but turned it down because he wanted to make member the right way at a meeting of the entire club.

A very much alive undercover law enforcement officer poses as a
murdered Mongols MC member for a staged photo used by the
undercover team in Operation Black Biscuit.
Photo by Jay Dobyns

In reality, had a group of prospects that had only been around for a
few months gone rogue and committed a murder of another club member in a foreign country and then been amateur enough to FedEx/bring
evidence of the crime back to the club with them, it would have been
such over the top, reckless, and suspicious behavior that they would
have not only not been made a member, but they would also have likely
been run-off by the club for their behavior and putting the club at
risk via their actions. The purpose of the prospect period is to get to
know the membership and for them to get to know you, so they can
decide if they even want you as their brother. The idea of a prospect
making member simply for committing a murder is a myth created by
law enforcement and has no basis in the realities of outlaw motorcycle club culture. Just because someone can commit a murder does not
mean they're loyal or honorable. Additionally, the Hells Angels charter Dobyns infiltrated was an official charter and had the authority to
make them members and give them their patches immediately, the fact
Dobyns never received a patch and does not have any photos of his or

Billy Long's patch ceremony is further clear evidence that Dobyns never made member and once again he is lying to inflate his own personal image and sensationalize the story.

Finally, it is totally unrealistic to believe that the ATF would shut down an undercover operation of the Hells Angels if multiple undercovers had been successfully gathering evidence that the Hells Angels were operating as a criminal enterprise. As members the undercovers would have had the ability to attend meetings, become officers in the organizations, transfer to any charter they chose, as well as once the agents made member, they would set the rules for their own personal behavior which would mean no more incidents where the agents would be forced to potentially use drugs, etc. If Dobyns had indeed made member, ATF would most likely have continued the operation because they would have had an all-access pass.

Instead, less than three months after Dobyns and the others went prospect, Operation Black Biscuit was shut down on July 8th, 2003, as planned due to the costs associated with continuing the operation and lack of value resulting from it. Just as we had seen with previous OMG investigations, there were numerous allegations of drug use, illegal recordings, filing false Reports of Investigation (ROI's), and other illegal acts by the undercover agents and informants, which in combination with internal government disputes resulted in numerous charges being dismissed or reduced, and Operation Black Biscuit could more accurately be described as an awfully expensive failure, rather than the heroic and triumphant undercover operation Dobyns and ATF like to make it out to be.

When the arrests from Black Biscuit happened, Dobyns and Special Agent in Charge Virginia O'Brien held a press conference that hailed the operation as a huge success and told reporters that they had undermined the Hells Angels propaganda that they were just a benevolent organization that could not be infiltrated. O'Brien's statement appears to be another spontaneous admission that their main goal is not justice but undermining the true narrative that motorcycle clubs are just clubs and not criminal enterprises. Of the over forty arrests made as a result of Operation Black Biscuit, the majority of the charges were dismissed. Hells Angel Joby Walters was charged with conspiracy to murder a member of the Mongols for giving Dobyns the gun for the staged Mongols murder, and he got a second conspiracy to murder members of the Bandidos for Dobyns fictitious COC attack. Hells Angels Teddy Toth and Bobby Reinstra were also charged for the fake COC attack.

In the fall of 2005, the judge assigned to the case chastised prosecutors for failing to turn over discovery and being "inaccurate, inconsistent and sometimes legally incorrect.", and the government admitted that they had deliberately tried to burry defense attorneys with voluminous amounts of less or irrelevant documents but claimed they did it in an attempt to protect government witnesses from the Hells Angels. The Mesa chapter of the Hells Angels President Bob Johnston was not charged with any drug or gun charges but indicted for simply being part of the criminal enterprise by wearing his patch.

Joby Walters charge for the staged Mongols murder as well as all the charges against the all the Hells Angels that resulted from Dobyns fictitious COC attack were all dismissed. Kevin Augustiniak was convicted of murdering Cynthia Garcia, Eischeid would remain a fugitive until July of 2018, when he was extradited to the U.S., he is still awaiting trial on Garcia's murder, and Hells Angel and contract informant Mike Kramer was sentenced to only five years' probation for murdering Cynthia Garcia and did not spend a day in jail for the killing and attempted beheading.

While ATF and federal prosecutors did their best to hide it, Mesa Mike Kramer would become a source of great controversy for ATF surrounding Operation Black Biscuit, and his role would shed even more light on ATF's tactics when it comes to the use of contract informants and their outlaw motorcycle gang investigation tactics. Amongst the Hells Angels, Kramer was known to be violent and volatile, and this proved to make him a difficult informant for Ciccone to control. Combined with ATF's questionable undercover tactics, Kramer's involvement in the operation produced at least two very troubling incidents. The first incident occurred in March 2002 when Kramer was drunk at a bar and witnessed bouncers kick a man out, after which Kramer ran out and kicked and stomped the man. "He was screaming like a little bitch," Kramer would brag when recounting the incident later. The beating was captured on an ATF recording device hidden inside Kramer's cell phone battery and would become one of many pieces of evidence of CI and UC misconduct that ATF attempted to or did hide.

In another incident, Ciccone sent Kramer to buy four machine guns from a man in Woodland Hills, California for $3,000. Two of the guns turned out to be replicas and the other two were completely inoperable. After Ciccone scolded Kramer for buying the fake guns, Kramer returned to the gun dealer's house and stole a motorcycle from a man named Peter Joseph who was staying at the house. When Joseph complained, Kramer beat Joseph with a baseball bat and just like the previous incident, it is clear Ciccone and ATF covered for Kramer's criminal activity. In fact, it appears Ciccone covered for Kramer throughout Operation Dequaillo to be able to keep him in play. Kramer was known publicly in the motorcycle club community to be a raging alcoholic and meth addict, but Ciccone reported in internal ATF reports that Kramer has never used methamphetamine in the past while working on behalf of the ATF, does not have a drug history and has never been convicted of a drug offense. In fact, Kramer was regularly stealing portions of the drugs he would buy for the ATF before handing over the drugs over to Ciccone and Kramer would brag about the method he had devised to do so.

Between 2001 and 2008 Kramer was paid or reimbursed an average of almost $60,000 a year to work as a contract source of information for

ATF in their operations and assist in the prosecutions of the Hells Angels in Arizona and California. In addition, after Black Biscuit closed, Kramer was paid a secret sum by ATF and was enrolled in the United States Marshall's Witness Security program. Excluding performance bonuses, ATF officially paid or reimbursed Mike Kramer $197,220.05 for his work, and during that time Kramer committed at least two violent felony assaults, an armed robbery, and he stole and used an undetermined amount of narcotics he purchased on behalf of ATF using their buy money in his official capacity as a contract informant. Then the Marshal's Service spent $99,079 to relocate Kramer in March 2004 and protect him for the remainder of that year, and his protection at the expense of the taxpayers continues to this day. Not a bad deal when you consider that he was the ringleader in the cold-blooded murder of Ms. Garcia and should be spending the rest of his life in prison.

This next part is critical because this is where the agents began their criminal conspiracy, violated ATF policy, committed multiple U.S. federal and Mexican crimes to further their enterprise and be able to launch Operation Black Biscuit, enrich themselves via case bonuses, overtime pay, and pursue fortune and fame.

By this point in the book, you understand that Operation Black Biscuit started from three ongoing ATF undercover operations against the Hells Angels that had been running for a year and a half and resulted in almost no intelligence and no indictable criminal activity, those operations were on the verge of being shut down but the three ops were rolled together into Operation Black Biscuit when ATF agent Jay Dobyns was able to start a chapter of the real Solos Angeles CM. We have learned that in order to prospect for or start a chapter of an existing motorcycle club, you must at very least go to that club and announce your intentions. Additionally, you know that the Solos Angeles one and only chapter is in Tijuana Mexico, so at least one of the U.C.'s from the Operation Black Biscuit chapter or Rudy Kramer would have had to go to Mexico to pay the $500 fee to the Solos Angeles CM mother chapter to obtain the charter certificate and initial sets of colors. The problem with Rudy Kramer going to Mexico is it does not provide good cover because if the HA were to call the Solos in Mexico, they would only be able to describe or a have pics of Rudy, which would not resolve any HA suspicions and raise more red flags about why Rudy was not in the club, and why guys would want to be in a club they have no connection to. Regardless, undercover agents and their C.I.'s cannot just go operating anywhere they want, and cross-border undercover operations are extraordinarily complex operations that must be approved by not only the undercover agents' lead agency and Department of Justice, but also foreign authorities, so agencies do not want to go there unless they absolutely must, have excellent probable cause, and even then, they don't like to because of operational security reasons and risk to benefit. There is no way that when ATF was wanting to shut down the operations against the Angels due to costs and lack of results that they would approve a cross-border undercover operation or even want to use the political capital it would take to make it happen, just so that Dobyns could by a Solos Angeles CM chapter to dynamite the pond. It would be much easier to dress the UC's up in seized colors from an American club and send the agents out on the town like Dobyns did in the Sons of Silence operation.

I believe the reason for the conflicting stories by Dobyns and Ciccone as to whether Dobyns paid the $500 for the chapter or Rudy Kramer paid it, and why ATF would be concerned about claims by the defense for the use of a real MC, is because the reality is the agents are deliberately lying to cover their criminal activity, and Jay Dobyns and their C.I. "Pops" crossed into Mexico in their undercover roles without authority to purchase the chapter and obtain credibility photos at the annual Solos Angeles CM Toy Run in Tijuana, and in doing so they violated ATF policy, and numerous U.S. and Mexican laws. If they did, in order to maintain their cover, they would have used their ATF supplied cover identification and been riding ATF owned motorcycles, which would be additional serious crimes. In fact, it would be over a decade after the Hells Angels who were indicted in Black Biscuit had their homes raided, were arrested, their lives, destroyed, and had their cases adjudicated with some forced into taking pleas, that the public would come to find out from Jay Dobyns best friend and partner of 20 years, former ATF agent Vincent Cefalu who writes in his book *Ratsnakes: Cheating Death by Living a Lie… Inside the Explosive World of ATF's Undercover Agents and How We Changed the Game*, that in fact Jay Dobyns did violate ATF authority at the highest level when he crossed into Mexico with their contract source of information Pops to purchase the Solos Angeles CM chapter and take credibility pics to backstop their cover.

There you have it and straight from a respected ATF agent, that in order to keep the operations against the Hells Angels from being totally shut down, undercover ATF agent Jay Dobyns and a contract employee violated ATF policy, numerous U.S. and Mexican laws, they did it with the knowledge of other ATF employees including at least Vincent Cefalu who did not attempt to stop or report the criminal action, making it a criminal conspiracy and Operation Black Biscuit the fruits of their criminal enterprise. Which begs the question, if ATF had been running three investigations against the Hells Angels for over a year and a half which failed to develop any intelligence or indictable criminal offenses, then when facing being shut down, ATF conspires to violate ATF policy, and commits multiple Arizona, federal and Mexican criminal offenses to be able to continue to investigate the Hells Angels, who is the real criminal organization? Before the agents had ever developed evidence of criminal activity by the Hells Angels or Operation Black Biscuit was launched, the ATF undercover agents and CSOI were operating as a provable multi-national criminal enterprise.

10

THE IN-BETWEEN
YEARS

In a culture based on loyalty, honor, respect, and where your commitment to your club is supposed to be until death, should a member leave the club whether that be because the member quit or the member was kicked out for acts of dishonor, there are only two possible out statuses for the member leaving the club; "Out Good" or "Out Bad". Out Bad is a dishonorable discharge from the outlaw motorcycle club and generally comes with a no-contact status that is observed by the other outlaw motorcycle clubs, meaning the out-bad former member cannot have contact with any other motorcycle clubs and other motorcycle clubs will not have contact with him. About a week and a half after Josh called me to say he had quit the Hells Angels, I got a call from the new Hells Angels Nomads Washington Sergeant at Arms who was clearly fishing to determine if I knew or would say where Josh was living, and when it became clear I wasn't going to give up anything, he informed me that Josh had stolen money and a motorcycle from the club, was out bad and demanded I tell him where Josh was if I knew. I told him I had not heard from Josh, could not help him, and I ended the call.

Over the next couple of weeks Josh, Lisa and Hannah would bounce back and forth between a friend's house in Tacoma and his parents on the other side of the state in Spokane, and it was clear to me that it was taking a toll on them. I had been living in a small town in the mountains about thirty minutes east of Seattle called North Bend, and Josh and Lisa had always talked about how much they enjoyed it out there when they came to visit. After discussing the fact the Hells Angels had put him "Out Bad", they were looking for him, and that bringing him and his family into our home to live could expose us to grave danger from the Hells Angels, my wife and I decided they were our family and protecting our family was worth the risk, so we invited Josh, Lisa and Hannah into our home to live until they could get into a new place of their own.

Hearing that the Hells Angels had given him "Out Bad" status really upset Josh after all the loyalty he showed the club, and he was not going to stand for that injustice without trying to right it. One night as we were sitting in my garage Josh told me that he had thought about it, and he was going to go to a club meeting at the Oakland HA clubhouse and ask them to change his status and let him become an Oakland Hells Angel. I almost snorted the sip of beer I had just taken out my nose as the words registered in my mind and I asked him, "Bro, you're Out Bad, the club is looking for you, and you're really going to go to the Oakland clubhouse for church, knock on the door and say I wanna talk?" He smiled his big Josh "This is gunna be fun smile" and said, "Yup!" Before Josh had left the Hells Angels, an Oakland member named Flash had suspected Smilin' Rick of committing some dishonorable acts against the club. Flash vaguely mentioned something to Josh about the issue, but Josh backed his brother and denied knowing what Flash was talking about even though, Flash was exactly right about what he suspected Smilin' of. When Josh left the club, he was mad about being given an "Out Bad" label and the lies the Washington Hells Angels charter were telling about him, especially since one of the things they were lying about and accusing him of doing was exactly what Flash had suspected Smilin' of. The Washington charter was attempting to use Josh as a scapegoat for Smilin' Rick's bad deeds because Josh was not in the club to defend himself. Josh sent a letter to Flash in Oakland explaining what had really happened, that he was being falsely accused and he wanted the opportunity to get in the same room with Smilin' Rick and figure this out.

We talked about his safety and a couple of days later he was in Oakland, and I was waiting for a phone call to say he was safe. Josh is bad to the bone, and he followed his plan, went to the clubhouse that night but because each Hells Angels charter is autonomous and they all have to abide by the other charters out-status, there was nothing the Oakland Hells Angels could do to help him, and Josh came home without so much as a black eye which told me Oakland really didn't agree with his out status or the allegations. He went to Oakland to make a statement that he was willing to back up his word by stepping into a room where he has no friends, only enemies, and risk everything to stand up for his honor. In the end Josh was told that they cannot take the word of a non-member over a member and that he should have brought the issue up while he was still a member.

Josh and his family lived with us for about six months while they found jobs and saved up for a place of their own in North Bend. During this time, I was asked several times by the Hells Angels both in person and via phone conversations if I knew where Josh was, and I always played dumb and denied I knew where he was. I would always let Josh know and we would get a good laugh at how little effort they were putting in to trying to find him. Eventually, Josh and Lisa found a cute little apartment at the base of Mt. Si in North Bend and just a couple of miles from my place. When he moved into that place, he deliberately had his name and address listed in the phone book and told me that the next time the Hells Angels asked me where he was to tell them he was listed in the phone book. The very next time one of them asked me if I knew where Josh was, I told them they must not be trying to find him awfully hard, because he is listed in the phone book. What I had seen firsthand with Josh's situation when he quit the Hells Angels was the first time, I saw a good member being falsely labeled "Out Bad" by the club, simply so the club could save face. I would come to see this become a matter of practice for many outlaw motorcycle clubs when a good member quits, since the status can't be questioned by other motorcycle clubs and it is a way for the club to save face when a good member quits because they are dissatisfied with the club, and it prevents them from joining another club. The Hells Angels never did pay Josh a visit, but ATF would in the coming years.

In the fall of 2004, I took my wife at the time to Europe for a month. We had a great time, traveling all over Europe and I got to clearly understand that European outlaw motorcycle clubs are totally different than American outlaw motorcycle clubs, and they run totally autonomous from their American counterparts. It was my wife's first time in Europe, and I had put together an amazing vacation that took us from Paris to the French and Italian Rivera, Monaco, London and ended with a week in Amsterdam. Prior to leaving I told Smilin' Rick that I would be in Amsterdam and thought it would be fun to meet the Amsterdam Hells Angels and visit their legendary clubhouse Angels Place. Angels Place was the elaborate longtime home of the Amsterdam charter of the Hells Angels MC, and it was allegedly given to them by the government to discourage them from going into bars and causing trouble. The Amsterdam Hells Angels had been around since the early 1970's and had a reputation as one of the most serious Hells Angels charters in Europe. Rick told me he would make a phone call and make it happen for me, and few minutes later I got a call back from Smilin' saying it was all set up.

I wanted to spend a day exploring Amsterdam with my wife before I went to the Angels clubhouse. My personal rule has always been that that my ol' lady doesn't go to any clubhouse including my own unless I invite her to go with me, and I never invited her to a strange clubhouse for a first visit for two reasons. First, safety because I have never met these guys and do not know them. Second, I am not going to really be able to get to know them unless they are comfortable and speak freely with me, and due to outlaw motorcycle club cultural protocols, that would not happen if I brought my wife along. We had a great first day in Amsterdam together, but my highlight was when we went to a well-known little coffee shop called De Dampkring. De Dampkring is the oldest coffee shop in Amsterdam, where you can buy and use various marijuana products. As Americans during an era of our national history when marijuana was still a forbidden drug, we wanted to fully experience the culture of Amsterdam, so after a tour of the Heineken Brewery, Anne Frank Haus, and taking in what turned out to be a super creepy live sex show in the Red Light District involving an out of shape middle aged couple wearing purple velvet capes and masks, we headed to De Dampkring for a joint of Amsterdam's finest. We ordered milkshakes at the bar and then went over to the weed counter where the budtender handed us a photo album with actual buds from various strains that we could choose to purchase in flower or pre-rolls. There were also several different types of great looking hash. We ended up choosing a one-gram joint of White Widow and I think it cost us the equivalent of about three dollars U.S.

First off, let me say that De Dampkring has one of the best milk-shakes you will ever have and when you pair it with their phenomenal pot and really cool atmosphere, it's an amazing experience. Well, by the time we were about halfway through that joint we were so high and paranoid that we were worried we were going to get in trouble for being too high in De Dampkring. Cheeched to the gills and making wise decisions, we headed outside for fresh air, where it actually was illegal to be too high in public. Once outside, we sat ourselves on a bench on a little cobblestone bridge that spanned one of the canals and tried to pull ourselves together as we each drank our milkshakes, not realizing we were holding them with two-handed G.I. Joe Kung Fu grips until we caught a group of passing tourists laughing at us. That was about all of Amsterdam we could take-in that day and we headed back to the hotel for some topless Dutch news and much needed sleep.

The next morning, I got up and walked towards the bathroom and noticed a local newspaper had been slid under the door to our hotel room. We were staying in an upscale five-star hotel so there was nothing alarming about its presence and I did not bother to pay attention to it, assuming it would be in Dutch, and I would not be able to read it. The plan was to get up and have breakfast then do some sightseeing together, after which I was supposed to meet with Big Willem the President of the Amsterdam Hells Angels for lunch at Angels Place. I was in the shower when my wife walked in and asked me if I had seen the paper that had been slid under the door. I told her I had but I did not pay attention to it. "Ummmm, I think you should read the front page." she said with a mischievous tone in her voice. I slid back the shower curtain and as I wiped the water from my eyes, I saw a photo of Angels place and Big Willem with the headline *"Hells Angels President Arrested for Plotting to Bomb Clubhouse with Members Inside."* What the fuck! I guess I'm not having lunch with Big Willem I chuckled. "Holy crap, they really are different over here." she said, the shock of the headline setting in. Yes, they are I told her. The way I remember it is Big Willem was allegedly involved in a plot to murder a close friend of the Hells Angels who was known to regularly visit Angels Place, and he was going to kill him by blowing up Angels Place while the target was inside with other Hells Angels. Big Willem was thrown out of the club in Bad Standing.

My time spent with the Hells Angels over the years taught me that you will be unfairly targeted and harassed by law enforcement simply for being a Hells Angel, prospect, hang-around or associate. I watched it happen and I experienced it myself for years. I would later learn that while the Hells Angels receive more law enforcement harassment than many clubs, it does not matter whether you are a Hells Angel, Outsider, Legacy Vet, or member of a Christian motorcycle club like Soldiers for Jesus, the unconstitutional practice of motorcycle profiling and harassment of motorcycle club members by law enforcement is rampant nationwide. There are bullies within law enforcement who look at their position as that of a member of an untouchable gang whose mission is to punish and eradicate, rather than protect and serve, and they have no problem violating the Civil Rights of American citizens for simply being members of a motorcycle club. One of the most prolific of these law enforcement bullies in Washington is Seattle Police Department Detective Ron Smith.

It was a sunny and crisp spring Seattle afternoon in 2005 when my phone rang and on the other end of the phone was a Hells Angel friend of mine named Anthony "A.J." Magnesi who sounded more excited than I had ever heard him in all the years I had known him. "Bro, I need to talk to you! Can you come down to my office?" Sure, I said and told him I would meet him there within the hour. I had known A.J. since before he was a Hells Angel and during the time I had known him, I had worked as a criminal defense investigator for him and helped him beat a shooting charge from when he was a prospect and resulted from an incident in which he was jumped by a couple of guys outside a bar, one of which was armed with a knife, so AJ fired into the ground to scare them away, and I was currently serving as his criminal defense investigator on a serious felony assault case in which the editor of a well-known biker magazine came into A.J.'s custom chopper shop soliciting advertising business after he had recently published an issue of the magazine which included a satirical Photo-Shopped photo of a billboard advertising Jack Daniels Wild Berry County Cocktails with a tag line that read "Because gay Hells Angels get thirsty too."

As you can imagine when this jackass came into A.J.'s shop asking for him to pay for advertising in the magazine that had publicly disrespected him, his brothers, and his club, A.J. had no problems telling the editor what he thought of him and his magazine. Failing to respect A.J.'s six foot plus, 230-pound frame and cauliflower ears that told the tale of his time as an elite wrestler, the editor took a swing at A.J. and A.J. defended himself. The editor called the police and A.J. was charged with felony assault. However, during his interview with myself and A.J.'s defense attorney, the editor made several statements that would later be used to impeach the version of events that he testified to on the stand and ultimately A.J. would be acquitted of all charges against him.

A.J. owned Lucky's Choppers which was located in the Georgetown district of Seattle, in a large old multi-story brick building that used to be one of the original Seattle brothels. It was the coolest chopper shop in Seattle and the crew there built some beautiful choppers. His office was in a loft area that looked out over the shop and lounge area. Hung above the stairs leading up to his office was a three-piece painting a friend of his had made for him which depicted law enforcement officers conducting surveillance from buildings which appeared to be the buildings surrounding Lucky's Choppers and a sniper shooting bikers who were standing in front of a business. It was an eerie and grim reminder of the daily reality you faced as a Hells Angel or member of any outlaw motorcycle club. No matter whether you were involved in criminal activity or not, law enforcement treated you as if you were and they would go so far as to kill you for simply being a member.

I know the thought of law enforcement harassing, framing and even killing bikers seems far-fetched, but it happens regularly to bikers and over the course of this book you will be given enough evidence that you will come to understand this for yourself. A.J. was a young, intelligent, successful business owner in Seattle and a Hells Angel, so he received more attention than most one-percenters from local, state, and federal law enforcement, and in particular from Seattle P.D. Detective Ron Smith.

I loved the way the roar from the pipes on my Harley echoed off the brick buildings lining the narrow Georgetown streets as I neared the shop and when I pulled up to the shop there was a prospect waiting to open the large iron gate and let me into the private secured parking lot in the rear of the building. Just like I did every time that I walked up the stairs to A.J.'s office, I took time to admire the mural and smile about the irony of it. When we got upstairs to his office, A.J.'s girlfriend, the beautiful daughter of a prominent commercial developer and several other people were hanging out in the chairs around the coffee table. A.J. politely asked them to give us some privacy and they all immediately jumped up and scurried down the stairs. A.J. took a seat at his desk, took his cell phone from the inside pocket of his colors, removed the battery, and sat the pieces separately on the desk in front him. A.J. is very surveillance aware, this was a common practice when he had something especially important that he wanted to talk to me about, and I reflexively did the same with my phone. A.J. smiled a giant smile like the cat that just ate the canary, and he opened his desk drawer and removed a small silver colored digital audio recorder. "I need you to listen to this and give me your advice." Standard A.J., he only says what he must and nothing more when it came to serious business. He pressed play and for the next couple of minutes I listened to a voice that while I could not identify the speaker by voice, it was clear he was a law enforcement officer, and it was clear he was directly threatening A.J. According to A.J., the voice on the tape was that of Detective Ron Smith of the Seattle P.D.'s Pawn Shop unit. A.J. told me that several of his friends who own businesses around his in Georgetown had been contacted by Det. Smith who told them that he was investigating A.J. and wanted anyone to contact them with any information they had on any criminal activity that A.J. was involved in. A.J. said that he took offense to this because he is simply the owner of a successful business and a Hells Angel, and Det. Smith was ruining his reputation. He told me that one of the business owners Smith contacted had provided him with the business card Smith gave him, so he decided to contact Smith and voice his displeasure. It was during this conversation that detective Smith began openly threatening him, so A.J. decided to start recording the conversation.

During the recorded conversation Det. Smith can be heard calling A.J. a "dirtbag" and taunting him about suspected criminal activity even though Smith acknowledged A.J. was not under official investigation and had never been convicted of a serious crime. Smith goes on to tell A.J. "You better watch your back." and he says that "Simply being a member of the Hells Angels outlaw motorcycle gang is a crime." What is most disturbing was when the corrupt detective boasts that "he is a member of the biggest "gang" of all: It's called law enforcement. You got it?" There is a point in the recording where it is clear that Smith realized A.J. was recording the conversation and he tells A.J. it's illegal to record a conversation without all parties' consent, Smith said he is going to charge A.J. criminally for recording the conversation, and shortly after that statement A.J. stopped the recording. I sat back in my seat, looked into A.J.'s eyes and let out a long drawn out "Wow!" I told A.J. that we needed to try and get out ahead of this and make copies of the recording and get a copy to his attorney who in turn can provide it to Seattle P.D.'s Office of Professional Accountability (OPA), which is exactly what happened. Smith did as he promised and charged A.J. with several misdemeanor charges related to recording the conversation. As a result of A.J's attorney providing the recording to OPA, an investigation was opened but, in the end, OPA simply referred the incident to Smith's supervisor as a training issue and no further action was taken against him. What Smith had done should have resulted in much worse than some training and because nothing was done to the bully this would not be Smith's last encounter with the Hells Angels, and Smith would get his revenge against the Angels for daring to stand up against as Smith put it, "the biggest gang there is."

In June 2005, ATF and other federal, state and local agencies executed nineteen warrants after a federal grand jury indicted 26 members of the Bandidos Motorcycle Club on charges including Violent Crime in Aid of Racketeering, Kidnaping (VICAR), Assault (VICAR), Conspiracy to Tamper with a Witness, Tampering with a Witness, Conspiracy to Distribute Marijuana and Methamphetamine; Distribution of Marijuana; Distribution of Methamphetamine, Carrying a Firearm During and in Relation to a Drug Trafficking Crime, Conspiracy to Traffic in Certain Motor Vehicles and Motor Vehicle Parts, Trafficking in Certain Motor Vehicle, Sale of a Firearm to Prohibited Person, and Felon in Possession of Firearm.

George Wegers, then Bandidos International President was indicted after he was caught on a wiretap during a phone call telling another Bandidos member "We don't talk to those people. Them feds. We don't have any conversations at all with those people" George would end up pleading guilty to racketeering charges for those statements, in exchange for fourteen other charges against him being dropped. As part of the deal, it was agreed that he would serve up to twenty months in prison. This is significantly less time than the twenty plus years that the federal sentencing guidelines could have forced him to endure had he been convicted at trial. As part of the plea deal George admitted that he along with other Bandidos members conspired to tamper with witnesses, traffic stolen motorcycles as well as conspire to commit other crimes. It was a garbage case that had been started by the Bellingham P.D. and D.E.A. but was not fruitful, apart from during that investigation, a couple of

Washington Bandidos along with Bandidos from Montana, had pulled the patches of members of an outlaw motorcycle club called the Kinsmen MC in Montana.

When the patch pulling occurred ATF contacted the investigator on the Bellingham case and suggested that ATF assist them in opening a federal case against the Bandidos, and that is how ATF got the warrants for the wiretaps they used against George. I was disappointed to see George go to prison because under his leadership there had been a lot of positive changes in the Bandidos MC, and I was worried those might not continue. George's conviction was a lesson to the club community and demonstrated that the feds really would build a case against you for nothing more than what you say on the phone, even if it was something, we as outlaw motorcycle club members felt was no big deal. George never said anything nefarious, he just repeated a code of the culture, that we as outlaw motorcycle club members do not talk to the cops, ever. Whether you are a suspect, victim or a witness, outlaw motorcycle club members do not talk to cops and George repeating that ethic earned him a R.I.C.O. beef. Before we really bring ATF into the story, I want to introduce you to another character who is central to that portion of the story and at the same time I will tell you one of my favorite tattoo stories.

One of the scariest human beings I have ever called my friend is Rod Rollness. Rod was a Washington Hells Angel when I started hanging around and one of the most serious individuals I have ever met. Just being around Rod you know he is a man to be taken seriously that is capable of great violence and not to be disrespected. That said, once he gets to know you and determines he likes you he lets you see he has got a kind side. It took Rod and I a few years before we got to know each other to the point I even saw him smile for the first time, but we ended up becoming good friends and I enjoyed the time I spent with him and his family. I had a tattoo that I wanted covered, and Rod had offered to cover it for me. Over the next couple weeks, he designed an elaborate Viking battle scene that would take up my entire right calf and included a one percent diamond, the phrase "Snitches are a dying breed.", and the tattoo even has my company logo hidden in the design. When it was done, Rod called me and told me to come over and get tattooed. Rod, his wife, three sons and two daughters lived in a small three-room cabin in the woods just outside of the small town of Snohomish Washington. The cabin was located on a sloped lot in a clearing at the top of a quarter mile gravel driveway. About halfway up the driveway was a metal chain link kennel which housed an angry white Pitbull named Gypsy who barked at anything that came near the driveway or yard, and who I never saw anywhere but that kennel. Chained to a stake in the middle of the lawn on the top third of the clearing was a wolf that served as the same type of unpredictable sentry as the Pitbull but was the more approachable of the two animals.

As I arrived to get my tattoo, Gypsy was normal Gypsy and freaked the fuck out as I drove past her kennel. The wolf looked at me and gave a bark and then went back to laying in the sun. Rod's two middle sons and his youngest daughter were playing in the yard and greeted me as soon as I got out of my car. As I walked across the yard, I could hear the familiar buzz of a tattoo needle being adjusted with Skynyrd's Sweet Home Alabama playing in the background and I got excited. Rod was a respected one-percenter and enforcer, so it was an honor to have him give me my first one percent tattoo. I walked into the house, Rod got up, greeted me with a big bear hug and asked, "Are you ready to have some fun?" Fuck yeah, there is nothing better than living room tattoos! I said. He proudly unrolled the large piece of parchment style paper and showed me the Viking battle scene he had drawn by hand. I commended him on his work and told him let's get to work.

Just as Rod finished laying down the stencil transfer his youngest daughter came flying through the door, her tiny face bright red and tears streaming from her eyes, she screamed "Daddy, daddy come quick. Gypsy's out and she's killing the wolf!" Rod and I sprang to our feet and ran outside where we found that Gypsy had broken out of her chain link kennel and had attacked the wolf in the upper yard and had it by the throat in a death grip. Rod tried to pull Gypsy off the wolf but there was no prying her free. He straddled the dog, dropped down on Gypsy's back and gave her two huge right punches to the face. Blood, teeth, and slobber sprayed from Gypsy's mouth with each punch, but Gypsy was still not letting go, so Rod wrapped his giant hands around the beast's massive neck and began to strangle it to death. When the dog went limp and released the wolf, Rod threw Gypsy's lifeless body across the yard. Almost as soon as her body hit the ground she came-to and immediately charged back across the yard and had the wolf by the throat again. Rod dropped down across Gypsy's back again and yelled to one of his sons to get him a rope. I pulled out my knife and offered to cut the dog's throat and Rod told me it would be too messy. His son scrambled into the garage and after a minute or so Rod yelled to him demanding to know what was taking him so long. His son came back into view and said in a panic that he could not find a rope to which Rod instructed him to find something to wrap around the dog's neck. Thirty seconds later his son emerged from the garage and brought Rod a large rainbow striped beach towel. Rod wrapped the towel around Gypsy's neck and strangled her until she went limp and released the wolf again, this time tying off the towel tightly round the dog's neck to ensure its death. When he was done, he tossed the dogs lifeless body off the upper lawn onto the concrete driveway below and instructed his sons to bury the dog and to bury it deep because he did not want anything digging it up. Then he and I went back inside.

The whole incident lasted just a few minutes and was very violent and chaotic. I had just watched my friend kill his dog; I did not expect Rod to want to give me a tattoo that would take several hours after an incident like that. We did not talk as we came back into the house and then I spoke first and told him I was sorry he had to put his dog down and we don't have to do my tattoo today. Rod looked at me and smiled, reached into his chest pocket of the red and white flannel shirt he was wearing, and retrieved a joint. He said, shit happens bro, let's get stoned and have some fun. I laughed and we got down to work.

We had a great time as he worked. We talked and joked and laughed. The kids were running in and out of the house the entire time and did not seem bothered by what had transpired earlier. After about eight hours of work Rod told me that he was done. When I looked down at my leg, I instantly realized that he had misspelled the word snitches when he had given me my "Snitches are a Dying Breed" tattoo, and instead it appeared as Snitch's, and to make matters worse there did not appear to be any way to fix it. Now let me remind you that Rod is probably the scariest human being I have ever met and so confronting him about his spelling error and insulting his work was not my most desirable course of action, but I wasn't not going to not say something about it. I looked at Rod and laughed. "Why the fuck are you laughing at me?" he growled at me from behind his thick black beard. I pointed out his spelling error and said "I don't think there's any way to fix that bro. Now I've got to tell anyone who points out the spelling error that my friend Rod got too stoned after he killed his dog and misspelled my Snitches are a Dying Breed tattoo." "Fuck that shit!" he yelled, "I didn't misspell shit! Vernon, go get my Snitches are a Dying Breed shirt!" he demanded. A few minutes later his son Vernon came into the living room holding a t-shirt, his face clearly nervous and his little hand trembled as he held out the shirt to his father. "What's wrong with you?" Rod demanded to know. "Nothing dad", Vernon said softly. "It's just, you did spell Jeff's tattoo wrong." Rod angrily commanded Vernon to get out. He looked down at the shirt. Looked at my ankle and then back to the shirt before looking at me and saying, "Sorry bro, wanna T-shirt?" We had a good laugh about the situation. It may be a misspelled tattoo but there is one hell of a story behind it and I wouldn't have it any other way. Little did I know but the hug goodbye I gave Rod as I left that night would be the last hug, I would ever be able to give Rod.

Now back to ATF. On the morning of February 14th, 2006, Josh got up and went to go fill their car with gas so that his wife Lisa would have gas to get to work that morning. ATF, state, and local law enforcement had his home under surveillance at the time and arrested him without incident a short distance from his home. Since the feds had his home under surveillance, they knew that Lisa and little Hannah were alone inside the home, yet they still felt it necessary to use a SWAT team and armored vehicle to assault his residence and detain Lisa and Hannah, while ATF deliberately and maliciously destroyed their home and personal property during their search. What happened to their home was not the professional execution of a search warrant but a willful violation of their Civil Rights, the deliberate destruction of personal property intended to punish, and an abuse of power that occurred because law enforcement knows they can get away with that kind of corruption, and it is present in varying degrees in almost every search warrant executed on every member of an outlaw motorcycle club who has been the target of an ATF warrant. It was wrong, it disgusted me, and no matter how hard I tried to justify ATF's actions and let it go, in my mind and heart I have never been able to accept the way ATF deliberately violates Civil Rights and their extrajudicial punishment of outlaw motorcycle club members.

At the same time the feds were hitting Josh's house they hit Rod's house. Once again at Rod's house law enforcement was conducting preoperational surveillance and had the home under surveillance and they used a SWAT team and armored vehicle in the raid. It was in the twenties that morning and law enforcement laid all six young children facedown in the snow at rifle point where they were held for over an hour while the raiding agents destroyed personal property. Just as in Josh's case, I felt ATF's treatment of the families in those raids was unduly harsh and beyond justification.

**Local, state, and federal officers outside the Hells Angels clubhouse
in Spokane, WA. February 14h, 2006.**
Photo by Jesse Tinsley / The Spokesman-Review

Meanwhile, in Spokane Washington, federal authorities were serving warrants on the clubhouse, Hells Angels Nomads Washington President and West Coast President Smilin' Rick Fabel's home, and then Hells Angels Sargent at Arms Ricky Jenks home. Within minutes news of the raids was all over national news, touting that the president of the Washington Hells Angels and three other current or former members had been arrested for various racketeering crimes, the most serious of which were related to Josh and Rod who faced numerous charges including Murder in Aid of Racketeering and Violent Crimes in Aid of Racketeering (VICAR), which meant they would both be eligible for the death penalty if convicted.

The raids were the result of a newly unsealed indictment in the federal district court in Seattle that accused Smilin', Josh, Rod and Ricky of federal racketeering crimes including murder, robbery, extortion, and trafficking in stolen motorcycles. The racketeering (RICO) indictment alleged Smilin' Rick and the other named defendants engaged in an "organized criminal enterprise" since 1999 that was held together by a series of crimes. Specifically, they were accused of the murder of Michael "Santa" Walsh, armed robbery, trafficking in stolen motorcycles, extortion, and mail fraud. All of the defendants were held without bail and housed at Federal Detention Center SeaTac (FDC SeaTac) while they awaited trial.

This is probably a good point for me to share another part of my story that is critical. While I chose not to continue to pursue becoming a Hells Angel after Josh and Rod quit the club, I remained close with the Hells Angels MC as an organization up until I left the motorcycle club world behind in 2017. During my time spent with the Angels I volunteered my professional skillset as an investigator to assist with the criminal defense of multiple Hells Angels members over the years on cases ranging from assault with a deadly weapon to murder, and my work helped result in good outcomes including acquittals. In one case we were able to get a murder charge resolved with a plea to manslaughter and a five-year sentence, and in another case, I helped get a member an acquitted on a serious felony assault with a firearm case. In fact, during the course of my time in the club world I would end up volunteering my professional skillset to assist members from every major one percent club in the country with matters ranging from motorcycle profiling, harassment and excessive use of force by law enforcement, to the most serious RICO offenses. What I would come to understand from the perspective as a professional investigator is that when it comes to outlaw motorcycle clubs, the Constitution does not apply and there is never a presumption of innocence until proven guilty, rather it is a presumption of organized criminal activity until proven innocent.

Naturally, when the HA Washington RICO arrests went down, I reached out to Smilin' Rick and volunteered to assist free of charge. Several years earlier when I was in my early twenties and made that first trip to California to go to my first H.A. party, I made the conscious decision that I was more than likely going to be captured on law enforcement surveillance and ultimately identified as a Hells Angels associate which law enforcement considers a gang/criminal organization and that would make it impossible for me to ever pass a law enforcement background investigation and get a job in that career field should I ever choose to go that way and use my skill-set and education, but that consequence didn't matter to me because I wanted to be part of a culture based on loyalty, honor, respect and brotherhood with strict accountability for a man's actions, and I believed law enforcement was misidentifying outlaw motorcycle clubs as outlaw motorcycle gangs and unfairly targeting them. I also believed that with no criminal history, and with my professional and educational background, that I could be a credible voice for the outlaw motorcycle club community someday, if I could stay out of prison and stay alive. RICO is no joke and when this case kicked off, I knew that I could help, and I volunteered my services to the Hells Angels, Josh, and Rod. I knew that I needed to start to distance myself from the Angels and build my professional resume to allow me to be a more credible professional witness and appear impartial, should my testimony be needed in the RICO trial.

In April 2006, I was offered a job as an Investigator with the State of Washington. It was an undercover position and I only had to work four days a week which would allow me plenty of time for motorcycle fun, travel, and short-term high-threat protection contracts. The job security and benefits that come with a state investigations job made it very attractive but my hang-up on it was the fact that the position was a law enforcement position which should make me ineligible to ever be a one-percenter. After weighing the benefits that having this position would have on my credibility should I be called to testify in the RICO case or future outlaw motorcycle club member cases, against the fact that I would probably never be able to become a one-percenter, I determined that the credibility and potential benefit to men I considered my brothers and friends was worth the personal sacrifice, and I approached the Hells Angels as well as Josh and Rod and I let them know that I would be taking the job and hoped this wouldn't affect our relationships. All parties responded the same and agreed that I had established who I was, what my motivations are, where my loyalties lie, and my professional choice would not be a conflict.

I would hold that undercover position for ten years, and during that time my caseload came to include criminal street gangs, drug cartels, and organized crime groups, yet I never once investigated a case involving a member of an outlaw motorcycle club. Ultimately, what resulted was that for the remaining eleven years I spent in the outlaw motorcycle club world, I had made a decision that forced me to deliberately retard my professional career in order to remain eligible to be a member of an outlaw motorcycle club, but it was a decision I made freely believing that at some point my credibility as a voice for the outlaw motorcycle culture would be worth my personal sacrifice.

Shortly before the raids on the Hells Angels in Washington, I had started a Washington chapter of a traditional motorcycle club. I had never stopped being part of the Washington motorcycle club community or wanting the brotherhood of a motorcycle club and when the opportunity presented itself, I decided to move forward. I am sharing this experience because law enforcement experts frequently mislead juries and the media to believe that to start a motorcycle club or new chapter of an out of state motorcycle club that you either need to get permission from the "Dominant Club" that controls the state, or you have to get permission from the Confederation / Council of Clubs (COC) for that state. This assertion is totally false.

Based on my own personal knowledge and experience I can attest that there are slight differences to the process from state to state, but pretty universally, asking permission to do anything in the motorcycle club world will not get you respect because you are approaching the situation from a position of subservience. Furthermore, all Confederation /Council of Clubs (COC) have a policy that they are not a sanctioning body, and no club business is to be discussed at the meetings. This policy is in place to help avoid confrontations and violence between clubs as well as prevent any behavior that could expose the organization (COC) and its participants to any legal liability, because motorcycle clubs whether they are an outlaw motorcycle club or not are hyper aware that law enforcement is constantly looking for ways to indict them on seemingly anything. Thus, the COC is definitely not granting permission for new clubs because they know that would expose them to RICO.

That said, here is how I started that motorcycle club in Washington State. In Washington State there is no such thing as a "Dominant Club." While the Bandidos had by far the most members and support clubs in the state, at the time I brought that club into Washington there were actually four respected outlaw motorcycle clubs who all shared the state and needed to be approached. They included in order of length of time in the state, the Gypsy Joker MC, Outsiders MC, and Bandidos MC both of whose Washington chapters started in 1974, and the Hells Angels MC. Because of the club relationships I had developed by that time, reaching out to the Jokers happened over the course of a motorcycle ride over Snoqualmie Pass with their President on a warm spring day, and since this all occurred before the Hells Angels raids, Smilin' Rick was still free, showing the Angels the respect due was simply the matter of a phone call to Smilin' to announce my intentions.

Smilin' happened to be out of the country at the time and it took him a few days to call back. I was in Las Vegas when Smilin returned my call from Rio de Janeiro, Brazil. We chit chatted briefly about both our travels and as we spoke, in the background I began to hear what I knew to be the distinctive clack, clack, clack, clack of AK-47 fire, followed by the sound of return fire from a small caliber automatic machine gun. "What the fuck is going on there bro?" I asked in amazement. Smilin' liked nice things, was security aware from being a Hells Angel for over thirty years and up until that point I imagined him relaxing in a fine luxury resort on a beach with a couple beautiful twenty something Brazil-ian hotties and not a care in the world. "Ahhh, it's no big deal, I'm spending the night at one of the brothers and his favela is like this every night. The gunfire is mostly going out not in, so it's all good." He said casually with a confident chuckle. I told Smilin', "I'm going to be starting a chapter of a traditional motorcycle club in Washington and out of respect I just wanted to give him a heads up and let him know we don't plan on stepping on anyone's toes and we're just going to do our own thing," Without more than a pause for a quick breath Smilin' responded "That sounds good but are you sure you don't want to be a Hells Angel Jeff? I can make that happen for you." To which I respectfully declined his offer.

I had an almost identical conversation with the Regional President of the Bandidos a week later at the Oyster Run in Anacortes, WA, and the only difference in his response was that he asked us to become a support club for the Bandidos, and again I respectfully declined the offer.

There were no black eyes, no taxes paid to the "dominant club", no seeking COC sanctioning, no stolen colors and motorcycles, and nobody died. I just established a reputation for myself within the motorcycle club community, had a good plan and the experience to pull it off, and then showed the respect to the clubs who had earned it, and they in turn showed me the respect I had earned. The only real difference in the process is when it comes to the rare state like Texas where up until very recently the Bandidos were the only one-percent outlaw motorcycle club in the state, so up until recently you would simply talk to them. Again, the Confederation of Clubs or Council of Clubs as they are called depending on state, are never a sanctioning body and despite law enforcement's false assertions, they do not tax motorcycle clubs so they can exist in that state, that is just law enforcement lies designed to make the COC's appear as if they are a criminal organization.

It was winter of 2005 when I got a call from a Spokane number that I did not recognize. I ignored the first call but when the same number called back repeatedly, I answered it. The guy on the other end of the phone introduced himself as T-Rex or some shit like that. He said he was from a motorcycle club called the Iron Order and my National President had given him my number and told him I might be willing to make some introductions for him in Washington. I was shocked, I do not make introductions for anyone I don't know. That said, I had heard about the Iron Order. They were a new club that was only a few months old and was founded by a Secret Service Agent, ATF Agent, an executive from Papa Johns, and a bunch of other cops and goofballs that could not make it in any real motorcycle clubs. Beyond that, I did not know shit about those Iron Order douche-bags at this point and I was willing to at least hear this guy out so I could learn more about his organization and why he was in Spokane, and I had never heard of him.

T-Rex confirmed what I had heard about the Iron Order but told me that they wanted to do things right in Washington, which is why he was hoping I could help clue him in on the process for Washington. Fuck, this guy was green. I told him that the first thing he needed to do before he starts flying that black and white patch around in the Northwest, was to go find out what the Gypsy Joker MC think about that idea. I told him that if they are cool with it then he should do the same with the Hells Angels, and then make a trip to the west side and introduce himself to the Outsiders in Tacoma.

Next green guy question was "Can you give me their numbers?" Really man, you don't know anybody? I asked. "No, and I was hoping you could make some introductions for me." I told him that was not going to happen but what I would do is give him the name and email of the Secretary of the Washington Confederation of Clubs, and he could arrange through him to go to the next COC meeting, introduce himself and his club, and meet the people he needs to meet. This fucking guy's response was that he can't go to C.O.C. meetings or interact with C.O.C. member clubs because the C.O.C. is a criminal organization. I was shocked and disgusted, and quickly educated the lame on the fact

that the C.O.C. was a motorcycle communication and rights organization and is not involved in any criminal activity. He told me that his
clubs' national policy is not to participate in any C.O.C. activities because they are criminal organizations and have felons as members. At
this point in time the clubs in Washington were still pulling patches
from clubs that did not follow the process, and in my opinion, if you
did not show respect for the motorcycle club community or the process,
you should get what's coming to you. That is the rules of the culture
and if you change those rules, you change the culture. So, if you are
too soft to live by the rules, stay the fuck out of the culture. The Iron
Order started a new breed of internet generated money-making enterprises masquerading as motorcycle clubs, who insulate themselves with
membership consisting of law enforcement and claims they are on some
holy crusade to restore motorcycle club culture to what it once was and
what it's supposed to be. In reality, the Iron Order and the cop clubs like
them are all jokes. They have no idea what it means to be a real patch-
holder. They have lowered the bar for membership to the point where
they're behavior is disgraceful, and they are one of the most negative and
poisonous influences the motorcycle club culture has ever seen.

The next call was to my National President who I gave an earful for
giving that lame my number and interacting with that club. I had been
elected National Vice President a few months earlier and in the last couple weeks my relationship with him had taken a vastly different turn. He
had gotten focused on expansion of our club, while I believed that being spread across three regions was enough and expansion would lead to
conflict we did not want or need. Within three weeks of giving that Iron
Order lame my phone number, I heard that our National President uni-
laterally took it upon himself to violate an agreement that I had personally made with the Bandidos MC, that we would not open chapters in
Idaho, but he was he approving an Idaho prospect chapter that didn't
even have the membership numbers to be an official chapter. I was livid.
I called my chapter and we held a meeting where I told them what was
being done and that we could either go to war with the Bandidos over

our National President's violation of an agreement he told us to make, we could take a trip to the south and beat that old man's ass, take his patch and takeover the club, or we could simply shut down our chapter in Washington and do our own thing. The couple of members that voted to stay course with the club, knowing the National President had violated an agreement made by our chapter which would jeopardize our chapter and cause conflict for us and the entire club, were beaten, had their patches pulled, and were expelled from the club for failing to stand up for themselves and their brothers. We officially shut down the chapter and went a new direction.

From the time he was arrested, Josh had been housed in the SHU or Security Housing Unit of FDC SeaTac, and this intense isolation and twenty-three hour a day lockdown gave Josh a good look at how he could potentially spend the rest of his life. To Josh, cooperating with the government and implicating others was against the 1% code and simply not an option, but the thought of fighting the death penalty only to spend the rest of his life in prison was equally unattractive and left him facing a difficult decision. Does he fight the death penalty or just take the case to trial and if convicted not appeal his death sentence and hopefully get a quick execution? Ultimately, it came down to beautiful little Hannah and his loyalty to that little girl, and Josh decided to fight the death penalty. His attorney Gil Levy and Rod's attorney Terry Kellogg flew back to D.C. and made their argument that the death sentence was inappropriate for their indictments. When they returned to Washington Gil briefed Josh on the trip and told him, "Now we wait." U.S. Attorney General Alberto Gonzalez would be the one to make the determination on whether Josh and Rod would be put to death if convicted, and on September 20th, 2006, Gonzalez sent a letter to John McKay the United States District Attorney for the Western District of Washington, informing him that he was "authorized not to seek the death penalty" in Josh and Rod's case. The news was not a victory, but it was good news, and I was glad the government would not get the chance to kill my brother.

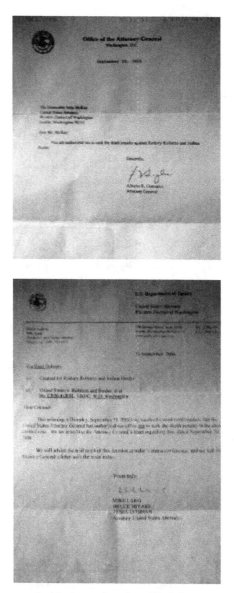

Josh's personal copies of the letters
informing him of the death sentence decision.

In March 2007, the Washington Hells Angels RICO trial kicked off and for the next ten weeks the jury would hear evidence intended to establish that the Washington Hells Angels MC were not just a brotherhood of men who loved Harley Davidson motorcycles, but were in fact a sophisticated criminal enterprise responsible for trafficking in stolen property, insurance fraud, intimidating witnesses, and even murder. The case was one of a string of cases in which the federal government had used the RICO act to prosecute members of motorcycle clubs. Convicting members of an outlaw motorcycle club of charges relating to the club being a gang is incredibly difficult and, in a March 11, 2007, article in the Seattle P-I, Agent Scott Thomasson of the Bureau of Alcohol Tobacco, Firearms and Explosives explained "It's difficult to prove, only because most of these guys are committing individual acts to line their own pockets, not for the gang." The article goes on to point out that while a courtroom victory would not eliminate the Hells Angels, it would allow the Justice Department to seize the motorcycle club's property – even the clubs precious trademarked "death head" logo.

The men on trial faced a total of nineteen felony counts stemming from the trafficking and sales of stolen motorcycles and parts, intimidating witnesses after a beating in Spokane, WA, and using the Hells Angels reputation and threats of violence to intimidate and further the enterprise, stealing motorcycles, and the murder of Michael "Santa" Walsh for falsely claiming to be a Hells Angels member. The trial was expected to last ten weeks, involve up to two hundred witnesses, and 1,000 exhibits. The high profile, high security trial took place on the ninth floor of the U.S. Federal District for the Western District of Washington in the heavily guarded courtroom of U.S. District Judge Robert Lasnik and utilized a twelve-member anonymous jury. Authorities claimed that it was necessary to identify the jurors only by number to reduce witness intimidation which they claimed was a hallmark of outlaw motorcycle clubs. To get to the courtroom you had to show U.S. Marshals at the main entrance your I.D., take off your shoes, remove all items from your pockets, all of which were then passed through an x-ray machine while you walked through a metal detector and in some cases, you were then physically searched. Once on the ninth floor where the courtroom was you repeated the process to enter the courtroom where inside, the courtroom was ringed with armed U.S. Marshal's as well as monitored via closed circuit surveillance cameras that law enforcement was using to capture photos of the attendees there to support the defendants, to use for intelligence purposes.

Over the next ten weeks I was in the courtroom almost every day and it was unlike any other criminal trial I have ever been involved in. The government's argument was simple, the Hells Angels are a criminal organization whose world revolves around the death head logo, and they use violence and intimidation to commit crimes in furtherance of the organization. The defense would counter that any crimes committed were done so by individuals and not with the sanctioning of the organization and allege that the prosecution was attempting to use a string of corrupt witnesses with motives to lie in exchange for leniency with their own independent pending criminal charges and sentences to prove the case.

The case was the result of an incident involving a former Hells Angels hang-around named Michael Kordash who called police to report that Josh and Rod had stolen his motorcycle in January 2004. Even though this incident took place long after both Josh and Rod had quit the Hells Angels, the government was alleging that Josh and Rod committed the crime in furtherance of the Hells Angels. The first time I met Kordash I thought he was a lame and wondered why the Angels would allow him around, but it was not my place to question the club. Kordash was a weak man who lacked confidence unless he had others around that he knew would back him up. He was one of those guys who talked the talk, but it was all show, and in the end, he would be sent down the road by the Hells Angels for being a drunk and not representing himself or the club well. To add insult to injury, his girlfriend decided he was not the one for her, she dumped Kordash and took up with Smilin Rick. When Kordash approached the cops, he was put in the witness protection program and moved outside of Washington State. On the day he was driving to Seattle to testify in the case he was stopped by police who found a loaded handgun and marijuana in his van. Now since this was prior to marijuana becoming legal in Washington, the gun and weed should have been a problem for him but because he was on his way to testify in the Hells Angels RICO trial he was let go and the government helped him out of the trouble he was in for the marijuana and gun charge in exchange for his testimony in the H.A. case.

The star witness for the prosecution was former Hells Angel Johnathon, J.T. "Thunder" Yates, a meth addict who made a lifestyle out of lying, was paid by the government to testify, had a history of witness intimidation, had been convicted of his own violent felonies, and was serving time in prison at the time he reached out to federal investigators and offered to cooperate and provide information on the Hells Angels in exchange for a reduced prison sentence and a book deal. J.T. was one of the biggest pieces of human trash I have ever met, a former porn actor and male stripper, J.T. had once threatened to staple a man's penis to a bar, set it on fire and then hand the man a knife and let him decide whether to cut it off. After signing his contract with ATF, J.T. committed a kidnapping but the feds helped him out and he was given his freedom and a new life in the witness protection program in exchange for his testimony in the Washington Hells Angels trial.

Another prosecution witness in the trial was Shawn Lundy, a career criminal who acknowledged on the witness stand that he had once been convicted of possession of stolen puppies. Lundy approached law enforcement and offered to testify against Rod in exchange for a reduced sentence that Lundy himself faced for marijuana charges, money laundering, and escape. Lundy was a weaselly, creepy looking little man who claimed that Rod admitted to the murder of Michael "Santa" Walsh while the two were in FDC SeaTac together. Now remember, Rod is the same guy who I did not even see crack a smile for years but allegedly he confessed to committing a murder to a convicted puppy thief that he just met in federal lockup. Does not make sense to me but the government was all-in on Lundy's information.

Throughout the trial I saw numerous prosecution witnesses take the stand only to testify that they had been threatened by law enforcement that if they did not appear as a witness and make specific statements against the defendants that they knew were false, law enforcement would charge them with crimes. One of the investigators from the Monroe Police Department had so many witnesses make claims of intimidation, threats, and other unethical behavior against him that the judge refused to allow the detective to take the stand and testify in the case he had been one of the primary investigators on.

Then there was Detective Ron Smith. That is right, the same Seattle P.D. detective who had previously harassed and been caught on tape making threats against Hells Angel Anthony "A.J." Magnesi. Smith had somehow managed to insert himself into the Hells Angels RICO trial even though what he had to testify to would just establish that some Hells Angels members carry firearms and possess concealed pistol licenses. During the RICO trial, Smith testified that when he was on patrol, he and other officers responded to a disturbance call at the Hurricane Café and confronted two Hells Angels who when searched, the officers found them to both be in possession of firearms. Smith would later identify the Hells Angels as J.T. "Thunder Yates" who had become an informant in this case, and Josh Binder, who Smith classified as an enforcer for the motorcycle club. Smith went on to testify that the day after the incident, Yates called him to apologize and ask him out for a beer, but Smith refused. Smith testified that later that day a group of six to eight bikes pulled up in front of the precinct and he saw some of the riders wearing Hells Angels colors. Smith said the bikes idled for a few minutes, nobody got off their bikes and then they left eastbound on Virginia. All in all, a whole lot of nothing but it got Smith what he wanted desperately, association with the Hells Angels RICO trial, the chance to paint himself as an Outlaw Motorcycle Gang (OMG) investigator, and it gave him a way to try and stick it to the Angels because he hates the Hells Angels.

After over ten weeks of testimony the federal jury returned guilty verdicts against Josh, Rod and Smilin' Rick, and hung on the charges against Ricky, giving the government a rare victory in its campaign to brand outlaw motorcycle clubs as sophisticated criminal organizations. More importantly, the jury's conclusion that the Hells Angels Nomads Washington charter operated as a "criminal enterprise" was a major win after disappointing results the government had received in the Laughlin River Run cases in Nevada, and the hugely expensive and unorthodox Operation Black Biscuit in which several undercover agents and paid informants with the ATF infiltrated the Hells Angels in Arizona. When interviewed by the media after the trial the U.S. attorney for the Western District of Washington conceded "the history of cases brought against outlaw motorcycle gangs, and in particular the Hells Angels, have met with spotty results." Sullivan went on to state that this has allowed motorcycle clubs to portray themselves as well-meaning organizations with a few bad apples who occasionally run afoul of the law.

At the time of Sullivan's statement, I had been around outlaw motorcycle clubs long enough to know that the truth was outlaw motorcycle clubs were really just brotherhoods formed around their love of motorcycles that genuinely enjoyed doing good for their communities, and whose membership just like with any organization does contain a few bad apples who occasionally run afoul of the law and give the entire motorcycle club culture a bad name, not just their club. Little did I know but I would spend most of my adult life defending this viewpoint and the motorcycle club culture. The victory was by no means complete and the jury returned a not-guilty verdict on the witness-tampering charge and deadlocked on ten other charges. The government immediately made it known that they would seek a new trial for all four defendants for each of those ten charges, which meant Josh would be re-tried on the murder charge and be facing life without the possibility of parole again.

Smilin' Rick was the first to be sentenced by Judge Lasnik. In a courtroom packed with Hells Angels and his friends, Smilin' Rick received a sentence of seven and a half years in prison which exceeded the sentencing guidelines range. He was also ordered to pay $50,000 in restitution mostly related to restitution for the insurance fraud. The U.S. attorney's office had recommended a 10-year sentence, $50,000 fine, $55,000 in restitution and an order that Smilin' be barred from associating with any Hells Angels members following his release. "For two decades, Rick Fabel's life has been dedicated to glorifying violence and a criminal subculture," prosecutors wrote in a sentencing memorandum. "Fabel brought together a toxic blend of sociopaths and anti-social personalities, giving their violent tendencies a place to flourish. Fabel himself extorted, robbed, and victimized numerous people."

In October, Rod was sentenced, and he was not going quietly. "It's clear this man is a predator. It's also clear he doesn't respect human life," assistant U.S. Attorney Bruce Miyake said. "For his lifetime of crime … it's appropriate he spend his lifetime behind bars." Before being sentenced Rod called the government's case against him a sham based on the lies of drug addicts, crooked cops, and a biased judge. That same judge then sentenced him to life in prison without the possibility of parole for the murder of Michael "Santa" Walsh. Rod responded by lashing out at the judge and prosecutors vowing to file an appeal, clear his name, and earn his freedom. "I was railroaded, I'm not guilty here. I'm only guilty of standing up for my family against crooked cops. You're illegally sentencing an innocent man." Rod told Judge Lasnik before being taken from the courtroom by eight U.S. Marshals.

Since the jury was unable to reach a verdict on Josh's charges involving the 2001 murder of Michael Walsh, who was killed because he had falsely claimed to be a member of the Hells Angels, rather than face a retrial and another shot for the government to give him a sentence of life without the possibility of parole, Josh plead guilty to a deal that recommended a prison sentence from 13 to 15 years, and he admitted to having a role in the Walsh murder. What would prove to be a recurring tool used by law enforcement to "prove" the false narrative that outlaw motorcycle clubs are criminal enterprises, and critical to future of outlaw motorcycle club culture as you will read over the course of this book, the government drafted Josh's plea agreement and as a condition of his offered plea agreement, the government made Josh declare under penalty of perjury that the Hells Angels Motorcycle Club are a criminal enterprise, and he committed his crimes on behalf of the enterprise. This would be the first of approximately one hundred similar plea agreements I would see members of various outlaw motorcycle clubs coerced into signing over the coming years in which they were forced to agree under penalty of perjury that their motorcycle clubs are criminal enterprises, or they would face huge prison sentences for crimes the government had weak cases or no cases on at all. Finally, in December 2007 it was Josh's turn to be sentenced. Assistant U.S. Attorney Tessa Gorman called Josh's conduct as the former sergeant-at-arms for the Hells Angels Nomads Washington "inhumane and depraved." "He was the brawn. He was the enforcer," Gorman said during his sentencing. "If you said you were what you were not, then Joshua Binder would punish you." After a brief statement to the court by Michel Walsh's niece, Josh stood up and simply said "I apologize," then sat back down, turned, and gave me a smile and a wink. That would be the last time I would see or speak to my brother Josh until May of 2018.

What was most disturbing for me having watched the trial was the outright lies prosecutors and law enforcement told about not only the Hells Angels but outlaw motorcycle clubs in general, and it became very clear to me that the government, more specifically ATF had begun a mission to have all outlaw motorcycle clubs wrongfully branded as criminal organizations, yet I knew them to be clubs not gangs, and there was really nobody fighting back, including the clubs.

Before I move on, I want to talk about Josh's "Out Bad" status. You see when Josh quit the club in 2003, the Hells Angels Nomads Washington charter gave him an "Out Bad / No Contact" status, but when he was later arrested on the RICO charges, facing the death penalty, refused to cooperate and took his charges to trial, the Hells Angels Nomads Washington charter changed his status to "Out Good" during the trial. However, as soon as he signed his plea agreement stating that the HAMC was a criminal enterprise, the charter changed his status to "Out Bad / No Contact" again. It is important to understand that while the Hells Angels Motorcycle Club is an international club, each charter operates totally autonomously and makes their own operational decisions, including membership status. The reason I share this with you is because I learned over my twenty two years in the one percent world that just because someone is labeled "out bad" it does not necessarily mean they were a bad member or did something dishonorable, and in many cases I found the "out bad" status is used by the clubs to save face when a respected member is dissatisfied with the motorcycle club and quits.

11

OUTLAW MOTORCYCLE GANG (OMG) TRAINING

Over the course of my professional career, I have completed approximately one hundred hours of specialized law enforcement Outlaw Motorcycle Gang (OMG) training, and what I can say without hesitation is that it is all crap, which is why I stopped at one hundred hours. While I cannot say for sure, based on other respected Outlaw Motorcycle Club (OMC) expert's analysis and my own research, I believe that my formal OMG training eclipses most if not all the top recognized law enforcement "OMG experts." The reason I say their training is crap is because it is all based on either outdated inaccurate information, speculation, or straight up lies told to law enforcement by a club member looking for a chance to avoid criminal charges or reduce a sentence resulting from their own personal criminal activity. Most disturbing is the law enforcement officers who portray themselves to be OMG experts and get paid big money to teach outlaw motorcycle gang training classes to other law enforcement, then deliberately lie to the students and feed them misinformation designed to give them a false and prejudiced attitude towards outlaw motorcycle clubs. For some reason, the "experts" who preach this bullshit narrative are almost always associated with the Bureau of Alcohol, Tobacco, Firearms and Explosives (ATF) whether they be an actual agent or members of other law enforcement agencies who serve as ATF Tactical Field Officers.

Over the last year, I had watched my caseload at work evolve to include a significant percentage of cases that focused on members of criminal street gangs and major criminal organizations, so in the spring of 2007, I attended a one-week gang investigators training conference. The curriculum for the conference was remarkably interesting and some of the top experts on various types of gangs from all over the country were going to speak. Of particular interest to me was a portion of the conference that focused on gangs and the military. Additionally, there was a portion of the conference which focused specifically on Outlaw Motorcycle Gangs (OMG's). While I had already completed extensive law enforcement outlaw motorcycle gang (OMG) training over the course of my professional career and always found it to be slightly different versions of the same outdated lies and misinformation, I had high hopes that this course might be different because the description made it sound groundbreaking. It was different indeed.

Just like with most OMG training courses the name of the instructor was withheld for security reasons. Knowing the culture like I do, the thought of any American outlaw motorcycle club targeting a law enforcement officer is unrealistic, and the notion of an American outlaw motorcycle club targeting an "OMG Expert" at a conference full of hundreds of gang investigators is utterly ridiculous. I believe this is done to further law enforcements propaganda campaign that outlaw motorcycle clubs are really dangerous criminal organizations and pose a threat to America, as well as build mystique for the investigators who do the work.

The "expert" who taught the OMG portion of the conference was a clean-cut Seattle P.D. detective about my age who serves on ATF's Regional Outlaw Motorcycle Gang (OMG) Task Force out of the Seattle office. His presentation started off just as almost every other OMG training course I had ever been through. First, he discussed the histories of the various "Big Four" outlaw motorcycle clubs. The term Big Four was coined by law enforcement and refers to the Hells Angels, Bandidos, Outlaws and Pagans. Based on my experience to that point and the dynamics of the outlaw motorcycle club world at the time, I felt the correct term should have been Big Six to include the Mongols and Vagos as well. The information was fairly accurate but nothing that could not have been found in numerous books or on the internet. So far, I was not impressed.

Next, he used the Hells Angels as his example of how all clubs operate and broke down patch meaning and protocols of the outlaw motorcycle club world. While his information about the H.A. and their patches was mostly correct, he incorrectly told the class that the 1% diamond patch is worn to signify the wearer's commitment to living a criminal lifestyle and claimed that the Filthy Few patch is awarded to members of the Hells Angels who have killed on behalf of the motorcycle club. We'll discuss the actual meaning of these specific patches later on in this book but my point is that it was just more inflammatory false information being presented as accurate information and intelligence to hundreds of law enforcement officers who risk their lives every day to protect us and depend on this training to help them understand and address the threats they face each day in the field, but this "OMG expert" was deliberately furthering an inaccurate and prejudicial stereotype of outlaw motorcycle clubs as outlaw motorcycle gangs. He went on to discuss the Hells Angels and he falsely presented a string of incidents that involved the criminality of individual Hells Angels members from various chapters as a pattern of criminal activity of the entire motorcycle club, and then the skinny, wholesome looking and cocky detective really turned things up.

Standing in front of the room of almost three hundred gang investigators from all over the country, wearing his blue polo shirt with the ATF Regional OMG Task Force logo embroidered on the left chest, the wholesome looking detective with an arrogance that made him appear as if he was overcompensating for a lack of experience and self-confidence, rather than an expert who had been there and done that, gave a dramatic pause. "I want to share a story from just a few years ago about just how dangerous these guys (Hells Angels) really are, so you understand." the detective said before taking another dramatic pause while he stared at the floor as if trying to wipe the horrors of what he has been through fighting the evil bikers from his mind and compose himself before speaking. Still looking at the floor intensely, he took another deep breath before looking up into the sea of gang investigators, his face shrouded with sadness, and he began his tale.

A few years ago," there was a case involving a Hells Angel from California that was arrested for running a major prostitution ring out of the bay area, the young detective said. During his case one of the girls, he had held hostage and forced to work as a prostitute bravely came forward and testified against him, and for her security, she was placed in the Witness Security Program. The Hells Angels tracked her for years before tracking her down to a tiny town in Oregon at which point the Angels dispatched a hit team to kill her, he said. Wait, what the fuck? I was familiar with every major H.A. criminal case in U.S. history and the only case I could think of that matched the facts laid out by the detective in any way, was the case of Margo Compton, but that was not from "A few years ago" as the "OMG expert" was teaching these investigators, it was from August 1977. As he went on to describe the crimes leading up to Compton's testimony, he was careful not to provide the names of any Hells Angels involved or dates of incidents that could have been used by the class attendees to track down more information on the incident or fact check what he was teaching them as an expert. Then he turned it up and things really got disturbing.

As he neared the portion in his story where he began to discuss Compton (still not identified to the class) being tracked down by the Hells Angels, his voice began to tremble as if he was trying to keep himself from crying. As he described to the room how Compton's twin daughters were murdered while still clutching their teddy bears, the detective who due to his close proximity in age to mine couldn't have been more than two or three years old at the time of Compton's murder, began to cry in front of the room of hundreds of gang investigators. While the incident the young detective was describing was horrific and deplorable just like he was saying, it was not a club incident even though it involved a member of the Hells Angels and a prospect. The harming, let alone killing of children is intolerable in the one-percent culture, and the killing of Margo Compton and her twins was the act of Otis "Buck" Garrett, a psycho meth addict and dealer who happened to be a Hells Angel and his equally sick tweeker prospect Robert "Bug-Eyed Bob" McClure, and in 1995 the pair would go on trial in Oregon for the murders after Mike "Iron Mike" Thompson, the former leader of the Aryan Brotherhood came forward to tell investigators that Garrett had bragged about the murders to him while they were in prison together at San Quentin. McClure had done the same to other prison gangsters in Fulsom, and the Aryan Brotherhood members testified in the trial that the only reason they came forward and were cooperating witnesses was because the killing of children is not even tolerated by prison gangs, just as it is not tolerated by outlaw motorcycle clubs.

The propaganda minion continued to vomit his bullshit over the course of an entire day. He was not just delivering inaccurate information but outright lies concocted by law enforcement intended to intentionally mislead and prejudice other law enforcement officers. A prime example of this was when he discussed the one percent motorcycle club that I was getting ready to go prospect for at the time, the Outsiders Motorcycle Club. As he showed photos of the clubs' patches, discussed their alleged meanings, club protocols etc., he once again got overly dramatic and told the audience of gang investigators from across America and Canada, "I want you guys to understand something so you can make sure you take adequate precautions, so that you can go home to your families if you come across one of these guys. Outsiders kill cops and they will kill you in a second if they get the chance!" He went on to show a photo of an Outsiders members club tattoo and explained to the audience that if they see an Outsiders member with that tattoo it means that the member has killed a cop to earn it. What the fuck? I was floored! I knew for a fact that tattoo was awarded after the member had completed their first year of membership in the club and received full member status, and nothing more. Moreover, the detective's statement was lunacy. There have been hundreds of Outsiders MC members over the almost fifty years the club had been in existence and if every Outsider member with a club tattoo had killed a cop to earn it there would be hundreds of missing and murdered cops which you think you might hear about, but I sure hadn't and at this point I had almost ten years inside the one percent world and spent my life growing up in Washington where the Outsiders MC had been operating my entire life. To drive home his point, he told another story from "Just a few years ago" that involved the Outsiders MC.

Forgoing the tears, the so-called expert who now because of his lies, I had such disdain for that I was struggling to control myself from walking to the front of the room and socking him in the mouth, switched to anger as he told the audience the story about law enforcement serving a search warrant on the Outsiders clubhouse "just a few years back". He told the audience that after officers knocked and announced their presence, an Outsiders MC member named Robert "Pigpen" Christopher shot a Portland Police Bureau Narcotics Task Force officer in the face with a shotgun, killing the officer. Now, what the shitbag corrupt detective and so-called "OMG expert" did not tell the audience was that while it is true that Pigpen did kill Officer David Crowther, it was in self-defense and in defense of his club brothers and their ol'ladies who were in the clubhouse that night. The incident was not from just a few years ago, but from 1979, and most importantly, he did not tell the audience that Pigpen's conviction was overturned and ultimately led to the discovery of what still is the biggest corruption scandal in Portland police history. We will get to that story a little later because even though the incident occurred in 1979, the impact it had on law enforcement and their willful misrepresentation and lies about the incident would come back to haunt me and in fact still haunts me and shapes law enforcement's interactions with and treatment of me to this day.

I was disgusted at not only this so-called OMG expert's deliberate delivery of false information, but at the extreme dramatics he used to intentionally mislead and prejudice the audience who came there to learn the truth about outlaw motorcycle clubs. More importantly, this type of egregious display of misinformation was the reason outlaw motorcycle clubs had been vilified by the media and why law enforcement harassment and civil rights violations of motorcycle club members is rampant across America. I knew it needed to be stopped before the entire outlaw motorcycle club culture was made illegal as was being pursued at the time in Australia with the assistance of the U.S. Bureau of Alcohol Tobacco, Firearms & Explosives, and it would ultimately become reality in Queensland in 2013 with the establishment of the Vicious Lawless Association Disestablishment (VLAD) Act which was enacted to "severely punish" members of criminal organizations and includes anti-consorting laws which prohibit outlaw motorcycle club members from associating with each other even if they are family members.

My hope by attending the conference was to obtain credible accurate information about criminal gangs that would allow me to do my job as an investigator more effectively and safely, and while I feel that I received that information from the rest of the instructors, what I had learned from the "outlaw motorcycle gang expert", the guy who was and still is a member of the ATF Regional Outlaw Motorcycle Gang Task Force, was total bullshit as was the majority of every other minute of the approximately one hundred hours of law enforcement Outlaw Motorcycle Gang training I have completed during my career. This is when I decided I had enough OMG training, and it made no sense to waste the public's money and my time to learn things I knew to be absolute lies. Additionally, I was about to permanently commit myself to a life of falsely being labeled a gang member and I was hoping that I would have learned something I didn't know about outlaw motorcycle clubs, something that would help me understand why law enforcement is so adamant that outlaw motorcycle clubs are really gangs involved in sophisticated organized crime, so that I could make a critical change in the direction of my life before it was too late, but that hadn't happened. The detective's immoral and prejudiced display taught me that law enforcement OMG training is not just bullshit, it is immoral propaganda designed to teach law enforcement prejudice and hate towards outlaw motorcycle clubs and their members and knowing that reinforced my determination to do the outlaw motorcycle club life the "right" way and prove them all wrong.

I began studying outlaw motorcycle clubs as a child and at one point in my life I could say that I had read every book written and watched every documentary ever produced on outlaw motorcycle clubs, studied every incident of major violence involving an outlaw motorcycle club, and every major criminal case. Today, the simple fact of the matter is that with the increased mainstream popularity of outlaw motorcycle clubs in the media and pop culture, there are many books that are just crap and I have refused to read because the author lacks the experience to be able to provide me with any information that I have not already learned through my own personal experience in the culture, and or I know their story to be full of self-serving lies. From the books written by ATF agents who infiltrated an outlaw motorcycle club like Billy Queen or Jay Dobyns, the writing and teachings of the egomaniacal Steve Cook who even though he failed to be able to infiltrate a motorcycle club he still claims he is America's top OMG expert, or the books and teachings of snitches like Charles Falco and Pat Matter, all law enforcement OMG experts have a consistent agenda and a mission to spread lies about the outlaw motorcycle gang threat to the world, and they do it in order to advance their careers and make themselves as much money as they can off their manufactured myth that outlaw motorcycle clubs are really sophisticated criminal enterprises. Even former outlaw motorcycle club members like Big Pete from the Outlaws MC whose book *The Last Chicago Boss* appears to be written simply for profit and a need to try and make himself feel important, dramatically over inflates his significance in the club world, his book is full of lies about the COC that are consistent with ATF's narrative, and the author of his book just happens to be one of the prosecutors from Operation Black Biscuit. Every one of these "experts" has the same motive to write their book on outlaw motorcycle clubs or teach their class, and it all comes down to making money rather than education, which is why they all spew the same narrative. In law enforcement terms they call this type of organized lying involving a group of people who are acting in concert to further an enterprise, a conspiracy, but because these are cops and informants working for the cops that we are talking about, it is just a matter of business. This book is no different, I most certainly have a goal with this book and that is to educate the public, the media, legislators, and law enforcement on the realities of outlaw motorcycle clubs in order to protect the culture, but unfortunately for me, I do not have the benefit of ATF using their connections to get me a lucrative book deal, so I'll be lucky if this book sells fifty copies.

While I've personally chosen to never to be part of the outlaw motorcycle club world ever again, it is a culture that I believe is part of American history, a culture that is on the front lines of a war with a corrupt element of law enforcement working against freedom and Constitutional rights, a culture that needs to be protected, and because of my unique access within the culture and my experience, I have the ability to provide insight on level and tell the truth about the culture better than anyone else. I am never going back to club life, I am not a cop or a snitch over-inflating my importance and experiences in order to keep an audience interested enough to sell books, get movies deals, or make huge speaking and expert witness money. I am Twitch and I am pretty sure that you'll find even this watered-down version of my story to be interesting as fuck. Moreover, what you will find by reading this book and considering the information I present, is that what I have to say about outlaw motorcycle club culture makes vastly more sense than law enforcement's narrative. What I will present to you over the course of this adventure is my first-hand experience over twenty plus years and it exposes a pattern of unconstitutional civil rights violations, harassment, assault, and criminal activity committed by corrupt members of law enforcement, for the express purpose of vilifying and eliminating outlaw motorcycle clubs in America, and they are doing it for money and fame. I can guarantee you I will take heat from law enforcement for sharing my views on the subject with the world, but it is necessary to defend our Constitution, the motorcycle club culture, and it is what's best for America.

12

PAPA IS KILLED AND STONEY CATCHES A RICO FOR IT.

With the mystique and misinformation surrounding outlaw motorcycle clubs thanks to T.V. shows like Gangland and Sons of Anarchy, motorcycle clubs tend to organically develop a highly effective civilian intelligence network made up of friends, hangers-on, wannabes, and groupies that unprompted will report the presence of any club members from motorcycle clubs not normally seen in the area, or what they perceive to be "rival" clubs to the indigenous outlaw motorcycle clubs. Due to the length of their presence in the bay area and their respect, the Hells Angels have one of the most effective civilian intelligence networks I have ever seen, and when a civilian made a call to the Hells Angels the night of September 2nd, 2008 in San Francisco, it would tip off a series of events that would lead to the death of Hells Angels San Francisco charter President Mark "Papa" Guardado, and a RICO conviction for Christopher "Stoney" Ablett, a member of the Modesto Chapter of the Mongols MC.

My recount and opinion of this incident is based on witness statements and testimony from Ablett's criminal trial, as well as the testimony I personally heard Ablett give under oath in federal court in 2018, as part of the U.S.A. vs Mongol Nation trial. I am not taking sides here, my opinion is looking at the incident from the standpoint of an uninterested third party and based on the evidence.

Ablett had gone to San Francisco to meet up with an old girlfriend of his. He knew things were hot with the Hells Angels, and with the Mongols not having any chapters in the bay area at the time, Ablett wanted to keep a low profile and avoid trouble, so he took care to make sure he was not displaying any Mongols indicia before he left for San Francisco. Ablett rode to San Francisco and met up with his friend Amie Marvel and her friend Joyce Yu. The women suggested the three of them go down the street to the Dirty Thieves bar. The Dirty Thieves unbeknownst to Ablett is only about a mile from the San Francisco Hells Angels clubhouse. When they left for Dirty Thieves, Ablett was wearing a set of Mongols Virginia "soft colors", a T-shirt with the Mongols patch on the back of it bearing a Virginia bottom rocker, covered by a black leather jacket, but it was likely his M.F.F.M. one percent diamond tattoo on his neck that betrayed his attempts to conceal his identity and resulted in the call from the civilian to the Hells Angels.

Christopher "Stoney" Ablett
Photo by Bartlesville Police Department

Ablett had ridden his Harley Davidson Electra Glide bagger to the Dirty Thieves bar and the women rode together in a pickup truck. Once there they drank and played pool. Ablett took off his jacket during the visit and went outside the bar multiple times to smoke cigarettes and check on his bike. We know this because of Ablett's and witness testimony, plus his DNA was found on cigarette butts and an empty pack recovered by police at the scene where he said he had smoked. We also know that a local motorcycle mechanic and friend of the Hells Angels named George Jimenez observed Ablett wearing his Mongols shirt.

When Ablett tried to leave the Dirty Thieves that night he had to stop quickly to avoid crashing into the back of Marvel's truck and dropped the bike. The Electra-Glide Ablett was riding was equipped with an electronic fuel injection and tip over sensor that automatically shuts off the fuel when the bike tips past forty-five degrees, called a Base Angle Sensor, and when Ablett dropped his bike, it activated the BAS which means that the bike would not start until the BAS was reset by turning the ignition off and then turning it back on again. It is reasonable to believe that Jimenez as a motorcycle mechanic would have known this and while he helped Ablett lift his bike, he never informed Ablett that his bike would start if he gave it a try rather than wait. As a result, Ablett waited with Marvel and Yu for at least ten minutes, during which time Jimenez placed a call to another friend of the Hells Angels named Samuel Thunder Sun Watso. Watso would later testify that he was the one that called Mark "Papa" Guardado at the Hells Angels clubhouse and told him "There are Mongols down on Treat."

Guardado who was about two inches shorter than Ablett, but eighty pounds heavier arrived at the scene. Marvel and Yu got into the pickup truck as Ablett was attacked by Guardado at the rear of the pickup truck. As the men fought, Marvel got out of the truck and yelled at the men to stop-it. Someone yelled at Marvel to "Get the fuck out of here."

According to Ablett, Guardado, attacked him while three men in a green sport utility vehicle observed the fight from a distance. According to multiple witnesses one of the men in the SUV weighed about three hundred pounds and had both arms sleeved with tattoos. As Guardado wrestled Ablett to the ground, Ablett produced a knife and stabbed Guardado in the forearm, upper arm and back. At the same time, according to Ablett, he observed a second man running toward them from less than a block away. As Ablett struggled to his feet, he stabbed Guardado a fourth time in Guardado's left armpit. It was a potentially lethal wound, but Guardado may have survived it if he had not been shot by Ablett, however Ablett maintains that Guardado kept coming at him. Ablett has testified that as the second assailant arrived, Guardado called out to him "He keeps sticking me." Ablett said the second assailant raised his shirt, and Ablett feared that man was about to pull a gun he had concealed in the small of his back, so Ablett then drew a .357 magnum revolver from inside his jacket. As Ablett drew, just after the second assailant arrived, the green SUV pulled up to the scene. The men inside were cursing and shouting.

Ablett fired a total of five shots fanning from left to right and back again. He fired the first shot in Guardado's chest and Guardado, who had already been stabbed four times, dropped. The shot was probably fatal but not instantly fatal. Ablett says he then addressed the next most urgent threat and fired his second shot at the second assailant. The shot may have hit that man in the leg, but he has never been identified, however a witness described someone at the scene limping away which supports Ablett's claim. Ablett fired the third and fourth shots at the green SUV. At least one of the shots broke glass. Another shot may have broken the windshield. The occupants of the SUV probably fired three shots at Ablett from an unknown gun before they sped off. Ablett testified that there was a gun battle and witnesses have been uncertain about how many shots were fired in all, some witnesses testifying they heard four shots and others have said they heard eight. Ablett testified that after the SUV drove away, he turned back and saw the second assailant was gone and Guardado was laid out on the ground but was still moving, so he fired again. Ablett has testified that he then started his motorcycle and fled. The two women fled. A witness stood over the body and called 911 at 10:29pm, and a man who apparently knew Guardado is heard sobbing on that call.

Crime scene photo of Hells Angels President of Mark "Papa"
Guardado.
San Francisco Police Department

Ablett argued that he acted in self-defense during the trial, but the jury rejected his claim. Prosecutors alleged that Ablett killed Guardado to better his standing with the Mongols. The jury ultimately found Ablett guilty of murder in aid of racketeering, assault with a deadly weapon in aid of racketeering, use of a firearm during a crime of violence, and use of a firearm causing murder. In May 2012, Ablett was sentenced in federal court to two concurrent life sentences and a consecutive life sentence, and it is important to note that Federal life terms do not allow for parole.

In my opinion which is based on my experience as a one-percenter, Ablett going to San Francisco with only soft colors on is consistent with his statements that he tried to avoid trouble when he made that trip. While it may have been a bad idea to wear those soft colors the tattoo on his neck would have given him away, so I can understand him thinking fuck it and wearing the soft colors. The allegation that Ablett killed Guardado to better his standing in the Mongols MC is total nonsense. I am unaware of any outlaw motorcycle club where you get elected an officer for killing a member of another club, it's just not the way things work, and if you're trying to increase your standing in the club by attacking a member of another club, wouldn't you take some of your club brothers to be witnesses and have your back rather than a couple of women who have nothing to do with and no standing in your club? Additionally, no matter why you pull the trigger, it better be for a righteous reason the club will back and going rogue to kill a Hells Angel in San Francisco would not only start a war with the Hells Angels but would also put the big steel-toed boot of law enforcement squarely up your club's ass, and nobody wants that. It has been over a decade since this incident and there has been no major war between the Mongols and Hells Angels because of this incident, but the feds have been up the Mongols ass ever since and still use this incident as evidence of the Mongols ongoing criminal enterprise. In my opinion this is simply a case of the random, senseless violence that occurs sometimes when you get an ultra-loyal one percenter like Guardado who takes it upon themselves to incite a confrontation with a member of another one percent club and things blow up. They go looking for a fist fight and it quickly escalates to something much more. The code is the code, and it does not allow for you to back down, so if there is any disrespect there will be violence and that never turns out good for anybody. Especially in this era of cell phones, GPS tracking, and cameras everywhere.

13

PRAHHH-SPECT!

No matter which one-percent motorcycle club a man decides to prospect for, up until recent years it was common to hear that you should be prepared to lose everything as a prospect to become a member of the club, including your wife/girlfriend, job, house, car, friends, possibly your freedom, and life. I was determined not to let this happen to me, so I tried to set myself up for success by making deliberate adjustments to my life before I went prospect for the Outsiders MC. I had a good legal source of income which I thought would minimize law enforcement harassment and I only worked four days a week which was great for prospecting. I had a solid bike to prospect on, purchased a giant set of throw-over saddle bags to make prospecting easier, and I was in good physical shape, prepared to handle the physical strain. Up until about six months prior to prospecting for the Outsiders I had been dating an incredible woman named Lisa. I had met Lisa in the fall of 2004, when a friend referred me to her when I needed a haircut. I will never forget the first time I saw Lisa. My partner told me she was "Just my type." So, I was eager so see what her interpretation of my type was. The place she had referred me to was inside a mall and was your typical chain hair salon, but watching Lisa walk across the room to greet me as her sheer skirt and long golden hair flowed behind her with the light amplifying off her tan face and ample cleavage giving her this golden aura made it seem like it was like a scene out of a movie, and I will never forget it. We had a great conversation as she cut my hair and when she was done, I asked her out.

That Friday we went on our first date. I picked Lisa up at her apartment in Everett which overlooked Puget Sound and we drove a short distance to a restaurant on the waterfront. Just like the first time I saw her Lisa was stunning. For our first date she wore some distressed jeans with strategically placed holes, black six-inch stiletto heels, and a black top that appeared to have been tailored specifically for her amazing breasts. I was speechless. I might have been smooth asking her out, but when it came to walking her from the car to the restaurant on our first date, I was anything but smooth. Normally, I position myself between traffic and the woman I'm with, but I guess it was nerves because this time I took the inside as we walked from the car to the restaurant which allowed a big truck that came from behind us to clip Lisa in the shoulder with its mirror as they passed. Fortunately, she was not hurt but she was quick to point out that I had failed to protect her, and it was a lesson I took to heart and have not made that mistake since. We had a great date that night, got to see a seal swimming from the dock we had dinner on, she called her parents to tell them the date was going great and made sure to tell them I had let her get hit by a truck.

Lisa and I ended up having an amazing relationship, she had a tremendous influence on shaping me as a partner romantically and as a gentleman. She helped me discover my love for working dogs, and I am proud to be able to say that to this day Lisa is still one of my very best friends and I will always consider her family. However, I knew she was just not the right type of woman to survive the outlaw motorcycle club world. It would have destroyed her and to protect her and our relationship, it would have meant me leaving her at home every time I wanted to be around the club, which ultimately would have destroyed our relationship and friendship. For the first time in my life, rather than just roll the dice and take Lisa with me on an adventure I knew would probably destroy her, I did what I thought was best and ended our relationship. She will always be the one that got away for me.

Jeff & Lisa, circa. 2006.
Photo by Lisa S.

Josh had taught me early on that behind every great Hells Angel there was a great woman who gave her man the freedom he needed to be there for the club, did not ask a lot of questions, and knew how to handle herself around the club members and in public. That principal made sense to me and was my primary motivator and the only way I was able to justify making the decision to end my relationship with Lisa, and it became my primary selection criteria for my next relationship.

Another one of the many misconceptions about the outlaw motor-cycle club world is that men get involved in it for the women. While that may have been slightly true in the 60's and 70's when the average motorcycle club member was in their 20's or 30's and as a result there were plenty of women in their 20's and 30's hanging around motorcycle clubs, it is not the case today. Because all respected American outlaw motorcycle clubs require their prospects and members to own an American motorcycle, the price of a Harley Davidson that is ideal for use by a one-percenter starts at $20 grand and goes up from there, as well as the fact that most club members need both a reliable automobile and a motorcycle to survive unless they happen to live in one of the few places where you can ride year round, the average age of American motorcy-cle club members has dramatically increased because it's expensive to be in an outlaw motorcycle club. Today, the average motorcycle club member is in their late forties to early fifties, which means the age of the women hanging around the clubs has increased as well. The exception to this is in the warmer states and metro areas located near military bases where the average age tends to be a little lower due to the ability of members and prospects to be able to survive with just a motorcycle as transportation. As a result, for the decade plus that I had been involved with outlaw motorcycle clubs to that point, I was not accustomed to seeing beautiful women in the clubhouses I had visited, unless they were in California or Europe. That all changed when I walked into the Outsiders Tacoma clubhouse for my first Wednesday night open-house night.

The Outsiders MC clubhouse is located smack-dab in the middle of Tacoma's notoriously dangerous Hilltop neighborhood, a predominantly African American low-income neighborhood with a history of bloody gang violence. The house itself was built in 1905 and has been the clubhouse for the Outsiders MC Tacoma chapter since 1975. It is a multistory house that sits on two lots and has been described as looking like a haunted house by numerous members of other motorcycle clubs. When the club first purchased the property there were two houses but back in the late 70's some tweaked out members who stayed home from a club run and had too much fun ended up making some remodeling decisions while high and they tore the second house down while the brothers were away. The front door to the clubhouse was a gift from Brother Speed MC and is a large five foot wide by eight foot tall by four-inch-thick solid wood door that has the stereotypical haunted house creek when you open and close it, and a large iron hasp that makes an intimidating sound when it is slid closed behind you. There's steel grating over the front window to prevent IED's from being thrown into the house, and numerous bullet holes visible in the front of the house making it look even more ominous, especially at night.

Outsiders Motorcycle Club, Tacoma clubhouse.

As I walked through the front door of the clubhouse my eyes scanned the room to assess who was there, identify potential exits, weapons, potential threats, etc. As I scanned the room my eyes locked on this tall beautiful raven-haired woman in her early 20's. She was unlike any woman I had ever seen in a clubhouse before, she was beautiful and seemed too innocent to be hanging out in a 1% clubhouse, but she was holding her own just fine and even the members treated her with respect which was really strange for the culture. Now, just swooping in and talking to the hot chick in a situation like that is likely to get your ass kicked and I knew that, so I went on about my business and over the course of the evening I would come to learn her name was Candace and she was dating the son of the Vice President of the Outsiders MC Tacoma chapter.

Over the next several months I would get to know Candace and discover that she is one of the coolest women I have ever met, but I did not ever try and make a move on her because she was dating the VP's son and I did not want to complicate my life with that kind of nonsense knowing that someday I was going to go prospect for the Outsiders MC.

About three months before I went prospect the VP's son dumped Candace. Candace might be nice and sweet, but she is a strong woman and will not allow herself to be mistreated, so she used the opportunity to move on with her life. However, because she was Outsider Spanky's wife's best friend and very well-liked by the Tacoma members, she continued to come to the Outsiders open house every Wednesday night. Candace and I got closer, but I had not grown the balls to ask her out yet, wanting to wait until I had gone prospect and it no longer mattered that her ex was the VP's son, because he was just a citizen, and I would be an Outsider prospect. Since the motorcycle club world is supposed to be all about loyalty, honor, and respect, I went to Candace's ex and told him that I was not trying to step on his toes, but I was going to ask Candace out. He told me he did not like it but there was nothing he could do about it. While I knew I had gone above and beyond what I needed to do I still did not make my move on Candace, not wanting to cause any problems for myself amongst the members that were friends with the VP's son because I needed their vote to go prospect, but fate stepped in and forced me to grow a pair.

I was hanging around the Outsiders MC almost daily at this point whether it was at the clubhouse, Easystreet Custom Cycles the motorcycle shop owned by one of the Tacoma members, or running around town with them. A few months prior a member of the Resurrection Motorcycle Club out of Seattle named Mad Dash had moved to Tacoma and in doing so, he followed the one percenter code and stopped by the Outsiders clubhouse to introduce himself. Over the course of the next few months, I would assist him by providing TASER and Use of Force expert consulting assistance with his Excessive Force lawsuit against Seattle Police Department and we became very close friends. With Mad Dash hanging around the Tacoma Outsiders that resulted in his club brothers and then his club started hanging around the Outsiders MC. We, and I say we because while I was not a member of the club, I was hanging around every day and contributed to the unusual atmosphere of brotherhood that radiated from the Tacoma chapter of the Outsiders MC at the time. It was infectious which is how I came around the club, and Mad Dash and other respected 1%er's would tell me many times over the years that if they hadn't put so many years into their club they would quit and move to Tacoma to become an Outsider. It was a cool environment and I wish it would have lasted forever.

Back to Candace and the Resurrection MC. About a month before I was going to go prospect, we had all gone out to a party at the Gypsy Joker MC Pierce County clubhouse, and Mad Dash and several Resurrection members joined us. When we returned to the Outsiders clubhouse several more Resurrection members met us to party at our clubhouse. The Resurrection were very much like the Gypsy Joker in that methamphetamine use amongst the members was common as were all the problems that come along with that type of activity, and as a result I tried to limit my exposure to them, but there are some good guys in the bunch that don't touch that shit and I really enjoyed those guys. On this sunny Hilltop afternoon one of the Resurrection members who was known for his love of meth and history of domestic violence had taken an interest in Candace. I was watching the situation develop as I tried to socialize and play the politics game and I figured that it would lead nowhere because this guy seemed like nothing that she would be interested in, but that is what I thought about her ex, and the next thing I knew she was borrowing Spanky's wife's helmet and heading off for a motorcycle ride with this guy. I happened to be outside when they came back and Candace stepped off the bike, took off her helmet, shook out her long black hair and immediately gave me a big smile and said, "That was fun!" I knew I could not stall anymore and trying to be slick I threw out what I intended to be a smooth opener to ask her out, but because of nerves came out like a garbled mess, and to try and salvage it I bummed a cigarette off of her even though I wasn't a smoker. That cigarette turned into an amazing first date, but it would not lead to a relationship easily.

After that amazing first date Candace and I started spending time together but within a few days I was told by my club sponsor Spanky that because she was the VP's son's ex-girlfriend it wasn't cool that I was dating her, he didn't want it to have a negative impact on me with the club membership and he told me I had to stop seeing her. Well, when you are a prospect and a member, especially when your sponsor tells you to do something, you do it. Ironically, shortly after Spanky told me I had to stop seeing Candace, she showed up at his house and I took her outside and sitting on the steps with her I explained that I could not see her anymore. She understood and for the next couple weeks our behavior towards each other changed enough that Ric, one of the Lifetime/Charter members of the Tacoma chapter who happened to be Spanky's sponsor asked me why I didn't ask Candace out. I explained to Ric what had happened and Spanky's directions and Ric told me that was bullshit, I was going to be an Outsider prospect and could do what I wanted. Having the blessing of a lifetime / charter member and my sponsors, sponsor's blessing, I immediately called Candace and told her what Ric had told me, asked her out, and that began the story of Twitch and Candace.

Twitch & Candace

The Outsiders Motorcycle Club is a one-percent outlaw motorcycle club that was started in 1968 in Portland, Oregon. The club was initially formed by thirteen close friends or "Brothers" to stand up to the Gypsy Joker Motorcycle Club who had been run out of California by the Hells Angels, only to come to Washington then Oregon with a chip on their shoulder, a raging meth problem, and they would terrorize the motorcycle club community with violence and motorcycle thefts. The Outsiders would form an alliance with two other Northwest outlaw motorcycle clubs, Brother Speed MC and the Free Souls MC, both clubs which also started around the same time, and they would work together to keep the Gypsy Joker in check.

In December 1979, the Outsiders MC became infamous in Northwest outlaw motorcycle club history when a corrupt team of narcotics officers from the Portland Police Bureau raided the Outsiders MC clubhouse in Portland Oregon with an illegally obtained search warrant and the intention of planting drugs to frame Outsider members. According to Pigpen the officers failed to knock, announce, or even identify themselves, they were dressed in plain clothes like bikers with no identifying law enforcement markers, and just began beating in the clubhouse door trying to break it down. As several of his brothers and their ol' ladies were upstairs on the phone trying to call 911, Pigpen says that he was on the stairs with a 20g shotgun telling the raiders he was armed and not to come in, and when the door came open and a guy with long hair and dressed like a biker pointed a revolver at him, Pigpen fired the shotgun hitting the man in the face and dropping him. A barrage of bullets came through the walls and Pigpen fled up the stairs as plaster showered down on him from the massive number of bullets coming from the outside through the clubhouse walls. Upstairs, one of the brothers H.K. was on the phone with the police trying to figure out what was going on. Dispatch informed him it was the police outside and they needed to surrender. Knowing they were likely going to be beaten and or killed by the police, H.K. offered to go first. H.K. had been Marine Force Recon in Vietnam, was tough as they come and a giant of a man. He surrendered peacefully and the way the brothers described it the cops tried to beat him to death. One by one the members and their ol' ladies were called out of the clubhouse by Portland Police, and one by one they were all viciously beaten just like they had watched H.K. be beaten. Even the women were savagely beaten with one of the pregnant ol' ladies being kicked in the stomach by male police officers while they told her they were going to "abort her Outsider baby for her." This brutality is not sensationalized for the book, it is the way it went down and during my time in the club I got to know the woman and her son who is now a grown man and they both struggle to bear this tragic incident as part of their family history to this day, as well as the developmental and psychological scars that it has left.

Eventually one of the officers involved in the raid would be busted for his own criminal drug activity and to save his own ass and his pension, he agreed to become a cooperating witness against the rest of the narcotics unit, and he would start by ratting them out for the raid on the

Outsiders MC clubhouse. It would be proven that the cops had made up information they used to get the search warrant, the informant identified in the warrant never even existed, and the dirty cops came to the clubhouse with drugs they intended to plant and frame Outsiders MC members with. Pigpen and several of the brothers involved in the incident that cold December night in 1979 had already been convicted and sent to Oregon State Penitentiary (OSP). Pigpen's sentence would be overturned as a result of the extreme law enforcement corruption, but prosecutors told him he killed a cop and was not going to get away with it, so either he could plead guilty to Manslaughter and go home, or they would keep him locked up in OSP and tied up on appeals for the next seven years until their appeals were exhausted. Facing the prospect of seven more years in prison for doing nothing wrong or going home to his brothers, Pigpen plead guilty and was released shortly thereafter. Upon his release, law enforcement told him he had an hour to get out of Oregon and never come back or he was fair game and would be hunted and killed by law enforcement.

The story of the raid on the Outsiders clubhouse and the subsequent exposure of police corruption would be soaked up by the media in this day and age, but in 1979 the only ears that heard about it were the motorcycle club community via word of mouth, and to their ears the way Pigpen protected his brothers and his club against the corrupt police force, went to trial, and did his time made him a legend in the Northwest biker community as well as inside OSP where they made him president of the prison's motorcycle club, the Screamin' Eagles MC. That is right, back in those days while you could not have individual motorcycle clubs in prison, you could all join the prison MC which had their own prison-based custom chopper shop and held bike shows in the prison yard that their club brothers and members from all the motorcycle clubs could attend. It was a different time.

Pigpen with his trusty chopper on the prison yard at OSP. A Gypsy
Joker MC member can be seen wearing his club colors in the
background.
Photo by T-Mike

I had met the Tacoma chapter of the Outsiders MC in 2002, and at
that time it was a small chapter with a fierce reputation. However, the
youngest member must have been in his late forty's and the twenty plus
year age difference did not make the idea of becoming an Outsider attractive to me. Over the next few years, the demographics of the Outsiders Tacoma chapter would begin to change and by 2007, the Tacoma
chapter had multiple members around my age. The Outsiders and their
new younger members were a lot of fun to spend time with and the
more time I spent with them, I began to believe the brotherhood I
thought I was seeing was genuine, that I had found exactly what I was
looking for in an outlaw motorcycle club, and I decided I wanted to
prospect for the Outsiders MC Tacoma chapter.

My time spent around the Hells Angels and the long conversations with Josh and Marvin about being a one-percenter and a Hells Angel had instilled a fierce dedication to living my life by the one percenter code of loyalty, honor, and respect. A code of no snitching no matter what and no matter who it was against, even if it was the cops. The constant threat of violence and need for good personal and club security that comes from such a close association with a motorcycle club like the Hells Angels who have been at war for decades had given me a level of operational sophistication that was not common amongst prospects for one percent clubs in the northwest, I was known in the club community, and I had developed a level of respect due to my actions to that point that made me really attractive as a prospective member to any outlaw motorcycle club.

Geographical and sociological influences have resulted in some slight to major differences in outlaw motorcycle club culture across America. One of those differences is how outlaw motorcycle clubs identify their prospective members. Out here on the west coast we call prospective members "Prospect's", but if the club started east of the Mississippi, it is likely they identify their prospective members as "Probates." Whatever term they use the prospect process is likely to be very similar which starts with the prospective member hanging around the club for a period of time, the purpose of which is to get to know the club, its membership, and it lets the club get to know the individual. This hang-around period is so that you can all decide if your membership is a life-long commitment that both sides want to make. The "Hang-around" may be officially identified as such with a patch or even special patch set sometimes referred to "hang-around colors." In my case, the Outsiders MC do not officially recognize their hang-arounds or the hang-around period. You are either an Outsider, a prospect, a friend or a civilian. The path to membership in the Outsiders MC is something that evolves out of the individual's relationship with the club and at some point, subtle to pointed suggestions are made that you find a sponsor and come in front of the club to state your intentions. You do not ask for permission to go prospect, or at least you should not as it shows subservience and weakness, but in this day and age the hardline one percenter protocol I was taught has been lost and the newer generation are much softer than those of us that experienced the tail end of the club wars in the 90's and early 2000's.

Outlaw motorcycle clubs identify their prospects differently. Some like the Outsiders MC have their prospects wear their top and bottom rocker and they earn the center patch and MC. The Hells Angels only allow prospects to wear the bottom rocker with the MC cube, and they earn their center patch and top rocker. The Bandidos use only a top rocker that says "Prospect" on it, and there are more variations for other motorcycle clubs.

Bandidos prospect

Hells Angels prospect.

Outlaws probate

Outsiders prospect.

Having spent almost every day around the Outsiders Tacoma chapter for the last six months, I had grown very close with the President Double D, and over the course of that time he gave me subtle hints that I should find a sponsor and go prospect. In the Outsiders as in most outlaw motorcycle clubs, the individual who wants to go prospect needs to find a club sponsor and while I would have asked Double D to sponsor me, I did not want to do so because I was worried about him taking it easy on me and the animosity it may cause in some of the membership and other prospects. The Tacoma chapter sergeant at arms at the time was a new member named Spanky. Just like with all new members of an outlaw motorcycle club he had a big attitude, but unlike what I was used to in outlaw motorcycle club members, he had spent almost no time around outlaw motorcycle clubs prior to prospecting. Spanky's sponsor in the club was Ric, a Lifetime / Charter member of the Tacoma chapter who had a lot of influence in the club, he treated me well and really encouraged my membership in the club. I figured if Spanky was my sponsor his new guy attitude would force me to work extra hard to earn my patch which would gain me respect amongst the membership and club community, and Ric's influence in the club could help keep me out of hot water. It was a rainy Wednesday night during open house at the Outsiders clubhouse on Hilltop in Tacoma when I asked Spanky if we could talk.

The conversation was short, simple, and I remember it to this day. "Hey Spank, I want to prospect for the Outsiders, and I'd like you to be my sponsor because if anybody is going to make me earn it, you will. What do ya think?" His face lit up and the cold attitude he had shown me for months suddenly melted away and with a big smile he said sure. Before I could leave for home that night, he would give me one of the giant safety pins that Outsiders are known for giving each other and the people they care about to keep them safe, like the little bells some bikers hang from the bottom of their Harley's to protect them from road gremlins. Now if you ask law enforcement, they will tell you the reason outlaw bikers carry giant safety pins is to use them as weapons but that is just more ridiculous law enforcement bullshit because every outlaw biker understands that when it comes to defending yourself, a gun or knife is much more effective than a fucking safety pin. In some states on the east coast the giant safety pins are used as a visual symbol when traveling to show the prominent one percent clubs of the area that the member(s) traveling through are from out of the area and have contacted all the prominent one percent clubs of the area to advise they are traveling through, kind of like a passport. That is another part of the one percent code that I was taught and is largely ignored or forgotten now; out of respect when traveling you always notify the one percent clubs where you are traveling that you will be there or passing through. This practice started as a means to avoid conflicts between clubs when their members traveled and led to several clubs building friendly long-term relationships that continue to this day.

I had always been taught that before you go prospect for any outlaw motorcycle club, you can expect the club to always conduct a thorough background investigation on you. With most outlaw and even non-outlaw motorcycle clubs a prospective member can expect this to include the club running a criminal history check and talking to people in the community who may know the prospective member, to get their insight and opinion on the individual. In some cases, outlaw motorcycle clubs will use fee-based background investigation services available to the public on the internet, hire private investigators, or have members of the club who are private investigators conduct a criminal history check on the individual. Contrary to law enforcement's assertion that this background investigation is performed in an attempt to identify undercover law enforcement, it is actually done to identify men who have been convicted of sex crimes, crimes against children, or who have an on-going pattern of criminal activity that indicates that if that individual becomes a member of the club his activities would create potential liability for the club from having that individuals criminal activity incorrectly attributed as club activity, or that their personal activities could expose the clubs membership to danger.

In my case, the Outsiders did not conduct any background investigation on me other than making some phone calls, and it was clear the night that I went prospect that they had never gathered any real intelligence on me the entire time I had been hanging around. This really disappointed me as it showed the Outsiders totally lacked the sophistication necessary for an outlaw motorcycle club at that time, but I figured I could change that. More importantly, it meant they were doing nothing from preventing a rapist or pedophile from gaining membership in the club which would be devastating for the club's reputation if discovered. When they spoke to the people in the outlaw motorcycle club community who knew me, all of them gave me extremely high recommendations. While I knew this process would take place, I was totally unaware of who they were talking to or what was said until once I made member and my chapter President Double D shared the details with me.

At the time I went prospect, Smilin Rick was locked up in FDC SeaTac, so when Double D contacted the Hells Angels Nomads Washington charter to inquire about me, he contacted Ron, the acting President who had known me for years. Ron told him that I was the real deal, could be a Hells Angel anytime I wanted to, and came with the Hells Angels highest recommendation. As I expected Double D asked him about my investigator job and whether the HA President felt I was a risk as an undercover or informant, to which the President definitively and incontrovertibly said "Absolutely not, cops don't testify on behalf of the Hells Angels!" a reference to my investigative work and court testimony I had given in AJ's felony assault case. That was it, I was the most highly endorsed prospect the Outsiders MC ever had, and I was ready to go in front of the club, but before I could do that something would happen that would change how the motorcycle club world identified me.

I had continued to ski professionally and that winter I had taken a crash at approximately 80 mph and suffered what was by my count my thirteenth serious concussion. Like the others, I ignored it and continued to train for the remainder of the day, but I could feel something was different about this one. Over the next couple of weeks, I experienced nausea, memory loss, and my vision was in black and white. Eventually my vision would return, I began to go back to life at one hundred percent and hanging out with the Outsiders every day. I would get off work each day in Everett and fight two plus hours of rush hour traffic south to the clubhouse which was in the tough Hilltop neighborhood in Tacoma and is infamous for its history of gang activity. I would stay at the clubhouse until the last Outsider was ready to leave and then I would call it a night and make the long ride home to Kirkland. I was never able to leave before midnight, I would have to make the long ride back home, then get up at four in the morning for work and repeat the process. On the weekends, I would get up at three in the morning, drive to the mountain, coach ski racing for eight hours, drive the three hours home from the mountain, shower, and hop on my Harley and head to the clubhouse in Tacoma.

On Saturday night the week prior to going prospect I was at the clubhouse hanging out with the fellas and just like every other night my plan was to leave when the last Outsider did. Well, that night when we were getting ready to leave Double D invited me to come back to his place and hangout while he worked on his music. Double D never had a job the entire time I knew him, but he is multitalented, a genius, and a master of bullshitting people. Double D's father was a charter member of the Tacoma chapter making him the first second generation Outsiders member, but he was not a biker and only began riding motorcycles after his father's death in 2004. Growing up, Double D focused on his education, excelled in debate in high school earning himself a college scholarship and eventually he went on to become a national debate champion as well as a debate coach at the University of Michigan. He was also a rapper; his group had recorded a song which ended up being used as the theme song for a major video game and that was earning him royalties.

That night he was working on a song that had a very hypnotic hook and as I sat there, I began to feel uneasy but assumed it was just auditory response to the high-volume hook being played over and over again. This uneasy feeling would soon turn to an intense sense that something was very wrong with me. As I sat there in Double D's studio this feeling grew to the point where I knew something was wrong. I stepped outside thinking the fresh air might help and if something embarrassing like me passing out happened, I would be out of Double D's view, pull myself together when I came-to and just come back inside like nothing happened. I stood there pissing in his backyard, but the cold air was doing nothing to ease the feeling that something seriously bad was about to happen to me health-wise, and I began to feel like whatever was going to happen I needed a witness that could get help. I staggered to the door, inside and back to my chair. I sat down in the 1970's office swivel chair and as I leaned back, I felt it start to happen, turned to Double D and said, "Hey man, something's not right." as I reached for the radiator next to me like a life-line, then I launched into my very first seizure. While I do not remember much of what happened, I do remember coming back around and Double D was punching me in the chest yelling "Jeff, Jeff. You alright bro? Fuck! Fuck! I'm going to get Marla!" I remember slurring to him, "No, don't call 911." not wanting to be the guy that got the cops called to the Outsiders President's house. Plus, even though his wife Marla did work at a local hospital, she worked in administration, so I did not know what good she was going to do me other than help fill out the paperwork at the hospital. I forced myself to come back around, not wanting to be "that guy" and Double D began to calm down and told me I just had a seizure. I told him I did not feel like it was a good idea for me to ride all the way back home and asked if I could crash on his couch. He started to help me inside and when we were about six feet from that swivel chair I collapsed and launched into a seizure again, but before I could hit the ground Double D was able to catch me and sweep the swivel chair with his leg, pulling it under me and catching me. At that point, terrified I was going to die in his studio he ran inside and got Marla who immediately wanted to call 911. Again, I told them not to because in my view I would have failed to hold my mud which would have been dishonorable in my hardcore one-percenter views. The next day I would seek medical assistance and it was confirmed that I had a seizure related to my head injuries.

Wednesday night is always open house night at the Outsiders Tacoma clubhouse, and the Wednesday following my seizure I was sitting at the bar in the Tacoma clubhouse when the Hells Angels stopped by for a drink. I was seated in the middle of the long bar talking to Double D and some others while Spanky was at the far end talking to Ron and Jammer from the Hells Angels. Spanky's speaking volume tends to raise with his beer count and I heard him begin to tell the story of my seizure to Ron and Jammer and he say's "Yeah, old Twitch over there seized-out at Double D's house and almost died the other day, but it's ok because we would have just rolled him out into the ally and left him for the dumpster diving druggies to find." The entire clubhouse erupted in laughter at his use of the name Twitch to identify me, it stuck, and that is how I got my club name. Initially I hated the name as people often mistook it for "Tweek" and I hate tweekers (methamphetamine addicts), so it instantly drew an aggressive correction from me, but after a few corrections of other club members in very public places, that problem stopped. As Double D and I gained notoriety in the club world and international reputations in the motorcycle club culture, I became very protective and proud of my name, and I would go to great lengths to protect my name and the honor and sacrifice it represented to me from those who would try and adopt my name as their nickname. Sadly, when I was in southern California at the USA v. Mongol Nation trial in November 2018, attorney and motorcycle club groupie Steven Stubbs would tell me about a new gay motorcycle club that has started in Las Vegas, and he had just gone to their President Twitch's wedding. The motorcycle club world has and is changing, and everything that was once honorable and held meaning whether it's the one percent code or the names of one-percenter's who have shaped the culture whether it be Sonny's, mine, Double D's, J.R.'s, Taco's, etc., the meanings of certain patches, almost everything about outlaw motorcycle culture has been stolen and degraded by the new generation of one-percenters and motorcycle club members who wear the patch but won't and can't back it up.

Because of my experience in the club world up to that point in my life, I felt like I knew what my role was as a prospect was, I knew what I brought to the table, I knew what was expected of me, and I took the entire process very seriously. Outsiders MC members do not wear their colors on a leather or denim vest like other outlaw motorcycle clubs, and instead have opted to wear their colors on vests made from Mexican serape blankets. The practice of wearing your club colors on serape vests became popular amongst outlaw motorcycle clubs across the United States during the 1960's, and the Outsiders MC is the last holdout from the period who still wear their colors on serapes.

An Outlaws MC member shown with Outlaws colors being worn on a
serape vest in 1967.
*Photo by Jim "Flash 1%er" Miteff, courtesy of Beverly Roberts, Flash
Productions LLC*

Prospecting as was my membership in the club, was something I took very seriously and tried to embrace the tradition and significance of it. Rather than just use a serape blanket I found at a swap meet or had laying around the house, I called a friend of mine in Mexico and had her send me three different blankets made with the club's cardinal red, white and black colors so that I could choose the perfect blanket. Another second-generation Outsiders member's aunt had made vests for him and a few of the fellas and she had agreed to make mine. Rather than just let her make it, Single D and I spent time at her place together where he helped make a significant portion of my serape vest which meant and still does mean a lot to me. The blanket I had chosen was stunning and matched the club's colors perfectly. I designed the vest with a waterproof, breathable liner and built in interior and exterior pockets to allow me to carry my prospect kit and eight beers, which would allow me to be more efficient as a prospect at runs and events. The vest was beautiful when it was done and was the most progressive serape vest at the time which while it did not cause any problems for me in Tacoma, it would become a target of some Portland member's jealousy and resentment in later months and years, just as everything else about me would.

At the time I went prospect for the Outsiders the process of becoming a prospect was a closely guarded secret and I really did not know how it was going to go down. I knew how it worked when I went to the table with the Hells Angels, but the Outsiders are a different club, so I did not know what to expect. However, thanks to Mavrick and Paul, a couple of Tacoma prospects with big mouths who had started the process a few months earlier, I knew that I was going to be brought in and asked to explain in twenty words or less why I wanted to be an Outsider, at which point I would be sent back out front with the rest of the prospects. If I received the clubs vote to proceed as a prospect, I would be brought back in and must drink a pitcher of beer without stopping, and if I vomited into the pitcher, I would be required to consume the contents until it was empty, and I had completed the task. That Thursday night was cold and as we waited outside the clubhouse Mavrick and Paul seemed more eager to see me struggle with the pitcher of beer and potentially fail than have me succeed, and along with the fact that they were both recovering tweekers with no real outlaw motorcycle club experience that raised huge red flags with me, but I figured the club knew what they were doing with those two guys.

The Outsiders clubhouse in Tacoma has been in operation in the same location on Hilltop since 1975, and at the time I came around it was in such disrepair it really looked like a haunted house. Today it is not much better but in 2016, the chapter spent a lot of money to remodel the interior of the main bar and it looks very nice today. At the time I went prospect though the front door of the clubhouse was and still is a large eight foot tall by five foot wide by four-inch-thick wooden door that was a gift to the Outsider Tacoma chapter by the Portland chapter of another outlaw motorcycle club called Brother Speed MC. The door creaked just like your stereotypical haunted house door every time you opened or closed it and was secured with a giant iron hasp that made an ominous sound. I will never forget the sound it made that night as Spanky threw it back and swung open that big door or the way his footsteps sounded as he walked down the wooden porch before yelling "Twitch!" I ran up the front steps and to the front door where Spanky was waiting and pulled myself into serious mood prior to entering the room. The members were seated all over the barroom of the clubhouse and I was told to stand in front of the pool table. "We hear you want to go prospect for the Outsiders MC, and you want Spank to be your sponsor, is that correct?" Double D asked. Yes sir, I said. Well then in twenty words or less, tell us why you want to be an Outsider, Double D said. "Because I want to be part of a brotherhood and culture based on loyalty, honor and respect." I confidently told the room. The room looked stunned, and several members started counting my words on their fingers in disbelief that my response had been so immediate and complied with their requirements. OK, Double D said, back outside. And back outside with the prospects I went.

After about another hour or so of meeting I was still standing outside with Mavrick and Paul who were now telling me how this was not how it went for them, and things were not looking good for me. Then the door opened again and Spanky yelled for the prospects and me to come inside, however when we got inside the meeting was on a break. After a couple of beers with the fellas inside with no hint as to my future it was back outside into the cold Hilltop night air and the sound of gunshots from the ongoing gang war. After about forty more minutes the door opened, and they called out to us and announced that they were adjourned for the evening. What the fuck, I didn't make prospect? I thought to myself silently, trying to stifle the rage. As I walked through the door Double D commanded me to stand in front of the bar. This was a good sign, there is either hope or there's going to be a fight and either way it was better than things ending with nothing. Spanky pulled my Tacoma bottom rocker from behind the bar and told me, "Before you get this, you've gotta drink that." as he pointed to the pitcher of beer Buell Greg had in front of him, "And you can't let your lips leave the pitcher or you'll have to start all over." I grabbed hold of the glass pitcher with both hands, raised a cheers to the fellas, and began to drink. It was Budweiser, not my favorite but it could have been worse, and when I was about thirty seconds in and halfway through, my stomach started to get full of foamy warm Budweiser and I started to feel like I was going to puke. Without letting the pitcher leave my lips I took a short break to let my stomach settle and get some air.

To try and make things more difficult for me, Buell Gregg had noticed that my serape had small gold threads woven in it and he started joking about me being the Rhine Stone Prospect. "He's a Rhine Stone Prospect. Duh, Duh, Duhhhh", he would sing at the top of his lungs over and over again before laughing and patting me on the back only to start again. It took me just over a minute, but I finished the damn pitcher, and when I was done Spanky handed me my top and bottom rockers and told me "Now sew these on and never let anyone take them from you." With pride I took the red and white rockers. I had come prepared and had stashed a prospect kit which included a sewing kit inside my serape vest where it would be handy for me to begin sewing as soon as I made prospect and I could really show some class. It was about then that the Budweiser started to kick in, making sewing even more difficult than just protecting my rockers from the members who were jokingly trying to steal them from me as I sewed. Just as I would see him do with almost every Tacoma prospect over the next ten years, Single D helped me sew my rockers on once my fingers started to bleed from forcing the needle through the heavy vest and rockers. Pigpen had taken me under his wing, and we spent the remainder of the night talking about what it meant to be a good Outsider and what he expected from me.

The next afternoon when I got off work, I grabbed a quick shower and made the four-and-a-half-hour trip from my place to the Outsiders clubhouse in Portland, Oregon. It was important to me that I was in their face busting my ass so they could see I knew my shit and wanted to make me a member. When I got to the Portland clubhouse that night, I was greeted by the sergeant at arms Spike who immediately sent me to get fourteen cases of pop and beer with only my Harley Davidson motorcycle as transportation. Being part crafty and part circus performer, I stuffed the oversized saddle bags I specifically had gotten for prospecting situations like this as full as I could possibly get them, then bungeed another three cases to my sissy bar. The rest I balanced on my lap and handlebars as I carefully and slowly rode the mile or so back from the store. Spike being a new member had the Portland version of Spanky's new guy attitude, and as soon as I was done restocking the cooler and the snacks, he immediately put me to work tending bar. It was an unusually hot night in Portland which meant I could expect the clubhouse to be busy.

By eight o'clock that night the clubhouse was full. Almost the entire Portland chapter was there, as were members of Brother Speed, the Gypsy Joker, and a few guys from a Gypsy Joker support club that the Jokers had just re-started in the northwest called Road Brother MC. As the night went on, I realized just how strung-out on meth the Portland chapter of the Outsiders MC was which was in stark contrast to their Tacoma brothers who except for Pigpen only drank and or smoked pot. In the motorcycle club world, when we refer to someone who is able to handle their partying or serious and dangerous situations, we say they can "hold their mud.", however when it came to the Portland Outsiders, the only member I was seeing that could hold their mud was a quiet but very security aware member named Raven who spent most nights in his room in the clubhouse with his cat Spot or out front keeping an eye on the neighborhood. As the night dwindled so did the crowd until there was nobody left but me and the "Tweeker Dawn Patrol" as I called them, and it was torture to me. I don't and have never used meth, so to me when you get so fucked up that you start chewing air, speaking gibberish, rewire the vacuum or take your motorcycle apart and can't put it back together (all typical tweeker behavior), that's not cool, and to watch my prospective Portland brothers and their friends devolve into this type of meth zombie disgusted me, but I bit my tongue like a good prospect should and reassured myself that the harder I worked, the sooner I would make member and the sooner I would be able to control how much I had to see of these tweeked out lames.

Around 10:00am Saturday morning we all headed over to a bar called the Queen of Hearts. Riding over there was nothing like riding in the disciplined Tacoma Outsider packs where you rode side by side with your brother and eighteen inches off the tire in front of you, moving as a cohesive unit. Portland was the exact opposite. The pack had no structure except at stop lights and as soon as the light turned green it was time to twist the throttle wide open until the pack's path of travel was blocked by a vehicle, then jam on the brakes causing the back of the pack to almost crash into the front. It lacked structure, was dangerous, looked unprofessional, and was no fun, but once again I just wrote it off because I figured they started the club and just had a different way of doing things. Well, that and I figured all the meth, booze, pills, and old age had something to do with it, as the average age for Portland members was late fifties. When we arrived at the Queen of Hearts the street was closed and there were table's set-up on the sidewalk. We backed the bikes to the curb and parked directly in front of the main entrance. At this point I had been up since 4:00am the previous day due to the Tweeker Dawn Patrol, it was already over one hundred degrees, and I was the only prospect, so I knew it was going to be a rough day and I would have to stay hydrated and sneak food regularly so that I would not succumb to heat stroke.

Just like Portland is the dirty, tweeked out, uneducated little sister of Seattle, the same is true of the Portland chapter of the Outsiders MC when compared to the Tacoma chapter. Not only is the average members age significantly greater than that of Tacoma, but they tolerate and, in many cases, promote meth use which the Tacoma chapter does not like, and it creates a lot of internal problems for the club and brotherhood because they just refuse to see that shit for what it is, pure evil. Prospecting in Portland as a Tacoma prospect was different as well. It was not about teaching me about how to be a good Outsider or getting to know each other, it was about having a slave and nothing more. What I would come to find out is that the harder I worked, the more I would stand up for my prospective brothers, the club and the community, the more respect I earned, the worse the Outsiders Portland chapter would treat me.

The fellas drank while I fetched drinks, ran to the store for cigarettes, stood guard, and did all the other tasks I expected to as a prospect. By noon it was one hundred-twelve degrees, and the Queen of Hearts was packed with motorcycle club members from the Outsiders, Gypsy Joker, Brother Speed, a few veterans' motorcycle club members, and members of the public. The Outsiders Portland President Magic Mike and several other Outsiders had taken tables on the sidewalk by the bikes, and I had taken a spot against the building behind Magic Mike, next to the front door where I was still close enough that I could effectively protect him but also interact with the members of the other clubs as they came in and out of the bar.

Around 1:30pm the fellas had gotten a good buzz on and so had the local drunks. My feet hurt, the sweat running down my body into my boots had soaked my socks hours ago and now my heels had half-dollar sized blisters on them, and I was getting grumpy but doing my job. One of the Queen of Hearts regular drunks had taken a seat with Magic Mike at his table on the sidewalk while I had been sent on a task and I could hear the drunk rambling on with a thick slur about how he used to be a Gypsy Joker. I scanned the guy up and down and aside from his Gypsy Joker support shirt there was nothing about the guy that indicated he had ever been a Gypsy Joker. On top of that, the fact that

Magic Mike had been an Outsider in Portland for almost thirty years and his normally loud jovial attitude had changed to silence as he listened to the drunk, told me that this drunk was about to get popped. I knew my job as a prospect was to let Mike do whatever it was that he was going to do and then immediately react appropriately to his move while making sure no harm can come to him at the same time. Magic Mike is not a big man. He is in his late fifties, about six feet tall, missing a leg and some fingers from a bike accident, and weighs about one hundred sixty pounds, with long greasy salt and pepper hair. He reminds me of a tweeked out version Captain Morgan, the fictional rum pirate.

All of the sudden Mike asks the drunk to tell me what he had just told him, at which point the drunk turns to me and introduces himself as a Gypsy Joker and Mike immediately delivered a decent right hook to the drunk's jaw knocking him from the plastic chair, he was in. I came in and scooped up the semi-conscious drunk and the Portland VP told me to take the drunk around the corner, which I didn't think was a good idea because I was sure the cops were on their way and the last thing we needed around was a victim, but whatever, I was a prospect and my job was to follow orders.

Once we got the drunk around the corner, I went into damage control since clearly the Portland Outsiders were even less sophisticated than the Tacoma chapter. I went inside the Queen of Hearts and had one of the waitresses get me a five-gallon bucket with some bleach and a scrub brush and went back outside and scrubbed the blood off the concrete where the drunk had fallen and bled. When I was done, I ditched the scrub brush and bucket in a neighbor's garbage can down the street and came back to find the drunk still laying where we had left him. Not good I thought. It had already been about three minutes since the incident, and I knew the cops would be there soon. The Portland V.P. and I walked the drunk across the street to the small park and left him to take a nap in the sun and work on his tan, then walked back to the Queen of Hearts and went about the day as if nothing had happened. The cops showed up about a minute later but by that time there was nothing to see, nobody at the bar was going to say anything, the cops could care less about the drunk asleep in the sun across the street in the park and they went on their way. The Portland V.P. would later tell me I did a good job handling the incident but when that kind of quick thinking and action became a pattern from me and caused me to stand out as a patchholder, he would eventually become one of my greatest enemies in the Outsiders MC and was certainly never a brother to me.

While some of you are reading this thinking that I just committed a gang crime, I did not look at it that way at the time, and I think it's important to explain how a true one percenter looks at what I did, because we do not view it as a gang crime even though per the law you could potentially charge it as one. In the one percent world, there are strict protocols that govern your personal behavior, and it is a serious offense to claim you are/were a member of a one percent club if you are not. It is just like stolen valor with the military and men such as Michael "Santa" Walsh have been killed for making these types of false claims. In my eyes, that drunk deserved a sock in the mouth because he must have known what he was doing was wrong. He was hanging out in a biker bar wearing a Gypsy Joker support shirt, running his mouth to real outlaw motorcycle club members, so per the one percent code Mike was honor-bound to give him a punch in the mouth for his lies. What I did after that, I did of my own free will, nobody asked me to do it, and it certainly was not done to advance the reputation of the club, further the enterprise or any of that bullshit. I did it to protect Magic Mike and make sure he did not go to jail because my obligation as a brother is to protect him. It is that attitude and circular thinking though that is prevalent across a percentage of hardcore members in every outlaw motorcycle club, and it is incidents like this one that are then charged as gang crimes and used to justify calling outlaw motorcycle clubs, "outlaw motorcycle gangs."

As things wore down at the Queen of Hearts the decision was made to head back to the clubhouse. Back at the Portland clubhouse it was just like my first night. Kenny the "Wiz" or National President of the Gypsy Joker MC, Mark the Portland Gypsy Joker chapter President, several of the Gypsy Joker members from Salem and Portland, and a handful of members of a newly reestablished chapter of a Gypsy Joker support club called the Road Brother MC showed up to party.

Before I go on, let me explain the history of the Road Brother MC because they love to claim they are not a support club for the Jokers but that is a fucking lie, they are absolutely a support club for the Gypsy Joker MC, take their orders from the Jokers, and when they fuck up it's the Jokers who intervene on their behalf and keep them from being held publicly accountable for their actions. The Road Brother MC originally was started as a support club for the Gypsy Joker MC in the mid 1990's, with their first chapter located just off I-5 south of Olympia, Washington. However, at the time the Road Brother MC was started, the motorcycle clubs of Washington state were living a very tense and volatile existence, there was periodic violence between some of the four one-percent motorcycle clubs that existed in Washington, and the Jokers did not extend the respect of talking to all the other one-percent clubs before they opened a new support club, they just did it. That led to the brand-new Road Brother MC chapter becoming a target for the other one-percent clubs as well as brought direct heat on the Jokers for their disrespect. That original Road Brother chapter was shut down within a few months of opening and most of the members joined one-percent clubs because the Jokers had left them hanging like they did and failed to have their "brothers" backs. A set of original Road Brother colors hung in the Seattle Gypsy Joker clubhouse for years.

In the spring of 2008, the Gypsy Joker MC decided to bring back the Road Brother MC as a support club. This time, the Jokers did the right thing and reached out to the other outlaw motorcycle clubs in Washington and Oregon to show respect and inform them of their intentions, and that they would be responsible for overseeing the Road Brother chapters they were planning on opening. While as a friend of the Outsiders and now a prospect, I should not have known any club business right out of the gate, because of my prior experience with the HA and my reputation, Double D and several of the lifetime members from the Tacoma Chapter had already shared with me that the Jokers had approached the Outsiders prior to starting the Road Brother to announce their intentions and offered to give the Outsiders half of the dues they were collecting from the Road Brother MC chapters in Washington and Oregon. The Outsiders members had approached me because of my experience doing criminal defense investigations for the Angels, more specifically the R.I.C.O. case, and my knowledge of how the government investigates and prosecutes R.I.C.O. Double D shared the same opinion I did which was that the Gypsy Joker are a bunch of unpredictable tweekers and he was concerned that if the Outsiders agreed to accept part of the Road Brother MC dues from the Jokers that it would make the Outsiders vulnerable to a R.I.C.O. indictment if the Jokers got themselves into legal trouble. I ran down a myriad of reasons why I thought accepting the dues was a horrible idea and in the end the Outsiders told the Jokers they could re-open the Road Brother MC but refused to accept any money from the Gypsy Joker. For a couple of years after I made member, I would hear Kenny talk about how much money they were making off the Road Brother from dues and again offer to cut us in, but the offer was always refused, and I am really glad it was because my concerns about the Jokers would prove correct.

I had a couple of friends in the Gypsy Joker MC, but they were not a motorcycle club that I enjoyed spending time around because for the most part they were all spun out on methamphetamine, from the leadership to the prospects. They had members that had been convicted of rape, a public reputation for raping women in Portland and at clubhouse parties and were more tweekers on wheels than they were modern one-percenters. Just like with the Portland Outsiders MC chapter, the meth culture of the Gypsy Joker MC has frozen them in time, as the rest of the one-percent world evolved they have stayed trapped in the 1980's, and as a result they are not taken seriously as a one-percent club on the national level and their only influence in the MC world is within the state of Oregon where they're shown respect for their length of time in operation, or overseas in Europe and Australia where existing clubs adopted the Jokers name because of their reputation from the 60's and 70's here in the U.S.

With Kenny and Mark was a Road Brother MC prospect named Josh. Josh was about six feet tall with a steroid enhanced muscular build, tattoos, a black mohawk, and he oozed arrogance. While I busted my ass as a prospect for my club, he sat around drinking beer and acting like a respected member. It was our clubhouse, so I did not expect him to be behind our bar as that was not allowed, but I at least expected him to be protecting an officer, keeping an eye on their bikes, etc. I was not impressed but I tried to be friendly with him and as the night went on, we began to get along and I thought he was an alright guy that fell in with the wrong clubs. He was excited to be in a motorcycle club even though his club had no history or respect, was green as they come when it came to the biker world, his ultimate goal was to someday get the opportunity to be a Gypsy Joker, and as I stood outside that night watching the pack of Jokers ride away with him at the back, I couldn't help but wondering how long it would be before he was dead or in prison. It would not be long before he got his wish and that decent guy that I had met turned into a horrible piece of shit that committed once of the most heinous acts I can recall a motorcycle club member committing.

When the Jokers left the party continued, with me being the lone bar tender for the Tweeker Dawn Patrol once again. Let me tell you, you have not lived until you have bartended for drunk tweekers, listening to them tell the same part of the same story repeatedly for thirty minutes before moving on to a new piece of a different story until the sun comes up and they retreat from the daylight like vampires, and watching them chew air is an experience. Well, that was my life that hot Portland night until about 8:00am when the last member went home, and I was finally allowed to catch an hour of sleep before Spanky showed up to ride back to Tacoma with me.

I was exhausted, a little disgusted by what I had seen in Portland because it was so different from the Tacoma Outsiders, and I needed a fucking shower after spending since Friday in the same clothes and 110+ degree heat. I had been tested in just about every way you can test a prospect and it had happened in a matter of less than forty-eight hours. That said, I was on such a high from having completed my first three days as an Outsider prospect that I could not wait to get a photo with my sponsor Spanky in front of the Portland clubhouse. It was not until I looked at the photo later that I realized I had sweated so much you could see the salt stains on my shirt.

Outsider Prospect Twitch and Outsider Spanky in front of the Outsiders Motorcycle Club, Portland clubhouse.

When Spanky got there, we stayed and hung out with Raven for a little while before heading back to Tacoma. Once back at the Tacoma clubhouse I continued my prospecting duties until about 8:00pm before I was finally sent home. At the time I was living in Kirkland which was an hour ride from the Tacoma clubhouse with no traffic, and because I had only had one hour of sleep in the last three days I was exhausted, so much so that I ended up falling asleep as I made the long ride home, woke up startled about two miles past my exit, and it took me a couple miles to figure out where I was before turning around and going home, where I got about five hours sleep before I had to get up for work at 4:00am, going to work, and then fighting two hours of rush hour traffic to go back the clubhouse to keep up my hard work as a prospect. The schedule was grueling, but I was committed, I saw a brotherhood in the Tacoma Outsiders that I believed was worth the effort, and I was loving prospecting.

I knew when I went prospect that I was going to get more heat from law enforcement and I accepted they were going to fuck with me, but it really pissed me off when they fucked with and intimidated the people, I love in order to fuck with me. There was an incident shortly after I went prospect when my daughter and I had ridden the three blocks through a residential neighborhood to my sister's house for dinner. My bike was parked outside on the curb in front of her house and at some point, Kirkland P.D. had driven by, seen it, and decided to set up surveillance. Way to protect and serve. Anyway, during the course of the evening I noticed them watching my bike but figured they would be gone by the time we were done with dinner, however to my surprise they were still there over two hours later. Because of the late hour, I needed to get my daughter home and figured I was only going a couple of blocks and they would not fuck with me in that short distance. As we pulled away from the curb, I watched the cop car pull out and follow us. I made sure not to make any traffic violations along the short trip and as I pulled into my driveway, they pulled across the driveway blocking it and turned their spotlight on me. Not wanting my daughter see police harass her father, I sent her inside to bed and turned to face the officers. "What are you doing in Kirkland Jeff?" Really, this is why you guys sat on my sister's house and followed me home? I asked. "You aren't going to start a chapter up here Jeff." Yeah, Yeah, Yeah, I said. "You understand that would be really bad for you, ...really bad for you Jeff." The officer said menacingly. Whatever dude go fuck yourselves! I said as I turned and walked into the house.

On another occasion Candace had followed me home from the clubhouse in her car. We were stopped at a red light at an intersection just a mile or so from my house. Stopped at a red-light perpendicular to us in the intersection was a Kirkland P.D. car. I was worried they would fuck with me, and once the light turned green, I proceeded through the intersection with Candace behind me. As soon as we passed through the intersection and the cop car, he crossed over the lane to the right of him, ran the red light, dropped in behind Candace and me, and immediately turned his lights on and pulled Candace over. I knew what was going on, this was one of those dickhead cops that wants to know what I am doing in Kirkland and now they are going to fuck with my girlfriend in an attempt to intimidate her, ruin my relationship with her, and or get information on me and the club out of her. The cop told Candace he smelled alcohol on her even though she had not been drinking and he told her he wanted her to take some field sobriety tests.

I'm watching this go down from across the street at this point and have got Spanky on the phone telling him I think the cop's going to arrest Candace for a bullshit DUI. During the stop the cop started to threaten her with a DUI and ask her questions about me, then saw me watching with my phone up and thought I was filming, so he left mid field sobriety test. That's how it started, later on the harassment of my loved ones would get much more extreme, but it was this kind of continued pattern of behavior by certain corrupt members of law enforcement that had become an epidemic for outlaw motorcycle club members, it was occurring across the nation, had been occurring and getting worse since the 1960's, and this fueled my desire to be part of the outlaw motorcycle club community, fight for motorcyclists civil rights and protect the Constitution.

"The pack is where it's at!" You will hear that regularly from Pigpen if you have the pleasure of being around him and it means so much. Different clubs ride differently but when clubs ride together as a group it is called "The pack", and it is an amazing thing to be part of. As a prospect, Pigpen taught me that the pack is part of the club's identity and Outsiders were known for being the best riders around. Our packs were visually distinct because we rode eighteen inches or less off the wheel of the bike in front of you with a bike right next to you and were so disciplined that when we accelerated or changed lanes it was one seamless transition. It was a stunning thing to see and an amazing thing to be part of. To ride like that is some next level shit and incredibly dangerous because whatever happens to the guy in front of you is going to happen to you. That meant we had to be constantly riding together so that we could practice, and we all got exceptionally good at riding our motorcycles. So good, that when we would ride together with other one percent clubs and stack up right on their rear tires like Outsiders, they would see how close we were when they looked in their mirrors, freak out and you could see them get visibly stressed because they were not used to riding that close, and their riding would go to shit. More than once I had a member of another one percent club pull out of the pack and fall in further back because they could not handle someone riding so tight on them like that. That is how we did it in Tacoma back then, and if you could not handle it then get the hell out of our way, was our attitude.

In August, the Outsiders had a mandatory run to the annual Mudd Creek Run held by the Unknown MC. The Unknown MC are an outlaw motorcycle club that started in the Midwest back in the 1960's, and eventually migrated out to California and settled in Half Moon Bay. I always really liked the Unknown MC. They weren't a very big club but they were tight as a brotherhood and meth wasn't a big issue for their club, so they were a bunch of really cool guys that were a lot of fun to hang out with, and their annual Mudd Creek Run was one that a lot of us in the Outsiders as well as a lot of the other prominent west coast outlaw motorcycle clubs all looked forward to and talked about all year long. The Mudd Creek Run takes place in a campground located in the mountains just on the Oregon side of the border with California about midway across the state. I had heard the fellas tell stories about Mudd Creek since before I went prospect and while there were some great stories there were also sad stories like the time one of our packs was plowed into by a drunk driver on the way down to Mudd Creek and a member lost his leg, several were injured, one members old lady was killed, and several others with us were hurt, or the story from the year before where the bees were so bad that several people were attacked and stung, and one person died after going into anaphylactic shock when a bee flew into their beer and stung them when they accidently drank the bee without noticing it. I had been prospecting for about three months when Mudd Creek rolled around, and I was excited. I had already reached my five mandatory days prospecting in Portland, and I figured I would go for some extra credit. I showed up in Portland the Thursday afternoon before Mudd Creek so that I could be there for church and prospect in Portland until we left for Mudd Creek. It was forty full hours of Portland style prospecting with members being deliberately rude to both prospects and other members, and substance abuse that totally repelled me and confused me. I could not believe that Portland was so different from Tacoma, and they were only one hundred forty-seven miles away from each other. I would later come to find out that this is common to some degree with every motorcycle club.

We rolled out of the Portland clubhouse for Mudd Creek at 10:00am on Saturday morning and I was excited. We had a big pack that consisted of Outsiders as well as members of Brother Speed MC, Free Souls MC, Rogues MC from Holland, and probably fifty guests. As a prospect, I was assigned to ride road-guard for the pack along with the other prospects and the Sergeant at Arms from Tacoma and Portland. As road guard your job is to block traffic at strategic predetermined intersections along the pack's route, so that the pack may pass through unimpeded. This is done for the purpose of safety, because it is safer for a pack that stretches out over a great distance to be able to proceed through the intersection unimpeded, rather than be broken up by a red light that occurs as the pack is partially through the intersection and forces riders to jam on their brakes causing an accordion effect in the pack and creating the high likelihood for an accident involving multiple riders. When you are riding in a pack, whatever happens to the guy in front of you is most likely going to happen to you, so at eighteen inches off the tire of the guy in front of you, jamming on your breaks creates a domino effect that can wipe out entire packs. Riding road-guard can mean that you will go from thirty miles per hour to over a hundred miles per hour for short distances before having to stop quickly. You may have to ride towards oncoming traffic in their lane, you will certainly face pissed off drivers, you definitely risk a serious ticket for multiple traffic offences, and it can be sketchy as hell to say the least. When I was a prospect, I liked running road-guard but after some really close calls, I began to do everything I could to avoid it. We took a route from the Portland clubhouse that took us out through Gresham and over Mt. Hood. We had a beautiful but windy ride over Hood, before stopping at a bar for lunch after about two hours. The Jokers and a handful of Road Brother met up with us, and our bikes lined both sides of the street all the way up and down the main street in the quiet little town.

As a prospect, I did not get lunch unless I could do it without abandoning my duties, so I stayed outside to provide security and be onhand for our members staying outside, I counted bikes and kept an eye on the unmarked Chevy Blazer that was not with us but had clearly been conducting leap-frog style surveillance on the pack since we left the clubhouse in Portland. Being outside was great because it was such a nice day and several of the members of the other clubs were outside hanging out, which meant I was able to do my job as a prospect and have good conversations with a lot of guys from the Oregon clubs that I had not really had a chance to get to know yet. After about twenty minutes, the Portland Sergeant at Arms Gutz came out of the restaurant and gave a big deep yell, "Prahhh-spect!" I immediately set down my lunch and ran from my observation post to where Gutz was standing by the front door of the restaurant. Yes sir, I said. "Nuthin, I just wanted to see what you were doing.", he said. Gutz was my favorite Portland brother and always treated me with respect. We had a lot of fun together over the years and this time would be no exception. You are on task, come with me. He said. Gutz started to walk ahead of me with purpose as we headed away from our club's bikes, we were clearly on a mission, but I had no idea what it was and Gutz was not going to give me any clues. We walked about a block down the street and rounded the corner to where one of the chase vehicles was parked. A chase vehicle is a vehicle that follows the pack and carries tools for breakdowns, camping gear, food, cooking equipment, etc. For a run of this size, we had multiple chase vehicles and as Gutz slid open the door to the van, I reflexively got a big smile on my face as this was the chase vehicle that had the club's alcohol. Gutz dug through the first big white cooler, grumbling a string of swear words, before finally handing me a Corona and demanding, "Here, drink this!" Fuck yeah, I thought. I am on task, and I was just tasked with drinking this beer, I'm all in. Gutz continued to dig through the large coolers until I heard an "Ah Ha!" He pulled his arm from the big cooler spilling ice all over the floor of the van and in his hand was a bottle of Jameson. Whoa, Whoa, Whoa, you're leaving evidence. I joked. Prospect, clean up the evidence and then come sit in the shade with me. I picked up the ice and we went and sat in the shade and enjoyed a couple of drinks. He had seen how hard I had been working as a prospect in the days prior to leaving for the run, and that was his way of making sure I got some down time before the remainder of the long ride to Mudd Creek and what would be an exhausting trip.

After two hours we finally got back on the road. The ride to southern Oregon was great. As we were rolling through Bend, Oregon we were stopped by a red light, and when the light turned green, I rolled on the throttle and ended up snapping my throttle cable. I coasted out of the pack and to the right side of the road into a parking lot. Single D, the Tacoma Sergeant at Arms and Raven from the Portland chapter joined me. Single D owns a Harley shop in Tacoma and lent me his bike to go to the Harley shop in Bend and pick up a new throttle cable. It took us over two and a half hours to change the throttle cable but once on the road again we were determined to catch the pack and we knew they were going to stop for a fuel break, so we figured if we really got after it, we could catch them and roll into Mudd Creek together. The three of us rode at over one hundred miles per hour for over three hours. It was exhausting. Single D was leading, and he had me riding on his right with Raven tucked in behind us with his front wheel between our rear tires. The sun was just starting to set, and we were passing a beautiful high alpine lake and riding over a series rolling hills when I thought I could see a pack out in the distance ahead of us. Like I said earlier, you can tell an Outsider pack by the way they ride and as we topped the next rolling hill, I got a good enough look that I was sure it was our pack. I looked to my left at Single D, he smiled at me and nodded then cranked on the throttle and we were off like missiles. As we closed in on the pack there was no doubt it was our pack, and it was an amazing feeling to catch the pack and pull right back into the spots we had fallen out of.

We rode with the pack for about three miles before coming to a stoplight in the middle of nowhere. I have no idea why it was there or what it is controlling because it's not an intersection, but it was there, and we caught it when it was red. When it turned green, this time it was Slow Jim's turn for some bad luck and his bike stalled out. Single D, Raven and I fell out again, and as Jim struggled to get his bike started, we all talked about how great it was to have fixed that kind of mechanical issue and been able to catch the pack, and we decided we could do it again if we got Jim's bike going. After about five minutes we got Slow Jim's bike fired back up and were playing catch the pack again. We had come around a long sweeping left hand curve at over one hundred thirty miles per hour and headed into a hard right that dropped over the top of a steep hill, Single D and Slow Jim accelerated and walked away from us like we were standing still, when I said fuck this, and backed off thinking that it would be hard to prospect without a license. Raven pulled back with me and just before we started into the hard right, we both looked ahead and saw Single D and Slow Jim drop over the hill at the same time as an Oregon State Patrol unit was dropping over the hill on the other side of the canyon coming right at us. If he had not seen and lasered the fellas, he certainly was going to. Raven and I dropped down to the fifty-five mile per hour speed limit and as we crested the hill, the cop had his lights on and was in the process of turning around and hauling ass after Single D and Slow Jim. The protocol in the club is if a member(s) gets stopped by law enforcement, the remaining member(s) ride ahead to the next exit and wait for the member that had been stopped by law enforcement to catch up. We only give them one Outsider or prospect for each law enforcement unit. As we rode past the fellas Single D gave us a shrug like "oops". Raven and I continued up the road about a mile to the first side road we came to and pulled over to wait. When Single D and Slow Jim caught up, they said that the trooper had been really cool and let them off because they were going so fast it caused an error on his radar, but he did tell them to slow way down. Not letting that deter us, we were off again and determined to catch the pack in the short ride to Mudd Creek, and as we got to the spot where you turn off the highway onto the long dirt road into the campground, we met up with the rest of the pack who had to stop due to a couple of riders having a minor fender bender as they made the turn.

Once everybody was ready, the big pack made the ride down the long dirt road into the campground. The sun was almost set, and the deer were everywhere which made it a neat ride as we slowly cruised the long road towards the campground. When we arrived at the run site it was like a scene out of a biker movie from the 1970's. All the old school west coast outlaw motorcycle clubs were there, and each club had set up their own individual campsites. One of the members of the Unknown MC is a well-known chef and brought a full commercial catering trailer to cater all the meals. The Unknown had set up a cool covered bar with a bar top that had been signed by numerous members from various motorcycle clubs over the last thirty years that the Mudd Creek Run had been held, and they had a great sound system that made the entire campground one big party. It was an awesome time. Right away, I was put on task setting up members' tents, fetching drinks, and other various jobs. To me prospecting required teamwork, but it was competitive, and my goal was to outshine and outlast all the other prospects regardless of whether they were Outsider prospects or from another club. As a prospect it is just as essential that you earn the respect of the community as it is your own club's respect.

As our first night at Mudd Creek wore on, eventually the other prospects were released to get some sleep. When it was my turn, I told Double D that I wanted to stay up and hangout with him and the rest of the Tacoma guys that were still up. Tacoma was a very tight chapter, and we spent every day together, rode and partied together, so I welcomed the opportunity to get to spend time with him, Spanky, Buell Greg and Single D. The other reason I wanted to stay up was because Single D had always been a hard-ass on me, but since the breakdown he had changed and was starting to be really cool, so I wanted to continue that. We hung out at the bar and socialized with the members of the other clubs. It was a great time, and it was cool getting to meet some of the long-term members of these old school outlaw motorcycle clubs and hear their stories. The fellas decided we were all going to have shots together, and they were being served as triple shots in Solo cups. Double D is not a big drinker and so he took a sip when we toasted but after that, every time I would turn away to engage someone else, he would pour his whiskey into my cup. Very quickly, I noticed what he had done, but the fellas continued the game, and every time I would turn away or be sent away on some trivial task intended to separate me from my drink, they would pour some whiskey in my cup, until the red Solo cup was almost full. As a prospect, you've gotta do what you are told, and a willingness to do outrageous things is referred to as a "show of class" in the motorcycle club world. Because of this, when Double D ordered me to finish my drink, I finished my drink. Now, I think that I forgot to mention that Mudd Creek sits at over 8,600 feet in elevation, so I would really regret my actions later. I held my mud as we say and eventually Double D, Spanky and Bueller went to bed, leaving Single D and I to finish out the night. We hung out all night long and I really enjoyed that night. The next morning, I was still on task running errands and getting drinks for the Portland members, while the rest of the prospects were still sleeping. The whiskey and fatigue from four continuous days of prospecting was really taking its toll but I was determined to be super prospect. It was about 8:30am, when the Portland President sent me to get him coffee with Carol Anne's. As I stumbled across the campground towards the food trailer, I ran into Double D. Good morning prospect, he said to me cheerfully. What are you up to? I am going to get Magic coffee with Koreans. I said. What? He said. Magic wants coffee with Koreans. What are you talking about prospect? Man, I'm trying to get Magic coffee with Koreans. I exclaimed. Do you mean coffee with Carol Anne's? Yeah, man. No, you are going to bed, and you are going now. Go get some sleep and don't come out of your tent for at least four hours, he ordered. I would hear the story about me looking for Koreans for Magic's coffee at Mudd Creek the duration of my time in the club, but honestly that night with the men who I would eventually call brothers was very special to me.

As soon as we got home from Mudd Creek I got together with Single D at the club's shop, Easystreet Custom Cycles. At the time, the shop was owned by a good friend of the club, Single D worked in the shop, and we pretty much had free run of the place. Easystreet was and still is a place that you can stop by any time and find Outsiders and members of various motorcycle clubs hanging out, working on their bikes, and maybe having a beer or two together. I am not a mechanic, so Single D and Spanky helped me install gear driven cams, new lifters, Mikuni racing carburetor, programmable ignition, Thuderheader pipes, and eighteen-inch ape hanger handlebars with chromed-out controls and cables. Working on your bike with your brothers is part of the culture and being around the shop let me learn hands-on about everything from Pan-heads and Knuckleheads to V-Rods. When we were done, my bike was sexy as hell and really fast. Do not get me wrong, I am not a motorcycle mechanic, it does not interest me, and I would rather leave that work to the experts with a passion for it. But I felt like it was important that I had a basic knowledge if I was going to be a true outlaw biker and my prospective brothers were a great source of knowledge.

The bi-monthly Washington Confederation of Clubs (COC) meeting in September of 2008 would prove to be historical. I was a prospect, but because I was smart and had been involved in the COC in the past, I was allowed to attend the COC meetings. The main topic of the night would be an incident from June of 2008, when a member of a traditional club called the Society's Deviants MC from Olympia had been pulled over by Washington State Patrol trooper Pigott. Basically, he was pulled over simply for wearing a patch and being a motorcycle club member. Before you go and assume that he was a "motorcycle gang" member and probably deserved to be pulled over, I will let you know that this individual was an engineer for Boeing with multiple degrees, no criminal history, and never committed any infraction to warrant the stop. In the dashcam version of the event which I later posted on YouTube, Trooper Pigott can be seen and heard approaching the polite biker and demands that he takes of his helmet or "I'll arrest you for, uh, yeah I'll think of something." Then the trooper proceeds to arrest the biker. While the club member is locked in the back of the car, Pigott and another trooper can be heard making several derogatory comments about bikers. This was just one more egregious example of the motorcycle profiling problem that is occurring across America, and it was the last straw as far as the motorcycle clubs of Washington were concerned.

Before the meeting, we met with the Bandidos, the Gypsy Joker and the other clubs making up the COC Board of Directors, and we came to the consensus that the motorcycle clubs of Washington needed to do what the COC was intended to do, and that was unite for the purposes of protecting the culture, and in this case that meant cooperating as a grass-roots rights movement to try and pass the first motorcycle profiling law in the nation. The Washington COC first began trying to obtain sponsorship for a motorcycle profiling bill modeled after our states racial profiling law back in 2005, but up to this point we had limited participation from the clubs and difficulty obtaining a sponsor for our bill. Times had changed though, this time we had several passionate and intelligent younger generation patch-holders involved, we understood that the situation for the motorcycle club culture was near critical and were committed to doing something about it.

The COC meeting at Jules Maes Saloon was packed that night with the crowd overflowing out of the building and people standing outside crowded around the back doors trying to hear what was going on. When the meeting started and the reading of the minutes from the last meeting was finished being read, PigPen told the crowd of patch-holders about the stop that had occurred back in June, and that the C.O.C. attorney Martin Fox would be representing the club member in a civil rights lawsuit against the Washington State Patrol. He went on to tell the crowd about how we have the stop on dash cam video, and we are going to use it to evidence the problem of motorcycle profiling by law enforcement and attempt to get a motorcycle profiling bill passed. At this point, the Sergeant at Arms of the C.O.C., a Gypsy Joker, chimes in and says "Yeah, basically, all our clubs at the front of this room fought to exist and now it's your clubs turn. We're all doing this and if your club and most of your people aren't involved, you won't be recognized as a club if ya get what I'm saying." While it is policy that the COC is not a sanctioning body, in this case we needed manpower and there were starting to be too many clubs that were isolating themselves away until it was time for a COC meeting and then they would show up to use it as a social event. Our clubs were in this to protect our existence and the existence of the culture, and we do not give up, so if they wanted to exist in Washington, they would have to be involved and not just take up space like a bunch of posers. Right or wrong, it worked, and that historical meeting would forever change the motorcycle club culture of Washington state and America for the better.

Like I said, prospecting for me and the other prospects was what you would expect. Learning about the club, learning how to ride like the club (side by side, eighteen inches off the guy in front of you.), tending bar, cleaning the clubhouse, and providing security for the club both around the clubhouse and in public. Apart from the Portland chapter, I was not treated like a slave, but I went into prospecting knowing what the expectations are of a one percent club prospect and determined to excel. I knew to keep my mouth shut, do what needed to be done before I was told, and always be there for the club. My favorite part about prospecting was learning the club history from the old-timers. There are not a lot of one-percenters left who were charter members of their clubs or have been in the club forty years or more.

Late that fall, one of the younger Portland members that I had gotten close to was found dead in his room in the clubhouse. None of the Portland members had seen him in twenty-four hours and when he did not show up for church, they went into his room and found him dead. They immediately called Tacoma who was having their church meeting and even though I was a prospect, because of my professional training and experience, I was sent down with one of the Tacoma lifetime/charter members to investigate his death. It was clear when we got there that his death was accidental and while I really didn't do anything other than take a trip in a car and share my observations and opinion, the fact that I had been asked to go and he hadn't, irritated the shit out of Mavrick, and he began to exhibit a pattern of behavior that made it clear, he was out to get me, I couldn't trust him, and I never would be able to. This incident was a major turning point for our relationship.

One of the most well-known Outsiders and a Lifetime/Charter member of the Tacoma chapter of the Outsiders MC is Robert "Pig-Pen" Christopher. I had known PigPen for a few years before prospecting and when I went prospect, I was lucky enough to have him take me under his wing to teach me what he knew about club security and how to be a good Outsider and one-percenter. At the same time, his ol'lady Sandy Jo took Candace under her wing and taught Candace how to be a good ol'lady from and old school one-percenter ol'lady's perspective. It made it incredibly special for Candace and me both to have them helping us succeed. On December 12th that year Candace and I were at the clubhouse by ourselves when just before 8:00pm, PigPen opened the front door, immediately locked eyes with me standing behind the bar, and with a serious tone in his raspy voice began "Brother, I love you." He said before a long pause as he walked across the bar and put a manila folder down on the bar top before taking a seat. "It's 12/12 brother, do you understand why that's important?" he said. Yeah Pen, I think I do. I said trying to portray that I understood it was the anniversary of the worst day in the Outsiders MC history. PigPen stared at me affectionately and took a deep breath then told me, "I know you do brother and that's why you're here tonight, to stand guard with me." Let me tell you why it is important we are here and let me tell you why it is important we're involved in the Confederation of Clubs he said, referring to the Washington motorcycle rights group made up of the motorcycle clubs of Washington State. He went on to share with me his experience from December 12th, 1979, when the Portland Police Bureau raided the Portland chapters clubhouse using an illegal warrant and PigPen was forced to defend himself and the club by shooting what turned out to be a dirty cop. Having him tell me that story from the heart like he did and getting to share that memory with him was a special moment for both Candace and me. To be clear, we were not celebrating that he killed a cop or even that later his conviction was overturned and he was released, but we were having a solemn memorial for the most unfortunate night in the history of the Outsiders MC, to serve as a reminder that a corrupt element of law enforcement has been waging an unconstitutional war against outlaw motorcycle clubs for decades, and it is our responsibility to defend the club, the culture, and the Constitution from the abuses of this corrupt law enforcement, as best we can.

Outsider PigPen 1%er, Tacoma and Outsider Prospect Twitch at the clubhouse on 12/12. You can see my Mudd Creek Run pin on my left chest.
Photo by Candace Burns

When you are a prospect, you are expected, well back in those days you were expected to ride your motorcycle everywhere. I continued to live in Kirkland and over the ten and a half months I prospected, I put over twenty-seven thousand miles on my bike, riding in all sorts of conditions. The worst trip I took as a prospect was a trip, I made to Portland the last week of December with Mavrick. The Portland clubhouse is an easy one-hundred forty-seven-mile trip south on I-5 and would usually take Mavrick and I two and a half hours or less, but this trip was different because it was during one of the worst snow storms the Northwest had seen in years. Because I was coming from Kirkland and the Tacoma clubhouse on Hilltop was inaccessible due to snow, I met Mavrick at a gas station just off I-5 in Tacoma around 6:30pm. It was thirty degrees, snowing heavily and the roads and highways were covered in snow when Mavrick and I left for Portland. Because we were both still young, dumb, and trying to be "old school", we were wearing leather jackets, chaps, boots, and wintered ourselves up by using full-face helmets, rather than being professional bikers and dressing accordingly like we should have. You learn some shit as you get older, I guess.

It took us three and a half miserable hours to get to Portland that night, riding with our feet down like outriggers at times. When we showed up out front of the clubhouse, we had over an inch of compact snow and ice frozen to our chaps and it was shortly after that we both learned that you could look just as cool with a heated/waterproof jacket under your really badass leather jacket and colors and keep your hands nice and toasty with heated gloves.

Prospecting was different for me because of my experience and relationship with the Hells Angels, my knowledge of the one-percent clubs, and my security skillset. I was often brought in to consult on matters with the HA, foster relationships with them, and provide security during meetings between the Angels and other one percent clubs. While I knew it was a violation of club rules and one-percent protocol for a prospect to be read-in on club business, it made sense to me because I had an established reputation for keeping my mouth closed and I understood the benefit I brought the club in terms of my skills and experience.

All my training and experience in dignitary and executive protection was directly transferrable to motorcycle club security. During one of those conversations with Josh years ago, he told me that he had been taught that one of the way's a one-percent club establishes respect is by demonstrating they run a tight ship with professional security. He explained that it does not mean that you are being aggressive, it is defensive and it makes you a hard target which makes another club less likely to make a move on you. This made sense to me as it is consistent with my professional training and experience, so it is something I put into play as soon as I became a prospect and was able to assist to some degree in club security. I was not a bar-room tough guy, but a high-threat protection specialist and security for me was much more than just being a tough guy. It meant creating threat models and conducting threat assessments, identifying weaknesses, developing countermeasures, and avoiding exposure to risk of anything that could potentially harm or embarrass the club, whether we were at home or traveling. Mavrick and Paul saw that I was getting positive attention from applying myself to club security, they started joining in and together along with the sergeant at arms we were able to provide an effective and professional look to Outsiders MC security which garnered comments and respect from other one-percent clubs.

One of the Tacoma members, Tommy No Guns, had decided to buy a restaurant in a tiny town in eastern Washington with a member of the Gypsy Joker. The move did not make a lot of sense to any of us because the town they were moving to was in the middle of nowhere and a five-hour ride from the Tacoma clubhouse which would make being in the club really difficult for Tommy, but he was our brother, so we all supported him. Tommy made it work as best he could, and I made several trips over to visit Tommy and the restaurant. It was a cute run-down little place, and I had a hard time believing that the town had enough on an economy to support the restaurant since it had been closed for quite some time before Tommy bought it. It was around 2:00am in morning when I got a call from Double D, and he told me to get to the clubhouse and to come prepared. I did not know what was going on or what to be prepared for, so I tossed a trauma kit, body armor, some guns, ammo, gloves, a burner phone, some protein bars, and bottles of water in a duffle bag with my prospect kit, and I headed for the clubhouse. When I got to the clubhouse Double D explained that Tommy had been having some issues with some Hispanic gangbangers that were coming into his restaurant, Tommy stood up to them, now his restaurant had been burnt down and I was being sent with the sergeant at arms to protect Tommy, his family, and gather intel so we could figure out what was going on. We loaded up in a car and headed for eastern Washington.

When we arrived at Tommy's it was clear things were not right. We walked inside and all the curtains and shades were closed, some of the windows were boarded over with plywood, there were rifles and pistols strategically placed by certain windows and throughout the house, all the furniture in his home was gone except for the kitchen table, a bed had been set up in the family room, and there was a picnic bench in one of the back bedrooms which they were using as a smoking room to avoid going outside. Tommy looked pale and stressed, and his wife was out of her mind and shoveling handfuls of unknown pills into her mouth. He told us about the gangbangers that had been coming into his restaurant causing problems, threatening him, and that he has not been putting up with their shit but said neither side had gotten violent yet. He said that they had come in the previous day and when he stood up to them, they threatened to burn down his restaurant, and it appears they made good, and he did not know how far this was going to go. We spent a couple of days in town making sure nothing would happen to Tommy and his family and trying to dig up leads without any luck before heading back home. When I walked into the house that night Candace was asleep in my bed. I put the duffle bag of guns in the closet, took off my clothes and tried to sneak into bed without waking her. I figured like most women, she would be pissed that I just up and left in the middle of the night, did not tell her where I was going, and did not call or come home for a few days. I was right, she was pissed but Candace was so cool and worked so hard at trying to be a good ol'lady for me that she did not ever ask me any questions and didn't give me any drama, she just let it slide. That is when I knew I had myself a great ol'lady Years later when I would praise her for how she handled the situation she revealed how angry she had been but said she knew what she was getting into when she decided to date me.

Now, let's talk about the worst experience I had as a prospect. During my time as a prospect, I spent over thirty-seven days prospecting in Portland and it was during one of those trips as a prospect that my attitude of disdain for Portland would be cemented by the actions of one of their lifetime members and then president of the Portland chapter, T-Bob. As an Outsider prospect the by-laws state that you must spend five days prospecting in Portland if you are a Tacoma prospect, and five days in Tacoma if you are a Portland prospect. Well, Portland prospects had developed a bad habit of taking an extraordinarily long time to complete those five days and as a result they were not eligible to be brought up for membership until they did, and the length of their prospect periods grew because of Portland's laziness. The Portland prospect who made member shortly after I went prospect took a full year to get his five days in Tacoma completed. Tacoma prospects were the exact opposite, and we got our five days done as quickly as possible. This helped all Tacoma prospects look good which as the quality of the Tacoma prospects increased and the quality of Portland's stagnated, the jealously from Portland towards the Tacoma chapter increased and the Portland members responded like little bitches, taking it out on the Tacoma prospects. This trip was about six months into our prospecting period and Prospect Paul, and I had already completed over twenty days prospecting in Portland. We were going down to be in their faces so there was no excuse not to make us members. We were both busting our asses tending bar with a full house of guests from other motorcycle clubs and civilians on a busy Friday night. T-Bob, the president of the Portland chapter at the time, a tweeker and alcoholic with a horrible stutter, was drinking at the booth in the corner by the window with some of his tweeker buddies. Suddenly, he yells for Paul to bring him more tequila. Paul had just had open heart surgery a few weeks earlier, was still recovering, should not have even been in Portland but came anyway, and the physical toll of his decision was starting to show. When he took too long to bring T-Bob his tequila, T-Bob decided to make a spectacle of him by having him do fifty pushups, but since Paul was over fifty years old and had just had open heart surgery he tried to explain to T-bob that he couldn't for medical reasons, at which point T-Bob threatened to "no-vote" him for membership if he didn't do the push-ups. I stepped in and explained to T-Bob that Paul had just had open heart surgery and was physically unable to do the push-ups and told him I would do the push-ups for Paul.

Rather than commending me for having my prospective brothers back, T-Bob responded by ordering us to take off all our clothes and race around the block naked. We are talking a Portland city block which is over a mile all the way around and sits in the middle of a school zone. This was the most idiotic thing I had ever heard of in the outlaw motorcycle club world, but there was no talking T-Bob out of it and now he was threatening both our memberships. We were not going to get out of this so I said let's get this over with, knowing that the Tacoma members would not approve, and I would be raising hell once I got back. Paul asked for a few minutes to call his sponsor who advised him to do what he was told and just made the situation worse for us both with T-Bob. T-Bob ordered us to strip to nothing but our colors and boots and line up on the sidewalk in front of the clubhouse. "T-t-t-t-ch-ch-ch-ch-wh-wh-wh-when I s-s-s-say go, you, you guys race around the block and I'm going to t-t-time you." T-Bob stuttered his red face and drunken state making him look even stupider than he really is. He held his hand in the air like a starter pistol and stuttered go at the top of his lungs. Paul was in no shape to run and I did not want to risk getting caught running around naked in Outsiders prospect colors in a school zone, getting beat up and having my rockers stolen by the cops then having to register as a sex offender for the rest of my life because some fat old tweeked out idiot with suppressed homosexual fantasies wanted to watch me and a middle aged man recovering from open heart surgery and a meth addiction, run around naked for him. It did not seem like a good idea, and I figured Paul was probably going to have a heart attack and die before he made the first corner. I decided the best plan was to run the block as fast as I possibly could, get my pants on and then go back and help Paul.

I was only thirty years old and still skiing professionally, so I was in pretty good shape at the time and ran the block in about seven minutes. When I was about halfway down the second side of the block, I passed a house with a large picture window full of people looking out on the street who clearly saw me. I was horribly embarrassed that these people had just seen this kind of bullshit from an outlaw motorcycle club with a respected reputation like the Outsiders. What T-Bob had us do was not honorable and just as I had feared it had now tarnished our reputation. As I planned, I did not stop when I finished the block, I ran straight into the clubhouse, pulled on my pants, slipped my boots on and ran back for Paul. I found Paul throwing-up and leaning against a fence about halfway down the second side of the block, just passed the dinner party who were still in the window clearly talking and laughing about what they had seen. I let Paul pull himself back together as best he could, and I picked him up over my shoulder and carried him to the corner on the last side of the block leading to the clubhouse. Paul was in bad shape when I put him down, but I knew if I carried him back like I probably should have it would have caused more problems with T-Bob. I helped him pull himself together and told him I was not going to let him not finish and we'd do it together. I put his arm over my shoulder, supported his body weight as best I could, and Paul gave his best effort to make it look like he was trying to run while I helped him finish the run. When we got back, T-Bob had lost interest and gone back in and secluded himself away in the member's room to fill his nose full of more devil dust. From that day on I vowed I would never demean a prospect or damage the club's reputation like T-Bob did and I have hated him ever since. He is a piece of shit as a human being, a poser when it comes to being an outlaw biker, and nothing more than a meth junkie who uses being an "outlaw biker" as justification for his inadequacies and wrongdoings, and as tool to feel important. I was very open with the brothers when I was in the club that if they made me go to that geriatric tweekers funeral when he died, I would piss on his casket rather than throw dirt on it, and I fucking meant it.

When we got back to Tacoma and informed them of T-Bob's gay prospect Olympics, the Tacoma chapter was pissed and called a special meeting. While I stood guard outside the special meeting and heard all the yelling, we could not tell what was being said and we rode home with a pissed off Tacoma chapter and went on with our prospect lives. I would later learn once I made member that nothing had been resolved because the old members in Tacoma sided with the old members in Portland who backed T-Bob, the issue was tabled and I would have to deal with the issue repeatedly for the first three years I was a member before I finally put my foot down and ordered T-Bob's prized prospect and bag-buddy/meth lacky prospect to run around the block after he told me to get my own drink at a party when he was tending bar in our clubhouse. Had it been most other one-percent clubs I would have been OK to sock that prospect in the fucking mouth for his disrespect, but the Outsiders have a rule that we don't hit our own, so that is the one and only time I gave the order to run around the block, and like a bitch he went running to T-Bob to try and get out of it. If it was good enough for me to do for the club, it is good enough for him and he should do it without question. That's the one-percent code. However when it came to me making his meth buddy run, T-Bob had a change of heart and decided that we shouldn't have prospects run around the block anymore, claimed he got that idea from something he saw another club do back in the 70's, and finally admitted that he didn't actually done it himself as a prospect like he had told me and Paul when I asked him before we ran.

In my opinion prospecting should be about getting to know the protocols, traditions, and history of the club you are attempting to join, and the clubs in the community which you will be interacting with. It is a time to evaluate and identify your role in the club and how you can best benefit the club, learn to keep the club and your brothers safe from violence, criminal and civil liability, addiction problems, learn to interact with the community and for your prospective brothers to get to know you by educating you. It is not a time to demean, shame and generally treat prospects like bartenders or slave labor. Neither the prospect or the club learns anything from that type of behavior, it lacks class when observed by other clubs, and makes your club look unprofessional. Yes, prospects need to tend bar, provide security, watch the bikes and run some errands for members when necessary, but if they were a good enough man to earn your vote to prospect for the club you love, they should be shown the respect you will show them as a brother until they prove they are not worthy of that respect, at which point they need to be sent down the road. Additionally, if a guy is not working out the chapter needs to assess why their prospect is having problems, determine if he is "fixable", and if so, develop a plan with the prospects sponsor to fix the issue. If he is not fixable, he needs to be sent down the road rather than strung out hoping that any "no-vote's" will abstain or be pressured into changing their votes and he will make member. I saw that kind of bullshit with the Portland chapter all the time. They would bring a guy to the table who while he may have been a good friend of a couple of members, he was either not physically fit enough to prospect or a tweeker that was going to be a problem for the club. Tacoma understood the damage meth does to motorcycle clubs, and myself in particular was very vocal about my hate for that drug and tweekers. On numerous occasions I made it known that I would no-vote any prospect who used meth, and twice I made motions that were brought to vote, to have the drug's use banned in the club. Bottom line, set a standard and curriculum you expect a prospect to thoroughly learn and comprehend during their prospect period, and then stick to that. Do not lower the bar unless it is truly in the best interest of the club that you lower the bar.

I came to the Outsiders with an existing reputation in the motorcycle club community for being a stand-up guy who could take care of business, and while they did not take it easy on me as a prospect, I was shown the respect I had earned in Tacoma. Portland was a different story. When I went prospect there were already three prospects in Portland, two in Tacoma and out of all of them, I stood out as something special. I should have been, I had prior training and experience in the club world. I am not trying to pat myself on the back, it's just the way it was, and it led to a lot of animosity and problems for me with the Portland chapter and with Mavrick which at first manifested themselves in different ways and I could manage, but years later when Mavrick and Portland teamed up it would push me to my breaking point.

With Portland, it was a few specific members in particular; Gordy, T-Bob, Squeeze and Rod who went out of their way to be disrespectful to me, and because of how significantly my reputation in the club community contrasted with my profession, they knew I would stand up for myself and as a prospect they knew I was not allowed to, so T-Bob, Squeeze, and Rod loved to push my buttons by calling me a cop. While it was true that I was in law enforcement at the time and carried a badge, I was doing it with the motorcycle club community's blessing and because it was the only legal job that would allow me to use my professional skill set and still be around to be part of the club enough to prospect and be a member. When I got involved in the motorcycle club world, I was determined not to become a criminal and never wanted a criminal lifestyle. The entire Outsiders MC knew what I did for a living when they first met me and that had not changed, so to me it was totally disrespectful that these Portland members would call me a cop and when they would do it, I would issue a stern correction which was all I could do as a prospect without risking my future membership in the club. That changed one night at the Portland clubhouse but first let me tell you about my brother Gordy.

Gordy had been well-known and respected in the northwest outlaw motorcycle club community for decades. He had been a respected member of Brother Speed MC's Portland chapter before becoming a Tacoma Outsider, and dying as a Portland Outsider. I am not sure how old Gordy was when he died but he was fucking old and until the very end he was too cool for school, the ladies loved him, and he rode a beautiful blue Panhead until the day he died. You had to earn Gordy's friendship and respect but once you did, he was loyal till the end. For the first six months of my prospect period Gordy had been not just a hard ass, but a total dick to me until late one night at the Outsiders Tacoma Halloween Party.

It was about 3:00am, all the other prospects had gone to sleep, and I was the lone prospect left to tend bar for Gordy and a handful of the few of Portland's tweeker crew that were still awake partying. Gordy had been drinking all night and was grumpier than usual, so I was just trying to keep myself busy cleaning up behind the bar and in the kitchen to try and avoid him. All of the sudden I heard Gordy yell Praahhhh-spect! I bolted from the kitchen and was in front of him at attention within the blink of an eye. "Who the fuck are you, and what do you know about being an outlaw biker?" Gordy growled at me. "I had some respected patch-holders show me what's up, been around the community for over 10 years, and seen and done some shit." I said, not wanting to name drop as that goes against one-percent protocol. "Just what the fuck is that supposed to mean prospect?" he yelled. "I was trying to show class and not name drop and figured you were aware of my background, but I've been close with the HA since the late 90's, almost went that route, did a bunch of criminal defense investigation work for them, helped with the HA RICO defense, brought a motorcycle club into Washington, and then found the Outsiders and decided this was where I belong." I said. Gordy glared at me like he was sizing me up and then he asked, "Do you live in North Bend?" I told him that I used to and asked how he knew. His tone took a dramatic and friendly change in tone, and he said, "We've got a mutual brother." It was at that point that it clicked for me, and I realized that this is the Gordy from Tacoma that Josh used to speak so highly of. "Josh!" I exclaimed with a big smile. "I considered him a brother and he spoke very highly of you for years." "Any brother of Josh's is a brother of mine." Gordy said and got up and gave me a hug, then told me to get him a new drink. From then on Gordy treated me like a brother, not like a prospect. He still expected me to work like a prospect but that's because Gordy never stopped working like a prospect himself.

There was a period of time when I was prospecting when Gordy got in some sort of trouble with the club and since I was a prospect, I wasn't clued in on what he did, but he had his colors taken by the club and his membership suspended temporarily, and during that period of time he had to stand outside with us prospects. We were standing outside at a special meeting in Tacoma with Gordy when he went into his saddle bags and pulled out a soft rag and a can of lemon pledge, then used it to shine up the President and Vice Presidents' bikes. "If you wanna be stylie, you and your brother's rides gotta be stylie." Gordy said with a smile. "Get to work on your brother's bikes and lets all look good together he said." With that we all went to work shining all the fella's bikes and when the meeting broke everyone was thrilled to see their bikes gleaming in the Hilltop sun. Gordy was one of those old timers who took the lessons he learned as a prospect to heart, never stopped prospecting, and always tried to adhere to the one-percent code as best he could.

With Gordy, his initial attitude towards me as a prospect was because he did not know me, and he had high expectations for any prospect that wanted to be a member of the motorcycle club he cherished. With T-Bob, Rod and Squeeze, their attitude was the result of them being insecure, out of touch, irrelevant addicts who were jealous that a highly functional younger generation of Outsiders were beginning to make the Tacoma chapter something very special, eclipsing the reputation that the Portland chapter was so proud of, and I was one of those young Tacoma Outsiders.

About eight months into prospecting, it became clear that my membership vote was being deliberately delayed, and it was frustrating the hell out of me. We were all hanging out at the clubhouse watching a UFC fight one night, I was talking to Double D, and he flat out told me he was frustrated with Portland delaying me and suggested I talk to my sponsor to see what I could do. I asked Spanky to talk and he had me follow him outside on the front porch to talk. It was a cold February night and a thick fog had rolled in on Hilltop making it so you could barely see the bikes parked on the curb in front of the clubhouse. We sat down at a high round bar table on the porch and Spank pulled a maroon and silver metal pot pipe out of the pocket of his sweatshirt and took a long hit off it. As he held his breath, he looked at me and in a raspy voice choked out "What's up?" I told Spank that I was felt like I had learned what I needed to learn, demonstrated I am totally committed to the club, and felt like I was being held up and wanted to know what I could do. Spanky told me that there were some people in Portland who said they have not seen me in Portland and that I need to spend more time in Portland before they will vote for me. What the fuck? I have spent thirty-six days in Portland already Spank, we are only required to spend five and I'm done dealing with their bullshit. Spanky had no answers on how to resolve the issue and just said there were people in Portland who said they have not seen me down there. It was bullshit but I was a prospect, so the following Friday I got off work and rode straight to Portland to spend the weekend prospecting.

When I got to the Portland clubhouse Friday evening it was a standard Friday night. Prospect Paul from Tacoma had gotten down there earlier in the day and was tending bar for the couple of Portland chapter members who had shown up to start their weekend early. The night started slow, Portland Outsiders and friends of the club trickled in, and the party slowly picked up pace. Around 7:00pm, I was tending bar and the Portland chapter President's daughter asked me to make her another Snake Bite. As I made her drink, she asked me about Candace, and talked about what a hard-working prospect she thought I was. I was halfway listening to her as she spoke but really, I was paying attention to the sound of Harley Davidson's approaching the clubhouse. As I slid her drink across the bar to her, she reached out and grabbed my wrist, pinning my hand to the bar. Our eyes locked and she asked me,"Can I suck your cock?" Wow, this is an outlaw motorcycle club and all, but she was only one drink in for the night, knew I had an ol'lady, and knew she was nowhere near the same class of woman as Candace, and while I could have gotten away with it, there was no way I was cheating on Candace with a skanky Amazon. I should have read it as a sign that I was going to be tested in Portland that night, but I did not.

As the night went on, things picked up and by 8:00pm, the clubhouse was full of members of Brother Speed MC and the Gypsy Joker MC, along with a handful of Road Brother, including Road Brother Josh that the Jokers had brought with them. Within minutes of the Jokers arriving and getting their drinks, Kenny from the Jokers and T-Bob disappeared into the member's room. Every clubhouse has a "member's room" which is a room for members only and their invited guests and is just a quiet place to get away from the party. For many outlaw motorcycle clubs that have been around for decades and still have members with methamphetamine addictions that have been around equally as long, the members room has become the place that the members of the clubs that do meth are relegated to during parties. Contrary to law enforcement and media portrayals, outlaw motorcycle clubs are generally not involved in methamphetamine. Methamphetamine has been one of the most destructive influences on motorcycle club culture and since it came into the culture via the outlaw motorcycle clubs, they have experienced its devastating effects firsthand and as a result many clubs, including major one percenter clubs like the Bandidos, are instituting "No-Meth" policies. While others like the Outsiders are taking the much less effective route of hoping it dies out as the old guys die out. The problem with this second method is that meth addicts like to have other meth addicts around them to make themselves feel normal and like they are not such a shit-bag, and as a result they will either convince one of the young guys to be "old school" and try meth one night or they champion prospects with addiction problems and this just continues the cycle and poisons the club. Having meth users in your motorcycle club will always bring with it unnecessary chaos and drama that will negatively impact the brotherhood and operations of the motorcycle club, but even worse these meth users lie, steal, sell drugs, and commit other crimes to fuel their addictions and survive, and all of that is always blamed on the club, even though they were the independent acts of the addict member. The motorcycle clubs that are trying to run meth out of the culture in their own ways is an attempt to clean up the clubs and protect themselves from being blamed as a club for the crimes committed by addicts who are members. The "Members Room" is a way for the clubs to attempt to hide the embarrassing behavior of their meth using members by isolating them away from the party, so when Kenny and T-Bob and the rest of that crew disappeared into the members room, I knew I was in for a late night.

As soon as Kenny disappeared into the member's room, Road Brother Josh relaxed, and his ego began to inflate as he bragged openly about how he was getting ready to "Go white background." Going white-background is Gypsy Joker slang for a probationary member and refers to the white background behind the Simon center-patch used in the U.S. and some European Gypsy Joker colors. Unless the club is from east of the Mississippi where "Prospects" are generally called "Probates" or are patching-over from a respected one-percent club, getting your patch as a probationary member is looked at as getting your patch the easy way. As a result, probationary members are often treated worse than prospects by members and may even be bossed around by the prospects depending on the club.

A Probationary Gypsy Joker patch on the left and a full member
Gypsy Joker patch on the right.
Photo by Photo- Rogues-MC.com

Well, hearing that Josh was not going to be just a support club member anymore and was going to be in a respected one-percent club was all it took, and Skankzilla pounced. Next thing you know the cock-hungry amazon who had propositioned me was on her way to the bathroom to slum it and suck some Road Brother cock. I was disgusted and not just because unless the chapter has a ton of prospects or has cleaned specifically for an event, clubhouse bathrooms are the most disgusting bathrooms you will find in the United States and the last place a woman would want to get on her knees, but she was on a mission. What really disgusted me was that Josh had a beautiful girlfriend named Jessie at home who he had a daughter with, and I could not believe that he would cheat on Jessie and risk all that with a 6'2", 240lb linebacker of a woman who could not hold a candle to Jessie. I was hoping he was going to have better judgment than that but clearly, he did not have any concept of risk to benefit. Cheating in the club world happens but it is certainly not any more rampant than it is in the civilian world, and I never cheated on Candace even when we were having problems, because I viewed me breaking our marriage vow equivalent to me breaking my vow to my club.

With T-Bob off in the member's room, the Portland Outsiders Vice-President Squeeze seized the opportunity to stroke his own ego and began ordering around the prospects which now included a Portland prospect in addition to Paul and me. As Squeeze drank, he got louder and more obnoxious, telling over-blown stories about "this one time" that really were not all that interesting. On a positive note, at least since he was not high on meth his stories didn't spin into a circle of nonsense that just repeated itself like T-Bob's tweaked out tales, but what wasn't good is that as Squeeze told tales to his audience at the bar, the volume of his voice and ego continued to grow and he continued to snap orders at the prospects. Paul and I did our best to stay busy so that we would not give him any reason to fuck with us, but it was useless. Paul was standing towards the end of the bar talking to a Brother Speed member he had just served a drink to when Squeeze slid his empty cup down the bar past Paul off the end of the bar, crashing into the wall, the ice and remaining contents of the cup spilling all over the floor at the end of the bar. Squeezed looked at Paul and snapped "Prospect, what the fuck's wrong with you? Clean that shit up!" Squeeze turned back to the Brother Speed member he had been talking to and says, 'It's so hard to find good prospects these days." He then went on to tell a "Back in my day" story about when he had been a prospect, then suddenly he stopped and turned to his right and looked at me and sneered loudly, "Get me a drink Cop!" What the fuck? I thought. I could not believe this guy, a member of the club I was prospecting for, had just referred to me in such a derogatory manner. It was a deliberate disrespect and even worse, it had been done right in front members of other outlaw motorcycle clubs.

You see, while it was true that at that time professionally, I was a peace officer, it was something that all the one-percent clubs were aware of and a career I got into after I had proven my loyalty and commitment to the outlaw motorcycle club culture. The community viewed me as a one percenter first and foremost and my job was a paycheck that came after I had proven myself to the one percent world. In addition, I always kept my professional life and personal life separate. So, separate that for the ten years I worked in that position, I basically lived two separate lives. Over the last several months that I had been prospecting, T-Bob and Rod had taken cheap shots, referring to me as a cop, knowing that I could not really do anything about it, because I needed their vote to make member. Tonight, Squeeze decided that vice-president tab and his vote gave him enough power that it was his turn, and he was going to put me to the ultimate test by disrespecting me in front of numerous members of respected outlaw motorcycle clubs and guests.

Looking back on it, I'm can honestly say that having had to make split second life-or death decisions and training to make those decisions under extreme stress was very applicable in this situation, but rather than thinking about what the threat is doing, what's going on around us, my escalation/use of force, tactics, or how I was going to articulate all of those in the after-action report, while developing an immediate action plan for it all, processing it at a million miles an hour in my head, I was thinking about all of the criminal defense investigations I had done for various one-percenters and how they had helped them and their clubs. I was thinking about how when Double D vetted me with the Hells Angels and asked their president if he trusted me, the response was "Cops don't testify on behalf of Hells Angels." , referring to when I testified as a defense expert witness in A.J.'s assault case and resulted in a not guilty jury verdict. I was thinking about how in the one-percent world, honor and integrity is everything and this piece of shit who

I had always treated with respect had just totally disrespected my honor and integrity in front of the community, and the one percenter code demands I stand up for my honor because it was not just my honor, it was the clubs honor as well because I was wearing those rockers. If I acted, Squeeze would surely no-vote me, but if I did not respond I would have allowed myself to be punked in front of other outlaw clubs and I would never have any respect in the community again. My mind raced as I attempted to fight the rage that had been instantly triggered by Squeeze's disrespect and my thoughts became laser focused. Honor or my patch? Fuck it, I choose honor!

My right hand shot from my side, and I grabbed Squeeze by the throat, at the same time turning him and pinning the small of his back against the back bar and using it for leverage to bend him backwards and off balance leaving him unable to fight back. My rage-filled eyes locked with his fear filled eyes, now teary for the lack of blood and oxygen to his brain. He attempted to look away and I squeezed his throat harder until he looked back into my eyes, and then I leaned in and quietly explained that if he ever called me a cop again it would be one of the very last things he did, so he might want to be more careful how he addressed me. Paul had seen and heard the whole thing and was attempting to intervene, so I let Squeeze go. Teary eyed and struggling to maintain his balance and catch his breath, Squeeze tried to play it off like he was just joking to save face, but I knew there would be repercussions for me when church rolled around on Thursday. Squeeze grabbed another drink and then slipped away outside leaving the three prospects to tend bar for the approximately fifty guests from various clubs and handful of Portland Outsiders. As soon as Squeeze was out the back door, Paul came to me. "That was fucked up what he did man. You shouldn't get in trouble for that and I'm going to make sure my sponsor knows what really happened." I thanked Paul for his help because I was sure I was going to need it. You see, while my argument that Squeeze had committed the ultimate disrespect against me in front of other outlaw clubs and I was honor bound to respond was technically correct, I was sure that

Portland would make the argument that I was a prospect and Squeeze was a member and then use a broad interpretation of the Outsiders by-law that says you never hit another Outsider as a way justify terminating my prospecting. Whether or not it came with a black-eye, I could give a fuck about. What I was most concerned about was them terminating my prospecting because I loved the brothers in the Outsiders Tacoma chapter, I wanted to be their brother more than anything, and now that might not happen.

The Portland prospect was at the end of the bar talking and I was stressing big time, so I told Paul I was going to go out front and stand guard. As soon as I got outside, I sent texts to Spanky and Double D, giving them the text friendly version of what had transpired. Spanky's response came back almost immediately saying that I should not have done what I did, but Squeeze should not have done what he did. Not good but there was hope. After about thirty minutes of waiting with no response from Double D, I went back in the clubhouse and went on with the night. As things wound down, Gordy pulled me aside. "You know Twitch, brother. I saw what Squeeze did tonight and I do not want you to worry. You did the right thing." One of the many things that went through my head while processing Squeezes initial insult was Gordy being perched at the bar and what he would think if I did not respond, which in turn triggered thoughts of what would our brother Josh think if he finds out I did not stand up for myself. Knowing that Gordy had my back made me feel much better, but I would not be at ease until I heard from Double D and knew what he thought. If he thought I did the right thing, he could get the rest of the chapter to back me and while Portland would still try and make a big deal about it, it would get them nowhere, and most importantly as a prospect I would be standing guard outside during the meeting and would not have to deal with any of it.

Double D's text came the following morning as Paul, and I were getting ready to make the ride back to Tacoma. By then Paul had spoken with his sponsor and what had transpired had got around Tacoma, and the Tacoma chapter was angry. How dare Squeeze intentionally abuse and disrespect one of their prospects like that and put me in a situation where I might lose my vote if I respond to defend my honor, they thought it was total bullshit. While I knew that no matter how much Tacoma was on my side, I was still going to take heat over this from the Portland sect that was threatened by me and it would definitely extend my prospect period because Tacoma was very calculating with how they operated and always tried to foster brotherhood with Portland, so even though I might have been right and they backed me, they were not just going to shove me down Portland's throat and make me member right away after this.

I got back to Tacoma early Sunday afternoon and went straight to the clubhouse. Double D and Spanky met me at the clubhouse and by then the Tacoma members had all discussed what had happened and were all in agreement that Squeeze's actions were totally unacceptable. Double D told me that if Portland brought the issue up, Tacoma would back me, end of story. You see at the time, the way the Outsiders by-laws were set up, each chapter voted for their own members, and you needed a 100% vote of your own chapter to make member, which meant if Portland gave Tacoma any shit, they would just make me member and it would be a done issue. Starting with my group of prospects, as Tacoma would grow with younger generation guys, Portland would eventually work with some corrupt Tacoma members to change the by-laws to where a prospect needed 100% vote of the entire club to make member and this was done to control membership, the vote, and ultimately the club. Not very brotherly, but that is the Portland Outsiders. The rest of the week was uneventful. Because I was a prospect, the fellas really could not talk to me about what the members from both chapters were saying, but from time to time the Tacoma brothers would make statements to let me know I did the right thing, and they had my back. This made me feel loved and like I had chosen the right motorcycle club. I felt like my prospective brothers really did have my back.

When Thursday night rolled around, it was one hell of a Thursday night. The Outsiders Tacoma clubhouse is located on 19th and L, smack dab in the middle of Tacoma's Hilltop neighborhood which has long been regarded as the most dangerous and crime infested area in Washington, is notorious as the home of the Hilltop Crips criminal street gang and long-term bloody gang wars. The Outsiders have had their clubhouse in the same location on Hilltop since 1975, over the years they have bumped heads with the Hilltop Crips and there's an old Hilltop legend about an incident which involved a prominent Hilltop Crip pulling up in a car in front of the clubhouse and shooting at some Outsiders who then took the gun away from him, beat him with it, ducttaped him, put him in the trunk of his car and rolled him down the 21st street hill. Anyway, we have bumped heads with those guys over the years, but they stayed off our block and our presence kept the block crime free and made it the safest block on Hilltop. Over the previous year and a half several of the OG's from the Hilltop Crips who had been locked up on R.I.C.O. charges had started getting released and coming back to Hilltop. As they did, the gang activity increased and by the summer of 2008, Hilltop was in the middle of another gang war. Drive-by's and murders were common, but the violence stayed off our block. In the last month I had watched two guys get murdered at the end of our block on the corner of 19th and L while I was standing on the front steps of the clubhouse looking down the block one Sunday afternoon. Several of us had witnessed various shootings either enroute to or from the clubhouse, or simply while we were just standing out on the back porch that overlooks a church and Martin Luther King BLVD. These shootings were so common that when the cops would come cruising through the neighborhood after one and see us, they would just roll by, wave, and say, "I know, you guys didn't see anything." The Tacoma cops who patrolled our neighborhood were respectful and friendly to us because they saw firsthand that we kept the block safe, did not cause any problems and were easy to deal with. Because they watched us live our lives, we were not the big scary mystery to them that motorcycle clubs are to most cops and the public.

Thursday night's meeting started like every church did and the prospects were sent outside to stand guard during the meeting and the members began the meeting. There was not any yelling that we could hear from the sidewalk in front of the house but clearly this was a serious meeting because the guys usually took a break about an hour to an hour and a half into the meeting but tonight, they had been in for well over two hours. Just as Mavrick and Paul started hypothesizing out loud about my future with the Outsiders, we saw a car swoop up on a gangbanger who was standing on the corner of 21st and L selling dope about seventy feet from us. The car came to a screeching stop in front of the guy, there was yelling back and forth and then gunfire erupted from the vehicle. The gangbangers back exploded in four different spots as rounds penetrated through his body, before he crumpled to the ground with his last bits of life leaving his body in the form of a few violent convulsions on the bloody Hilltop sidewalk. The car took off and I turned to make sure Mavrick and Paul hadn't been hit, and they were alright. "Fuck, that dude had a bad night", I said, and we all laughed. Because close range gunfire on Hilltop had become the norm, the meeting never stopped, and nobody even came outside to check on the prospects.

About ten minutes after the shooting, we heard the first sirens. We watched the cops and forensic team come out, photograph, and process the scene, clean up the dead guy, and leave. All the while the fellas were locked in their meeting which I was sure was about the future of my membership. At about 11:00pm, Spanky came outside and told us they were on break but it was just going to be a short one so we could stay outside, then he asked us how things were going. "Oh, you mean aside from the dead guy?" I asked. What are you talking about? Spank asked. We all filled him in on what had transpired while they were in the meeting, and he told us to be careful out there. After about two minutes the meeting was called back to order and twenty minutes later, they adjourned, all without me ever being called inside. I knew this was a good sign and, I knew I would likely have to prospect longer but my prospect status was safe. Immediately after the meeting Spanky and Double D pulled me aside and told me that Tacoma had put Portland in their place on the incident and they explained that I did not have to go to Portland anymore, but I had a lot of support amongst the Portland membership, and they would like it if I continued to develop those relationships. I was safe, and not only was my prospect status safe, but I also did not have to go to Portland and deal with the tweeker madness unless it was a mandatory meeting or party. This was a great result; I should have choked that pill-popping bitch Squeeze sooner.

14

THE CONFEDERATION
OF CLUBS

From the time I got involved in the outlaw motorcycle club culture, I was exposed to an organization comprised of all the motorcycle clubs of Washington State called the Washington Confederation of Clubs (WACOC) which exists for the purpose of maintaining communication between the motorcycle clubs of the state and to defend motorcycle rights. The WACOC was formed in the mid 1990's. Amongst the founding clubs of the Washington COC were the Outsiders MC, Bandidos MC, Gypsy Joker MC, Vietnam Vets MC, and several others. The Hells Angels were not in Washington at the time but would get involved in the COC later. Confederation of Clubs, now often going by the name Council of Clubs, exist is most states, are totally independent, not controlled by one particular motorcycle club, and their membership consists of the various recognized motorcycle clubs of that state, whether they be outlaw, support clubs, traditional, veteran, Christian, community service oriented, etc. Some COC's allow female motorcycle clubs (chick or bitch clubs) to be members and ironically as progressive as the Washington COC was, they were one of the last COC's in the country to allow chick clubs to become members. At the last COC meeting that I attended in 2017, the chick clubs had recently been admitted as members with the contingency that they could never hold an officer position.

The idea for the COC's started back in 1986, at a meeting consisting of all the major motorcycle clubs of the United States, California personal injury attorney Richard Lester, and it took place in Las Vegas, NV. The meeting was based on the idea that motorcycle clubs across America were all fighting for their survival against a common enemy, law enforcement discrimination and profiling, so if the motorcycle clubs wanted to survive, they were stronger as a group and needed to unify for the common ground purpose of fighting this law enforcement discrimination. The meeting was groundbreaking, and the result of the meeting was the formation of the National Coalition of Motorcyclists or N.C.O.M. The idea was Lester's brainchild that he had pitched to various bikers he had represented; it made sense and was appealing to the clubs. No motorcycle club wants to be at war and motorcycle club history had taught them that there were members of law enforcement who would go so far as to plant evidence on you or outright murder you, lie about it, get away with it, and then use the media to paint an unfair portrait of motorcycle clubs as gangs. This was not just some simple profiling stops and harassment, this was send you to prison on a R.I.C.O. beef that was total bullshit, or just plain old execute you on the side of the road, blame it on another motorcycle club and claim it was part of some ongoing gang war. This was serious shit. One of the key players at this meeting was J.R. Reed, the National President of the Sons of Silence Motorcycle Club (SOS). I have had lots of friends who were S.O.S over the years and they were one of my favorite motorcycle clubs to spend time with. J.R. fully embraced this new idea and because of his respect in the motorcycle club community and his clubs' relationships with many of the other clubs at the time, J.R. was able to act as an intermediary and help the various clubs understand the concept and communicate effectively with each other, which was key to the successful result of the meeting and ultimately the organization. I am bummed he was gone before my time because he is the only one-percenter legend that I never got to meet, and I really would have liked to.

J.R. Reed, Sons of Silence M.C.
SonsofSilenceMC.com

Lester knew that if all the outlaw motorcycle clubs in the United States got together in the same place and had a meeting, the feds would look at it like 1931, when Salvatore Maranzano was killed and the mafia families called a meeting in Chicago in which they established a board of directors called The Commission to oversee all mafia activities in the U.S., mediate conflicts between the families, and they agreed to hold meetings every five years or as needed to discuss family problems. Even though there was nothing criminal about the meeting between the motorcycle clubs, Lester knew the feds would try to come up with some sort of way to unjustly indict everybody at the NCOM or COC meetings for conspiracy to commit organized crime and other R.I.C.O. related crimes, so Lester agreed to participate in the first meeting and act as legal counsel in case there were any undercovers and informants in the room, and nothing was said or done that would open the clubs up for indictment. Lester had built a successful nationwide personal injury attorney network called Aid to Injured Motorcyclists (A.I.M) and he had agreed to provide attorneys from his network to do the same at each of the state C.O.C. meetings. In exchange, the motorcycle club community agreed to promote his referral service and A.I.M. His concern was legitimate because as you will hear later, the response from law enforcement was almost dead-on consistent with Lester's concerns, and to this day law enforcement insists that the purpose of NCOM and the COC is to facilitate communication amongst the motorcycle clubs for the purpose of controlling territory and insulating their criminal activity, which is absolute horse shit. NCOM and the COC's are nothing more than communication and motorcycle rights organizations. They are not a sanctioning body for new motorcycle clubs, and they are certainly not criminal organizations. The new N.C.O.M. members went back to their home states and with the help of Lester's attorneys they formed legitimate non-profit organizations in their respective states, determined their own membership criteria, established their own dues and meeting schedules, and were responsible for their own fundraising.

The Washington C.O.C meets once every other month. For years, we met at the Eagles Club in Georgetown, an old industrial neighborhood in downtown Seattle, but the Eagles had just started a construction project that was going to last over a year, so we had moved the meetings to a cool little historical bar up the street called Jules Maes Saloon. It was a sunny Seattle spring day, and I was loving being an Outsider prospect. Since the meeting started at 7:00pm, I would not have time to fight traffic south to the clubhouse and decided it was a good night for a cruise across the 520 floating bridge and some dinner at the Saloon. I made it about two miles from my house when I was pulled over by Kirkland P.D. The cop in his early 50's walked up and asked me "Do you have your gun on you tonight Mr. Burns? " Oh shit, here we go. "Yes, sir, it's on my right hip and my concealed permit is in my wallet with my I.D., so rather than reach for my wallet, I'd prefer that I be allowed to leave my hands on the handlebars and give you permission to retrieve it from my wallet in my rear pocket.", I said. "Let me ask you Mr. Burns, your rocker says Tacoma, your license and bike say Kirkland and I'm contacting you here in Kirkland. Are you starting a chapter of the Outsiders motorcycle gang in my town?" Man, you guys know where I live, and I am out on a ride. What was my violation, I asked? "I'll get back with you, but for now keep those hands on your bars and don't fucking move or I'll fucking shoot you!" It was awesome protecting and serving, not! It was pure, fucked up harassment.

As I sat there, the cop took photos of my prospect rockers and tags. He asked me targeted questions about the club, patches, members, etc. It was a standard intelligence gathering stop and I just sat there and bit my tongue because I was furious inside and did not want to say or do something that would give him justification to arrest me and impound my bike, just to fuck with me and cost me money. That is one of the many games they play, and I had been educated in their ways, so rather than be a dick or play tough biker when cops fucked with me, I just went silent until they let me go. It's better to handle it that way because every now and then when you get pulled over for shit you deserve, you'll run across a really nice cop who treats you with respect and will say "It's all bullshit what they say about you guys. You guys are alright." and they'll let you slide. Respect gets respect in my book; it does not matter whether it is a member of another club or a cop. The only people who do not deserve any respect are pedophiles, rapists, and terrorists. Eventually, officer Friendly let me go with no citation and I was on my way. Next up the 520 bridge and the cruise across Lake Washington into downtown Seattle.

At 7,710 feet long the Evergreen Point Floating Bridge or 520 bridge as we call it is the longest floating bridge in the world and crosses Lake Washington from Bellevue into Seattle near the University of Washington campus. The ride across the bridge provides an amazing view of Mt. Rainer to the south and Seattle and the Olympic Mountains out in front of you. As I left the protection offered by the trees and surrounding houses and rode out onto the bridge, I caught a strong cross wind, and my bike almost blew into the car in the next lane. Oh shit! This is going to be interesting, I thought, and I guided the bike back into the center of my lane. As I rode down the steep incline of the bridge, I could see waves breaking across the bridge onto both lanes and I knew not only was I going to get wet, if I was not careful, I might get blasted off the bike by a wave. I rode onto the main expanse and immediately got blasted by cold lake water crashing over me and into me. It felt like it was everywhere, I was coughing up water like I had been water boarded but I was upright and moving forward towards the blast of cold lake water. I caught the second one as bad as the first one and at that point I was soaked, angry, and now it had become a clear sign that my night was going to suck, but did I pay attention? Hell no. I made it across the bridge and into Jules Maes with no further incidents and as I backed my bike to the curb by the front door, I breathed a big sigh of relief. Time to dry out and have some dinner and a Corona.

I took a seat at the main bar near the door where I could keep an eye on my bike, monitor who was arriving and hear the fella's approach when they came for the meeting. When you are in a motorcycle club and you ride with your brothers every day, you start to know the sound of each brother's bike and can identify your own pack by sound. I got my dinner and was enjoying it when I saw a rider with a New Mexico rocker backing his bike to the curb. Hmmmm, I wonder who invited that guy? I thought. The patch was from a club I had heard of out of the southwest region, but I had not ever seen it in Washington. When the rider took off his helmet, I immediately recognized him. It was Ted the Bear, the former San Diego President of the national club I helped bring into Washington. We had parted on good terms, and I was interested to see what had brought him up to Washington. As soon as he walked through the door, he made eye contact with me, and a look of recognition and relief washed over his face. Ted's history as he had told me was that he had been a national enforcer for the Misfits Motorcycle Club "back in the day", then left the club to raise his family and when he decided he wanted to get back involved with the motorcycle club, the Misfits had closed which is how he found our former club. How he got to this new patch and why was a story that I was eager to hear.

Ted walked right up to me and gave me his formal club introduction which is name, position if any, motorcycle club and chapter/charter. In Ted's case he was a state President. He explained that he had just been sent up to the area for work, was going to be running a Nomad rocker while he was in the area, and he had been invited to the meeting by the secretary of the C.O.C. so that he could make his introduction to the other clubs. Ted took a seat at the bar next to me and we caught up. I told him I had been prospecting for the Outsiders MC and was loving life, and I asked him if he needed help understanding who's who in the zoo up here and how we operated, so he wouldn't step on his dick. "Nah, I've got it all figured out." he said with a repulsive level of arrogance for any patch-holder from out of state. Alright, well when PigPen gets here, I will introduce you. I told him. It was then that I heard the distant rumble of my prospective brothers. Watching an Outsider pack roll in someplace back in those days was something special. We rode peg to peg, eighteen inches off the bike in front of you and when we pulled in somewhere the whole pack would swoop-in and back to the curb in unison. It was beautiful.

I met the fellas on the sidewalk. Since PigPen was chair of the C.O.C. and a lifetime/charter member of the Outsiders, I assumed my role protecting him while he took care of business. I advised him of Ted's arrival and what I knew about Ted's background as a Misfit. Like I said, PigPen has been in the club over forty years and during that time has become a nationally known and respected outlaw biker. He also partied with a lot of Misfit's back in the day, so his history with that club is deep and he knew them well, but he had never heard of Ted. PigPen tells me to go get Ted and bring him over for an introduction. When I get back with Ted, I introduce him as if PigPen did not already have the back-story and explained he had been a Misfit National Enforcer. They chit chatted for a few seconds and then PigPen realizing the guy is full of shit about being a Misfit asked to see his brand. Ted's face went white, and his knees buckled to the point he had to take a half step to steady himself. You see, back when the Misfits were originally around and even since they have re-formed, all new members get the club brand burnt into their chest over their heart when they make member. If he was a Misfit, if he was a National Enforcer, he'd have that brand, and PigPen knew it. Ted made up some bullshit excuse about how they did not make him get the brand because he was thinking about enlisting and did not want it to ruin his chances, and then immediately excused himself to go find the secretary of the C.O.C. During the meeting Ted made his introduction and let everybody know he was just visiting and did not want to step on any toes and then he disappeared. You would think he would want to stay around and get to know the community, but I guess he needed to get home for Sons of Anarchy.

After the meeting I rode back to Tacoma with the fellas and hung out at the clubhouse. The ride home was great, it was warm, and PigPen leads a great pack. Candace met me at the clubhouse and then followed me home to Kirkland to spend the night with me because it was the last night that we were going to see each other for a week since I was going to be leaving town to coach ski racing at the Junior Olympics. The next morning, I woke up at 4:00am, got packed and took my German Shepherd Enzo to the field behind the house and played Frisbee with him for about an hour before heading to the airport and off to the race. This was always a good way for me to re-center and do some thinking, and as I played with Enzo, I was starting to feel torn. Here I was getting ready to leave town and do something I have loved my entire life in an amazing place, and I did not want to leave because I was worried that I would miss out on something as a prospect. I had no idea how right I was.

As the plane touched down, I turned on my phone and I had three missed texts and a phone call from Double D. Something big must be going on back home but I was a prospect, so what the hell did they need me for, and his texts did not say anything other than call me ASAP. I got off the plane and found a place in the airport where I could talk and called Double D. "Twitcheroo!" He exclaimed as he answered the

phone. With the fellas, our nicknames kind of always evolved into multiple variations of the name and so with me there was Twitch, Twitchy,
Twitcheroo, etc. The Twitcheroo gave me hope that there was nothing wrong and his urgent messages were about good news. Once again,
I was wrong. "Bro, you haven't done anything wrong, but we've got a
problem." Oh yeah, what is that? I asked. Double D got serious and said
"You know that guy from your old club that you introduced to PigPen
at the C.O.C. meeting the other night? Well, that motherfucker sent an
email to the secretary of the C.O.C. calling you a snitch and saying he
was going to take care of you." "What the fuck are you talking about?"
I said in disbelief. "Yeah bro, this fucking guy sent an email to the secretary of the C.O.C. and called you, an Outsider prospect, a fucking
snitch and claims you snitched him out to the chairman of the C.O.C.
for being a Misfit and he was going 'take care of the snitch!' We can't
put up with this Twitch." Fucking right! I said. Can I take care of this
as soon as I get home next week? I asked him. Nah bro, we gotta handle
this now. I begged Double D to just wait the four days until I got home,
but he said this was urgent and there was no waiting. "This guy called
you a snitch and threatened you and did it in a very public way, so this
can't wait and we gotta take care of this ASAP, but we'll need you, so
you'll be part of it and you're still standing up for yourself." he told me.

In the motorcycle club world, there are certain things you just can't
say about another patch-holder without causing big problems, which is
part of the reason that the American motorcycle club culture is actually one of the politest cultures I've ever been exposed to. Calling someone a bitch, snitch, or cop in the one-percenter world is just begging to
get instantly beat up. Next to losing/having your patch taken or being
put out bad, those insults are the ultimate disrespect, but Ted took it a
couple steps further and threatened an Outsider prospect and he did it
to the President of another motorcycle club, an officer of the C.O.C.,
and this could not be tolerated. We were way past apologies at this point
and Ted would be educated on the error of his ways. He had threatened
and disrespected me, he had disrespected the Outsiders MC, and in the

motorcycle club world this could not be tolerated, and we were honor bound by the one percent code to respond.

That night after I got done with our ski team meeting, I drove into town and went to a grocery store with no cameras in the parking lot. I waited in my rental car until I spotted a woman in her mid-twenties who it was clear from her physical appearance that she loved her some methamphetamine, walking across the parking lot from her little red Suzuki toward the entrance of the store. I approached her and turned on the charm. After some brief flirting and tactical interviewing, I had gathered enough intelligence to confirm that she would gladly be a willing accomplice for whatever as long as there was money involved, and I offered her fifty bucks to go inside and buy me the cheapest pre-paid phone she could find and then give her another fifty bucks when she came back with the phone, and told her she could keep any change she had left from the purchase. She agreed and few minutes later she returned with the phone. I then drove to a different store and repeated the process with a different minion, but this time for a SIM card. Having what I needed to make the call to Ted, I made a two-hour drive until I crossed state lines, was outside my travel state and made the call. I played it like I was just calling him out of the blue, told him it was good to see him at the C.O.C. meeting the other night, and I wanted him to come down to the clubhouse and have a drink with me and get to know the fellas. He eagerly agreed, told me he would see me tomorrow night and thanked me for the invite multiple times before hanging up the phone. That would be the last conversation I would have with Ted. I removed the SIM card from the phone and crushed the phone into pieces on the concrete, before breaking the SIM card into multiple pieces, all of which was discarded at various locations before I made the long drive back to the hotel where the ski team was staying and going to bed.

I spent the next day on the mountain coaching. It was a beautiful day, cold but sunny and from the 8,000' plus elevation, you could see for miles. It was the women's downhill, speed events were my favorite and

I had gotten to take several really fast (80+mph) and really fun warm-up runs with my girls (my women's ski team) that morning while the mountain was still closed to the public, in order to help them get things dialed in with the tune on their skis and their skiing, and as a result I was in a great mood. My girls skied very well, and we ended up with one on the podium and three in the top five, so it was a great result.

Twitch preparing skis for his racers.

I had not heard from Double D all day but in my mind that was a good thing. He had told me he would make sure to let me know everything went ok, but it was hard for me not to be there and face danger with my prospective brothers. In my mind it was all for one and one for all, and while I knew that I had played a critical role, I would have much rather been on the front lines with my brothers. About 11:30pm that night I got text from Double D that simply said, we had a great time at the clubhouse tonight bro, but we missed you. We love you! I knew things had gone well.

I would later find out that when Ted showed up at the clubhouse, he came bearing a bottle of wine and two loaded .45 autos in shoulder holsters. He was greeted at the front door, immediately searched, and disarmed. At that point Ted knew he was not going to be doing any Hilltop wine tasting with the Tacoma Outsiders. He was told to take a seat at the bar, behind which Double D was standing. It was our house, and the fellas had the tactical advantage and had taken strategic positions in the barroom to maintain that advantage without giving away the true nature of his visit. Ted sat at the bar wide eyed and confused as the fellas surrounded him on all sides. PigPen took up a spot at the bar just to Ted's left as Double D began to question Ted. So, I hear you think our brother Twitch is a fucking snitch? Double D said. After a long pause, Ted denied knowing what Double D was talking about. Now, I fucked up during my time in the one-percent world, but I always held myself accountable and took what I had coming like a man. Ted decided to go a route that goes against the one percenter code and lied. Bad fucking move man. As Ted stammered about not knowing what Double D was talking about and how this was all a big misunderstanding, Double D bitch slapped Ted across the face, and turned over the white sheet of paper that was sitting on the bar between them. Calmly but clearly irritated, Double D began to read the email Ted had sent to the secretary of the C.O.C. out loud. Ted tried to explain what he meant when he said I had "snitched" him out to the chair of the C.O.C. and run my mouth about him. Desperate for a lifeline, Ted turned around and mistaking Spanky for me, he begged for me to help him and explain. Double D immediately stopped reading the email. Wait, do you know who the chair of the C.O.C. is? Double D asked. Yeah, I met him the other night. What is his name? Double D asked. Ted stammered as he tried to recall before admitting he could not remember. PigPen immediately delivered a hard-right to Ted's jaw which spun his head, "PigPen's the name!" he exclaimed. The fellas were supposed to wait for a pre-determined signal, but I guess they got jealous seeing PigPen and Double D having all the fun, and they pounced like a pack of lions, beating Ted out of his chair and onto the floor until he was begging for forgiveness.

The guys were fair and did not take it too far. They picked Ted up off the clubhouse floor and sat him back in this chair. Blood streamed from Ted's head, nose and mouth, and Double D handed him his email and told him to clean himself up and quit leaking on our bar. Double D explained to Ted that you do not ever threaten an Outsider or call them a snitch, and by doing so he had just earned himself an eviction from the Pacific Northwest. By this point, Spanky had moved around behind the bar and was standing next to Double D. Seeing Spanky and mistaking him for me again, Ted said "Jeff." at which point Spanky delivered a hard-left elbow to Ted's face and proudly said, "Outsider Spanky, Tacoma. And you wouldn't be fit to lick the dog shit off my brother Twitch's shoe!" Ted fell face first onto the bar, still clutching his now bloody email to his face attempting to control the bleeding. As Ted steadied himself on his barstool, hugging the bar to keep from falling to the ground in a pile, Double D told him, "You're a fucking mess, now get out of our clubhouse and out of our state." At which point Ted was helped to his vehicle and sent on his way back to where he came from, and a call was placed to his club informing them of his transgression and that he was not welcome in the Northwest anymore and would be coming home. They did not know what to say. All it took was one interaction in the Washington motorcycle club world for this guy to fuck up his club's reputation and get deported, and what made matters worse is that he did it with one of the oldest and most respected outlaw motorcycle clubs in the northwest. What Ted had learned that he should have already known had he really been in a one percent motorcycle club like the Misfits, is that calling someone a snitch is a very serious transgression in the motorcycle club world, so if you're going to use that word you better think about it very carefully and you better have some undisputable evidence to back it up.

I think one thing that is important to discuss about this incident is that there was never any attempt to take Ted's patch and per motorcycle club culture protocol, the Outsiders would have been well within their rights to take Ted's patch. The Outsiders were known as the "patch-police" in the northwest and for decades they displayed the numerous patches of various clubs they had pulled over the years, hung upside-down on the walls lining the entire clubhouse bar. It has been common historically for warriors to take trophies from their vanquished enemies, and taking a patch is the ultimate war trophy in the club world. It was not like we didn't want to take his patch as a sign that we had obtained justice for his disrespect of me and our club, but beginning in about the mid-2000's, the fed's began to charge motorcycle club members with Armed Robbery in Aid of Racketeering and various other R.I.C.O related offences for pulling patches, and they were doing twenty year sentences for simple bar fights that led to a patch pulling. As a result, beginning at this same time, the one percent clubs in the Pacific Northwest all independently made the decision that we were still going to take care of business as needed, but we would not pull patches anymore because we did not want to expose members or the club to a R.I.C.O. In my opinion, this was the best decision the clubs could make in this situation, but what I would realize later is that it opened the door for bullshit clubs like the Iron Order who are full of lames who learned to be bikers by watching T.V and which would ultimately have a devastating effect on the motorcycle club culture. You will see this kind of adaptation/concession of motorcycle club culture by the outlaw clubs again and again over the course of this book, and every time law enforcement comes up with a new way to attack the clubs, the clubs respond by doing away with the aspect of the culture which is exposing the clubs to criminal liability. Like a stone thrown in the middle of a mirror calm pond, that adaptation ripples across the entire American motorcycle club culture and ultimately changes the culture, and the change is not necessarily a positive one.

I want to make something really clear; I do not hate law enforcement or believe all cops are bad. To the contrary, I believe that it is a very small percentage of bad cops who commit civil rights violations and crimes against motorcycle club members and others, but the ringleaders

272 - JEFF "TWITCH" BURNS

of these bad cops are in powerful positions at the Bureau of Alcohol, Tobacco, Firearms and Explosives (ATF) and other federal, state, and local agencies, and this allows their prejudice to spread. As we know from PigPen and the Outsiders experience back in 1979, as well as numerous other motorcycle clubs' experiences of their own, the bad cops are really bad. I do not like to say this without any evidence, so let me back this up with an example from when I was prospecting.

In 2008, shortly after the Mongols opened chapters in Oregon, the major news outlet in the state, the Oregonian released an article titled *Police Hear Rumble as Mongols Motorcycle Club Roll In*. The article which was written by Brian Denson and includes quotes from multiple law enforcement officers, including ATF special agent Jimmy Packard, discusses the Mongols expansion into Oregon and the pending biker war law enforcement fears is coming due to the Mongols encroaching on the territory of the respected Oregon outlaw motorcycle clubs. In his article, Denson chronicles his ride-along with agent Packard while they conducted surveillance and profiling stops as part of an outlaw motorcycle gang intelligence gathering operation, they were conducting in conjunction with a Free Souls MC anniversary party. In the article Denson writes, "A few moments later, Special Agent Jimmy Packard, a veteran of the U.S. Bureau of Alcohol, Tobacco, Firearms and Explosives, pulled his SUV up to a pack of Mongols gathered in the parking lot of the Super 8 Motel in nearby Springfield. The Mongols listened as Packard, with a strong North Carolina twang and vocabulary as salty as any biker, told them police had just stopped rival club members out "Mongol huntin'."

This could not have been further from the truth. What had really happened was at the intelligence checkpoint by the Free Souls party, a Portland Outsider, a Gypsy Joker, and a member of Brother Speed were stopped together in a car. In the trunk of the vehicle, the Outsider had his legally possessed pistol. He was charged with driving on an expired license and released with no other charges. Nobody was out "Mongol huntin", they were simply on their way to the Free Souls birthday party and Packard's statements are a great example of how law enforcement, particularly ATF, uses the media to falsely portray motorcycle clubs as warring gangs to the public. What is more upsetting to me about this specific incident is that Packard deliberately lied to the Mongols about alleged rival club members out Mongol huntin in an attempt to create conflict and violence between the clubs. Fortunately, in this case, the Mongol Presidents who had brought the club into Oregon were former Outsiders prospects, great guys and know the political climate of the motorcycle club world in Oregon very well. Rather than cause conflict, the Mongols President Mooch picked up the phone and called Double D and said Hey, did you see that article in the Oregonian? Do we got a problem? Double D was just getting ready to call Mooch when he got the call and after a brief conversation about what a jackass agent Packard is and how scary it is that the feds deliberately lie to us and the media to try and start shit between the clubs, the article and agent Packard's lies were a non-issue. What I would come to realize later is that this deliberate use of the media to spread misinformation or lies about the clubs to vilify them and attempt to create violent conflicts between the clubs, is one of many very questionable techniques that ATF uses in their Enhanced Undercover Operations when they investigate outlaw motorcycle clubs.

What made this more disgusting to me is that before the Mongols started flying colors in Oregon, they met with all of the other outlaw clubs out of respect and none of us had any issue with their move. Present in that meeting were multiple ATF informants who were inside the Mongols and on ATF's payroll as part of Operation Black Rain, working as Contract Sources of Information. The ATF and special agent Packard knew that none of us had a problem with the Mongols and did not want a problem, but the ATF, Eugene P.D. and others were doing their best to try and stir up a biker war in Oregon. In my opinion they did this in an attempt to incite the Mongols to commit crimes that could be included in the indictments from Operation Black Rain that was coming to a close. Law enforcement does not want us getting along because it disproves their false narrative and that costs them huge, specialized anti-outlaw motorcycle gang grant money, cool surveillance vehicles and equipment, paid speaking engagements, lucrative book deals, movie deals, and international travel to preach their hate as "experts" on a global scale.

On May 2nd, we buried my first Outsider, a Portland charter member named Shorty. Because of some internal controversy surrounding the member who died in the clubhouse, the Portland chapter elected not to give him a funeral, meaning this was the first Outsider funeral I had participated in. Tacoma rode down to Portland the morning of the funeral and even though we were early, there were already about a hundred bikes lined up outside the clubhouse. As we backed our bikes to the curb, I noticed an electrical contractor's van parked across the street from the clubhouse. What made it stand out is that even though it was parked in front of a house, it had the whole curb but was parked well in front of the front door of the home making it appear out of place. Instantly, this stood out to me as poor cop surveillance tradecraft and the reason the van was so far forward of the front door was because in order for the cameras and hidden viewing ports in the van to have a view of the clubhouse, they had to get passed the tree in the front yard of the house and had to be pulled that far forward. The vehicle was consistent with several other specialized surveillance vehicles I had used in my professional career, right down to the large storage tubes on top used to conceal microphones and pinhole cameras. I pointed out the suspected surveillance vehicle to the fellas. Over the next couple of hours, the crowd would grow to several hundred and as the riders fired up their bikes, the suspicious electrical van drove off. A few minutes later the pack took off for the service. I was assigned road-guard and with a pack that size it means you are riding with your hair on fire down the center line, or into oncoming traffic to get out ahead of the pack and block your assigned intersection. We were on the freeway doing about eighty-five miles per hour into downtown Portland when all the sudden the traffic ahead of the pack was at a dead stop. Rather than slow down and move through in an orderly fashion, we just split and continued single file screaming past traffic in between vehicles coming within inches of disaster until finally we broke through traffic to the exit and the pack morphed back together.

As we made the right turn onto the street the funeral home was located on, there was a small dirt parking lot located directly across from mortuary. Parked in the middle of that lot with the best view possible of the funeral home was the same electrical van that had been in front of the clubhouse. In addition, there were two other vehicles that were backed in and had men watching us with binoculars and cameras. About this time, a fucking professional camera crew set up on a hill across the street from the funeral home and was clearly filming us. This was hugely disrespectful; all we were trying to do was bury our dead brother and they would not like it if we came to their funerals, treated them like circus freaks, took photos, and brought a professional camera crew. Double D asked me to go with him and T-Bob the Portland President to talk to the cops across the street. Double D explained that it was hugely offensive to us that they were there and asked to know why. The cop explained that the Mongols were having their 1st anniversary party in town tonight and they were there to protect us in-case the Mongols showed up, to make sure we did not try and go crash the Mongols party, and the cops said they were not leaving. Next, I went and approached the camera crew who told me they were making a documentary about outlaw motorcycle gangs and asked me to do an interview. Fuck your interview and fuck you! I said. You wouldn't like it if we came to your brother's funeral and filmed, so why the fuck are you going to do it to us? With that we walked back across the street and got on with the service.

This was just one more instance where law enforcement was deliberately harassing us, using the media to feed a false narrative about a pending biker war to the public to vilify motorcycle clubs, and attempting to create conflict between the clubs. In reality, the Mongols had invited the Outsiders and the other outlaw motorcycle clubs of Oregon to their anniversary party that night and there was absolutely no need for the law enforcement harassment or the flagrant waste of tax-payer money.

A couple of years later a documentary called *Gang World: The 1%ers*, would be featured on the National Geographic Channel and it would shed light on what really happened that day at Shorty's funeral. What the documentary revealed is that the ATF and multiple Oregon law enforcement agencies were involved in surveillance operations against the Outsiders Motorcycle Club and Mongols that day because they believed that the Oregon outlaw motorcycle clubs were angry at the Mongols for moving into Oregon and based on intelligence, they had there was going to be an attack by the Outsiders and other Oregon outlaw clubs against the Mongols at their anniversary party. The documentary includes footage that was shot at the Free Souls MC anniversary party and was mentioned in Denson's article in the Oregonian about rival clubs out Mongol Huntin', and it promotes an identical bullshit narrative of the Oregon outlaw motorcycle clubs on the verge of war with the Mongols. What is important about the footage is that when they show the Mongols anniversary party, there are Gypsy Joker and Mongols mingling together chatting and laughing on the sidewalk in front of the party. That is not the kind of behavior you would see if clubs were about to go to war. I would have loved to have been there at their party, but we had our own party, and the clubhouse was overflowing with motorcycle clubs from all over the west coast.

But Jeff, the cops might not have known you guys were invited to the party? To which I say, bullshit. They had multiple informants and undercovers in that meeting and inside the Mongols for over four years, they conducted extensive surveillance on all the outlaw clubs, knew we all got along in Oregon, and they deliberately chose to ignore everything they knew to be fact and then used the media to promote their false narrative to the public to try and incite conflict and violence between the clubs.

The next day we had a mandatory meeting at the Portland clubhouse. Mandatory meetings are held a couple of times per year and rotate between the Portland and Tacoma clubhouses. Mandatory's cover planning for upcoming events, discussing financial issues, issues of importance or concern to the club, membership issues, etc. Mavrick had been prospecting over a year when he made member the month before, and while I was at ten and a half months, I figured Portland would make me run to a full year or more for the Squeeze issue. I knew that I had more than earned my patch at that point and I was being held up because of the Squeeze incident and the politics between Portland and Tacoma, but during the party the night before several of the Portland members referred to me as brother and more than one Tacoma member got loose enough that they made it clear I would be coming up for a vote that day. Just like a regular meeting, when the meeting starts, the prospects head out front. In Portland, the prospects stand across the street from the clubhouse, so across the street we went. It was a cold day and the rain rolled in and out on us as the meeting went on inside. After about three hours they took a break for lunch while us prospects tended bar, and then it was back outside to stand across the street some more. The nice thing was the rain had stopped and now it was just cold.

After about two more hours we heard the lock work on the metal door of the clubhouse, and it swung open and the Portland Sergeant at arms yelled "Prospects!" What the fuck? I thought I was getting brought up. We ran across the street and took our place in front of the pool table facing the membership. The Portland Sarge slammed the metal door shut and locked it. T-Bob was the Portland President now, so he was leading the meeting since it was in Portland. "T-T-T-T-T-Twwwwwwww, T-T-T-T-T-Twwwwwwww, T-T-T-T-T-Twwwwwwww, Twitch. Wa, Wa, Wa, We wwwant to talk to you about the information you've been providing the cops.", the fat red-faced old tweeker stuttered. What the fuck! I was furious, they were pulling this shit again, and this time it was with Tacoma in the room. I was instantly ready to fight the entire room. I do not know what you're talking about T-Bob! I snapped and my death glare focused on T-Bob's bloodshot eyes. He eventually went on to stutter out that members had seen me signaling and passing information to the cops at Shorty's funeral the day before. That is bullshit T-Bob, you're fucking wrong! I snarled as I began to charge the bar that he was standing behind. As I crossed the room Spanky intercepted me with a big smile and a paper bag in his left hand. Whoa, whoa, whoa brother, you want this more than you want to kick his ass. Congratulation's brother he said as he slammed the bag into my chest and gave me a hug. I reached inside the bag and felt the center patch I had worked so hard for, ignored the congratulations from the room and retreated towards the pool table to sew it on. I was happy I had made member, but I was furious that I had made member by being accused of being an informant and passing information to the cops, and I was furious that Tacoma had allowed it to happen in their presence.

I would later come to find out that after my membership vote when the club was trying to decide how they were going to make me member, T-Bob chimed in that he had a great idea and asked if he could handle it and the club agreed without finding out what his idea was. I had busted my ass for ten and a half months and put over 27,000 miles on my bike during that period and now I wanted nothing to do with them other than beat on them for disrespecting me like that and ruining what is supposed to be the best experience in a patch-holders life. As I prepped to sew my center patch on, Pigpen could tell I was pissed and came over and apologized for how things went down, and he began to help me sew on my center patch. Shortly after my brother Single D came over and started to help. Then the announcement was made. Pack to Tacoma is leaving in ten minutes for all who are going. What the fuck? I just made member and now if I want to ride with my new Tacoma brothers, I somehow must get this patch sewed on by hand in ten minutes. Ain't no way that was going to happen. I guess I am going back to Tacoma dressed like a prospect. I changed my mind, I'll improvise and use safety pins to hold it on, I'm done being a prospect. Before I got the safety pins out a Portland member snapped this pic of me and Pigpen with my shiny new patch. Of course, Mavrick and his giant ego had to photo-bomb the pic. If you look close at the Outsiders Portland center patch painting in the background, the slashes were cut by Portland Police and several other pieces of memorabilia were deliberately destroyed when they illegally raided the clubhouse on that illegal warrant in 1979.

Outsider Twitch 1%er immediately after receiving his patch.

With my patch safety-pinned on, they let me ride up front with Double D on the way home to Tacoma. Back in Tacoma, Candace met us at the clubhouse. Most of the fellas were tired from the weekend and went home but Double D and Spanky stayed, along with Candace and Spank's wife Nicky who joined us at the clubhouse for dinner and drinks. It was then that I realized that no matter what, I was a Tacoma Outsider, and I was home with my brothers, so life was good.

At the annual Sturgis Motorcycle Rally in August 2008, Detective Ron Smith with the Seattle Police Department took his hate for the Hells Angels and outlaw bikers to the ultimate level when he tried to kill one. This was not an on-the-job incident though, this was something much more interesting and like all of the incidents involving dirty cops and bikers it would get covered up and Smith and the other members of his gang wouldn't even get a slap on the wrist, while the bikers would receive serious criminal charges.

Now I've never talked to any of the cops involved but their version of the story was that a "group of outlaw bikers" in reality an out of shape Hells Angel from California and a Prospect from Washington, came into the Loud American Road House in Sturgis and recognized Smith as the detective who had testified in the Hells Angels RICO case, so they assaulted him and he shot the Hells Angel in self-defense because he thought he was going to die.

I knew both the Hells Angel and the Prospect involved in this incident and their version goes something like this. Neither of them knew who Smith was but they knew the Iron Pigs MC was a cop club and Smith and the other four men with him were all wearing colors identifying them as members of the Iron Pigs MC, so they took the only spot they could find in the bar which was still within just feet of where the Iron Pigs were sitting. They both told me that Smith immediately started talking shit to the Washington Prospect about AJ, taunting him about sending his brothers to prison, and making over the top disrespectful comments about the Hells Angels, until he was honor bound to respond. They said it was a five on two bar fight and as soon as Smith got punched and went down, he pulled a gun and shot the Hells Angel who was unarmed. Once the shot was fired the cops all pulled badges and identified themselves as cops and rendered aid until local law en-

282 - JEFF "TWITCH" BURNS

forcement arrived and arrested the Hells Angel, the prospect, and all five members of the Iron Pigs MC. Almost immediately the cover up started.

Once the law enforcement figured out that all the Iron Pigs were either cops or firefighters the justice system split and rather than arresting the cops, including Smith who shot someone, taking them in for blood-draws like they did the Hells Angel and prospect, then send them to jail and force them to come up with ridiculously high bail, the cops got to go home with no blood draws to determine if the cops had been drinking or using other drugs while they partied like outlaw bikers at Sturgis. Smith had shot a Hells Angel in front of thousands of eyewitnesses at the most famous motorcycle rally in the world and he had done it in a bar fight while wearing motorcycle club colors, so there was going to have to be a little show before they could sweep this incident under the rug. A Mead County grand jury indicted Detective Smith for aggravated assault, perjury, and carrying a concealed weapon without a permit. Also charged in the incident were the four Iron Pigs who were with Smith at the Loud American and included Scott Lazalde of Bellingham, WA, James Rector of Ferndale, WA, Erik Pingel of Aurora, CO, and Seattle Police Sgt. Dennis McCoy of Seattle. Both Lazalde and Rector are longtime members of the U.S. Customs and Border Inspection. All were charged with carrying a concealed weapon in a bar. The Hells Angel member involved received the same charges as Smith and was facing fifteen years in prison.

The incident drew national attention because it was the first incident of its kind where a bunch of drunk shitbag cops in a cop motorcycle club wearing a three-piece patch like an outlaw club, and carrying guns, had started a bar fight and shot a Hells Angel, and they had done it at the most famous motorcycle rally on the planet. While the law enforcement agencies the Iron Pigs worked for vowed to launch their own investigations to determine any wrongdoing, the motorcycle club world knew the Hells Angel would end up with a criminal conviction, nothing would happen to Smith and the other dirty cops because it would be covered up, and that is exactly what happened. Since law enforcement deliberately did not conduct blood draws on the shitbag cops, they couldn't prove they were intoxicated at the time of the incident which would have been a crime and invalidate their right that they had as law enforcement officers to carry a concealed firearm interstate and into a bar. Witnesses in the bar confirmed the Iron Pigs had been talking shit to the Hells Angel and Prospect before the shooting. Ultimately the charge of aggravated assault against the officers was dropped because the prosecutor determined the attack by the Hells Angel was premeditated, the perjury charge was dismissed, and the charge of carrying a concealed weapon was dismissed as were those charges for the other cops involved since there was no blood evidence to prove intoxication. The Hells Angel and prospect involved were forced to take a sweetheart plea deal to avoid spending decades in prison for defending themselves against an attack by shitbag corrupt cops.

I have no reason to doubt what Joey and the prospect told me about the incident and that the drunk shitbag cops started it. They said they tolerated it for as long as they could because they knew they were all cops and they knew the cops would likely pull guns and shoot or arrest them for a bullshit RICO witness intimidation charge because of Smith's connection to the RICO, and that is totally reasonable to believe. Because we constantly must worry about the cops setting us up for anything they can, we have to be incredibly familiar with RICO and being a Hells Angel, Joey would be an expert because it was the biggest threat he faced on a day-to-day basis as a Hells Angel, whether he was involved in criminal activity or not.

15

OPERATION BLACK RAIN

Mongol Ruben "Doc" Cavazos, Mongol "Lil Rubes" Cavazos, Mongol
"Ogre" and Mongol "Bouncer" attend the Book Expo Celebrity
Dinner at Restaurant 208 on May 30, 2008 in Beverly Hills, California.
Photo by Getty Images

On August 30th, 2008, Doc Cavazos was exposed as a thief and a liar, and Doc, his son Lil' Rubes, and brother Al "The Suit" Cavazos were all kicked out of the Mongols MC in bad standing, at which point Hector "Largo" Gonzalez became national president, immediately changed the direction of the club and began the process of restoring the Mongols to a respected outlaw motorcycle club.

On October 21st, 2008, a massive Bureau of Alcohol, Tobacco, Firearms & Explosives (ATF) undercover operation targeting the Mongols wrapped up with the arrests of Doc Cavazos and 37 other Mongols

MC members, when 110 arrest warrants and 160 search warrants were executed in California, Nevada, Colorado, Ohio, Oregon, and Washington for various federal racketeering charges. It turns out that Doc's lax membership standards and process combined with his desire to expand the club to as many areas as possible had allowed twelve ATF undercover operatives to infiltrate the Mongols for a second time in less than ten years. I will never forget the morning the raids went down. I printed off a copy of the indictment and headed straight for Double D's house. Normally, I would not have been too concerned about an indictment involving the Mongols but this one was different. The feds were not just trying to put these guys in prison, the indictment made it clear that they were going to try and take the Mongols patch using trademark law and forfeit it as an asset using the R.I.C.O. statute, alleging that the Mongols were using the patch as a tool of intimidation to further the criminal enterprise. This was huge, the patch is the flag of the club and without that patch they have no identity, not to mention it appeared to me to be a violation of the First Amendment. Even worse, if they could do it to the Mongols, they could do it to any motorcycle club and effectively shut down every motorcycle club they could indict and convict.

I got to Double D's and walked in the front door to find him sitting on his couch, where he spends most days. Bro, did you see this shit with the Mongols? "Yeah, but they brought it on themselves." he said. I could not disagree. In my opinion, under Doc's influence the Mongols MC had gone from a righteous outlaw motorcycle club that was just trying to survive and turned it into a bunch of gangbangers on wheels. You still had some good chapters like the Oregon guys, but the Cali guys were not bikers. Double D was adamant that what the feds were trying to do by taking the Mongols patch was a violation of the First Amendment and would never be allowed.

As smart as Double D is, he really does not understand shit when it comes to criminal law, especially the R.I.C.O. Act and outlaw motorcycle clubs or how they are targeted and investigated. I on the other hand have studied every investigation, the resulting indictments, and resolutions of every outlaw biker R.I.C.O. case including the Outlaws various cases over the years, the Warlocks and Sons of Silence cases, the Bandidos RICO's, the Mongols cases, the Devils Disciples, and all the various Hells Angels cases including the Washington Hells Angels RICO which I provided investigative assistance on. Plus, at this point I had over one hundred hours of law enforcement outlaw motorcycle gang training and had received my undercover training from Charlie Fuller, the now retired head of the ATF's Undercover School, and Dave Reddeman, a detective with the Seattle P.D., who spent four years undercover in an outlaw motorcycle club as part of an undercover operation for ATF, so when it comes to outlaw motorcycle gang investigations and prosecutions, I could put the big picture together and what I understood was not only that law enforcement's undercover techniques and tactics they used against outlaw motorcycle clubs were getting much more sophisticated, aggressive, and questionable, but beginning with Josh's case they started to target the club's patch using the trademark the club held for their logo and name.

Why they didn't pursue trademark forfeiture in Josh's case, I don't know, but my guess is it is because the federal government believes that the Hells Angels are a much wealthier club than the Mongols, and since the HA have a proven track record of aggressively and successfully defending their trademark in civil cases, and Operation Black Rain was well underway at the time of Josh and the Washington Hells Angels convictions, I believe the feds viewed the Mongols as an easier, less sophisticated target, with fewer resources to fight for their patch and trademark which would give the feds a higher likelihood for success against the Mongols. In addition, I knew that the extra time they had to prep to take the Mongols patch would mean they would have done their homework, and the battle to save their patch would be incredibly sophisticated and expensive for the Mongols to fight.

We both had our positions on the situation and a few days later, on October 23rd, 2008, U.S. District Court Judge Florence-Marie Cooper granted an injunction that prohibited Mongols Motorcycle Club members, their family members, and associates from wearing, licensing, selling, or distributing the club's name or logo, because according to law enforcement they use the logo and name as an identity and as a form of intimidation to fulfill their goals and further the criminal enterprise. ATF began raiding Mongols member's residences and seizing their patches and any items bearing the clubs name and logo including cigarette lighters and a refrigerator door. Obviously, the motorcycle club world as a whole freaked out and some clubs which had their patches trademarked dropped their trademark thinking it would insulate them from a similar fate as the Mongols. Double D still insisted there was nothing to worry about, but I knew that the Mongols fight to save their patch was going to be a long and expensive one that would require the help of the entire motorcycle club community to fight, and it would end up taking over ten years to work its way through the courts system in multiple manifestations of the same case.

16

THE BEGINNING OF A REVOLUTION

Every January, the Washington C.O.C. and a motorcycle rights organization known as A.B.A.T.E. hold a legislative day at the state capitol in which bikers meet with their legislators to gain awareness and support for issues effecting the Washington motorcycle community that require legislative attention. In 2009, the Washington state motorcycle club community was starting to work together, and for the first time in years the Washington Confederation of Clubs had over one hundred bikes from various motorcycle clubs in the pack on the ride into the capitol. When we arrived, Washington State Patrol was set up and channeled us into a parking lot off to the side of the capitol that was ringed with tall hedges and had been specifically designated for us. While we were inside meeting with our legislators attempting to gain support for our motorcycle profiling bill to prohibit law enforcement harassment and discrimination, the W.S.P. had a trooper outside who was captured on video crawling through the bushes recording the license plate and identifying information from every motorcycle in the parking lot. Double D and I were inside the pavilion of the capitol when a member of one of the support clubs ran up and told us what one of their members had captured video of. This was crazy, we were all peacefully assembled at the state capitol for a prearranged legislative day and the cops are outside goin' Secret Squirrel crawling through the bushes to spy on us. They were not doing it to anyone else, so it was unacceptable they were

288

doing it to us, and it was an example of motorcycle profiling following us all the way to the steps of the state capitol that we would later use to evidence our need for legislative relief.

Our C.O.C. attorney Martin Fox, sent then Washington State Governor Christine Gregoire and the Chief of the Washington State Patrol a letter calling out W.S.P and complaining of their unconstitutional motorcycle profiling. In response, Chief Batiste responded that it was proper for the trooper to be gathering information on motorcycle club members because there is a high propensity for violence when motorcycle clubs gather, and the intelligence gathering would give law enforcement a list of potential witnesses should any violence occur. We were gathered in the same place, the state capitol, to exercise our Constitutional rights as American's to meet with our legislators, present our issues, and attempt to gain sponsors for a bill preventing law enforcement from profiling us, and in his written response the Chief of the State Police had given an incredibly strong piece of evidence that we needed to show that the problem of motorcycle profiling went all the way to the highest level of Washington state law enforcement. It also solidified with me the importance of the use of video to document incidents of motorcycle profiling, as well as the use of counter-surveillance at motorcycle rights events to document the harassment we were experiencing when we all gathered peacefully for the purpose of fighting for our civil rights. To me, that was inexcusable. They could fuck with us any other time and while I did not like it, I took it as part of the life I had chosen and a reminder of the battle that we were ALL fighting, and it just fueled my fire more.

The way I see it is the motorcycle club culture is at war for its survival. The enemy is formidable, sophisticated, and what makes it even worse is we must fight by the rules, and they do not have any rules. At this point in my professional career, I had extensive physical surveillance, counter-surveillance, and surveillance detection training and experience. I knew that if law enforcement was going to use surveillance to gather intelligence on our motorcycle rights movement, then we needed to use counter-surveillance to document their surveillance and motorcycle profiling that was occurring at our events, in order to use it as evidence in our push for motorcycle profiling legislation. In my personal life, I had been an outlaw biker dealing with law enforcement harassment and surveillance for over a decade at this point and I knew that the only person that hates getting their photo taken more than a biker is a cop, so I figured that could be exploited and may help chase away some of the hostile surveillance at our events.

I drafted a manual titled *Countering Hostile Surveillance* which presented the idea that if the Washington motorcycle clubs' Sergeant at Arms and prospects who were responsible for their clubs security at these events simply took on the task of filming any law enforcement surveillance or other profiling they experienced, whether it be at a Confederation of Clubs event or other incident and then forwarded that to me, I could maintain a central repository of profiling evidence that we could reference and use as needed in our push for profiling legislation. The manual also laid out basic surveillance detection and counter-surveillance techniques and their specific application to the motorcycle rights movement. When it was done, I was really proud of what I had produced for the motorcycle club community and the motorcycle rights movement, and I thought we were going to take civil rights movements to a whole new level of sophistication. Man was I fucking wrong. Before I got too proud of myself, I did a quick Google search and learned that over the years several other various American civil rights movements have suffered from the same plight and they used the same techniques I was proposing, but they took it even further and had trained each other to use various techniques and tactics to attempt to identify undercover agents and informants. We were not ever going there as I knew that was just inviting a world of complications and potential for drama for the movement, but I was convinced this manual and these new tactics and techniques would help with our effort and protect the movement.

At the next Confederation of Clubs meeting the topic of law enforcement harassment, surveillance and the Black Thursday incident was the primary focus of not only the meeting but the conversations that were taking place outside the meeting as well. Everyone was just as offended as I was that law enforcement would conduct intelligence gathering activities on us while we were at the capitol fighting for our rights from just such harassment, and they did it on all our dime because it was tax-payer money paying for it. I was just a member/officer of the Outsiders Motorcycle Club and not a C.O.C. officer, or even our club representative yet, but I was given the floor, copies of the manual were distributed to all the clubs, and I explained the process and my proposal. All the clubs responded enthusiastically to the idea. I think part of the reason the idea was so easily and well received by the clubs was because we all understood that it was time to go to war and this was a way to fight fair with an enemy who wasn't required to fight fair like us and use the same level of sophistication as our enemy, and that gave us all hope, a sense of unity and pride in our organizations, and the Washington motorcycle club community as a whole. Counter-surveillance proved to be a very effective tool for us here in Washington and I would end up teaching it at various state and regional C.O.C. meetings as well as national N.C.O.M. conventions all over the United States over the next several years, and my system would be adopted by every major motorcycle club in America.

ATF oversees developing and disseminating propaganda against outlaw motorcycle club culture and their word is considered gospel by gang investigators and law enforcement all over the country. In fact, in 2009, Jeremy Sheetz, one of their intelligence analysts who is assigned to ATF Office of Strategic Intelligence and Information, and sits on the board of directors for the International Outlaw Motorcycle Gang Investigators Association, a position that allows him to preach ATF's bullshit narrative on outlaw motorcycle clubs to law enforcement all over the world, Sheetz created and disseminated a report titled *Outlaw Motorcycle Gangs (OMGs) and the Military*. The report included the names, photos, and biographical information of outlaw motorcycle club members from all over the United States who were active or former military members or DoD contractors, most of whom had no criminal history whatsoever, yet the report described these men as national security threats, "Military Trained Gang Members (MTGM)", and domestic terrorists. It was distributed to local, state, federal, and military law enforcement agencies all over the United States, as well as to several foreign law enforcement agencies. The report included maps and charts depicting active duty, prior service, and or retired military personnel who were current members of one percent outlaw motorcycle clubs that according to the report, "are accepted by law enforcement to be specifically engaged in criminal activity." The report also included outlaw motorcycle club members who were employed on military compounds, bases, instillations, and Federal buildings in the United States and abroad.

What's particularly concerning about ATF labeling these men security threats and domestic terrorists without any criminal history or evidence of criminal activity beyond their membership in their motorcycle clubs, is that several of the outlaw motorcycle club members identified in the report held active security clearances, which means that they had passed comprehensive government background investigations that went well beyond just a simple criminal history check, and those investigations deemed the men were not a national security threat to the United States. But that does not matter to ATF because what they say without evidence is gospel and it does not matter that facts, evidence, and logic contradict what they say. Innocent until proven guilty is just not a concept that the ATF agents and intelligence specialists who investigate outlaw motorcycle clubs recognize, and according to the ATF, those men of honor with special skillsets who are trying to use them to make an honest living are really Military Trained Gang Members (MTGM's), a threat to our national security, and domestic terrorists, solely because they belong to an outlaw motorcycle club, and because of that membership they are someone to be feared and vilified rather than appreciated for their service to our country.

The ATF propaganda worked, the law enforcement world was clearly concerned by the thought of MTGM / Domestic Terrorists taking over their communities, and over the first few weeks following the report's release ATF received approximately thirty-six referrals from numerous law enforcement agencies with updated intelligence to include in a follow-up report. For the next year, ATF analysts coordinated with more than forty-five law enforcement agencies and the DoD to consolidate the follow-up report. ATF's unconstitutional propaganda war against outlaw motorcycle club members who had or were serving their country was born, and just because ATF said so, good men were now terrorists and not only had their honorable military service been disparaged by labeling them Military Trained Gang Members, but now they were terrorists which allowed for the involvement of the Department of Homeland Security and the ability for federal law enforcement to use the U.S. Patriot Act to circumvent the U.S. Constitution in their "Outlaw Motorcycle Gang" investigations, and hide all the evidence and records related to their investigations and operations as national security secrets, thus avoiding any scrutiny or accountability for their corruption. Over the years, ATF and law enforcement nationally would go on to publicly vilify outlaw motorcycle club members who are firefighters, a mayor, and even a former member of the Vagos during his campaign for City Council who fortunately was still elected by his community despite law enforcement's effort to destroy him.

On January 23rd, 2009, there was a huge development in the Mongols case. Doc Cavazos flipped and cut a plea agreement with the federal government in which he forfeited the rights to the Mongols trademarks to the Department of Justice. Hardly the hardcore gangster he wanted the world to believe he was, Doc was the very first Mongol to plead guilty to count one of the indictment and confessed in his plea agreement which was written by the government, that he directed a criminal organization called the Mongols Motorcycle Club which committed acts of murder and drug trafficking to enrich the members and organization. He went on to confess "that the Mongols Registered trademarks afforded a source of influence over the RICO enterprise that the defendant admits he established, operated, controlled, conducted and participated in the conduct of." In his guilty plea Cavazos agreed to the forfeiture of all rights, title, and interest in certain assets acquired or maintained by him as a result of his violation of (the RICO statute) including the Mongols registered trademarks or marks, and he admitted the marks were subject to forfeiture to the United States. The government also cited the guilty pleas to count one of the indictment by numerous defendants besides Cavazos as proof that the Mongols Motorcycle Club is a criminal conspiracy and the name and patch are subject to forfeiture, and argued that the pleas demonstrate "a nexus between the violation of which the defendant has been convicted (or to which he has pled) and the property sought." This was not good at all for the Mongols or any outlaw motorcycle club for that matter, and it appeared the Mongols fate was sealed. I knew that this patch issue could eventually become a threat for all of us and nationally we may all need to financially help support the Mongols legal battle if it came to it, as this case would set precedent one way or another that would impact the entire motorcycle club community, and we needed to make sure it was in our favor.

On a cold and sometimes rainy Saturday in March, the Washington C.O.C. held a special meeting at the King Oscar Hotel in Tacoma, for the purpose of a allowing a Bandido from Texas named Gimme Jimmy, introduce his U.S. Defenders program in an effort to get the Washington COC involved. The U.S. Defenders / Corps of Independent Riders (C.O.I.R.) that Jimmy created is essentially a networking program that allows rapid communications and calls for action to be disseminated amongst the club community. The way it works is each state chooses a "Commander" and "Lt. Commander" to organize, run, and publicly represent the program in that state. Each of the member motorcycle clubs appoints a Defender and alternate whose job is to monitor their emails daily for U.S. Defenders communications, brief their club on any communication or call to action immediately upon receipt, and then ensure that any call to action has timely and appropriate participation from their club.

Several clubs or their members who we were close with gathered at our clubhouse that morning. It was Tacoma's birthday party that night and some of the Portland brothers like Gordy and Gutz had come up Friday to hang out with Tacoma and go to the C.O.C. meeting. Everyone was in a good mood, excited, and it was not because of Jimmy's presentation, it was the fact that we all got to hang out together since there was a C.O.C. meeting. The more time the clubs spent focusing on our unified fight for survival, the more it fired us up, and genuine friendships were developing amongst all the member clubs of the Washington C.O.C. I knew the meeting was going to be a big one, but I would have never anticipated that there would be over five-hundred bikes in the parking lot when we made the left turn off Hosmer Street. Now, to you five hundred bikes might not sound like all that many, but in a state where it rains nine months out of the year in the part of the state where ninety percent of the population lives, the clubs do not have huge numbers, so five hundred patch-holders was a huge showing. All the one-percent clubs were there (Outsiders, Bandidos, Gypsy Joker, and Hells Angels), as were every support club, Christian, veteran, chick club, social interest club, and they came in large numbers. So many in fact that when we arrived, the conference room we were having the meeting in had reached capacity, overflowed and the river of people trying to be within ear shot of the meeting ran down the hallway, and down the first flight of stairs, leaving several hundred patch-holders outside socializing in between the cold intermittent winter Washington rain squalls.

Inside the conference room, Double D and PigPen took their seats at the C.O.C. officers table at the front of the room. I took a position standing within arms-reach of Double D and PigPen. After some brief statements from PigPen and Double D, the floor was given to Gimme Jimmy. I had initially met Jimmy a few months earlier when he had come up and met with the officers of the C.O.C. to discuss him coming to a meeting and introducing his program to the Washington C.O.C.

Jimmy was a Bandidos MC National Officer and the first Texas Bandido I had met other than Yankee, a Nomad who was now living in Tacoma, and just like Yankee, Jimmy was a loud and proud Bandido which I was totally cool with, but it was clear he was used to being in Texas because during our conversations he occasionally made comments that the Bandidos would just "tell people what to do.", and that was not going to fly with the Washington motorcycle clubs. Jimmy had a protection detail made up of Yankee and several Washington and Texas Bandidos, but his primary protection for that trip was Austin Walt. Walt was a big dude, 6'7", well over 300lbs, dressed all in black, with black gator skin boots, and a large gold chain with diamond and gold Bandidos pendant. I think the only thing I heard Austin Walt say that entire trip was "Austin Walt, Bandidos." When he introduced himself, everything about his presence screamed he was only there to protect Jimmy, and he would do whatever it took to make sure he did his job.

When Jimmy presented the U.S. Defenders, his tell people what to do attitude put-off everyone who was not wearing red and gold in that room. Jimmy went so far as to tell us who was going to be the Commander and Lt. Commander of the U.S. Defenders in Washington, and he had taken it upon himself to appoint a Bandido who had not been involved in the C.O.C. as Commander of the U.S. Defenders. Are you fucking kidding me? I thought as Jimmy and his Texan twang laid out a plan in a manner that was insulting to the motorcycle clubs of Washington, and I knew it would never fly in its current form in Washington State. When Jimmy got done and PigPen asked the room what we thought, there were some immediate objections, and it was clear the Washington C.O.C. was not going to be told what to do and we were not going be involved in the U.S. Defenders. The look of disbelief, shock, and confusion that painted Jimmy's face as club after club got up and voiced their opinion was great, and it was clear Jimmy had never had a room full of clubs speak to him like that. Nobody disrespected Jimmy or his club, but they made it clear they would not be pushed around, and Double D eventually stepped in before things got sideways and he politically correctly brought the meeting to a point where PigPen closed it out.

We went back to the Tacoma clubhouse for the birthday party. It was the Tacoma chapter's thirty fifth anniversary and motorcycle clubs had come from all over the west coast to celebrate with us. By 10:00pm, bikes lined both sides of the street up and down the entire block on L Street. The front lawn and both front and back yards were full of members of various motorcycle clubs socializing. Inside the bar was a who's-who of west coast outlaw motorcycle clubs partying and playing pool together. The motorcycle club world was changing, and the Outsiders Tacoma clubhouse was becoming an especially important place that was helping facilitate that change. At our clubhouse it was common to see Hells Angels, Bandidos, Outsiders, Gypsy Joker, and numerous other major one percent clubs playing pool and hanging out together. It was a safe place for them to come and relax and get to know guys in other outlaw motorcycle clubs, and that generated communication which led to friendships. Because of the security we exhibited, it was also a place that during time of conflict, clubs would turn to as a neutral host for sensitive meetings to attempt to resolve those conflicts, and I was always responsible for handling the security for those meetings.

It was about 10:45pm, I was out on the front lawn keeping an eye out for the neighborhood troublemakers when Gimme Jimmy and several other Banididos arrived. Jimmie had come to talk to PigPen and Double D about the C.O.C. meeting and how we had responded. Please pay close attention to this part of the story because this is an important example of how the Bandidos operate that you will want to remember later in my story. Law enforcement and the media will have you believe that as part of their alleged criminal enterprise, the Bandidos control the Confederation of Clubs and use it to tax and control the other motorcycle clubs. The U.S. Defenders and COIR are national programs, designed by a National Officer of the Bandidos MC, which are intended to be run through the C.O.C. and have a Bandido oversee it, and we just told that Bandido national officer that we (Washington C.O.C.) were not going to participate in his program. It is easy to see why the Bandidos might be perceived as controlling things because they do have the most numbers in the state, but the fact of the matter is we told Jimmy no and there was not shit the Bandidos could do about it even if they did have several hundred more members in Washington state at the time than any other motorcycle club, they would still have to go to war against all of us.

Because the Bandido's do not control the C.O.C.'s like law enforcement alleges, what really happened was that PigPen and Double D sat down with Jimmy who explained that he had come to the realization after the meeting that nothing was going to get done in Washington without the support of the Outsiders MC, and he wanted to know how he could get our support. Double D explained the aspects of the program we disagreed to and potential accommodations that could be made to the program that might make it attractive to the Washington clubs, and over the course of about forty-five minutes Jimmy agreed to the necessary concessions. At the close of the conversation, Jimmy asked Double D and PigPen for a commitment from our club and from the Washington C.O.C., and once again I got to see Jimmys' confused, shocked, speechless look when Double D explained that he could not speak for our club or the C.O.C. without talking to the respective parties first, and he said would have to take it back to everybody and let them decide. Jimmy just was not used to the club politics of Washington, but he quickly adapted and evolved, and I watched it have a positive impact on how he presented the U.S. Defenders program on a national level from there on.

Ultimately, the Washington C.O.C. would vote to participate in the U.S. Defenders program and it would serve to be a critical element in our success in mobilizing Washington State, as well as help grow the national motorcycle profiling movement. Double D was the best public speaker in the Washington motorcycle club community and was elected Commander of the U.S. Defenders program for the state. A very smart, organized, and enterprising businessman and Bandido named Lucky Les was elected Lt. Commander. I was elected Defender for the Outsiders MC. The structure of the U.S. Defenders was highly organized, represented by the most talented and passionate members of each motorcycle club, and as a result we were highly effective.

In April 2009, the Washington C.O.C. decided to test the effectiveness of the U.S. Defenders program and issued a Call to Action. A preformatted letter voicing objections to an overly broad anti-gang bill that was being proposed was emailed to the Defender for each motorcycle club in Washington state, along with instructions that they print copies for each of their members and any family or friends who are interested in participating, and have the letters signed, sent off to the senators, and then send a total count of signed letters back to the Commander so that we can determine the effectiveness of the call to action. That first Call to Action (C.T.A.) resulted in over 1,200 signed letters within one week, the anti-gang bill failed, and it was clear that the U.S. Defenders program was an effective tool in our civil rights battle.

Because of their large numbers, the C.O.C. decided to open membership in the U.S. Defenders program to any non-law enforcement motorcycle organization that wanted to participate in the motorcycle rights movement, and this would help bridge the gap and develop an effective working relationship between significant independent biker organizations like A.B.A.T.E. and the motorcycle club community. A.B.A.T.E. was concerned that the U.S. Defenders was a plan by the motorcycle club community to influence or take over their organization, so Double D and I spent time developing a relationship with one of their key players, Donnie "Mr. Breeze" Landsman, and we met with the A.B.A.T.E. of Washington Board of Directors to make sure they understood there was no nefarious intent and that this was simply a way for us to maximize the effectiveness of our organizations through cooperation.

On a cold sunny Saturday morning in May, we gathered at the Tacoma clubhouse for our annual Outsiders MC, Tacoma Memorial Run where we ride to the various cemeteries and pay tribute to the fallen Outsiders. When we rolled out of the clubhouse for the first cemetery, we had the entire Tacoma chapter as well as several Portland members, guests from other clubs, family members, and the public in the pack with us. If you are into the history of your club, memorial runs are cool because you get to hear stories from the old timers about back in the day while you share a drink with your brothers, and it really gives you a chance to understand where your club came from and be proud of your club.

We had just finished at the last cemetery and were headed through Lakewood on our way back to the clubhouse when we noticed a Lakewood P.D. unit following the pack. When the pack moved into the left turn lane and came to a stop at a red light, the officer slowly rolled up the right lane alongside the pack, snapping photos with his digital camera. I was pissed when I noticed what was going on. We were not speeding or doing anything wrong and here was this cop taking our pics for "intelligence." When the light turned green, the pack surged ahead and the cop changed into our lane of travel and initiated a traffic stop on one of our chase vehicles that was driven by Buell Greg, an Outsider member who was unable to ride due to a broken back. A few minutes after we got back to the clubhouse, Buell Greg arrived and told us that the cop never told him why he pulled him over and just asked him all sorts of questions about the club, all of which he refused to answer, and he was let go without a citation. This was blatant profiling during one of our solemn occasions and Double D and I were infuriated. Drawing on my professional knowledge I suggested we use a public records request to obtain the photos and associated police report to use as evidence of motorcycle profiling. I drafted a public records request using the date, time, location of the incident, and vehicle number we got off the police car. The response to my request was exactly what we were hoping for and provided a key piece of evidence of motorcycle profiling that was created by law enforcement and allowed us to use the law enforcement's officers' own words against them.

In the opening paragraph of his report the officer states that we were not committing any crimes or traffic offenses but "based on his twenty years of law enforcement training and experience he knows the Outsiders MC to be involved in criminal activity in the past, and initiated surveillance for the purpose of gathering intelligence on the club." Also included was a list of every license plate in the pack and the associated biographical information for the registered owners, but it did not differentiate between club members, prospects, and our guests, which included teachers and state employees. The report clearly indicated on it that its final dissemination was the F.B.I. Gang Unit, which means that all those individuals whether they were an Outsider or simply a friend of a deceased member who wanted to ride along with the club, they were all now officially identified as Outlaw Motorcycle Gang (OMG) members to the F.B.I Gang Unit, and most importantly they had done nothing wrong. The photos the officer took were less useful than the report, but we used them to evidence motorcycle profiling was occurring and they were good pics of us riding together, so I included the in a digital photo fame that I gave the club for the clubhouse.

The use of the public record request had only cost us the price of a stamp but had proven itself to be a priceless tool we could use to document and build a pattern of evidence of law enforcement discrimination and harassment. Just as with the manual I put together on countering hostile surveillance, I put together a public records guide for all fifty states which included contact information and instructions on using public records requests to document law enforcement profiling and harassment and included a pre-formatted public records request that patch-holders simply needed to fill in the proper agency and incident in-formation, then submit. I briefed the clubs of the Washington C.O.C. on the use of public records to document profiling and once again the community received these new tactics enthusiastically, and within a week we were being informed of incidents of motorcycle profiling by law enforcement and clubs were requesting my assistance in obtaining the public records. While I was hoping the community was going to be more self-reliant, I was happy to assist the clubs in learning how to use the requests and it allowed me to monitor and analyze the informa-tion being generated via the requests, with the useful evidence being in-cluded in our pattern of evidence we were building for the legislature.

Law enforcement surveillance photo taken by the Lakewood Police Department. Double D is leading the pack and I am behind him on the blue Softail with Candace in her purple serape vest. Candace is riding old school ol' lady style and is sitting directly on my rear fender with no seat.

Photo – Lakewood Police Department

In the coming years as Double D and I began to travel the country speaking, I would educate the nation on the techniques I developed here in Washington, and they would be utilized by motorcycle clubs across the nation and helped develop critical evidence used to pass Maryland's motorcycle profiling law and others.

In July 2009, Judge Florence-Marie Cooper sided with the ACLU in a case filed on behalf of Mongol member Ramon Rivera, and she issued a preliminary injunction against the restraining order that she herself had authorized in October of 2008 at the behest of the Department of Justice. Judge Cooper determined that even though Rivera did not own the Mongols trademarks, his First Amendment right to wear items bearing the marks of the Mongol Nation was clearly at issue. Because he could not be left without remedy to protect those rights, she reasoned he did have standing to challenge the governments attempted appropriation of the trademarks. Judge Cooper's ruling declared that the government had overreached and that Doc and the other indicted defendants did not own the trademarks, which meant they were in no position to forfeit them to the Department of Justice because the government itself had argued that the trademarks at issue are collective membership marks which signify membership in an organization, and the law is clear that only an organization, not an individual, can own a collective membership mark. In this case, the club acquired the trademarks by first using it forty years ago, long before Cavazos joined the club, so they were not his to give away.

A major milestone in the American motorcycle rights movement occurred in Washington State in September of 2009. Several bars, night clubs, restaurants, and even county fairgrounds had adopted no-colors policies, refusing admission to motorcycle club members wearing their patch or any indicia of club membership. It was a hot summer afternoon and I had swung by Double D's house to hang out and kill time before we rode up to the clubhouse. I spent time with Double D literally every single day that I was in the club unless I was traveling, we were incredibly close, and our personalities worked well together. After-noons at his house gave us a chance one on one to talk and brainstorm about the club and the motorcycle rights movement. We came up with some great ideas, one of which was to use a protest run to counter the es-tablishments with no-colors policies. After discussing the idea with the C.O.C., it was decided that we would once again test the effectiveness of the U.S. Defenders program by conducting a protest run.

To limit law enforcement's ability to set up surveillance on the run and interfere, the meeting place and stops were kept a closely guarded secret, with only the officers of the C.O.C and myself knowing the meet-up location and various stops, until just before the run. A Call to Action (CTA) was sent out via the U.S. Defenders requesting that all available motorcycle club members and independent riders meet at the Lighthouse Tavern in Everett, WA on Saturday September 12th, 2009, at 10:00am. Everyone in the community knew the C.T.A was coming and there was a good buzz of excitement amongst the various Washing-ton clubs. We were excited to do something extraordinary together and uniting as a community to fight for our rights. I knew that the motorcy-cle club community unifying like this had never happened before, and we needed to capture the historical event on film. I reached out to the leadership of several of the major clubs, explained that I wanted to make a video that we could use to document the protest run and motivate the community, and I requested the clubs provide a member's ol' lady with a video camera to work with my ol' lady Candace to help film the run. Everyone understood the historical significance of the event and when the day of the protest run rolled around, I had plenty of camera help, pre-planned camera positions, and the ten-minute short video that re-sulted served as a great motivational tool. Over the course of our push for profiling legislation, I would film several major events and personal interviews that I would weave into a feature length documentary film ti-tled *What It's All About*.

Candace and I got to the clubhouse early the morning of the protest run. Pigpen was going through cancer treatment and was too weak to ride but he wasn't going to miss the protest run for the world, so Candace had agreed to drive him, and he was going to help direct the ol' ladies into their camera positions. I got some coffee going, turned on the music, and within a few minutes the fellas and members from other clubs began to arrive. T-Bob, Gutz, and Prospect Matlock came up from Portland to participate in the run and I was excited to see the Portland fellas showing interest.

We rolled out of the clubhouse for Everett at about 8:30am with a pack of about fifty bikes. Because I was working in Everett at the time and I thought I knew where we were going, I was asked to ride up front with Double D so that I could help lead us in. I was so excited, I was a new member, a new officer, and I got to lead a pack of not just Outsiders, but a pack that included members of multiple respected outlaw motorcycle clubs into one of the most historical motorcycle events in history. The ride to Everett from Tacoma was beautiful and took us just under an hour. As we rolled into Everett, I signaled to Double D that we needed to take the Broadway exit and we guided the pack off I-5 and onto Broadway Avenue in Everett. The large pack thundered down Broadway and I took us left onto Hewitt and headed towards the water. Unfortunately, when we got to the bar that I thought was the Lighthouse, I was wrong. I took the pack right trying to locate the bar, thinking I was only one street off and that took us onto a street that had been closed and forced us to go right again, which took the big pack right into the middle of a breast cancer marathon and runners dressed in pink. I looked over at Double D and he flipped up the visor of his helmet and threw his hands in the air in frustration. I could tell he was pissed, the new member in me freaked and I took us right again in an attempt to get us out of the marathon and then once we were free, I pulled the pack over so I could consult my iPhone for directions, not realizing I left half of the large pack hanging out in the road blocking traffic.

Double D was pissed, and Spank's wife Nicky knew it, and since Double D always loved to push Nicky's buttons, she decided right now would be a great time to push his, walked up to him and said "Smile, Double D. You look like you could use a cigarette." then handed the non-smoker one of her Marlboro's before giving me a wink, giggling, and skipping off into the convenience store we were stopped in front of. Turns out I had us about five blocks away on the wrong side of town and when we rolled up to the Lighthouse there were at least two hundred bikes waiting there already. Now, two hundred bikes might not seem like a lot to some of you, but in a state where it rains or snows nine months a year, the club community and motorcycle population is not that big so two hundred is a ton of bikes for Washington state, especially since ninety eight percent of them were motorcycle club members and almost every respected motorcycle club in the state was represented.

Staging for the protest run at the Lighthouse Tavern, Evert, WA.
September 2009.
Photo by Irish McKinney

When you move a pack of several hundred bikes it takes a lot of planning and precision to do it safely and efficiently. Single D is a second-generation Outsider, arguably the best rider in the club, at the time of the protest run he was the Tacoma Sergeant at Arms, responsible for establishing the route and road-guard tactics whenever we moved the club, and most importantly he has a track record of doing it safely. Just before we headed out to the first stop, Single D decided that he was going to run the riders meeting because he did not trust anyone else to do it. Single D grabbed a chair from inside the bar and came out onto the sidewalk where the majority of crowd was mingling because the bar had long since reached its capacity. He hopped on the chair and called everyone together for a riders meeting, during which he briefed them on our first destination, route, pack rules, selected his road guards from all the other clubs and briefed them on their assignments.

Single D standing on his chair, leading the riders meeting.
Photo by Irish McKinney

We started up the bikes and the noise shook the entire neighborhood as the sound reverberated off the buildings and homes surrounding the Lighthouse. Double D and Lucky Les from the Bandidos led the pack. It was important to us that we all rode as one giant pack and did not leave in stages, so we lined the pack up prior to heading out. Even stationary, lined up wheel to wheel, the pack stretched for over three blocks and once we took off it was one of the most beautiful sights I have ever seen. It was not Outsiders riding with Outsiders and Bandidos riding with Bandidos, we were all intermingled as one unified force headed out to fight for our rights as Americans and patriots, and it was fucking glorious.

Bandido Lucky Les and Outsider Double D with the pack staging to take off behind them.
Photo by Irish McKinney

The first bar we stopped at was called Foxy's. We brought along our C.O.C attorney Martin Fox and a form letter that read:

Attention Management,

The Washington State Confederation of Clubs has recently been made aware that your establishment has recently practiced the policy of denying motorcycle club members entrance and/or service if they are wearing their club colors. This practice is based on discriminatory stereotyping blatantly violating the First and Fourteenth Amendments of the U.S. Constitution. Your right to deny service to anyone does not include discrimination against the basic freedom of expression even if it is based on the belief that motorcycle club wearing colors may result in unrest. Absent tangible, specific and empirical examples there is no basis for denying access to an entire class of American and Washington State citizens.

The Washington State Confederation of Clubs respectfully requests that your establishment permanently discontinue the practice of denying motorcycle club members access or service. The Confederation of Clubs represents a massive constituency, and we are determined to gain access tour tights base at every level through legitimate protest and political activism.

Any questions or inquiries may be directed to Martin Fox, attorney for the Washington State Confederation of Clubs.

The ride to Foxy's was amazing and the pack stretched further than I could see in my mirrors. I had been a road guard at one of the first intersections and ended up getting to blast up the length of the impressive pack to get back into my spot near the front. Pigpen and Candace had gone on ahead of us so Candace could film our arrival, and when we pulled into the strip mall the bar was in, Pigpen was in front of the bar jumping up and down with his hands in the air cheering as patrons of the neighboring businesses in all directions poured outside to see what was happening.

We all parked our bikes and had a brief meeting in the parking lot before anyone went inside. Double D reminded everyone that we needed to be on out best behavior to achieve our goal. He explained that he, the C.O.C attorney, Pigpen, and a few others of us were going to go inside to speak with the manager. He asked people to let him, and Marty do the talking and to show respect.

Double D briefing the crew just before we entered Foxy's in Everett, WA.
Photo by Irish McKinney

Double D, Marty, Pigpen, Big Jim from the Gypsy Joker, Lucky Les, and myself headed for the front door. I was so focused on trying to get the door and run my camera that I did not notice that we had over two hundred brothers flowing through the door right behind us, having our back to the fullest because everyone wanted to be on the front lines of this battle. As we came through the door, the manager was already walking towards us in an attempt to intercept us. Are you the manager? Double D said to the woman in her late thirties who looked like she had just crapped her pants. Uhhhhm, yes. How can I help you?

Double D explained the situation as it was laid out in the letter he had written and asked her to change her policy. She stated that she had prior issues with members of other clubs and some of her customers are afraid that if members of different outlaw clubs come in at the same time there will be violence. Double D explained that if that were true, we would not all be gathered together in her bar right now asking her if she would change her policy so we can all come in, hangout together, and spend a bunch of money in her bar. He also let her know that this was the Confederation of Clubs asking her to reverse the policy and if there was ever a problem with any clubs in her place, she could call us, and the Confederation would police itself. You could see the light click on in her head as she realized that he was right, and we were about to make her Saturday the most successful Saturday she has ever had. She reversed her policy on the spot and over the next couple of hours we all had a good time and made a new friend.

We left Foxy's in Everett and headed south to SeaTac to a little bar on International Boulevard called First Class Pub & Grill. It was about a forty-minute ride south on I-405 to the next stop and all along the route traffic on the freeway just stopped and pulled to the side as the pack came up from behind and overtook them, even though we were in our own lane. Washington drivers are not used to giant packs of bikes, let alone a pack consisting of every respected motorcycle club in the state, and it was truly a sight to behold. I was at the front of the pack when we arrived, I immediately hopped off my bike and headed into the middle of International Boulevard and began to film the pack arriving. Even riding wheel to wheel it took the pack over five minutes to finish arriving at the bar. Pigpen and Candace had arrived first and told us that the bar did not open for another hour and even though we could see and hear people inside prepping to open, nobody responded to our knocks at the door, so we had no choice but to wait.

It was almost one hundred degrees that day, but nobody minded the wait because it gave us all a chance to be proud of what we were doing together and spend time getting to know each other. With no shade to hide in, the heat became a concern and I thought it showed a ton of class when a women's Bandido support motorcycle club called Buscadors del Sol MC, stepped up and took it upon themselves to go find the run enough water to prevent anyone from getting heat stroke while we waited. While Washington State may be the most progressive state when it comes to motorcycle rights, we were one of the last states to recognize and accept chick clubs, and life was not easy for the Buscadors when they started in Washington, but they have represented themselves with a lot of class, worked hard, and today they are one of the women's clubs I respect the most in the U.S. Them identifying a threat to our mission then taking action and going and getting that water to support our mission, the mission of the community, showed they really wanted to be an active part of the community, earned my respect that day, and I openly supported the Buscadors obtaining membership in the C.O.C. from that day on. Double D's very chauvinistic, his attitude was "Fuck them bitches!", and he would use his influence to continue to prevent the Buscadors from gaining membership in the C.O.C. for several more years.

At 1:00pm, the First Class opened the front door and desperate for drinks and air conditioning, the group flooded inside. Behind the bar was a female bartender and a middle-aged male who I noticed was wearing a watch and bracelet that was far too nice to afford on a bar tenders' salary, as well as a Washington State Department of Corrections retiree belt buckle. Double D, Marty Fox, Pigpen, Big Jim, and Lucky Les approached the bar and asked to speak to the manager. The female bartender who had frozen the instant the bar began to fill with hundreds of motorcycle club members just stared in disbelief and failed to even muster any response, while the male was quick to tell us the manager was not in. Double D asked if the owner was in? And again, the male was quick to respond that the owner was not in either. We had all noticed the only two cars in the parking lot when we arrived were an old beater Toyota and a brand-new Corvette, and it was clear the fancy jewelry wearing, Corvette driving retired prison guard was the owner of the First Class. I called the guy out in front of the group, at which point he told us we could not be in there and cited his no colors policy. Double D chimed in and told him that was exactly what we were there to talk to him about and explained how his policy was violating our First and Fourteenth Amendment rights, and introduced him to the C.O.C. attorney, Marty.

The guy's whole demeanor changed and while he continued to deny that he was the owner or manager and he could not explain why he was behind the bar, then gave a long explanation about how he had problems in there before with motorcycle clubs and the policy was in place to prevent that. One of the Bandidos from that area and the President of the Resurrection MC whose clubhouse is just up the street refuted the guy's statement and said if there were ever any problems with club members in their establishment, he could call them. Double D and Pigpen restated the same offer from the C.O.C and made it clear that there would be no problems. After some back and forth, the unknown male of authority agreed that they would remove the no colors signs and do away with their policy. We all celebrated with a drink.

This protest run was huge success and not only proved that the U.S. Defenders program worked, but most importantly it really inspired and unified the motorcycle club community. We may not have fought with violence, but we set aside our differences, stood side by side, and fought for our Constitutional rights together, and as American bikers and true patriots, that was a great feeling that we could embrace with pride. For all the clubs that participated, we were suddenly brothers in arms, it was the turning point for the dynamics of the Washington motorcycle club community, and the birth of what would eventually become the most successful national grassroots motorcycle rights movement in American history. In addition, the protest run and the video footage I shot was powerful visual evidence that not only are motorcycle clubs not prone to violence when they gather, but with unity and grassroots political activism, we could effect change for the motorcycle club culture and defend the constitution. I ended up posting the video I had shot of the protest run on YouTube so that everyone who participated could watch it and be proud of what we did, and within a few days I was being contacted by patch-holders from Canada, Netherlands, Norway, U.K. and Australia, saying how cool it was to see all the clubs coming together to fight for their rights and getting along like we were. The response from within the American motorcycle club community was huge as well which made it abundantly clear to me that even though I had no filmmaking experience, because the club community was ok with me filming us which was traditionally a no-go, it was my duty to try and fill a media role for the community and use film to document this historical movement, and social media to help motivate the community and gain public awareness of motorcycle profiling. I decided that with each public record request we received that clearly evidenced the problem of motorcycle profiling, I would post the video on YouTube so the public could see firsthand what motorcycle profiling really is and why it is a problem. I knew doing this would make me a prime target for law enforcement, but someone had to do it and since nobody else was stepping up and this was a war I believed in, I volunteered to take the heat no matter what that may be.

With a successful protest run under our belt, relations between the clubs of Washington state better than they had ever been, and the 2010 legislative session right around the corner, the C.O.C. was more motivated than ever to pass a bill addressing motorcycle profiling. A.B.A.T.E. of Washington had almost no participation in the protest run but of the few members they did have show up, two of them, Irish McKinney, and Donnie "Mr. Breeze" Landsman would play major roles in the Washington motorcycle rights movement. When I first met them both, I thought they were goof balls, but what we would achieve together would ultimately lead me to view them both as brothers. Mr. Breeze had been appointed the new Legislative Representative for A.B.A.T.E. and for the first time he was able to get A.B.A.T.E. to agree to adopt the same legislative agenda as the C.O.C., and Irish had been appointed the A.B.A.T.E. Liaison to the C.O.C., and very quickly he was able to bridge the communication and trust gap that existed towards the C.O.C. by A.B.A.T.E.

With A.B.A.T.E on board and committed, we were able to arrange a meeting with Representative Steve Kirby to discuss the possibility of him sponsoring our proposed motorcycle profiling legislation. It was a cold Tuesday when Double D, me, Mr. Breeze, Irish, and a couple other representatives from A.B.A.T.E met with Steve Kirby at a little dive of a restaurant that he chose on Pacific Avenue in Tacoma. The meeting went really well, and we spent a little over an hour sharing stories of law enforcement profiling and harassment that had impacted each of us. Representative Kirby was supportive and while he was explicit in saying that he would make no promises of success, he assured us he would push the legislation because he believed the problem was real and this was a viable cost-free remedy.

Twitch, Double D, and members of A.B.A.T.E. of Washington discuss motorcycle profiling with Representative Steve Kirby.
Photo by Irish McKinney

Twitch, Double D, and members of A.B.A.T.E. including Mr. Breeze (blue hoodie) meeting with Rep. Steve Kirby (Tan/stripe sweater).
Photos by Irish McKinney

Sponsorship for a motorcycle profiling bill was another major milestone for the motorcycle club community and armed with a sponsor, solid evidence package and a plan, we were looking forward to the 2010 legislative session. Our success and momentum were beginning to get noticed, not just in Washington but in other states as well. Because the Bandidos have chapters in so many states, as their Washington brothers shared stories of what was going on in the Washington motorcycle club community with their brothers from other states, those stories were filtering out into those communities and the nation was starting to be intrigued by how all the clubs in Washington were getting along, what we were accomplishing together, and they really liked what they were seeing.

17

UNITED WE STAND

2010 started strong with the entire motorcycle club community in Washington State more motivated and united than ever before. The general attitude of the community was one of brotherhood and if you were not participating then you were missing out. What we were all accomplishing together was fueling our drive to fight and we refused to be defeated.

The Black Thursday event in January 2010 had the most participation I had ever seen. I had decided that I wanted use all the footage I was capturing to make a feature length guerilla style documentary that chronicled the unification of the Washington motorcycle club community and birth of the motorcycle profiling movement. We may not have had any financing or professional equipment for the project, but I had a plan and the community's support, so I knew that even if it were not the most polished film ever made, it would be impactful and probably the most accurate and important documentary made about the culture to that point.

Just as with the protest run, I developed a shot list prior to the event, identifying what shots I wanted and then recruited camera volunteers from the various motorcycle clubs and gave them specific assignments. With the protest run video I included footage shot by all the different clubs which allowed everyone to feel proud of the product, and it generated even more eager volunteers for this event. Irish McKinney had a nice digital still camera and volunteered to shoot stills of the event for me. Over the last several months I had spent quite a bit of time around Irish, and he had started to become a very close friend of mine and the club community as a whole. He was so motivated to help effect change for the community and had a lot of talents that really helped the movement.

Like every Black Thursday event, all the clubs met at the Hawks Prairie Casino so that we could all ride into the capitol together. Irish had met us at the clubhouse and rode down to Hawks Prairie with us, along with Mad Dash from the Resurrection, and several other members of various clubs and guests. When we arrived, members from every respected motorcycle club in Washington mingled in the parking lot, while inside the same thing was occurring over breakfast in the bar. It was a beautiful thing and as the minutes passed the enthusiasm of the group and enjoyment of the experience grew. I have never seen Pigpen so proud. He was the Chairman of the Washington C.O.C. and had been tirelessly working for this type of unity and political activism from the Washington motorcycle club community for over fifteen years. He was clearly enjoying seeing all the hard work and commitment from important players in the community who believed in the concept of the Confederation of Clubs like him, Billy Two Weeks and Big Jim from the Gypsy Joker, and George Weggers from the Bandidos, finally pay off. He knew that what he was watching was an indicator of true and permanent change for the Washington motorcycle club community.

Outsider Pigpen at Black Thursday 2010.
Photo by Irish McKinney

Of course, just like with every previous Black Thursday, the cops were there to conduct surveillance and gather intelligence. You see, no civil rights event is complete without plenty of law enforcement surveillance, and we had gotten used to being surveilled from the time we arrived at Hawks Prairie until the time we left the state Capitol campus, but this year their tactics would change.

All we were doing was having breakfast and going for a ride to the state capitol but there were plenty of police on hand to take our photos and intimidate us.
Photo by Irish McKinney

We had almost three hundred bikes in the pack when we rolled out of Hawks Prairie and when we arrived at the state Capitol, law enforcement was waiting for us and making a definite show of force. Just like the previous year, we had designated parking but this year it was a spot that was in the open and could be easily and discreetly surveilled from multiple observation posts in the surrounding buildings. As we arrived, state employees and law makers poured out of the various buildings on the Capitol campus to watch the sea of arriving motorcycle club members. They stood in amazement, some waving and cheering as the wave of bikes rolled across the main drive of the Capitol.

The motorcycle clubs of the Washington COC arriving at the
Washington state capitol for Black Thursday 2010.
Photo by Irish McKinney

Law enforcement had used concrete barriers, police cars, and uniformed officers to block access from our parking area to the capitol, and the only way to get to the front steps of the capitol where we were all to meet and listen to Double D and Mr. Breeze speak, was by walking through a choke point of law enforcement officers and K9 units they had set up. It was clear that the gauntlet of law enforcement that we were forced to pass through to reach the steps of the capitol was deliberately set up for us and the photos and video we obtained provide excellent evidence of blatant profiling, discrimination, and a gross misuse of taxpayer funds to violate the civil rights of hundreds of Americans who were peacefully gathering to attempt to gain sponsors for a bill preventing this exact type of discrimination and harassment. It was totally un-American and infuriating to me. I was always taught growing up that the legislative process was established to give average citizens a way to protect their rights and effect positive change in their communities, however law enforcement was doing their best to tarnish our image by making us look like a security threat, and they were deliberately trying to intimidate us and discourage us from our pursuit.

The motorcycle club members were forced to walk through a
gauntlet of law enforcement officers and K9 units just to get to the
steps of the capitol at Black Thursday 2010.
Photo by Irish McKinney

Going into Black Thursday that year we had two specific goals. First,
since our primary sponsorship for our motorcycle profiling bill was in
the House of Representatives, we decided to use those relationships to
continue to develop additional sponsors in the House that could urge
a public hearing for our bill. Second, we wanted to try and generate
a primary sponsor for a bill in the Senate. With a short, sixty-day legislative session that year, we were fighting an uphill battle. Our House
bill was titled HB 2511, "A Bill Addressing the Issue of Motorcycle
Profiling" had garnered nearly unanimous support from the House of
Representatives and it appeared that the Chairman of the Public Safety

and Emergency Preparedness committee was going to schedule a public hearing for our bill which really motivated the motorcycle club community.

The clubs of the Washington Confederation of Clubs on the steps of the state Capitol. Black Thursday 2010.
Photo by Irish McKinney

The Senate was a different story. We had previously arranged a meeting with Republican Senator Pam Roach of the 31st Legislative District, for the express purpose of discussing the issue of motorcycle profiling with her and to attempt to gain her sponsorship for a companion bill addressing motorcycle profiling in the Senate. However, Senator Roach had a different intent for the meeting, and we would soon come to find out that she had set up an ambush for us. Because the meeting was to take place in the Senator's office with limited space, it was decided that Double D, Lucky Les, and myself would be the ones to meet with Senator Roach. We left the large crowd of our brothers and various club members on the sidewalk outside the Senator's office building, and the three of us headed inside expecting a meeting like the ones we had with Representative Kirby and other legislators regarding our bill.

When we walked in Senator Roach's small office there were three men waiting with her in her office already, one of which I identified by his uniform as Captain DeVries from the Washington State Patrol. The oldest of the group was introduced by Senator Roach as Don Pierce, the Executive Director of the Washington Association of Sheriffs and Police Chief's (WASPC), and the third escapes me because he was low enough on the totem pole, he was not a shot-caller, and he did not say anything during the entire meeting. The law enforcement officers were seated in comfortable chairs with Captain DeVries and Don Pierce seated against the north wall, the silent cop against the south wall, the Senator was behind her desk at the east end of the room, and there were three simple desk chairs lined up for us that had been positioned so they were just forward of the doorway, placing us between the cops and leaving us with no way to effectively respond to the door being rushed. I had brought my video camera with me and even though I was not filming as soon as Senator Roach saw the camera she freaked out and wanted to know why I had a camera in the room and then demanded that all recording devices be left outside the room. I compromised by offering to leave it off and she agreed. It was clear Senator Roach did not want any evidence of what was about to occur.

The Senator said she understood that we had found sponsors and had developed significant support for HB2511 in the House but said that she decided that all of the motorcycle communities' issues with law enforcement profiling and harassment could be most effectively addressed through dialogue between us and law enforcement, rather than legislation. She went on to tell us that our bill had no chance of ever passing, and she wanted to help us find some reasonable solutions for our issues. Double D had been preparing for the Black Thursday meetings and potential hearings for weeks and he began to systematically articulate a pattern of motorcycle profiling evidence, much of which involved Washington State Patrol, and our need for motorcycle profiling legislation. As Double D spoke, I watched Don Pierce's face gradually turn darker shades of red and little beads of sweat developed on his forehead. Pierce only lasted about a minute and a half into Double D's skillfully presented motorcycle profiling lesson when all of the sudden Pierce fucking lost it, he came flying out of his chair towards Double D and screamed "Do you think we're stupid? Don't you think we know who you guys are? We know what you have been doing since this '70's! This is just a smoke screen!"

Lucky Les and I immediately redirected ourselves in our chairs towards Pierce, and while we stayed professional it was clear that we did not give a fuck they were cops and had guns, if this fucking cop assaulted Double D for no reason, we were going to use force to defend him, no matter what. DeVries reached out and gently grabbed Pierce by the forearm as Senator Roach jumped up, her arms outstretched saying "Don, Don, have a seat so we can all talk." The look of shock on Double D's face when Pierce lost his shit was priceless. I knew inside he was frustrated as hell. Double D is a debate superstar and had prepped for this meeting for weeks, but Pierce's inability to have a calm and reasonable conversation had totally derailed Double D's plan to dismantle any opposition that the Senator could raise. We had no idea Senator Roach had invited those cops and the fact that the cops were there to ambush us was the icing on the cake because he knew they were no match for him, and he made them look stupid in front of the Senator. None of us in that room were even old enough to be in a motorcycle club in the 1970's, so Pierce's explosion had just demonstrated that dialogue was clearly not the solution, it was not even possible with these irrational, prejudiced jackasses, and legislation was our only option.

Double D's voice raised, and he started to get more animated and said, "Do you see how they treat us? If they treat us this way in front of a Senator, how do you think they treat us when you're not around.?" "They crawl through the bushes and conduct investigations based on an outdated stereotype. Law enforcement doesn't even have enough respect to refrain from discrimination and profiling on the grounds of the state Capitol!" he exclaimed. His arguments were strong, but I knew as soon as I saw the cops in the Senator's office that this meeting was going to be a waste of time, and while Pierce was back in his chair, he still looked like he was about to have an aneurysm and now a big blue vein had appeared on the left side of his forehead, so clearly, he was not calming down. Les and I glanced at each other and shared an amused smile. DeVries tried to play us like idiots and chimed in saying that W.S.P. takes profiling of any type very seriously and if we have problems with motorcycle profiling, we should file a complaint with W.S.P. and they will make sure to investigate it. Bullshit! That is no solution and Double D countered his offer by referencing the cop crawling through the bushes the prior year and the response we got from the Chief of W.S.P. The cops had no credible arguments, they knew it and Senator Roach knew it, and they were undeniably and deliberately trying to intimidate us into giving up our pursuit of legislative relief for their history of violating our civil rights and abusing our subculture.

As I thought it would, the meeting continued to fall apart, and after Senator Roach reminded us that we would never pass our bill and it had no support, we left her office without her sponsorship or support. It did not matter how convincing our pattern of evidence was or Double D's oral arguments, the Senator was never really interested in sponsoring our legislation. Roach's interests arose from her desire to protect her political support from her law enforcement constituents by helping derail our legislative effort, and she figured we were just a bunch of dumb bikers, and they could okeydokey us into giving up the fight. We do not back down, and we do not quit. Ironically, once Senator Roach realized that the motorcycle constituency can be enormously powerful, and with her re-election up for grabs, she would try to convince us that she was a friend to the motorcycle constituency, and in 2011, she was a vocal supporter and voted in favor of an identical version of our motorcycle profiling bill that she had refused to support and tried to derail.

In February 2010, we got the hearing in front of the House of Representatives Public Safety and Emergency Preparedness committee we had been wanting so bad. Double D testified on behalf of the Confederation of Clubs and Mr. Breeze testified on behalf of A.B.A.T.E and independent motorcyclists. I set up a tripod and camera right behind the table Double D and Breeze were sitting at, so I could be sure we at least got good audio of this historical hearing and then took a seat in the gallery next to Pigpen. There was so much interest and support in the motorcycle club community that the hearing room was over-flowing.

Double D had been preparing for the hearing for weeks and began by defining motorcycle profiling and explaining its legal and legislative background. Next, he established a clear argument that the entire motorcycle community was being profiled based on law enforcement's false belief that motorcycle club members are more likely to commit crimes or engage in acts of violence, and he used the evidence we had amassed as exhibits to back up his argument. He went on to explain how law enforcement was training each other in discriminatory practices using inflammatory training materials like Basic Biker 101, an Outlaw Motorcycle Gang training manual produced by Washington State Patrol. A few years prior, Marty Fox had gotten an injunction against W.S.P. preventing them from using the training manual because it was inflammatory and taught discriminatory and unethical practices. Double D held a copy of the 2002 permanent injunction granted against Basic Biker 101 high in the air, displaying it to the committee members. He then produced a transcript from a trial that occurred a few months earlier in which Marty Fox had cross-examined W.S.P trooper Pigott and the trooper admitted that Basic Biker 101 tactics are how troopers are taught to deal with bikers, and he knew nothing about the permanent injunction against the use of the tactics outlined in Basic Biker 101, which further drove home the point that our legislation was a perfect solution to the problem, since clearly judicial reprimands were not working. He then drove it all home by pointing out the potential exposure to massive civil liability and financial damages resulting from lawsuits.

Double D's testimony was masterful, was so well received by the committee and they were so engaged that they inadvertently let him go several minutes over his allotted time limit. When they finally cut him off several committee members asked him the standard questions about motorcycle clubs and crime. He explained that just like law enforcement officers who are involved in crime, it is a very small percentage of club members who are involved in criminal activity and that most club members are just your average hardworking Americans. However, with motorcycle clubs law enforcement and the media define an entire class of people based on the individual activities of a few. He went on to explain that traffic code should not be used conduct criminal investigations when there would otherwise not be enough evidence to obtain a warrant.

When the hearing was done the committee did something unexpected and moved into Executive Session and reported the bill out of committee right then. They told us that this was unusual but based on the strength of the testimony the discussion of motorcycle profiling deserved to continue.

For the first time anywhere in the United States, a bill to address the problem of motorcycle profiling had made it past a policy committee, just a week later the bill passed the House of Representatives by a vote of 96-2 and it was headed for the Senate. Even though this was a short sixty-day session, we were elated to have made it this far and there was still time for us to get a hearing in the Senate.

With no time to take a break, the U.S. Defenders sent out another Call to Action urging members of the Senate Judiciary committee to schedule a hearing on HB 2511, and a few days later the bill was added to the agenda of the final Judiciary hearing of the 2010 session. It was crazy, the community kept working together and supporting the mission, the bill kept moving forward, and now we actually had a chance of passing it. Unfortunately, less than twenty-four hours before the hearing our bill was removed from the agenda, replaced with a budget bill from the Governor's office and killed in committee.

18

OUTLAW MOTORCYCLE CLUB FUNERALS

I am going to use this chapter to tell you about the Outsider who was hardest for me to bury, while at the same time give you an inside look at what an outlaw motorcycle club funeral is like.

I have already told you about one of my very favorite brothers Gordy. Well in approximately 2008, Gordy was diagnosed with cancer and by the winter of 2010, Gordy's health had deteriorated to the point that it was clear we were going to lose him. March 12th, 2010, was the last time I spoke to my brother Gordy. I was away coaching at a ski race and having a great time. Women's Super-G. Super-G or Super Giant Slalom is an alpine ski racing discipline that consists of widely set gates that racers must pass through. The course is set so that skiers achieve much greater speed than events like slalom and giant slalom but is slower than Downhill. Each racer only has one run to try and accomplish the fastest run and speeds typically exceed 70mph.

Speed events are my favorite. It was a beautiful sunny day that was warm but not too warm, so the skiing was good, and my racers were all in a great mood. We had finished course inspection and I was assigned to the start, prepping my racers skis, going over line and tactics, and helping them get mentally ready. My girls were skiing great, and we had several in the top ten, when suddenly my phone rang during a break between racers. I retrieved my cell phone from my pocket and seeing it was Spanky, I answered. Hey bro, what are you up to? He said. Just hangin' out on the side of a mountain bro. I could tell something was wrong. "Hey bro, Nicky and I came down to Portland. Gordy's not doing good, so I wanted to give you a call." Fuck, bro! I quietly exclaimed. How long does he have? "Not long bro, he's at the clubhouse with us now having a drink and he's just going to enjoy his time. They say he's not going to make it through the night."

I was devastated, no matter what I did my brother was going to die before I could give him one last hug and say goodbye, and even harder for me was that I was not going to get the opportunity to be by his side at the end. Spank knew that was going to be hard for me, so he made sure he called me so he could put Gordy on the phone with me.

"Hello, my brother." Gordy's weakened voice said as he tried to sound enthusiastic. "I love you bro! I'm sorry." I said, as I tried to hold myself together in front of the other coaches and athletes in the start arena. "I love you too Twitch, and I'm going to miss you.", Gordy said before telling me about all the beautiful women who had gathered at the clubhouse to take care of him and say goodbye. Gordy was the coolest and he always had a way for finding the silver lining in a shitty situation. He was so weak that we could not talk long, but it was long enough that I got to tell my brother goodbye and remind him one last time that I loved him. He died later that evening. A week later we laid Gordy to rest in the cemetery in Portland where we lay all our fallen Portland brothers to rest.

An outlaw motorcycle club funeral is a celebration of the member's life and depending on the member's club and their standing in the community, members of their own club and other clubs may come from all over the world to pay their respects to the fallen motorcycle club mem-

ber. Gordy's was no exception and members from one-percent motorcycle clubs and others came from Washington, Oregon, California,
Idaho, Utah, and the Netherlands, to gather at the Outsiders MC, Portland clubhouse and tell stories about Gordy, socialize, and ride over to
the cemetery with us to lay him to rest. During this time, the prospects
are tending bar and handling any last-minute details associated with the
funeral or party afterwards, while the members are free to socialize and
remember their brother. I spent my time floating from club to club, saying my hellos and vising with friends from other states.

Members of various motorcycle clubs gather outside the Outsiders
MC's Portland clubhouse for Outsider Gordy's funeral.
Photo by Candace Burns

When it is time to head to the cemetery, the pack structure is a little
more formal due to it being an Outsiders funeral. Outsider officers rode
at the front of the pack, followed by Outsider membership, followed by
the membership and prospects of the other clubs, followed by civilians,
and there are always Outsider prospects at the back of the pack to use as
road-guards and in case of break downs. The pack for Gordy's funeral

was so long that the end of the pack had just left the clubhouse when the front of the pack arrived at the cemetery, and it was a fitting tribute for a righteous brother. When we arrived at the cemetery there was more socializing as we awaited the arrival of the color guard.

The pack rolling into the cemetery for Outsider Gordy's funeral.
Photo by Candace Burns

We sat around Gordy's open grave site with him, telling stories about his Viet Nam service, his wild times in the club, and the various adventures we had with him, while we all shared a bottle of liquor. Between the guests, flowers, and stories, you really understood how loved and respected a member he was.

Telling stories with Gordy before we buried him. Notice the head of
the casket is open so Gordy can be part of the fun and get a tan.
Twitch is in the center-top of the photo.
Photo by Candace Burns

Some examples of typical floral arrangements sent by other outlaw
motorcycle clubs to pay their respect and honor to the deceased
member and club.
Photo by Candace Burns

At the clubhouse, the funeral home, and grave site, you will find
elaborate floral arrangements and photos of the deceased member. The
fallen member's chapter and club will generally provide the most elaborate of the arrangements, designed to honor the fallen member and his
commitment to the club. Other outlaw clubs that respected the member or his club will also send arrangements to show their respect, and
these floral arrangements will often be in the colors of the club sending the arrangement but may also be in the club colors of the deceased
member.

Once the color guard arrived, we proceeded with the ceremony. Generally, it is tradition with outlaw motorcycle clubs that we bury our
own, which means we literally bury our own. After the service was concluded, we lowered Gordy and his custom serape wrapped casket into

the ground and buried him ourselves. For me, I find that burying your brothers this way gives you a lot of closure.

Outsider Twitch (plaid shirt) burying Outsider Gordy. Rest in peace my brother.
Photo by Candace Burns

Back in the day when the fellas were all in their twenties and dumb, there might have been an outlaw style twenty-one-gun salute with live ammunition, but in this day in age we understand that what goes up must come down somewhere, so we leave the twenty-one-gun salute to the color guard.

After the funeral it is back to the clubhouse for one hell of a party to celebrate your brother's life.

That is it. There is nothing mysterious or nefarious about an outlaw motorcycle club funeral, they are just like anybody else's, except there is probably a more impressive and genuine display of love for the decedent. For those of you that think like I used to, and that the funeral would make the club life worth it, I will remind you that you will not be around to see it.

19

NEVER LETTING OFF

The Tacoma chapter of the Outsiders MC was really clicking on all cylinders, our brotherhood was tight, and it was infectious. We spent every evening together at the clubhouse and running around town. If we were not spending time riding together or at the clubhouse, we were spending time together at Easystreet or sharing our other personal interests. Double D taught me to Bass fish, and we would go multiple times a week. He had this beautiful bass boat that I called the U.S.S. Lop-Dropper, and we would spend the entire day fishing and discussing the club, motorcycle community and culture.

Twitch with a 5 ½ lb. bass.

The Outsiders MC Tacoma clubhouse was the hub of outlaw motorcycle club activity for the Pacific Northwest, and we had members of other motorcycle clubs from all over Washington and the country visiting us all the time. It was common to walk into our clubhouse and see Outsiders, Hells Angels, Bandidos, and Gypsy Joker members playing pool, drinking, and laughing together. Not only was the motorcycle profiling movement changing Washington motorcycle club culture, but the Outsiders Tacoma chapter and the dynamic we brought to the table was changing the community as well. It was fucking cool, and it was great when the guys from the other clubs would stay late, get loose, and the next thing you know they're telling you how they'd be an Outsider if they had it all to do over again. Hell, several guys actually left their respected motorcycle clubs to become members of the Tacoma chapter, because we were just that much fun to be around back then.

Double D on the far bike, Twitch on the near bike.

With our profiling bill being killed in committee, we had a full year to prep for our next legislative run at it, but we had to make sure that we did not lose the momentum we had developed as a community. The Washington C.O.C. is funded off the minimal annual dues collected from the member clubs as well as donations obtained via an annual fundraiser held early each summer. The Northwest motorcycle club community was really starting to love the Tacoma Outsiders, and that along with our get things done attitude landed the C.O.C. fundraiser run in Tacoma that year.

We all met up at the 48th Street Pub & Grill in Tacoma and the participation was just as impressive as it had been at the rights events and C.O.C. meetings. Hundreds of motorcycle club members from various clubs and independents showed up, and for the first time we had a large participation from A.B.A.T.E. members. It was a simple poker run, although due to the threat of being charged with some sort of gambling RICO offense, we did not call it that or advertise it as such. Within minutes of our arrival at the 48th Street the cops showed up. Once again, we were not doing anything other than gathering peacefully for the purpose of conducting a fundraiser for a civil rights group, but the cops had surrounded us like we were getting ready to go to war. We did our part and started taking pics of them and they quickly backed off and left.

C.O.C. clubs and independents gathering outside the 45th Street.
Photo by Irish McKinney

**Tacoma P.D. contacts an Outsider member after I start taking photos
of the cop.**
Photo by Irish McKinney

All along the route we endured a coordinated multi-agency law enforcement physical surveillance operation. When we would stop, they
would move in close to take photos, and I'd start taking pics of them
causing them to back off. The run went great, and we raised a bunch of
money for the C.O.C. that would allow us to send multiple representatives of the Washington C.O.C. to the upcoming national N.C.O.M.
convention. The next day, I filed public record requests for the reports
and photos taken by the law enforcement officers from all the various
law enforcement agencies and the responses gave us more evidence for
the upcoming legislative session.

20

TWITCH GOES GATOR HUNTIN'

In May 2010, Double D, PigPen, Tommy No Guns, and I went to Orlando, Florida for the annual N.C.O.M. Convention. It was the first time I got to experience the national motorcycle club scene and I was excited. Gutz and T-Bob from the Portland chapter joined us on the trip, along with a lifetime/charter member from Portland named Old' Poop who was the Chairman of the Oregon C.O.C. Gutz had originally been a Tacoma member of the Outsiders MC, had been involved with the Washington C.O.C. and supported it and the rights movement. When he moved to Portland, he got involved with the Oregon C.O.C. We had started to pick up momentum with our motorcycle profiling movement here in Washington, the community was communicating well, and friendships were developing between the Washington state clubs who had lived a tense and sometime tumultuous existence. At that time, almost every Tacoma Outsider was involved in the C.O.C., with PigPen, Double D and I all starting to emerge as leaders in the Washington motorcycle profiling movement and motorcycle community, the Outsiders MC was getting a lot of positive attention from every club in the region and starting to develop a bit of a national buzz. Gutz wanted to be part of it and help bring the movement to Oregon, but T-Bob just wanted a free trip on the Oregon C.O.C.'s dime which he had never been active in, and an opportunity to try and feel important.

The motorcycle club world can be a dangerous place but at this point in time, it was an incredibly dangerous place and I understood it. There were a lot of active conflicts between various clubs, and the clubs involved in all of them were going to be there. N.C.O.M. conventions have an agreed policy between the clubs that absolutely no club business or violence is to take place, and everybody gets a free in and out. Before we arrived, I had conducted a threat assessment and advance for the convention and created an op's plan for our personal security. PigPen had been going to these conventions for years, but things had really heated up over the last few years and we were a handful of Outsiders wearing red and white rockers, going into Outlaw territory, and even though we had begun to develop a relationship with the Outlaws MC the year before, that is a big club with a lot of members and that could lead to issues. On top of that, with the conflicts that were going on in the club world at the time and the fact that we were building relationships with almost all the major one percent clubs in the country, I believed there was a threat that we could inadvertently find ourselves caught in the middle of a dispute between two motorcycle clubs. Before we left for Florida, Tommy and I briefed on everything. He had protected Double D at the convention the previous year and perceived the same threats I did. We worked really well together when it came to protecting Double D and the club, and this trip to Orlando would give us a chance to take the clubs security to a new level on the national stage, which would be noticed and earn respect for the club.

I am glad I took the time to put all the effort and attention into our security because when we arrived at the hotel in Orlando on Thursday, there were multiple SWAT teams surrounding the perimeter of the hotel, another SWAT team with K9 unit in the lobby, and a whole floor full of cops where they set up their command center and were monitoring us via the hotels CCTV system. Clearly, the cops were expecting World War Three. There were already about a thousand bikes in the parking lot of the hotel which meant there was no warming up to a dangerous environment, we were just jumping right in, and it was only going to get worse since the bulk of the attendees would be rolling in Friday and Saturday.

I took the lead and Tommy trailed with Double D and PigPen in between us as we walked into the lobby. We walked to the front desk and as PigPen and Double D checked us in, Tommy and I stood watch. Members of various clubs from all over the United States were everywhere and the atmosphere was incredibly tense. It was clear the Outlaws had booked the mezzanine level for their accommodations because there were several Outlaws and only OL's, strategically placed along the mezzanine looking down onto the lobby, keeping watch and gathering intel. On the far side of the lobby was a set of stairs that led to the hotel bar/night club and a hallway leading to what appeared to be a large convention hall, a Starbucks was conveniently placed at the entrance to the hallway. We had been standing at the front desk for about three minutes when all of the sudden one of the largest men I have ever seen in my life strides out onto the top of the steps with purpose, locks eyes with me from across the lobby and heads straight for me. Fuck, we've been here less than five minutes and I'm already going to have to shoot somebody because this dude was fucking huge, and he was on a mission. Well over 6'8", at least 450lbs, with white power and Outlaw tattoos covering every visible square inch of skin, he was an intimidating mountain of a man.

Here we go I thought. I moved towards him to keep distance between him and PigPen, stuck out my hand and said, Outsider Twitch, Tacoma. The giant loomed over me, looking down, stuck out his massive hand and said "Mountain, Outlaws 1%er" in a deep voice. His giant hand enveloped mine like I was trying to shake hands with a baseball mitt, and as he squeezed my hand to shake it, I felt something pop. As we shook hands, he maintained his grip on my hand, pulled me closer and leaned in. Oh great, here is the meet us here for a drink but we are really gunna fuck you up whisper, I thought. Mountain looked at me and all the sudden the tone of his voice went full-on stoner and he said, "Hey man, you got any groover?"

I do not do meth, never have and never will, so I do not know what they call meth in the south but groover sounded like a pretty good name for it to me. I told Mountain, "Nah man, I don't do that shit." Mountain looked confused and said no, no. You know, groover. "Grover?" I said, confused as hell. Mountain was getting visibly frustrated with our lack of communication like we were from two foreign lands, but he was doing his best to try and overcome it and next thing I know the giant squints his eyes, presses his thumb and index finger together and then presses them against his lips like he was smoking a joint and says, "No, you know. Groooooooover!" Bingo! Now we are speaking the same language. Ohhhhh Grooooover. I said. Yeah, man, we've got groover. We both laughed, and I invited the big man to meet us out back to smoke. You see, while the Outsiders Motorcycle Club does not manufacture, traffic, or distribute drugs as a club, the Tacoma Outsiders have always loved marijuana, individual members had grown marijuana as part of their own personal activities in the past, and their pot was truly world-class. Unbeknownst to me, Mountain had smoked weed with Double D, Spanky and PigPen at the NCOM convention the year before, and he had been knocked on his ass by some of Washington's finest. When Mountain saw us walk in the front door, he was eager to repeat the experience. On top of that, he had mistaken me for Spanky, which is why he got so frustrated when I didn't recognize him and wasn't understanding him. Mountain invited us to all come to the Outlaws floor when we were done dropping our bags off, gave us all hugs and headed back up to the Outlaws floor.

Yeah, that's right I said floor. They had an entire floor and they had it on lock down. When we got off the elevator on their floor there were guards posted at the elevators, as well as guards posted around the mezzanine, and at the entrances to all the hallways. Black electrical tape covered the lenses of all the security cameras on the floor giving them the privacy not afforded to the clubs that shared floors with the public. The Outlaws (OL) security at the elevator looked at us like we were crazy and asked why we were there. We told them we were there to see Mountain, who happened to be the OL's National Sargent at Arms at the time. Is he expecting you the Outlaw asked? Yeah, tell him Double D and the Tacoma Outsiders are here to see him. Still looking confused, the Outlaw and a probate escorted us back down an adjacent hallway to a room with the door open and led us in. Inside, Mountain sat in the desk chair making it look like he was sitting in a chair from a child's playhouse. There were six or seven Outlaws from all over the U.S. lounging about the room watching T.V. and drinking. A bank of two-way radios and scanners was plugged in on the desk with a list that appeared to be keeping track of members who had left the floor and hotel and their movements.

"Outsiders, I love these guys!" Mountain exclaimed as we walked into the room. Double D, Pigpen, Tommy, and I made our introductions, and Mountain offered us a seat and a drink. I had never met any Outlaws before and the only thing I knew about them at that point was things I had learned from people who had never met them, or from people who did not like them and had more than likely never met them, and what I had learned from the media and law enforcement. This introduction to the OL's was eye opening and I had a great time that afternoon in that hotel room with Mountain and the boys. The Outlaws are a bad-ass, motorcycle riding one percent motorcycle club with a lot of class, and over the years I would develop several close relationships in that club and a lot of respect for the Outlaws MC.

After we left the Outlaws floor, we went downstairs to the lobby to mingle with all the patch-holders that were hanging out and meet arriving club members. There were patch-holders from all sorts of clubs from all over the country there. Double D saw the President of an African American club that he had met the prior year and walked over to say hello. As that conversation ended, we turned and there was the

President of the Outcast MC out of Detroit and one of their prospects. The Outcast was initially an African American one percent motorcycle club that was founded in Detroit, Michigan in 1969. In the last several years the club has integrated and is multiracial now. We introduced ourselves to the president, while the Outcast prospect just stood next to the president staring straight ahead with his Malcolm X sunglasses, head cocked back, and angry militant look on his face. I could understand why the guy might be angry, instead of a rocker or rockers, this prospect simply had a duct tape "P" on the back of his vest. After talking to the president, I was getting bored, the angry militant prospect had not moved and his angry militant attitude was beginning to irritate the shit out of me, so I decided to amuse myself with an act of kindness. I remember how it was being a prospect and nobody showing any interest in you, so I stuck my hand out to prospect Grumpy X and gave my formal club introduction. He didn't fucking move. Are you fucking kidding me dude? You don't have enough respect to introduce yourself? I exclaimed. The Outcast President realizing what had happened and that it was a cultural misunderstanding intervened and apologized for his prospect who still had not moved. The President explained that in their club the prospects are not allowed to talk to anyone until they make member. I asked him how they were supposed to get to know anybody in the community until they made member and he said, they are not. We laughed and after a few more minutes of chit chat it was on to the next club and the next conversation.

Just because clubs like the Outcast MC wear a one percent diamond, does not mean they operate like traditional one percent clubs, and the black and integrated clubs operate very differently, with a lower level of commitment, and on a lower tier in the hierarchy than traditional one percent clubs. I use the term traditional one percent clubs in lieu of white one percent clubs as law enforcement likes to identify them, because one percent motorcycle clubs are generally not racist, even though they may have some members who are. During my time in the club world, I have met members of many different races in every major one percent motorcycle club. In fact, I have met African American members of the Bandidos, Outlaws and even the Hells Angels, over the years. The other thing I would come to find out about the motorcycle club world, including the one percent clubs is that members of the same motorcycle club will dress and behave very different based on their geographical locations and the environmental and sociological influences of that region.

While we were in the lobby, Gutz was having his own adventure. T-Bob was taking a nap and Gutz got bored, so he decided to explore the hotel a little. He was walking down our hall and found an odd door which opened into a stairwell. He followed the stairwell up to see where it led and ended up coming out on a floor that turned out to be the law enforcement command center where numerous plain clothes cops with guns were watching a wall of monitors that showed the views of the CCTV cameras in and around the hotel. They quickly kicked him off the floor, back into the stairwell and Gutz followed it down until it came to another door which opened onto a different floor in the hotel. Well, as Gutz wandered this new floor he came to a room full of Outlaws, one of which was Mountain because it happened to be their security command post that he had wandered into. The Outlaws were stunned to see him unescorted on their secured floor and when he explained that he got there via the one door on the entire floor they forgot to secure, they all got a good laugh. Then a probate was sent to secure the door. Gutz broke out a joint of some of the Northwest's finest and proceeded to get this room full of Outlaws Sergeant at Arms wrecked. We would later find out that they were all still so stoned hours later when they had an important national meeting that they got reprimanded by the National President. Gutz left a lasting impression, and the Outlaws would joke about that story with us repeatedly over the next decade.

From the lobby, we met up with Gutz and T-Bob and we all headed into the bar for some dinner. The bar was packed with hundreds of members of the Outlaws MC and their various support clubs. We took tables along the partial wall that separated the bar from the lobby and were enjoying our drinks when Ivan, who at the time was one of the Regional Presidents of the Outlaws was walking past the bar in the lobby and saw us sitting there. Ivan had met Double D and PigPen the year before and once again he mistook me for Spanky and spoke to me like we went way back. Ivan said that he had been hearing good things about what we were doing with uniting the clubs and our push for motorcycle profiling in Washington, and he wanted to hear more. He said he had a meeting he had to go to and excused himself. Before leaving, Ivan stuck his fingers to his lips, made a loud whistle, and at the top of his lungs he yells "Attention Outlaws!" The bar of hundreds of Outlaws MC members fell instantly silent. "You see these guys right here. These are the Outsiders Motorcycle Club and they're a bad-ass outlaw motorcycle club out of Tacoma Washington. They're friends of the Outlaws Motorcycle club and they're friends of mine, so you guys make sure you show them the utmost respect! Carry on." With that Ivan and his protection detail turned and walked away. T-Bob looked pissed, and we all knew why and were loving it. Not only had Ivan identified the club as being out of Tacoma and T-Bob likes to think Portland is the only chapter anyone knows about, but the fact that PigPen and the younger generation of Outsiders had earned that kind of respect on the national level incensed T-Bob and his fragile ego. T-Bob had not left the state of Oregon in years, let alone ever met any Outlaws, and he was visibly uncomfortable around all the other motorcycle clubs. Pigpen, Double, and I looked at NCOM as a critical opportunity to meet and develop relationships with anyone and everyone we wanted to and seized the opportunity. T-Bob called it an evening early and the rest of us stayed up socializing with the other clubs into the early morning hours. PigPen was off spending time with one of his good friends from the Gypsy Joker MC, while Double D, Tommy, and I went back out to the lobby and were socializing with the members of the various motorcycle clubs.

The lobby was a great place to spend time because it allowed us to monitor who was arriving as well as the overall tension of the environment. We were standing in the lobby when an older member of the Vagos came walking through the door with a couple of younger Vagos members. I scanned the Vagos tattoos, and it was clear that the older one had been in the club for a long time based on the evolution of the Vagos MC artwork which covered him, including his face. The patches on his cut identified him as a National Officer as well as a Nomad. As he walked into the lobby, he made a quick scan, locked eyes with me and b-lined it right towards Double D and I. As he reaches me, his smile broadens and he sticks out his hand and jovially says "Quicky John, Vagos MC Nomad. I shake his hand and introduce myself. Outsider Twitch, Tacoma. As soon as I uttered the word Tacoma, Quicky says, I love the Outsiders and asks me how PigPen is. He is doing good, he's upstairs in his room. Well, you tell him Quicky John says hello and I can't wait to see him. Quicky then went on to tell us all a story about how back in the day he had gotten in a jam in California and came up to Washington and the Outsiders and PigPen helped hide him out while he was waiting for things to blow over. It was clear that what we had done for him back in the day was not forgotten and he still held a lot of respect for our club. Over the years I would get to know Quicky better and come to respect him as an important part of the Vagos MC history, a good communicator, he would really help grow the relationship between the Vagos and Outsiders, as well as help get the Vagos involved in N.C.O.M. and the motorcycle profiling movement. Most importantly, I would come to know and respect Quicky John as a peacemaker.

The next morning, I was up early and headed downstairs to check things out before we brought Double D and PigPen down for the day. The Outlaws still had guards posted all over the lobby and mezzanine, the only thing that changed about the extreme law enforcement presence was a personnel change, giving us a fresh batch of angry looking militarized cops and swapping the Malinois K9 unit from the day before for a gorgeous German Shepherd who looked like he was having the time of his life hanging out in the air-conditioned lobby with all the bikers. The Sons of Silence MC and Devils Diciples MC had started to arrive overnight, and they both had posted guards in the lobby. We were all doing the same thing in that lobby, gathering intel on who was there, trying to gauge the attitude of the clubs with conflicts, assess the threat law enforcement posed, and enjoying the opportunity to meet guys from clubs we had never had any experience with before. It was like being in a foreign country, but this was just Orlando.

As I was headed back up to the room to brief Tommy and wait to bring Double D and Pig Pen back down, I ran into Gutz who was looking for a place to smoke a joint. The hotel bar opened to the pool area which had its own outdoor bar, all of which was surrounded by this beautiful lawn that gently sloped down into a small lake. There was a paved path that circled the perimeter of the lake. Just behind the outdoor bar was a long dock that ran out approximately one hundred feet onto the lake, was elevated about eight feet off the water and had a gazebo at the end of it. As Gutz and I walked the paved path, looking for a spot that was out of view of the hotel surveillance cameras which we knew were being monitored real-time by the floor full of cops and the SWAT teams on the exterior of the hotel, we came across a sign that warned that alligators were present and advised of a fine for feeding them. "Fuck yeah bro, check this out!" I said with excitement as I showed him the sign I had found along the water's edge. "I'm going to kill a gator while we're here and take it home." Yeah bro, you're fucking crazy. You're going to get eaten by an alligator while we're here. He joked. Besides, you're here to protect Double D and PigPen, and Double D isn't going to let you go alligator hunting. He was right but I was determined to take a crack at an alligator while I was there. As we walked back to the hotel, we stopped and spoke with the bartender who was restocking the pool bar and asked him if there were really alligators in the lake. "Sure, are!" he said. "Don't get too close to the edge of the water. We had to have a thirteen-footer pulled out of the swimming pool the day before yesterday." he said.

When we got upstairs to the rooms PigPen and Double D were awake. With great excitement I told Double D and PigPen about our gator discovery and my desire to go gator hunting. I figured that between all my special operations training, and my superior alligator hunting expertise obtained from watching seasons one and two of *Gator Hunters*, I had all the skills necessary to kill a fucking alligator. Double

D's response was exactly what Gutz said it would be. "You're fucking crazy Twitch and you're not going gator hunting." He said with all seriousness. Yeah, yeah, yeah, I said. I'm a member now, I'll take the heat on Thursday. I said defiantly.

We headed back downstairs, grabbed Double D a coffee at Starbucks, and then into the convention center for our seminars. N.C.O.M. conventions are not just a chance for all the clubs to get together and socialize, which for me was always the main draw. The conventions are packed with various seminars from industry experts, attorneys, etc., discussing topics like motorcycle safety, motorcycle rights, clean and sober roundtable, veterans' issues, Christian unity, etc. On Saturday of the convention, there is a general patch-holders meeting in which all the clubs from all over the country meet in one room with each state represented by their C.O.C. chair, and we discuss issues that were impacting the welfare of the motorcycle club community in the particular states and regions. There was also a banquet and party on Saturday night that was always fun to attend. Eventually Double D and I would become featured speakers at both the national and regional N.C.O.M. conventions. Honestly, the seminars were not that interesting to me because as I write this the only ones that I can remember were the ones about motorcycle profiling which really were born out of this N.C.O.M. trip, and the one where the Christian clubs got in a fight, that was fucking great.

The Pagans MC arrived early Friday afternoon and it was not just a few, it was the entire Pagan nation, and as soon as they arrived because of the conflict between them and the Outlaws at the time, the tension in the environment went through the roof. The Pagans had several guys posted up in the lobby and having never met any Pagans before and only knowing them from what I had read and seen on *Gangland*, we did what we had been doing since we got there, I told Double D we needed to meet them, and we walked right up to two of them and fearlessly introduced ourselves. The look of shock on their faces when we did was priceless.

I have mentioned that things are different depending on where you are at in the American motorcycle club world, well in the northeast where the Pagans are from, you do not just walk up and introduce yourself to a Pagan because that will likely get your ass kicked. You wait for that Pagan to invite you to come up for an introduction. Back then Tacoma Outsiders did not bow-down to anyone, so we refused to operate that way and played the game our way. Risky? Yeah, but you cannot sell your self-respect out for safety just because you are outnumbered in the one percent world. They introduced themselves as Mission and Lunatic, and then hit us with the first question of every club we met that has had conflict with the Hells Angels. "What's up with the red and white, are you guys support for the pink panties?" Mission asked. You see, it is commonly accepted that only the Hells Angels wear red and white rockers, and everyone assumed we were either undercover HA or a support club, and that made us instant enemies in their eyes. However, when they checked out the Outsiders history and learned the Outsiders have been doing their thing since 1968 and nobody has been able to stop that and saw how we carried ourselves on the national scene, their attitude started to change. We spent several minutes talking with them, and they were great guys. During our conversation, Lunatic says, "Hey, did you know they've got alligators in the lake out back?" "Hell yeah! I want to kill a gator, but Double D won't let me." I said. "Me too and my brothers won't let me either." Lunatic replied excitedly. "But I think I'm gunna take the fine." He said with a laugh. I told him I had told Double D the same thing.

Mission was a very respected and influential member of the Pagans MC, and while we stood talking to him, he introduced us to several of his brothers who stopped by to say hello to him, including the Philadelphia Pagans president Dominick "Tack" Dipietro. Tack is a well-known and respected long-time Pagan, and we clicked right off the bat. We were both take care of business guys, smart, and fiercely loyal to our brothers and our clubs. Over the years Tack would become a very dear friend of mine and someone I considered a brother, a leader in the motorcycle rights movement in his region, an excellent representative of the Pagans MC, and a man I highly respect. He is a true stand-up one percenter.

Tack is a full-on Pagan, really fucking cool, and sets his own style for the motorcycle club culture which is a mix between hardcore outlaw biker and Philly mobster. Tack always wears a beret, large leather gauntlets and plenty of jewelry. He carries himself with a confidence that screams don't fuck with me but is very approachable at the same time. In October 2009, Tack was indicted as part of a major R.I.C.O. indictment of the Pagans MC, and he along with several of his club brothers were charged with Interstate Travel in Aid of Racketeering, just for transporting the proceeds of raffle tickets for a club fundraiser across state lines. In Tack's case, all it took was $120 in raffle money and a motorcycle ride to the next state to earn an early morning raid by ATF, his wife was terrorized, his home destroyed, and he received a stay in a jail cell for the next year, before the feds finally dropped the charges and allowed him and the others to plead guilty to a minor state charge. I would have some good conversations with Tack during this trip, and over the years I would come to really respect and love the man for who he is and what he brings to the culture. He is the last of a dying breed of real one-percenters, so treat him good and pass on everything you learn from him.

The rest of the day was spent dropping in on seminars long enough to determine we were not interested and having meetings with the who's who of the motorcycle club world. Even though we had run out of time in our legislative session last year and didn't get a hearing on our motorcycle profiling bill in Washington, we had gotten sponsors for the bill, which had never been done before and that was huge not just for the Washington motorcycle community, but for the nation and it gave us hope that we would be able to fight a legitimate battle for our survival as a culture. There was a bit of a buzz beginning to develop amongst the motorcycle club community about how the Washington motorcycle club community had unified, our progress, hearing that we were starting to get along in Washington, and then seeing it firsthand as the other clubs from around the nation watched us have genuine, friendly interactions with not just the other motorcycle clubs from Washington state and the west coast, but from all over the country was intriguing to them. This was incredibly unique, had never happened before and the thought that we can all get along was appealing to motorcycle club members from every club.

One of my favorite motorcycle clubs I met this trip and one I would really enjoy spending time with over the years was the Warlocks Motorcycle Club. *Gangland* had aired an episode of the show a few months earlier that featured the Warlocks MC and included interviews with several of the members who I was now meeting in person and getting to spend time with. It was really interesting to have conversations with these men and discover how different they were from how they were portrayed by the creative editing in their segments on the show. Their National President at the time Big John and another influential member Diamond Dave showed a lot of interest in what we were doing in Washington, and we had multiple lengthy conversations with them. They told us about the problems they were having with motorcycle profiling in Florida, and we suggested techniques that could help them unify the community and start a legislative push. John, Dave, and the Warlocks MC are men of action, and they took the ideas and information we exchanged during our time together, put them to work, and over the years they would help lead the motorcycle rights movement in Florida.

It was on Saturday of this trip that I got to see how Bandidos protected their national officers when they travel. Gimme Jimmy, had come to N.C.O.M. to speak about the U.S. Defenders/C.O.I.R. program. Because of the danger of the club world at the time and his position in the Bandidos MC, when Jimmy traveled, he traveled with a full protection detail. I was impressed with how the Bandidos protected Jimmie because they were very professional. When they moved him, they would always send two advance guys who would go ahead of him to the destination and determine who was already there, where, and how many entrances/exits there were, they would secure seats for the group, and then Jimmy would be moved with a six-man protection detail using a modified diamond formation to create a protective perimeter around him. They had their shit dialed-in, and it was impressive. Along with Jimmy was Paul Landers, a member of a Bandidos support club out of Texas called the Escondidos MC. My initial impression of Jimmy was that of a Texan used car salesman and while he praised us for what we were doing in Washington, he immediately transitioned to trying to sell us on his U.S. Defenders program. We listened to Jimmy's pitch about the Kool-Aid we were already drinking for about five minutes before disengaging in search of food. Over the years, I would come to have great love and respect for both Jimmy and Paul.

Tata, the International President of the Vagos traveled with an even bigger protection detail than Gimme Jimmy. Though not nearly as professional as the Bandidos protection of Jimmy, the Vagos who protected Tata got the job done. We were passing by the Starbucks on the way out of the hotel and saw Tata sitting at a booth in the Starbucks with a couple of his national officers, one of which was Quicky John, along with an eight to ten-man protection detail watching over them. Double D and I stopped in our tracks, looked at each other and both said, "Let's go meet Tata!" With that we walked right in. When Quicky saw us, he motioned to the protection detail to allow us to pass, and we walked right up to Tata and introduced ourselves. Quicky told him that we were his good friends from Tacoma and go way back, at which point Tata told us he had heard what we were doing in Washington and thought it was interesting and liked what we were doing.

We left the hotel and went and got something to eat, unaware that back at the hotel tensions between the Outlaws and the Pagans were growing. N.C.O.M.'s have a no-violence policy but when you've got organizations that show up with several hundred members or even thousands, it is nearly impossible to prevent some hot-head in the group from doing something stupid that effects everyone, but the clubs try their best to prevent issues, including banishing members who get out of line to their rooms. As we pulled back into the hotel parking lot, I noticed that the SWAT teams had beefed up their numbers. We walked in the main entrance of the hotel, the mezzanine was ringed with Outlaws, and there were numerous Pagans in the lobby with ax-handle walking sticks and motorcycle helmets strapped to their belt loops. Tommy and I looked at each other knowing shit was about to go down and simultaneously we both said, "Room?" Yep. I said, and we took Double D up to his room then found PigPen safe and sound taking a nap in his room. Knowing there was an entire floor full of cops and the level of tensions downstairs, we figured that the safest thing we could do was keep Pig-Pen and Double D safe in the rooms while things played out downstairs. Double D took a nap and after a couple of hours I went downstairs to check things out. I was in the room, so I was not there to see how things resolved, but there was not any violence between the clubs and the show of force that had been going on in the lobby when we got back had reduced back to the normal lobby security presence from the two clubs. Clearly, something had happened between the two clubs, but they were obviously able to work it out. It does not always work out that way, but that was part of the goal of N.C.O.M., to get us all communicating so that hopefully we could resolve issues before they turned into conflict and violence.

As I made my way through the lobby, I ran into Ol' Poop. Ol Poop was a charter member of the Outsiders MC and got his name because at thirty years old in 1968, he was the old man in the club. Poop was a great guy and I really enjoyed him being involved in the club and the C.O.C., but he was getting on in years and you could tell he was becoming unaware at times. I did not want him to be roaming around by himself, so I took up with Poop and we went up to the N.C.O.M. hospitality suits which were on the opposite end of the mezzanine level from the Outlaws secured rooms. We were hanging out in one of the hospitality suites and both got engaged in separate conversations. With interest in what we were doing in Washington with the motorcycle profiling legislation, people from all over the country were wanting to talk to us about it and I found myself involved in a conversation that outlasted Ol' Poop's. When I finished my conversation, I looked around the room and saw that Poop's gone. Shit! Where did he go?

I headed out the door and looked to my right and saw Poop was all the way at the far end of the hall and he is headed for the Outlaws security checkpoint like he has no clue that he is headed for a clearly restricted area and potential danger zone. I couldn't run because that would freak people out, so I broke into a speed-walk for Ol' Poop, hoping that I could catch him and turn him around. As Poop wandered unaware towards the checkpoint, I called out to him, but he was pretty deaf and couldn't hear me. The Outlaw probates at the security checkpoint prepared to stop him but you could tell they were confused as to whether or not they should stop him or if he was just coming up to hang out with the Outlaws like we had several times over the previous days and recognizing me hurrying to catch up with him they just let him pass unimpeded. Poop wandered past the checkpoint guards and rounded the corner out of sight. Fuck! I thought. If these guys don't let me through, I've got a geriatric partially senile Outsiders charter member wandering alone and unannounced on the Outlaws secured floor and it happened on my watch. This situation is fucked!

As I approached the checkpoint the OL probates body language made it clear they were going to allow me to pass, and we all said hello as I hurried passed. I rounded the corner just in time to see a second set of probates do the same thing as the first, and Poop wandering into a secured conference room on the Outlaws secured floor. FUUUUU-UCK!! I hurried to the end of the hall and greeted the probates, who like the others recognized me from being on their floor multiple times over the past several days and like the prior probates they just let me pass. There was good distance between the interior security checkpoint and the room Poop wandered into and as I neared the room, I could tell he had wandered into a national meeting of the Outlaws MC. I could see the National President of the Outlaws MC, Milwaukee Jack speaking to a large room full of Outlaws members, some of which stared at Poop with shock while he had gone unnoticed to many others. Poop was standing by himself at a tall circular bar style table towards the rear right side of the room. Trying to go unnoticed myself, I silently and quickly entered the room and whispered to Poop that we needed to leave. As we turned to exit the room, Milwaukee Jack suddenly stopped talking. I turned to see Milwaukee Jack staring at us. Fortunately, I had met Jack earlier in the conference and we had a couple of good previous interactions, so I just apologized for interrupting and hustled Ol Poop out of the room, off their floor, and back up to his room.

We really made the most of the trip and over the course of it I met and began to develop relationships with national leadership from literally every respected one percent motorcycle club in the United States. I only met three Mongols from Florida at this N.C.O.M., but that would change as Doc Cavazos had been kicked out of the Mongols and under the leadership of Lil Dave the Mongols MC would become a strong and undeniably positive influence in the American motorcycle rights movement over the years to come.

Saturday night was the last night of N.C.O.M. and we spent it bouncing around from lobby and bar to various club members' rooms and hospitality suites. It was around 2:00am and Double D, Tommy and me were in the lobby talking to Tack and a couple of other Pagans members. Tommy and I had positioned ourselves where we each were maintaining a visual area of responsibility over the lobby since there were still several hundred members of various clubs milling about. I saw the automatic sliding door of the main entrance trigger in my peripheral vision and turned to see Mission and Lunatic from the Pagans walking in. Lunatic was carrying a clear plastic bag with a whole raw chicken inside in each hand, and when he saw me, he got a huge smile on his face, and they headed straight for us.

"Twitch, my brothers said I can go alligator huntin'. Wanna go?" Lunatic says excitedly in his West Virginia accent. Blood dripped on the marble hotel lobby floor from the corners of the plastic bags containing the raw chickens. "Nah man, I gotta watch Double D." I said. Just then, Tommy chimed in, "I got this. Go ahead bro." The atmosphere was much calmer and friendlier, and I figured I could sneak away for a little while at this point, so I politely interrupted Double D's conversation and asked if it was alright if I went alligator hunting with Lunatic. Double D turns to Tack and says, "Do you see what I have to deal with?" referring to me. "Our brother Twitch was off the hook already and he comes to Florida and hooks up with one of your brothers named fucking Lunatic of all things, and now they're going alligator hunting in Florida, and he doesn't know anything about alligator hunting. They're going to get eaten!" Tack laughed and said, yeah nothing good will come from this. Mission said he was not going miss watching us get eaten and was going with us. As we walked out onto the dock in the back of the hotel, we ran into a couple of Bandidos from Texas. We all exchanged introductions and seeing the bags of raw chickens, they asked what the fuck we were up to. When they heard that a Pagan from West Virginia and an Outsider from Tacoma, Washington were seriously going to try and kill an alligator right behind the fucking Orlando Marriot, the Bandidos decided they were going to stay and watch us get eaten too and we all headed down to the dock.

I pulled my Surefire flashlight out of the pocket of my vest and began to shine it in the grass and bushes that lined the edge of the small lake, until almost directly across the lake from us, my light lit up two large glowing red orbs. Jackpot! Watching *Gator Hunters* had taught me well and we had located a gator, but now we had to get it to come all the way across the little lake to us. Lunatic tore a large chunk of meat from the raw chicken and threw it as far as he could, which was almost halfway across the little lake. I tore off a piece, but my throw didn't make it any farther than Lunatic's. He and I both gave it another shot and came to the realization that we were never going to get anywhere close to the gator. Just as Mission started giving Lunatic shit about how he had told him he would never catch an alligator; the red orbs began to move out into the lake. I kept my light on the gators eyes as it slowly moved towards where we had thrown the chicken. Holy shit, that actually worked, one of the Bandidos said. The gator continued right to where we had thrown the raw chicken and we could see it clearly chomping its mouth in the water as if it were eating the floating chunks of chicken. It was like we had both got a shot of adrenaline and Lunatic and I began to throw more chicken out to the gator who continued to feed. Little by little we reduced our range until eventually we had lured the gator to where it was directly below where we were standing on the elevated boardwalk. The gator was about eight and a half feet long, and as we dropped the raw chicken to it, it would chomp it out of the air. Its big mouth making a powerful clapping noise as it slammed shut.

"We can't kill it from here. It will sink and we'll never be able to get to it." Lunatic said. This was a serious dilemma for both of us, because we had already talked about the Pagans/Outsiders South Florida Alligator Hunt trophies we were going to have made for each other's clubhouses, and the various items and gifts we were going to make from the hide. Not one to give up, I said, hold on I got this. I grabbed two handfuls of raw chicken and ran off the boardwalk, down to the water's edge and right into the water about mid-shin deep. We had been listening to the nature sounds of Florida since we got out there and I knew the familiar meep, meep, meep sound that we had been hearing was the call of baby alligators, but I could not tell where they were coming from when we were on the boardwalk. Well, now that I was down in the water, I could tell that those baby gators were hidden in a very large bush that was at my five o'clock and if this big son of a bitch that we had been getting all worked up feeding raw chicken wasn't their mama, then mama could be anywhere nearby, including the bush behind me getting ready to have a Twitchy snack.

Maybe it was the Corona, and I know the high of having a great time bonding doing crazy shit with one-percenters from these great clubs played a major role in my risky behavior. Regardless, I did not care, and I shoved my hands in the black lake water, shook them back and forth violently, and called out playfully in my best Australian accent. Heeeeere gator, gator, gator. The dock erupted in laughter. No response from the gator as it continued to hungrily stare up towards where Lunatic and the others were standing. I threw a piece of chicken directly at the gator, the chicken bouncing of the underside of the gators broad jaw. The gator dropped its head back to the water and squared off facing directly at me. I tossed the last piece of chicken mid-way between me and the gator, quickly checked my five o'clock to make sure I was not about to take a sneak attack and returned my focus to the alligator.

The light from the boardwalk clearly illuminated the big gator as it floated there motionless on the surface of the water below the end of the boardwalk. It just stared at me motionless for several seconds before Lunatic said, "Oh shit bro, I think you pissed it off!" Next thing you know it slowly sinks straight down just below the surface of the water and started off slowly, headed straight for me. Lunatic started to run off the boardwalk and frantically screams "Oh shit bro, you better get outta there. It's gunna eat you!" He bounced back and forth frantically on the boardwalk mid-way between me and the closing gator, yelling to me to get out of there and telling me I'm going to be eaten. The gator kept coming at me slowly, the distance between us narrowing, and Lunatic got even more frantic until he suddenly grabs an empty red Solo cup that was sitting on the railing of the boardwalk and throws it at the gator. The gator was just below the surface of the water, leaving an ominous wake like a shark and the empty red solo cup just bounced off the back of the gator, eliciting zero response from the gator who was clearly on a mission. Lunatic yelled "I can't watch this!" and ran from the dock while Mission and the Bandidos laughed and stayed to watch my demise. The gator was now within about eight feet of me. My right hand cleared my vest and shot to the grip of my 9mm pistol. Just as I began my draw stroke it dawned on me that if I fired a gun behind a hotel full of thousands of bikers, with a floor full of cops, and surrounded by SWAT teams, it might be bad. My draw stroke stopped and my pistol never broke leather. Just as I stopped the gator stopped, now only about six feet from me. "Holy fuck bro. You're ridiculous!" Mission yelled to me.

The gator just sat and stared at me then sank below the water and popped up to stare at me again. I backed out of the water and headed back up the lawn realizing that I did not think that one all the way through, and that wanting to have fun could have easily resulted me in being the biggest jackass in outlaw motorcycle club history had I pulled that trigger. As I got up by the end of the boardwalk Mission, Lunatic, and the Bandidos were all waiting. Lunatic just kept repeating "Holy shit bro, you're nuts!" Shaking his head and laughing, while Mission thanked me for the entertainment. We all talked about how much fun it had been before saying our goodbyes to the Bandidos. We found Double D, Tommy, and Tack right where we had left them, but now the crowd of patch-holders from various clubs socializing with them had started to wind down. Lunatic told them what had happened, we all had some more laughs and said our goodbyes to our new friends since we would be catching a plane back to the west coast in a matter of a couple of hours. Mission has since passed away but I am glad I got the opportunity to know him, he was a man of honor, and I feel very privileged that we shared this trip and its memories.

The trip was an amazing experience, I learned a lot about the clubs by watching them operate firsthand and getting to know their national leadership and members from multiple chapters. I had a great time traveling with my brothers and getting to experience the national club scene. Most importantly, we had really started to develop a lot of very positive key relationships and respect with the movers and shakers of the motorcycle club world, and this would end up proving crucial down the road.

Back home that Wednesday night at the clubhouse, Tabasco the Tacoma chapter President of the Bandidos and a handful of his guys showed up for open house. As he walked through the front door my eyes keyed in on an unknown item wrapped in a blue towel that was tucked under his arm. Double D and I walk out from behind the bar and Tabasco set the item on the pool table while he greeted us with big hugs. "Twitch, I heard a story about you." He grumbled cheerfully. Oh yeah, what's that? "Word travels fast in the Bandidos and I heard from all the way in Texas that you went alligator hunting with some of my brothers but couldn't shoot the gator because there were too many cops." He said with a big smile. Tabasco picked up the item and as he unwraps it, I could see it was a stuffed alligator head. Tabasco told us that one of his Louisiana brothers hunts alligators and killed the alligator, stuffed it, and gave it to him as a gift, and now Tabasco wanted me to have the head because he thought what I did was pretty cool and I had earned it. I was tremendously honored, and it is the most special gift any patch-holder has ever given me.

21

MOTORCYCLE CLUBS
AND RACING

By the summer of 2010, the Tacoma chapter of the Outsiders MC was running so tight, and we were having so much fun doing it that several of the older members that had retired began to ask to come back active. One of the old-time members that came out of retirement was an old Outsider named Bear. Bear was still in his teens and a member of another Portland area motorcycle club that existed back in the 1960's when he first met the Outsiders MC. He became a member of the Outsiders in 1969, and while he only was a member for less than five years the first time, he had a big impact on the club because he was responsible for starting a war between the Outsiders and Gypsy Joker.

The way I was told the story, Bear and another old school Portland Outsider were drinking and doing God knows what at the Gypsy Joker clubhouse when Bear and a Gypsy Joker got to bragging about who had the faster bike. That bragging led to Bear disrespecting the Joker, punches were thrown, shots were fired, and those two Outsiders were lucky to escape there with their lives. Things escalated from there with incidents going back and forth, and the next thing you know Bear finds a group of Outsiders building a bomb to blow up the Joker's clubhouse in the basement of the home he shared with his wife and daughter. That was enough for Bear, and he quit the club while we were still in a war he started. While I do not blame him for being pissed when he found the fellas in his basement, there are much better ways to handle that situation than quit the club but knowing Bear like I do now, I think things just got too outlaw for him and he got scared. The Jokers ended up deciding they wanted a truce when several Outsiders were stopped by police in a car on their way to go blow up the Gypsy Joker clubhouse. When you live by a code of honor that demands an eye for an eye, the stakes can get really high but it's what we all agree to when we join. Because of the way Bear quit the club, you had some Outsiders who looked at it as dishonorable as I did, and others that revered him because he had been around since 1969 and kept contact with the club after he quit.

I first met Bear when I was a prospect and we were on our Fourth of July Run in Ocean Shores, WA. Bear was a truck driver and seemed like a cool enough guy. I was not in the club yet, so I was not privy to why he quit and had not developed an opinion on it, and he mostly hung-out with the old timers in the club that had been there for forty years. That run was cool, we held it at T.D.'s beach house. The best part of the run was Saturday evening when Pigpen was teaching Double D's sons how to shoot cars with bottle rockets and the cops came. These were not just little pop bottle rockets; these were the big bad mammer-jammers.

I was pulling security, so part of my job was to control access to the main entry to the property. Pigpen had brought the boys down and was standing inside the fence-line walking them through how to aim and time their shots exactly right to hit passing cars. He demonstrated for the boys and launched a rocket at a passing BMW which exploded on the front window. The car came to an immediate stop and the man driving angrily looked towards us before picking up his cell phone and driving off. I warned Pigpen that the cops may show up and he just grumbled that they were not there now and handed each of the boys several rockets. Well just as their little arms were outstretched and the fuses had been lit, a cop car comes into view at the end of the block. As I turn to warn Pigpen about the cop car rolling towards us, the rockets fly out of the tubes the boys were launching them from, explode on the side of a passing Suburban causing the boys and PigPen to erupt in laughter. "Oh shit, it's the cops! Everybody scram!" Pigpen exclaims as he grabs the rockets from the boys. I took the rockets from Pigpen and made them disappear. I return to Pigpen just in time to meet the cops at the road and ask them if I could help them. After a couple of friendly hellos, they start to laugh and tell us that we can't be shooting rockets at cars anymore because they were getting complaints. We cooled it with the rockets but later in the evening, Single D lit off a string of 500,000 firecrackers in the middle of the road. Those firecrackers went off for over ten minutes and the smoke cloud from them was so thick that it stopped traffic on the road.

Sadly, the last day we were there, Bear opened the door to his motor-home and his little dog went running out into the road and was killed by a passing car. We buried his dog in the backyard of T.D.'s beach house. Over the next year Bear's marriage ended and by the spring of 2010, Bear was wanting to come back as an active member. Bear owned a nitro Harley dragster, was into drag racing, and when he started coming back around on a regular basis, Single D and I started crewing for his drag team. Racing has always been part of motorcycle club culture. It was where it all began and it was the motorcycle clubs that formed around racing which evolved into outlaw motorcycle club culture, so it should come as no surprise that many outlaw motorcycle clubs are still involved in motorcycle racing. Racing provides the riders with an amazing adrenaline rush, allows the rider and members of the team to spend time together bonding as brothers while they do something fun, and it exercises their drive for competition. In addition, the track is a great environment because it gives you a chance to socialize and spend time with members of other clubs.

The first big race we crewed for Bear was the A.H.D.R.A. Northwest Nationals in Woodburn, Oregon. Single D and I had ridden our bikes down with the motor-home towing the race trailer behind us. It was a beautiful ride down apart from the traffic we hit going through Portland, and we rolled into the racetrack around 11:00am. It was already close to one hundred degrees and the pits were filling up fast with racers and their crews. A couple of the big sponsored top fuel Harley drag teams with their million-dollar motorhomes and multi-level race trailers were already set-up and tuning their bikes. The roar from those bikes was deafening and I could not wait to see them make a pass down the track.

Twitch filming a friend racing in the stock class.

After setting up our pit and tuning the bike, we were ready for our first qualifying pass and had plenty of time to wander around the pits, check out the other bikes, and socialize. Brother Speed MC was there with a couple of bikes to run, along with a top fuel drag bike ridden by a Bandido from Mississippi. Our qualifying pass went well and that night the racers and teams stayed at the track, and it turned into a giant party. It was a great time.

Bear on his nitro Harley dragster making his qualifying pass. Twitch in the background at the starting line.

Saturday was race day and by 10:00am it was over one hundred de-grees; the stands were full, and almost every Oregon motorcycle club was there. Mooch and about ten Mongols along several members of a Mongols support club called the Raiders MC had shown up, and Single D and I had a good conversation with them before getting to work mak-ing the last-minute adjustments to the dragster's clutch pack and mixing the fuel for our pass. The dragster ran on nitro methane which had to be specifically mixed for each pass based on factors including air temp, track temp, humidity, and track length. Bear's crew chief "Just Dave" had been racing with Bear for years and spent the three days we were at the track teaching us the ins and outs of crewing a successful motorcycle drag race. We finished in the top three, so it was a good first race for us.

Twitch and Single D look on as Bear launches.

Single D is a second-generation Outsider, one of the younger members of the club, and for him being in a motorcycle club is mostly about the motorcycle and what he can do with it. He is a great mechanic and spent time learning to work on bikes as he was growing up from his dad and the guys in the club. When he started working at Easystreet Custom Cycles, he got a chance to immerse himself in his passion and his skills really began to develop. Over the years, he would become the trusted mechanic for not just the Outsiders MC, but for members of several south Puget Sound based motorcycle club members and become co-owner of Easystreet. He had just got done building himself a beautiful custom Dyna which was easily the fastest bike around, so working on a nitro drag bike was right up his ally. Getting the opportunity to be the mechanic for a nationally competitive nitro Harley drag team gave him the ability to take his skills to a whole new level and do some traveling.

I think the best time I had with Single D at a race was when we got invited out to race in Sturgis the first year that they brought the

Harley drag races back to the Sturgis Rally. Unfortunately, over the years there have been incidents of violence between clubs that have occurred at drag races and that has led several racetracks to either adopt no colors policies which drives away racers and teams associated with motorcycle clubs, or simply ban Harley drag races all together. Sturgis was one of these venues but this year they changed their mind and decided to host a Harley drag during the rally. Because it was Sturgis, several of us rode out there with the race team R.V. and trailer following us, and along the way stopped at various clubhouses to spend the night. Partying with various outlaw motorcycle clubs on the way out to Sturgis is a great way to start a trip like that. Sturgis was hot as fuck. Temperatures were over one hundred degrees each day with thunderstorms rolling through every evening.

Just like with every race, we stayed at the track and there were plenty of other motorcycle clubs to socialize with, which was good because there was only two bars in town that would allow motorcycle club members to enter, and to get there you had to navigate a deadly gauntlet of hundreds of thousands of wannabee's, weekend riders, tourists, and even first-timers who had bought a brand new Harley and had it shipped to Sturgis. At the track we had a full kitchen, restroom, shower, and a ton of great food and alcohol. Best of all, because there were so many motorcycle clubs there, there were none of the drunk lames causing problems that we would have had to deal with in town. Don't get me wrong, I'm not saying people weren't getting drunk out at the track, we were, but in the club world you have to maintain and hold your mud because if you lop out, you're gunna get knocked out. We were outside partying when it started raining on us, so we moved the party into the race trailer. Buell Greg had moved to Montana at this point but when he heard we were headed to Sturgis he hopped on his bike, met us along the way, and rode out to Sturgis with us. Bueller was one of those younger generation Outsiders that attracted me to the club, part of that core group of us younger generation guys that created such a unique dynamic for the chapter, and we all missed him. Having him with Single

D, Spanky, and I at Sturgis was awesome and we all partied in that race trailer until the sun started coming up.

Single D enjoying some whiskey on the Harley nitro dragster.

The next day it was hot as fuck again. We blew the motor on our first pass, so we were done racing for the trip, but rather than get bummed out we decided to fire up the barbeque, break out the alcohol, and start the party early. At the time of this Sturgis Rally, Washington and Colorado had not yet legalized recreational marijuana, so things like concentrates, oils, and dabs were just coming onto the medical marijuana scene in those states but the public was largely unaware of what a dab or a dab rig is. I am going to explain dabs here because there are a few funny stories from over the years which I talk about in this trilogy that involve dabs.

A dab is the term used for inhaling vaporized Butane Hash Oil (BHO), a highly concentrated form of THC, the main active chemical in marijuana. The process of taking a dab involves super-heating a glass bowl attached to a glass water pipe using a torch and then touching a metal spoon with a small amount of BHO on it to the glass bowl and inhaling the vapor. A dab rig is the glass pipe used to vaporize the BHO, and back then they were very simple and looked a lot like big crack pipes.

A few of us were in the back of the race trailer watching the crowd walk by and some of the fellas were doing dabs when a couple of members of the Sons of Silence MC stopped by to say hi. We had been getting to know the Sons over the last few years and when they saw us in the back of the trailer, they b-lined it right for us. After a few minutes of chit-chat, the Sons asked us if we knew where they could get some meth. As Spanky and I were explaining to the two Sons that we were not into that stuff, the two other guys with us fired up the torch and started heating up the dab rig. The Sons eyes got big, and Spank asked them if they wanted a dab. "Oh shit, you guys are into some hardcore shit! No thanks man, we're not into that stuff, we'll get kicked out of the club for doing that shit." one of the Sons said. The Sons thought the fellas were smoking crack and after Spanky explained that it was super concentrated TCH, we all had a good laugh. Even though it was just a marijuana derivative, they had never seen anything like it, said it was too "George Jetson" for them, and they passed on Spank's offer.

That is life at the racetrack. We are all there to race, have a good time, and try to leave any club drama on the street. That does not mean that incidents of violence have not occurred at races because they have, but they are usually sparked by a lone member or a couple of members who have had too much to drink and act out on their own, rather than a deliberate coordinated act of club violence. The acts of violence that have occurred and resulting no colors or no Harley drag policies, have made it much harder for motorcycle club members to be involved and be competitive in the sport of Harley Davidson motorcycle drag racing and it has had a negative impact on outlaw motorcycle club culture. Additionally, motorcycle clubs realize that racetracks are horrible locations to commit crimes and are full of innocent by-standers and witnesses, so every effort is taken by the clubs to avoid any conflict or violence at racetracks.

Bottom line, racing is part of the motorcycle club culture's heritage and a critical element of what they're all about, but between the huge financial expense of the sport and random incidents of violence that have occurred between clubs at races resulting in limited opportunities for racing, Harley drag racing is a dying sport, but the clubs are still trying to keep it alive by going back to the roots of the sport, renting private racetracks and holding their own outlaw races again. However, these outlaw races are usually at tracks that are too small to race the nitro methane or top fuel bikes and so they are limited and missing out on the big fun.

22

THE SWISS

We experienced back-to-back momentum boosts during the late summer and early fall of 2010. My use of the public records act to obtain dash cam video of WSP troopers profiling bikers had started to get under their skin and in August 2010, one of the most prolific law enforcement offenders and shitbag WSP Trooper named Kenyon Wiley showed his professionalism and helped reinforce the need for motorcycle profiling legislation and retraining, when he posted this comment to the video I had posted of WSP trooper Pigott arresting James Wegge for "Uhhh, uhhhh, yeah for something." This Trooper's internet temper tantrum was great evidence that we knew we could exploit with the legislature.

Tue, Apr 27, 2010 at 6:00 PM

Comment posted on "Profile Stop Performed By Trooper Pigott #963 of WSP"

help center | e-mail options | report spam

kenyonwiley has made a comment on Profile Stop Performed By Trooper Pigott #963 of WSP:

Bikers advertise that they are criminals... they wear patches advertising they assault police officers...screw bikers...they are all little girls unless they have their brothers with them.

You can reply to this comment by visiting the comments page.

© 2010 YouTube, LLC
901 Cherry Ave, San Bruno, CA 94066

Marty Fox had filed a lawsuit against the Washington State Patrol and WSP Trooper Pigott who arrested James Wegge for no lawful reason on the way home from our clubhouse back in 2008. On September 10th, 2010, the State of Washington Pierce County Superior Court found in favor of James Wegge and issued a stipulated judgment against the Washington State Patrol, Chief John Batiste, and Trooper Keith Pigott in the amount of $90,000. This was not only a significant win for the club member, but it was a win for the motorcycle club community, and it would allow us to put a price tag on motorcycle profiling offenses.

The misspelled No Cuts sign at the front door. C.O.C. attorney Marty
Fox's reflection can be seen in the door.
Photo by Irish McKinney

The next day the Washington C.O.C. held a protest run on a local Tacoma area landmark bar and grill called The Swiss that had recently instituted a no-colors policy. We were not going to tolerate a bar in our hometown having a no colors policy and were determined to change that using another protest run. The pack met up at the 48th Street Pub in Tacoma which is only about a mile and a half away from The Swiss in downtown Tacoma.

The pack was around two hundred bikes strong as we made the short ride to The Swiss. Once again, Single D oversaw the road guards and laid out a tactical plan that allowed us to efficiently block the intersections that needed to be blocked in order to allow the pack to pass through with minimal interference with the flow of traffic, and they got everybody there safely.

A member of one of the clubs was dating a graduate student named Julie from the University of Puget Sound and who worked in their media center. Julie had told her boss about the documentary I was shooting, educated him on the motorcycle profiling movement, and showed him my YouTube video of the protest run from the year prior. Next thing you know I get a call from Julie, and she asked if I would like to use some cameras and mics that U.P.S. had to shoot my documentary. It was not much but it was better than what we had and to me, having some-one take an interest in and support the communities work and my work meant the world. U.P.S. had given us several Flip cams which I passed out to various club member and their ol ladies. My goal was to have an ol' lady carry the flip cam and get footage from inside the pack, while I went ahead, and we used a tripod and one of the video cameras they loaned us to capture the pack as it came towards me and then turned past at a key intersection along the route.

**Me in the black beanie using one of the Flip cams provided by the
University of Puget Sound as Marty Fox addresses the bar owner
(bald head).**
Photo by Irish McKinney

When we arrived at the Swiss, Double D, Marty, and I entered the
bar. There was a tall bald man sitting at a table inside the main entry
with a group of women, and as we entered the bar, he got up and walked
towards us in a clear attempt to intercept us from making it to the bar.
Excuse me guys, I'm the owner and we have a no cuts policy and you're
not allowed in here. Double D told him that is what we had come to talk
to him about and asked him if he would rather speak to us outside. He
agreed and followed us outside.

Always there supporting me, the club, and the motorcycle profiling
movement, Candace can be seen on the left in the black and red
sweatshirt reaching for a camera in her purse, while Double D
speaks with the owner of the Swiss and I film it all from the middle of
the action.
Photo by Irish McKinney

Outnumbered and outsmarted, the owner of The Swiss and Double D
speak as the clubs of the Washington C.O.C and attorney Martin Fox.
Look on. (Photo by Irish McKinney)
Photo by Irish McKinney

As he walked out the front door his face turned white, and he could not hide the look of fear as he realized he was surrounded by over two hundred members of all the various motorcycle clubs of Washington State. Double D explained that his "No Cuts" policy was unconstitutional and violated the First and Fourteenth Amendments of the U.S. Constitution, and he provided the owner with a copy of the letter we had distributed to the bars during our protest run the previous year.

The owner brought up the typical objections we had heard, citing incidents like the 2002 Laughlin riot as proof that there will be violence if more than one motorcycle club came into his establishment. Double D smiled and then stretched out his arm to bring the owners attention to all the various patches peacefully gathered together to have a productive conversation with him about changing his policy that was excluding them and repeated his request for the owner to change the policy, reminding him that he would certainly make money if he did. At that point, the C.O.C. attorney Marty Fox suggested that the owner grant a one-day moratorium on his policy to give us a chance to prove that his line of thinking was outdated and false. Eventually the owner agreed to allow us in and after we filled his cash registers and left without incident, The Swiss permanently did away with their no cuts policy and the owner ended up hiring members from several different motorcycle clubs to work security together at the bar. It was another victory for the Washington C.O.C., proved to us that our success was not by chance, reinforced that working together we could accomplish anything, and the unity of the Washington motorcycle club community was undeniable. We backed each other.

23

STEPPING UP OUR GAME

There was a point in my life where I did not like Bandidos MC. I had no reason to not like them, but it is a mentality I learned from being around the Hells Angels early on. By the fall of 2010, I included multiple Bandido national officers and several members as my closest friends, and I felt stupid for having had the previous attitude I did about them. The Outsiders and Bandidos relationship was really getting strong, and a few weeks after the protest run at the Swiss, Double D, myself and several of our members, prospects, and hang-arounds rode up to the Bandidos annual Red Barn party on a farm in Snohomish, WA. The Red Barn party was a great time and we competed with the Bandits in traditional biker games like the keg push, slow races, etc. Each Bandido chapter in the state had their own campsite and after the biker games we had some great food and spent the next twelve hours bouncing from campsite to campsite visiting with all the different chapters. It was a fun time.

A few weeks later we spent the night partying with them in their compound at the annual Oyster Run. We witnessed one of their brothers get married and spent two full days bonding with Bandidos from Washington and all over the country. There was a genuine brotherhood developing between the two outlaw motorcycle clubs and it was not only changing the Washington motorcycle club community, but word was getting out around the country about how great it was to be a patch-holder in Washington and both clubs were getting a lot of positive national attention from the other motorcycle clubs for what we were doing.

In October, Double D and I were asked to speak at the Regional N.C.O.M Convention in Portland, OR. Regional N.C.O.M. conventions are smaller versions of the national conventions consisting of the clubs and motorcycle rights organizations that operate within that region. Washington State is part of Region-1, which consists of Alaska, California, Hawaii, Idaho, Oregon, and Washington. Just like at the larger national convention, there are speakers and seminars on legislative issues, motorcycle safety, clean and sober, and Christian issues, and a social event for all the participants on Saturday night. I had been to this event in previous years, and it had always been well attended but because of what was going on with the Washington C.O.C., we all showed up in force, as did the clubs from Oregon and California who were curious to see it for themselves and hear about how we were doing what we were doing. Even the Outsiders Portland chapter who traditionally had not participated in this event showed up.

If we were not in seminars, we were socializing with the various clubs from all over the region. The Bandidos showed up with over one hundred members and it was interesting for me to see how uncomfortable and intimidated our Portland brothers were around all those Washington clubs. So much so that they isolated themselves off in a corner of the bar with the Gypsy Joker and didn't really attend any of the seminar's, including the hour-long session where Double D and I spoke about our motorcycle profiling movement in Washington state and how to replicate it in their state, and I taught the convention how to use public records requests to document incidents of motorcycle profiling. We were very well received and after we were done Double D and I both spent a couple of hours having individual conversations with motorcycle club members from all over the region and answering questions. The brotherhood between the Washington clubs was evident to all the clubs from out of state and the entire conference fed off it, creating an awesome vibe. Our Portland fellas split early Saturday night, leaving us free to bounce from club to club, party in the bar, and have great private conversations with members of various clubs up in the hotel rooms.

All the clubs were partying down in the hotel bar. It was a great time but around midnight, Pigpen, Billy Two Weeks from the Gypsy Joker, and Spike from the Hessians MC decided to head up to Pigpen's suite for some drinks. As chair of the Washington C.O.C., Pigpen got a room paid for by the C.O.C., so we would generally try and book him a suite so there was room for members from our club and other clubs to crash, and it made for a great party spot. I was done with the noise level of the bar and decided to head up with Pigpen and the fellas and I am sure glad I did. Not only did Pigpen's room have the C.O.C. booze stash, but none of those guys had less than thirty years' experience in the outlaw motorcycle club world, and I spent the next several hours getting to listen to them tell stories about their time in the club world. What was really cool though is when Spike brought up the story about me and the alligator from Florida. The story had continued to spread amongst those that were in Orlando or had brothers in Orlando and it had made its way to southern California and Spike, and to have these respected outlaws including a story about me really made me feel honored and reminded me that I was doing things right.

PigPen, Billy Two Weeks, and Spike

Unlike Double D who feeds off it, public speaking has never been my thing, especially when it is in front of several hundred to several thousand motorcycle club members. That said, I was real and kept things simple enough when I spoke that no matter who you were in the room, you could understand what I was teaching, why it would help your club and your community, and how to do it. I had pieced together a rough cut of my documentary and began giving away copies and accepting donations to help raise money to pay for post-production work to try and help clean it up as best we could. People were starting to come up to Double D and me to thank us for what we were doing for the motorcycle club community. I was having a positive influence on the culture, and I was driven to keep stepping up my game however I could and seeing what we could accomplish with what the Washington motorcycle clubs were inspiring across the nation.

24

PULLING PATCHES

One of the traditions of the outlaw motorcycle club culture that is quickly dying out due to the feds use of R.I.C.O. is the tradition of pulling patches. A motorcycle clubs' patch is its flag, making it sacred to the clubs' members and something that they should be willing to sacrifice their life to protect and defend. Taking a club members patch is the ultimate disrespect to the member and his club, it is a profoundly serious thing and almost always involves some level of intimidation and violence. If a member had his patch taken, he was often expelled from his club, and if a club had their patches taken, they were permanently shut down. That said, over the last twenty years I've pulled my fair share of patches, because when I first got involved in the motorcycle club world patch pulling was a tool of communication and was routinely used to regulate the local motorcycle club community and prevent the problems that come with idiots that start their own clubs when they don't have any relationships in the motorcycle club community, don't understand the protocols, disrespect the motorcycle club community, and then behave like T.V. bikers, which gives everyone a bad reputation because the public can't differentiate between these bullshit pop-up clubs and an Outsider, Bandido, Hells Angel, Outlaw, Mongol, etc.

The primary reason the National Coalition of Motorcyclists (NCOM) and the various Confederation of Clubs were formed was because the outlaw motorcycle clubs realized that law enforcement was unfairly targeting them for the acts of individual members and R.I.C.O.

is law enforcements weapon of choice. The annual national N.C.O.M. conference provides seminars with attorneys on subjects such as trademark law, personal injury and even sessions that discuss major criminal cases against motorcycle clubs and R.I.C.O. These sessions gave the clubs the opportunity to ask questions of knowledgeable attorneys and compare the various investigative tactics and prosecution strategies the federal government was using against the clubs. It was these attorneys and the RICO prosecutions that helped the clubs understand we needed to stop pulling patches.

In the 1990's, ATF began to make outlaw motorcycle clubs one of their primary targets and started making what would prove to be regular infiltrations of outlaw motorcycle clubs. These infiltrations were based on the misconception that outlaw motorcycle clubs are really gangs that operate as criminal organizations like the mafia. ATF's first infiltration of the Warlocks MC in Florida yielded some charges against members of the club; however, it was a huge intel win for ATF and it taught them that outlaw clubs as a whole are not operating as criminal organizations, and the operation resulted in minimal convictions and sentences, and cost ATF a lot of money.

As a result of an ATF infiltration of the Outlaws Motorcycle Club that concluded in 1995, members of the Orlando and Daytona chapters were indicted for federal racketeering charges related to assault and robbery for a 1994 incident in which the Outlaws beat fourteen members of the Fifth Chapter MC, took their patches and club indicia, and told them they were shut down in Florida. For the first time a patch pulling would put outlaw motorcycle club members in prison for over twenty years on racketeering related offenses.

In 1999, the ATF began using an undercover technique I like to call to call "Dynamiting the pond.", in which they establish a club consisting of law enforcement officers in an area of the country where the existing outlaw clubs are known to be very territorial, all in the hopes of getting the undercover agents beat up and their patches pulled so that they could charge the offending real motorcycle club members with R.I.C.O. crimes, alleging they did it to enforce their territory and further the criminal enterprise. Patch pulling was a tradition of the motorcycle club culture that was used to enforce the protocols related to how new clubs were established in that area, as well as respond to major violations of a club's honor, and ATF knows this and was deliberately trying to instigate a violent incident, where but for the undercover agent's actions there would not be a problem.

A year earlier in 1998, two undercover ATF agents named Blake "Bo" Boteler and Cole Edwards hung-around, prospected, and were patched-in to the Sons of Silence MC in Colorado. The Sons of Silence MC started in Colorado in 1967, eventually spread throughout multiple states, and are a nationally respected old school one percent outlaw motorcycle club. The Sons are big, tough men who are known for standing up for themselves and being the original outlaw motorcycle club to call Colorado home. They are at the top of the political food chain of the motorcycle clubs in the state and were known to pull patches if a club came into their state or a new club tried to form without following proper protocol. ATF undercover agent Boetler's career to that point included work on ATF's Special Response Team during the L.A. Rodney King riots, the Branch Davidian standoff in Waco, TX, and the Ruby Ridge incident in Idaho. ATF had been running this operation for quite some time and it was not productive, so to bolster a flimsy case against the Sons, ATF decided to dynamite the pond.

ATF established a club called the Unforgiven MC that consisted entirely of undercover law enforcement officers, with the intent of getting their patches pulled to demonstrate that the Sons of Silence used intimidation and threats of violence to maintain their territory, and then roll those charges into the R.I.C.O. case being built by Boteler and Edwards. This was not a case where ATF started a club of undercovers and waited to see what happened, this was a case where ATF started a club of undercovers with the intent of exploiting existing motorcycle club culture protocols, disrespecting the existing outlaw motorcycle clubs publicly, picked a fight with the Sons of Silence to elicit an honor-bound response, and then indict the Sons for standing up for themselves. As Dobyns himself describes the incident in his book *No Angel*, he and agents John Carr and Chris Bayless, all wearing their new Unforgiven colors, went into a bar the Sons of Silence were known to regularly hangout in and the agents began drinking. When a member of the Sons of Silence approached agent Dobyns and asked him who he was, Dobyns responded with deliberately disrespectful and antagonistic comments. Honor bound; the Sons member blasted Dobyns tipping off a bar brawl. As they intended to, ATF rolled the charges from the brawl into the R.I.C.O. case and hailed the case as a victory, claiming they had totally dismantled and destroyed the Sons of Silence MC. However, of the forty-two people arrested in the R.I.C.O. case, twenty-one turned out not be members of the Sons of Silence, eight motorcycles had been illegally seized without warrants, one had "ATF" scratched into the custom paint job, and the ATF had vandalized some of the houses, for which ATF was eventually held accountable for by the courts. Most of the defendants had their cases dismissed, at trial evidence was suppressed because it had been improperly obtained or was fabricated, and many of the members who chose to take their cases to trial were acquitted. Larry Pozner, a former head of the American Criminal Defense Bar was quoted in the media saying the case epitomized taking, "relatively minor offenses and trumpeting them as the crime of the century. This is garden variety stuff made to sound like a major law enforcement coup." Nevertheless, in 2000, ATF undercover agent Boteler's work on the Sons of Silence case was hailed as a success and he was portrayed as a hero and nominated for the nations "Top Cop" award, was the July 2002 National Law Enforcement Officers Memorial Fund "Officer of the Month", and his work and the motorcycle used during the undercover operation were memorialized in the National Law Enforcement Museum.

In 2001, law enforcement used this technique again against the Galloping Goose MC, when Detective Steve Cook and others formed a club made up of undercover law enforcement officers that they named the Outsiders MC. The Galloping Goose are the oldest outlaw motorcycle club in the United States, having started in Sylmar California in 1943. By 1948, they had spread to the Midwest, establishing a base in Kansas City and by the late 1960's, they began enforcing a "fifty-mile rule", which meant no new motorcycle clubs were allowed to form within one fifty miles of Kansas City. For 18 months Cook and his fake "Outsiders" ran around Kansas City trying to antagonize the Galloping Goose. The Galloping Goose did not respond with violence but instead referred the Outsiders to a Bandidos support club in the area and told them they should join up with them. Cook was unsuccessful and achieved nothing with his attempt to dynamite the pond. In fact, Cook's team pulled the plug on that operation when they were referred to the support club because they could not target the Goose like they had wanted to. Cook continued to target the Goose and would be hailed as a hero for the few convictions they were able to get against the tweekers in the club in a subsequent investigation of the Galloping Goose.

By 2003, the dynamiting the pond technique was becoming a go-to approach for ATF, and agent Dobyns, and ATF used the technique to launch Operation Black Biscuit against the Hells Angels in Arizona. The Hells Angels Arizona charters were the result of a patch-over by the Dirty Dozen MC, Arizona's original and for over thirty years until they patched-over, they were the only outlaw motorcycle club in Arizona and were known for fiercely and violently defending Arizona as their state. In response to the Laughlin riot and agent Dobyns being able to buy an official charter of a real motorcycle club out of Mexico called the Solos Angeles CM, ATF combined multiple on-going undercover operations to launch operation Black Biscuit in Arizona with the intentions of either creating a patch pulling R.I.C.O. over territory or attempting to infiltrate the Hells Angels. Understanding just how easy it is to start a chapter of a motorcycle club, ATF agent Jay Dobyns and one of their Confidential Sources of Information illegally traveled to Mexico without ATF authorization and paid the five-hundred-dollar fee to start a chapter of the club, ATF provided its undercover agents and informants then launched an Arizona chapter of the Solos Angeles consisting of undercover law enforcement and one tweeker Contract Source of Information named Pops who was the team's credibility drug snorter. The Angels did not take the bait and just like had occurred with the Galloping Goose a couple of years earlier, the undercover agents were told they should just hang-around and prospect for a real motorcycle club (the Hells Angels), and just as easy as that, ATF was on its way to prospecting undercover agents for the most famous one percent outlaw motorcycle club in the world.

In 2005, the ATF took a failed undercover investigation led by the Bellingham Police and D.E.A. and used an incident in which several Bandidos from Washington and Montana pulled the patches of members of the Kinsmen MC, to reopen the investigation under federal jurisdiction and those Bandidos members were charged and convicted under the federal R.I.C.O. Act with various kidnapping, assault, robbery, and weapons charges related to that patch pulling. In addition, George Weggers, then International President of the Bandidos MC was indicted for simply telling another member "We don't talk to those guys, them feds.", when the member called to advise him that members involved in the patch pulling had been contacted by A.T.F. agents advising that they were reopening the case as a federal case. All George had done was restate the outlaw biker code of not talking to the cops and that was all it took for him to earn a RICO conviction.

In Grants Pass, Oregon in August 2007, six members of the Vagos MC beat a member when he was kicked out of the club in bad standing. He was then taken to his house and forced to surrender all property bearing the Vagos logo and his motorcycle, which is standard practice with many one percent clubs when a member leaves in bad standing. After the man reported the incident to police the six Vagos members were charged with first-degree burglary, second degree robbery, coercion, and second-degree kidnapping.

The Vagos indictments hit close to home for us, Oregon was our backyard and if they were getting popped for pulling their own members patches, we knew we were vulnerable. It was around this time that the outlaw motorcycle clubs of Washington all independently made the decision that they would no longer pull patches to avoid exposure to prosecution, significant criminal defense costs, and lengthy prison sentences. This was not to say that we were letting things slide, we would just fuck you up to get our message across, tell you never to be seen wearing that bullshit patch again, and leave you to bleed on it. The Washington clubs were looking at these incidents, paying attention, and adapting their behavior to attempt to play within the rules and avoid the lengthy prison sentences and organized crime and gang convictions.

Even when you play within the rules, the feds will still get you. In February 2010, our friend Ivan from the Outlaws MC was convicted of robbery and kidnapping charges related to pulling the patch of one of the Outlaws Knoxville chapter members. Ivan was a Regional President and he had come to the Knoxville chapter for their weekly meeting after they had learned that one of the members who had recently prospected and patched into the chapter was actually an undercover deputy with the Knox County Sheriff's Office named Joseph Linger. Linger's story is remarkably similar to notorious Hells Angel informant Anthony Tait. Linger had met the Outlaws while working at a local bar and when he learned he could prospect for the Outlaws, he contacted KCSO and offered to work as an undercover against the Outlaws if they would pay him and make him a deputy. After Linger was exposed by his own disgruntled wife, he was summoned to the clubhouse and told to turn in his colors and all property bearing the Outlaws logo. Linger did as he was told, and Ivan and the Knoxville chapter president were subsequently arrested and indicted. It turns out that the kidnapping and robbery charges stem from Linger saying that he felt threatened and like could not leave because he knew that Ivan had carried a firearm in the past, and the robbery was them forcing Linger to turn in his club property. Linger came to the meeting that night on his own free will, he was never restrained and free to leave at any time, voluntarily surrendered his club property when told he was kicked out of the club as the by-laws state you must return all property bearing the name of the club or center patch, and he left on his own without so much as a black eye. Ivan never threatened him, never brandished a firearm, never restricted Lingers movements, and acted in a manner that was consistent with the bylaws of his club, and now he was looking at robbery and kidnapping charges. Prosecutors let them sweat it out for over a year before finally dismissing the charges against Ivan and the Knoxville President.

As clubs across the country slowed down on the practice of patch pulling, new clubs began popping up left and right. Everyone wanted to be a biker, and everyone wanted to wear a three-piece patch. There were new military MC's, religious MC's, and special interest motorcycle clubs forming all over Tacoma and this same type of growth was happening all over the country. By now, the Iron Order MC had numerous internal revolts and disgruntled former members that had spawned dozens of pop-up "law-abiding" motorcycle clubs full of cops, giving birth to the ridiculous "law-abiding biker movement", making the role of outlaw motorcycle clubs as the patch police even more complicated. These new clubs were being started by guys that learned how to be a biker from watching T.V., guys that had washed out of other pop-ups or the Iron Order. They behaved like jackasses and were giving all the respected clubs a bad reputation. In Washington we tried to stick with tradition as long as we could, we adjusted our approach and started to work together on regulating the community, in an attempt to send the loudest message.

The Outsiders MC and the Bandidos MC have lived together in Tacoma since approximately 1974. While they have not always got along, by the fall of 2010 the two clubs were awfully close not only in

Tacoma but across the United States. It was a bit of a surprise when one Wednesday night a pack of Bandidos Sergeant at Arms', a Nomad, and a handful of their support club members stopped by the clubhouse. One of our prospects and I met the Bandits as they rolled in. I greeted the Nomad with a hug, and he pulled me aside and said, "Hey bro, stopped by to talk to you and Double D and see if you guys wanted to go have a little fun with us?" Oh yeah, let's go talk to the Commander, I said. "Commander" was a nickname we jokingly started using for Double D after he was elected U.S. Defenders Commander and it really irritated him when we called him it, so it got used in a myriad of ways, from a brass "Commander" plaque on a chair behind the bar, to naming the back-and-forth sway he does when he speaks in public, the Cobra Commander.

While the support club members stood watch over the bikes parked across the street, Double D, Spanky, me, and all the Bandidos gathered in a corner of the bar. The Nomad explained that the Bandidos had been approached by a new club that was wanting to start in Tacoma, right at the bottom of the hill from our clubhouse. He told us that the club had approached them for "permission" to start in Tacoma and when they asked them if they had talked to us yet, they told the Bandidos that they had and we did not have any problem with it, but the problem was they did not know who Double D or Twitch were and could not say who they talked to. Fuck that! Double D said, they did not talk to us. Well, they just opened a clubhouse down the hill from you guys after we told them that would be a bad idea, so we wanted to see if you guys wanted to go. I'm in, I said. Double D told me and Spanky to grab a prospect and said he was going to invite the Gypsy Joker members who were drinking with a couple of our members to go, and he would meet us outside.

I am a little twisted and enjoy the "Let's go to work." feeling, and as I sat there on my bike, the sound and feeling of about seventeen other idling Harley Davidson's reverberating off the old Hilltop houses, I was not just excited to go deal with this club, but I was really proud because we were all doing it together. What we were doing would be club secrets the three clubs would share together and a mutual demonstration of brotherhood and accountability for motorcycle club protocol by the Tacoma one-percent clubs. Double D and the Bandido Nomad led the pack and as we pulled away from the curb at the clubhouse, we all just intermingled together behind them with the prospects at the back of the pack. I broke into a smile that lasted until we made the right turn into this pop-up's clubhouse. We were all excited on the way down and as we made the short ride guys were exchanging nods, smiles, and other enthusiastic gestures with each other. Their clubhouse was in a warehouse just off the hill in an industrial section of old Tacoma. The metal siding of the warehouses made the echo of our bikes deafening and as we backed our bikes to the curb, the other club and their guests came running out to see who their unexpected visitors were. I hopped off my bike and took a position where I could cover Double D and the Nomad as the President of the other club approached.

"Haaa,haaaaa, how are you guys doing tonight?" he stammered with a weak, frightened smile as a finish. Double D extended his hand, took the guy's hand and said, "Double D, Outsiders Tacoma." I cannot even remember the name of the club now; they were that insignificant, but I remember the guy's introduction was one of the longest most ridiculous motorcycle club introductions that I have ever heard. We need to talk, Double D told him. Ahhh, ok. Please come in for a drink, the frightened President replied. He was not the only one who looked scared, there were about a dozen of these guys and at least as many of their guests, you could tell they were all short-circuiting from the sight of three of the four one-percent clubs of Washington state showing up for an unexpected drink, and they were being flooded with the memories of all the episodes of Gangland and Sons of Anarchy they had ever watched.

Inside, there were bathrooms and a kitchen to the right of the door, a makeshift bar set up directly inside the door that opened into a large dance floor with more tall round bar tables. Double D and the Bandido Nomad escorted the club president to a table against the far wall of the dance floor and told him to take a seat. Some of the members of this pop-up club gathered around a tall table by the bar, the looks of their faces told us they had watched enough Sons of Anarchy to know what was about to happen, but this wasn't the way it went down on T.V. and in real life things were much worse because instead of having just one pissed off outlaw motorcycle club to deal with, they had the three most powerful motorcycle clubs in Washington to contend with, and it was clear they just wanted a way out.

Some Bandidos wear a patch that simply says "Pterodactyl" which is a reference to how Pterodactyls/Bandidos hunt by encircling their prey before they attack. You can always tell when the Bandidos are getting ready to take care of business because they will make sure they have the tactical advantage by controlling the perimeter and all the entry and exit points of the potential conflict zone, and tonight was the first time I got to see Pterodactyl mode in action. In this case, the support club members were outside watching the bikes, driveway and main entrance, the Bandidos prospect and our prospect were in the bar area and able to cover and control the bar area and main bathrooms, a few of the Bandidos had taken one of the tall tables just on the dance floor where they could cover the group from the pop-up club and still watch the main door and their Nomad, while Spanky, me and the Jokers took positions around the table where Double D and the Nomad were now seated with the pop-up President.

As Double D and the Bandido Nomad began to lecture the President on his clubs disrespectful and dishonest ways, and how that shit wasn't going to be tolerated in Tacoma, I decided there were just too many of us for me to get a good chance to thump on the guy and moved out with the prospects in the bar. These guys were not used to someone coming into their house and absolutely controlling the environment without even brandishing a weapon and it had happened in such a seamless and professional manner like a wave sweeping through their clubhouse that they did not know how to respond other than cower and try to buy time. By this time most of the guests had realized that they were in the wrong place at wrong time and had split, leaving just these guys ol' ladies and this guy tending bar wearing a formal tuxedo jacket with long tails and a full members patch from this bullshit club on it. This was a new look I had never seen before, was even beyond some of the weird shit that motorcycle club guys wore back in the 1950's and 1960's, and since I was in the mood for a fight that night, I figured let's go fuck with the member at the bar in the stupid tux. I walked into the bar and B-lined it for our prospect.

Our prospect was in his late twenties, an Army veteran with no criminal history and no substance abuse issues, who met the club when he was working security at a bar several of us frequented in Tacoma for their amazing steaks. I am not going to give them a plug here because they would later fire him for being an Outsider and member of an outlaw motorcycle club. He hung around for a couple of years before going prospect, got to know us, and became a brother to many of us long before he wore the patch. You could count on him, he was serious when he needed to be serious but could make you laugh until your cheeks hurt, is a great motorcycle mechanic and loves to ride fast. When he went prospect, he came in full-on like I did which got my respect, so I took him under my wing and started teaching him about outlaw motorcycle club history, Outsiders MC history, protocol, club security, about the C.O.C., national scene, and motorcycle rights movement. I was happy he was here with us tonight and asked him to join me at the bar for a drink. Because of the layout of this place, a position at the bar would allow us to spread out our resources even more effectively and put us at a two on one advantage with the jackass wearing the tuxedo in case he tried to go for a firearm.

Twitch with one of my favorite prospects, Outsider Prospect Aaron.
Photo by Candace Burns

We walked up to the bar and without introducing myself (an act of disrespect in the club world.), I told him to give me a Corona and a Jameson on the rocks for our prospect. Our prospect loves his whiskey, and I figured the prospect deserved nothing less than their top-shelf stuff. We call this type of deliberate act designed to insight a response, a "mud-check." In the motorcycle club world, we conduct a mud-check to test an individual and see what they are made of and how they respond in certain situations. They can range from very simple mud-checks like asking a prospect or patch-holder from another club questions about their club to see if they'll adhere to the code or divulge information they shouldn't, to more extreme examples intended to illicit a more extreme response, like when T-Bob accused me of passing information to the cops in front of the entire club when the Outsiders made me their "brother." If you do not respond properly to a mud-check or show weakness, the mud-check will usually escalate, resulting in a good ass-kicking and education for the mud-checkee. They were a tool that was used to expose the posers while helping identify stand-up men, but they are no longer used as effectively as they used to be. I will normally not pick a fight, but we were there to take care of business and hold these guys accountable for their disrespect, so this was a different story and I wanted to see how this guy was going to respond to my disrespect. To my surprise, rather than standing up to me and calling me out like he should have, he responded with a chipper attitude, a smile, and off he went to fetch our drinks.

"Here ya go brothers." the weirdo said with a big goofy smile as he handed us our drinks. He seemed totally unaware of what was going on there and why, and this further confused me because he was wearing a patch just like all the other members. As our prospect and I stood there keeping an eye on the situation I decided to keep us entertained by turning up the heat with my mud-check. As the weirdo was telling us how nice it was to have us stop by, I took a long drink from my beer, sat it down hard on the bar and reached out, flipped the weirdo's lapel, and in a condescending tone asked, "Just what the fuck are you supposed to be man?" This was an act of disrespect that by the biker code required the jackass to standup for himself and warranted a violent response, but instead he responded the exact opposite and appeared to not even understand he was being mud-checked. "I'm the butler." he said. You are what? "I'm the club butler." he said. I wash the bikes, tend bar, and take care of whatever the members need, he said. Ohhhh, you are like the club mama, so do suck dick and fuck the members like a club mama too? I asked. Again, my actions warranted a violent response for my disrespect, but I got more smile and be nice. He seemed totally unaware he was being mud-checked which was no fun for me, so I explained to him that in a very masculine culture that was founded by manly men like the motorcycle club culture, being the club butler was the most bitch-ass thing I had ever seen, and still no response from him. This was not even going to be any fun because this dude was going to piss himself and submit as soon as shit popped off. This is why mud-checks existed and why it was important that the real motorcycle clubs regulated the motorcycle club community. It was not about controlling territory or being bullies, it was about protecting the integrity of the culture from those who did not understand it and whose interpretation of the culture or behavior was offensive and disrespectful to the culture, protocols, and traditions we dedicated our lives to. While we did not take their patches that night, that club did cease to exist from that night on, and in all my time traveling the motorcycle club world, I have never seen another club butler. Clearly, I am not the only one who thinks that is a stupid idea.

Motorcycle clubs are like individual tribal nations and just like mainstream foreign relations which require protocol and diplomacy, the same is true of the motorcycle club community, and this makes how a motorcycle club, and its members behave critically important because it will have an impact on the club community as a whole. For example, our Portland chapter decided they wanted to prospect a group of guys for a chapter out of Grants Pass, Oregon and they were allowing them to run around with serape vests with no rockers or patches. That was not how we did things in the Outsiders MC, but Portland was jealous of the way Tacoma was growing with quality younger member, so they viewed any opportunity to take in any prospective member as a good thing, and they made the move behind Tacoma's back.

I had been invited to the Vagos MC anniversary party down in Grants Pass, OR and figured it would be a good chance to check out the guy's Portland was letting run around telling other motorcycle clubs they were backed by the Outsiders and wanting to go prospect. These guys had developed a relationship with a bar in the middle of nowhere on Grants Pass that they treated like their clubhouse and were claiming it was going to be their clubhouse. Double D and I had earned enough respect from the motorcycle club community in the northwest and nationally that Mavrick was jealous of me and started inserting himself into any situation he could where I would have the potential to earn respect of or be shown respect by other respected one-percent motorcycle clubs, from photo bombing pictures of me with other respected one-percenters to attending COC meetings that were well beyond his level of intelligence or drive, and this Vagos party was no different. Even though we did not get along and he did not know any Vagos members, he and Paul were coming along. I had invited Gutz and T-Bob was on the same trip as Mavrick and used my existing relationship with the Vagos as an opportunity to get to meet the Oregon Vagos who had been in Grants Pass for years but because the Outsiders Portland chapter have always been very much isolationists, T-Bob had never met any Vagos and only knew the Vagos MC from what he had seen on Gangland and had heard from PigPen, me, and Double D. He also knew that I was going to make a full report to Tacoma on the Grants Pass guys that Portland was backing, and he needed to make sure that our visit with those guys went well.

The bar these guys claimed as their clubhouse was a cool enough place. It was in the woods at the top of Grants Pass, just off the highway. The bar appeared to have been built in the early eighties and had large ten-foot windows across the front of it. Inside, there was a long bar that had been built wide enough to dance on, with stripper poles and illuminated like a stage. The rest of the place was filled with comfy booths and decorated like a strip club. The rumble from the pack of Outsiders drew the occupants of the bar outside as we rolled into the parking lot. The only people in the place were the guys who were wanting to start the new chapter, the bartender who was the girlfriend of one of the Grants Pass guys, and the local drunk. I had met some of these guys before and never thought they were Outsider material, but this was the first time I was going to meet them as a crew in their place, so I came prepared to assess them from the time I laid eyes on them.

When I first meet and greet someone, I am scanning them for bulges that could indicate they have a firearm or other weapon on them. From a visual screen when I first see them, to a discreet physical search conducted by deliberately making contact with their body and strategically placing and sweeping my hand when I hug them to greet, I do everything I can to artfully and discreetly assess whether they have a weapon that could be a threat to me and my brothers. When the president of the Grants Pass crew came out of bar I was not impressed. He was holding a drink, visibly intoxicated, and looked like a tweeked out hillbilly wearing overalls with no shirt. The only weapon I saw on him was a hunting knife on his right hip. We got off our bikes and began our hellos. One of the lifetime/charter members from Portland who was going to sponsor the chapter and lived in Grants Pass met us there and as we stood in the parking lot catching up with him and talking to the Grants Pass crew, the guy who was going to be President seized the opportunity to run back inside and find himself a piece of garbage 1911 knock-off, which when he returned to the parking lot he now had prominently displayed simply tucked into the back pocket of his overalls. The motorcycle club culture was founded by veterans, which means it was founded by men who knew how to handle firearms, and today because the safety and security of the world includes men like myself who have training and experience in areas like advanced urban warfare, special operations, and hostage rescue, we have men who really understand firearms safety and we take it seriously. Seeing someone who is visibly drunk with a firearm and recklessly carrying it unsecured in a back pocket in a bar is disgusting to most outlaw motorcycle club members and will not earn respect. As soon as I saw this, I pointed it out to Gutz, knowing that he is very experienced with firearms himself would not approve and as a Portland member would be a voice in the room when it came time to discuss these guys as a prospect chapter. Like I thought, he agreed.

Once we got inside, the prospective President acted like he owned the place and fixed himself a drink behind the bar before he returned to the public side of the bar to drink with us. As he sat at the bar with an elbow rested on the bar telling me about how they did not care about the Vagos, they were going to be "the main game in town and keep Grants Pass on lock down" like we do in Portland and Tacoma. Gutz had positioned himself behind the guy who even though the room was lined with mirrors his situational awareness was so poor that he failed to notice Gutz gesturing like he was snatching the guy's gun and doing various acts with it. I had enough, not only was this guy a total poser, but he also clearly did not understand our relationship with the Vagos Motorcycle Club, and he had disrespected my friends. "Hey man, if you wanna be an Outsider, you better figure out who's who in the zoo and how we operate because you just insulted friends of ours, but first you need to quit being a motherfucking poser and take that pistol out of your back pocket and go secure it somewhere safe before someone snatches it and beats you with it or you shoot yourself. He looked at me dumbfounded for several seconds before saying, "Yeahhh, you're right." and then he got up and went and secured the weapon. When he returned, the night continued as it had started but with no reckless gun-play and showboat intimidation tactics, and the future President continued to drink himself to oblivion, in between trips to the bathroom for bumps of meth. That was all any of us from Tacoma needed to see and we knew we could not let those guys start running around southern Oregon representing themselves as a prospect chapter of the Outsiders MC because they had demonstrated from their behavior on their home ground that they were going to do nothing but cause problems in the club community, as well as be a negative representation of the Outsiders MC and outlaw motorcycle clubs in general. They were never allowed to prospect or wear a patch because based on their behavior if we did not end up taking their patches ourselves, someone else would have.

Whether it is a pop-up club like the Iron Order that is dishonest, disrespectful and does not follow proper protocol, or a respected motorcycle clubs' own member(s), patch-pulling was a necessary tool that was used for quality control, and to maintain cultural integrity and peace within the motorcycle club community. However, because of how law enforcement is targeting the practice of patch-pulling and applying state and federal criminal laws, motorcycle clubs are having to forgo using this tool and have adopted a policy of "You can do your thing but we won't acknowledge you and don't come anywhere near us attitude" and it's created two separate motorcycle club communities, one which consists of the recognized and respected motorcycle clubs, and one that is comprised of clubs like the Iron Order and all the other pop-up and internet clubs. That said, patch-pulling does still occur occasionally and is usually initiated by club members and leadership who are too archaic in their thinking to understand that patch pulling gives law enforcement a green-light to easily devastate your club and put members in prison for life while at the same time destroy the club financially with costly indictments and subsequent forfeitures. Bottom line, patch-pulling just does not accomplish anything positive anymore, so do not waste your time and put your club in jeopardy.

25

I KNEW I WAS GOING TO TAKE SOME HEAT

We had heard rumors that a Washington State Patrol cop had put a bounty on me for any other cop who could arrest me for on felony charge, but we thought that was a bunch of bullshit and dirty cop tough talk. Even though we knew that dirty Portland cops had tried to frame and kill Outsiders members back in 1979, we thought that was then and we did not really need to take the rumors about my safety seriously. I believed it was my Constitutional right to say what I wanted and believe in what I wanted, we were working within the law, and did not think we needed to worry about any major repercussions from my involvement in the motorcycle profiling movement. We were wrong, and in the summer of 2010, the cops struck back.

I was working undercover, in my undercover vehicle assigned by the state and driving down a main road when I saw a local police car approaching from the opposite direction. As the cop car passed me, I saw him turn his lights on and flip a U-turn. I knew I was not speeding and had good tabs, so I knew this was not going to be a good stop. I watched in the rear-view mirror as the cop exited his vehicle and drew his gun. Fuck! This is not good. I picked up my Nextel and hit the push to talk for my supervisor. Ahhh, Mike. I was on my way back to the office and now I am getting felony stopped. What do you mean, Mike asked? I gave him my location and was narrating what was happening as the cop slowly made his way towards my vehicle with his gun in a low ready position, when suddenly numerous cop cars came tearing into the parking lot in front of me with the officers exiting their vehicles and drawing down on me as well. Fuck, Fuck Fuck! It was a Thursday and I had church that night and figured I was not going to make it, but I would be the topic of the meeting.

The officer made his way down the driver's side of the vehicle until he was just behind the driver's door, then he backed down the vehicle toward the rear end, came around the rear of the vehicle, and worked his way up to the passenger window until he was pointing his gun at my face. I knew the reason he positioned himself where he did on the passenger's side was to give a clear shot on me to the other shooters. I had already pulled my badge and law enforcement credentials, and had them open and visible when he approached, then identified myself as an undercover and provided my agency information. "What's going on Twitch?" Oh fuck, this was definitely going to get bad, I thought. The officer snatched my credentials from my hand and threw them on the floor of the vehicle. The officer advised that he wanted to search my vehicle. I asked him why he stopped me, and he said they received a suspicious vehicle report and told me that if I just let him search my vehicle, they would send me on my way. I was pissed but at this point I had eleven officers on scene pointing guns at me and I knew there was no coming out on top for me in this situation because they were clearly looking for any excuse to shoot me. I have had lots of guns pointed at me over the years, but the worst feeling is when the cops pull guns on you as an outlaw biker, because both you and the cops know they get a free pass if they kill you, and cops are never held accountable when they shoot bikers, regardless of if it was unreasonable and unnecessary force. Plus, my status in the motorcycle club world and professional career in law enforcement had made me their ultimate enemy and one of their primary targets. There was absolutely no legitimate reason for the stop, so I figured they were going to shoot me dead that afternoon because it was clear they were looking for the slightest furtive movement that would have allowed them to open fire on me.

The officer went back and forth with me trying to get me to give him consent to search my state undercover vehicle, even saying "Come on, we're on the same side. I'd let you search mine." Being careful not to say anything that could be interpreted as consent, I told him that if he let me search his car first, we could revisit searching mine. At this point, the female sergeant who had been standing just behind the driver's window pointing her gun at my head, grabbed me by the hair and began to pull me out the driver's window. I immediately wanted to resist but knew that was exactly what they wanted me to do so they could shoot me, and instead I just went limp and forced the fat blonde female cop to earn the abuse I knew I was about to receive.

She pulled me out the window and I flopped onto the asphalt parking lot, deliberately not attempting to break my fall with my hands because I did not want to give them an excuse to say I was resisting or fighting and shoot me. Once on the ground someone used their boot to press my head into the asphalt as the chubby cop cuffed me and struggled to get back on her feet. Once Miss Piggy was back on her feet the boot party started, and she and other officers proceeded to kick and stomp me for what felt like several minutes. When they were finished with their beating, they took me to the back of my vehicle, sat me on the bumper and snapped several photos of me. There were several more law enforcement vehicles parked behind me including two unmarked detective's cars. The detectives were standing by one of their vehicles looking at what appeared to be a wanted poster and other documents they had on the hood. Then they approached me and told me that I was a suspect in a couple of kidnappings and armed robberies in Skagit County. I had not been to Skagit County in years and was not involved in crime, so I knew this was bullshit and told them to fuck off, they had the wrong guy. One of the detectives held up the wanted poster and said, "Are you telling us this isn't you?" Yeah, motherfucker, you know that is not me, the kid in that photo cannot be much more than eighteen years old and looks Hispanic and I am clearly Caucasian. It does not matter; we are going to make the club world turn their back on you and we are going to take you in for Attempted Child Luring and Attempted Kidnapping. My heart sank. I knew that it was the word of a bunch of dirty cops versus the outlaw biker and no jury was ever going to believe me even though I had done absolutely nothing wrong because I was a 1%er. I also knew that those charges, even with them being bogus, my bond amount would be set so high that I would not be able to afford bail or an attorney to fight them and would end up sitting in jail until they could force me to take a plea or convict me on the bullshit charges. On top of that, because they were charges involving a child, I knew the club world would turn their back on me. I was fucked, the cops knew it and had deliberately planned this whole fucked up framing with the intent of ruining me in the motorcycle club world to try and destroy what we were accomplishing with the motorcycle profiling movement.

We were about an hour and ten minutes into the arrest, they had contacted my agency and confirmed my identity and employment but told me that I was being detained and that they were going to search my undercover vehicle. They moved me to sitting on the ground in front of the detective's vehicle and as a couple officers began to search my vehicle, I saw my supervisor's car coming down the street in the distance. You guys are fucked now I said, my supervisor is a block down at the light, it is about to be my turn. . Hearing that the detective asked which car my supervisors was, and I pointed out his silver Ford Taurus with exempt plates. The detectives told the uniformed officers to get out of there and they would handle things. The uniformed officers all quickly piled into their various vehicles and left the scene, leaving me in the custody of the two detectives. When my supervisor arrived, he was professional but clearly incredibly angry. The detectives had my law enforcement credentials on the hood of their vehicle and explained to my supervisor that I was stopped due to a suspicious vehicle call and then refused to properly identify myself to the officers. My supervisor told them that was bullshit, pointed to my credentials issued by the state of Washington and signed by the Attorney General on the hood of the car, asked him how I failed to properly identify myself and then told him that he had heard everything on the Nextel. The detectives got frazzled and tried to justify their actions by insisting that I failed to cooperate with them and resisted the arresting officers while never elaborating how, and once again this was disputed by my supervisor. The detectives released me and they left the scene before even me or my supervisor could leave.

Once we got back to the office, we met with the Regional Director who had already been briefed on the incident. She explained how sorry she was that it happened and explained that the officers and detectives would be held accountable. The Regional Director and Supervisor could tell that something was wrong with me and told me that I would be put on a few days leave and required to go to critical incident debriefing. My supervisor asked me to request a copy of the police report and radio traffic for the stop, as well as the photos they took of me. I did as I was asked even though I knew that the police report would be nothing but lies, and when we got the response to my request it was just as I thought. However, rather than spending their time writing a bunch of lies, they just wrote a few short lies and the police report for the stop that lasted over an hour is less than half the page and makes it appear as if we had a brief and friendly traffic stop on a suspicious vehicle call and I was sent on my way. They also sent the photos which are still tough for me to look at to this day without reliving the incident in my head, but what was interesting was the radio traffic. Specifically, after about fifteen minutes into the stop an officer that was not initially able to respond radios the stopping officer and asked him if he still needs assistance. The stopping officer says "No but you're going to want to get in on this one. Give me a call on my Nextel and I'll fill you in.' Why would the officer have the other officer call him on his cell phone and not just discuss whatever he had to tell him about my stop over the radio? The answer is because all their radio traffic is recorded whereas Nextel and cellular traffic is not, and since they had illegally stopped me and assaulted me, and the cop was inviting the other officer to come over and join in on the fun and criminal assault, the stopping officer did not want to leave any evidence that could be used against them.

In the end, while the Director and my agency initially stood up for me and attempted to hold the police department accountable, even though they are not all bad, law enforcement really is the biggest gang there is, the power of law enforcement versus the outlaw biker won out, and the Director was told to drop it, I was ordered to turn over the police report, radio traffic and photos, they tried to make me sign a Non-Disclosure Agreement but I refused, and I was told to never discuss it again. The worst part was that the experience of being unlawfully stopped and assaulted had unlocked the P.T.S.D. resulting from my prior kidnappings that I had worked so hard to ignore, and it would take me years of living in hell to get my P.T.S.D. back under control.

26

MOTORCYCLE CLUB TATTOOS

Like many cultures, tattoos are an important element of motorcycle club culture, whether it be an outlaw motorcycle club, traditional motorcycle club, veterans, etc. For the intent of this chapter, I will be speaking specifically about tattoos associated with and from the perspective of outlaw motorcycle clubs. Regardless, just like with many cultures, in the motorcycle club culture, tattoos are used as a form of identification, serve as rites of passage, identify status and rank, are symbols of devotion, pay tribute to fallen members and can be decorations for bravery.

During my time in the outlaw motorcycle club world I observed the rules regarding tattoos change from being things that were earned and tightly controlled which made them a valuable intelligence tool for both other outlaw motorcycle clubs and law enforcement, to become simple decorations of pride in the members club due to much looser rules, and this allowed for the birth of "painted ponies", guys that have the tough-guy tattoos without ever having to put in the work to earn them. In the old days you could read a one-percenter by his tattoos and get a good idea of what their actual threat level was as soon as you saw them. Now, due to turnover in the club world, there are so many painted ponies that only a very small percentage has actually earned their tattoos or will back them up.

Additionally, motorcycle clubs have different rules regarding how their tattoos are earned. For example, in the Hells Angels, they take into consideration that motorcycle club tattoos are considered gang identifiers, so unless a new member has no tattoos, they are expected to get their Hells Angels member tattoo shortly after they make member. However, in the Outsiders MC the rules state that you must have been a member for one year and require the full vote of your chapter to be eligible for your member tattoo. Whatever their club's rules are, getting their club tattoo is usually a priority for most new outlaw motorcycle club members as it is a visual symbol of your accomplishment and commitment to the club. Generally, if a motorcycle club member is kicked out or leaves the club in bad standing their tattoos must be covered or removed. In the old days, this meant removal by knife, belt sander, steam iron or just simply blacked-out to leave the ex-member with a permanent mark of shame. Members leaving a club in good standing are allowed to keep their tattoos, but some clubs may require the former member to out-date the tattoo.

For me, I could not wait to get my Outsiders member tattoo. I was proud of the accomplishment of making member and I was proud of the national respect and reputation that I was helping build for the Outsiders MC with the other young Tacoma members, and I wanted my club tattoo to be a permanent visual demonstration of that, as well as so I could look like and have the same permanent brand as the rest of my Tacoma brothers. As I mentioned, the rule to get a club tattoo is that you must have been a member of the club for one year and have the vote of the entire chapter. As the Tacoma chapter grew with quality members and began to get a lot of positive recognition from the motorcycle club community nationally, some of the lifetime/charter members of the Portland chapter, the original chapter of the Outsiders, became jealous and along with the help of Ric a lifetime/charter member of the Tacoma chapter and Mavrick, they began to subtly attempt to use their numbers to influence the vote on club policies and bylaws in an attempt to stifle Tacoma's growth and influence. As my and Double D's reputation and respect grew across the country, they began to target us directly with this tactic. The first time I experienced it was with my Outsiders club tattoo.

As you have read, in my first year in the Outsiders MC I had busted my ass as a prospect, earned my patch and was elected an officer, I put in work for the club, took care of serious business, and I was personally responsible for helping the Outsiders MC build national respect as a top-tier one-percenter outlaw motorcycle club. I had seen members get their Outsider tattoos at the one-year mark having not demonstrated near the level of commitment to the club that I had, and I knew I deserved my club tattoo at the one-year mark. When it came and went without so much as a mention of my club tattoo, I began to suspect Portland was deliberately holding me up on my club tattoo. After some conversations with Double D and Spanky about the subject, I confirmed I was right.

It turned out T-Bob, Goose, Squeeze, and that tweeked-out lame Rod were saying that they were not quite sure that I had earned my tattoo yet and wanted me to be a member a little longer. When I heard that I was furious, and my attitude immediately changed to "Fuck Portland! I don't need a tattoo those lames can control me getting." Apart from Ric and Mavrick, the entire Tacoma chapter was eager to have me get my club tattoo but because of those two hold-ups' I had to wait. Mavrick still had not been approved to get his club tattoo yet and I am sure that a large part of his objection to me getting my tattoo was that he did not want me getting my tattoo first. Do not get me wrong, I still wanted to have the tattoo to show pride in my club, my accomplishment and to be like my brothers, but Portland had used their influence with a couple of out for themselves Tacoma members to hold me up. Fuck it! I said and just kept doing me and did not give a damn about my club tattoo.

As a big fuck you to Portland, I went out and got my right arm sleeved in tattoos that represented my club, my role and my commitment using several club specific symbols that the club did not have any rules controlling. Using symbols associated with the club without actually using the club name is common in one-percenter tattoos. In my sleeve, I got a devil gunfighter wearing a Tacoma t-shirt and serape vest with the same colors and pattern as my club serape. In addition, I incorporated the safety pin that Spanky gave me when he agreed to sponsor me, and I was the first Outsider to have the "Tacoma-T" tattooed on me. The Tacoma-T is a stylized T modified from a Templar cross with a pair of ape hanger handlebars, it was originally drawn by Gordy when he was a Tacoma member, and it is used to represent the Tacoma chapter. However, when I became a member, I really helped make the use of the symbol more popular when I began using the Tacoma-T as the T when I signed my name Twitch, got my tattoo, had a large silver ring made using the Tacoma-T, and from there the Tacoma chapter began to get Tacoma-T tattoos and use it in shirts, hats, etc. It is even carved into decorative bar-top in the Tacoma clubhouse that we had made for the clubhouse in 2016. Finally, I got some cemetery gates with headstones bearing O.F.F.O (Outsiders Forever, Forever Outsiders) on various headstones. Portland might have been holding me up from getting my club tattoo, but there was no way they could stop me from representing who or what I was to the world.

My "Fuck Portland!" attitude was not changing because no matter how much time I spent in Portland there was always the Tweeker Crew who were giving me attitude, fucking with me for no reason, and holding me up on my tattoo for no reason. My attitude extended to the entire chapter because in my opinion since the Portland brothers who claimed to support me were not standing up to the Tweeker Crew about their bullshit, they were not acting as my brothers, they did not have my back no matter what as the outlaw biker code says, they were not doing what was best for the club, and they were acquiescing to a bunch of tweekers and pill poppers who were targeting me because they were jealous of the respect and standing I had earned in the community and the club, which made them weak, and that disgusted me. You see, in my mind when you have a dispute between brothers or even chapters, and you must choose sides, you choose the side of right, not keep your fucking mouth shut like partisan bitches because you're afraid of conflict or personal and political repercussions. When you stay silent, when you pussy-out, it leads to small pieces of the integrity and righteousness of your motorcycle club being given away, and once you give that away you cannot get it back without major conflict and in many cases violence.

Finally, in December Tacoma had enough of Portland's stalling and decided that they were going to adhere to the Outsiders MC bylaws which at the time stated that a member was eligible for his club tattoo after one year of membership and upon one hundred percent vote from his chapter. At a church one snowy night a few days before Christmas, the chapter voted unanimously for me to get my Outsiders MC tattoo. Maverick's sponsor Single D brought him up for his tattoo and he was approved as well. After the meeting I was talking with Double D, Spanky and Tommy No Guns about how Portland was going to be pissed but we did not give a fuck, and because we stuck to the bylaws there was nothing, they could do about it. Of course, as soon as Portland called that night for their update on our meeting and found out that my tattoo had been approved, they were outraged and claimed that we did not follow the bylaws, that our copy of the bylaws was wrong, and they had the real bylaws in Portland. Double D told them ours were the original bylaws that are written by hand and signed by all the charter members, so if they have a copy that supersedes those, he would like to see them. T-Bob claimed that they would bring them to the next special meeting which was a few months off and told Double D that I needed to wait to get my tattoo. There was no mention of Mavrick waiting to get his tattoo until the next special as well, it was all about me. Double D laughed at T-Bob and told him he did not think I would listen to him now that I had the vote of the full chapter.

As soon as he got off the phone and told us what T-Bob had told him I exploded in a big "Fuck Portland!" and told a prospect to get me my phone which had been secured in another room for the meeting. I placed a call to a good friend of the club named Tattoo Rob who owned a tattoo shop in Tacoma. I told Rob that I had been approved for my club tattoo and that we were having a U.F.C. Fight Night at the clubhouse tomorrow night and asked him to come down to the clubhouse and give me my club tattoo. Rob thought that was a cool idea and said he would meet us at the clubhouse for the fights.

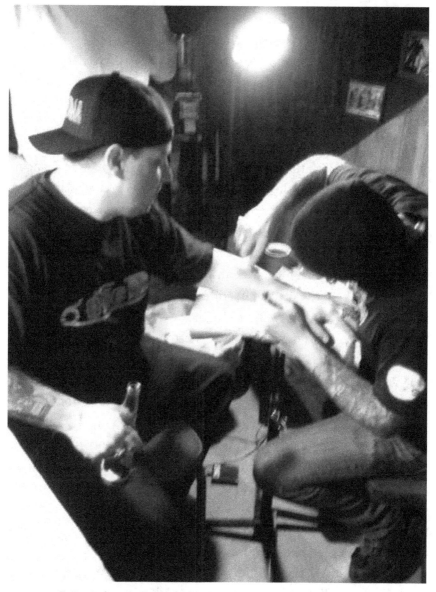

Tattoo Rob preps Twitch for his Outsiders MC member's tattoo in the Outsiders MC Tacoma clubhouse.
Photo by Candace Burns

I had always wanted to be riding my motorcycle when I got my club tattoo but that was not the way it worked out. That winter the entire Puget Sound area was blasted by a sudden winter storm and the only way to make it to the clubhouse at the top of Hilltop was by four-wheel drive vehicle. Even with the snow we had a full house for Fight Night, with all the Outsiders Tacoma chapter members there plus members of several other Washington motorcycle clubs. The Outsiders Tacoma clubhouse is the oldest continuously operating outlaw motorcycle clubhouse in the Northwest, the walls and ceiling are covered with outlaw motorcycle club history dating back to the early 1960's and stepping through the front door was like stepping back in time until we remodeled it in 2016. With the Tacoma chapter doing what we were doing in the motorcycle club world, our clubhouse had become a regular gathering spot for all the most respected clubs, and they did not let the weather keep them away. This night was no different as we had several Bandidos, a couple Resurrection MC Members, and several other guests. Rob had just started shaving my arm, and Double D was taking pics of me and sending them to Portland to stir the pot, when I hear what I knew from all my years in ski racing to be the sound of a pack of snowmobiles headed towards the clubhouse. We stopped what we were doing and headed out to the front yard just in time to see Ron the President of the Hells Angels Nomads Washington, Jammer their Sergeant at Arms, and a couple of prospects ride up on snowmobiles. Now, I have never seen snowmobiles on Hilltop, so that was unique to me, and most of the residents of low-income hilltop have never seen a snowmobile, but Hells Angels wearing their patches and riding snowmobiles on Hilltop, now that was really something different. The sound of the approaching snowmobiles had drawn several of the neighbors outside to investigate the strange noise, and just like during our parties, the sight of all the bikers and now Hells Angels on snowmobiles held their attention like we were the most interesting episode of Sons of Anarchy ever. After saying our hellos and talking in the front yard, we all went back inside, and I settled back in for my tattoo. Once Rob had finished mine, he ended up giving Tommy his members tattoo on the back of his head, and Mavrick got his on his upper left arm. When we were done Double D took a pic of all of us showing our tattoos and sent it to Portland to let them know it was done and they could either make an issue of it or shut the fuck up and move on. What we had done was consistent with the bylaws,

T-Bob's line about having a different set of by-laws was a total bullshit lie, and if they wanted to do something it was going to have to involve conflict and violence, and Portland knew they could never win against Tacoma.

Member tattoo is a term that describes any tattoo which requires the permission of the club for the member to get the tattoo. A traditional member tattoo will typically be the club's colors tattooed somewhere on the member's body. Most will try and put this tattoo in a visible location, while some may put them where they can easily conceal them. All my tattoos were strategically placed to where they could easily be covered with clothing and would not show below my sleeves if my arms were extended, with none above my collar line. Other club tattoos I had and which you will find versions stylized particular to the members respective outlaw motorcycle club and are used by other outlaw motorcycle clubs included my 1% diamond which contrary to what law enforcement claims means that I was proudly claiming I was part of the one-percent of motorcycle club world that lives outside the law, actually just meant that I was a proud member of a one-percent outlaw motorcycle club and part of the top one-percent of motorcycle clubs in the world, the elite of the elite. I know their version sounds way more ominous, sexy, and they have maintained it unopposed for almost seventy years, but mine definition is the reality, and I will evidence this with the fact that we were very much living and working within the law, trying to pass laws, and helping other outlaw motorcycle clubs try and pass laws that protected the constitution and civil rights. That is hardly a criminal lifestyle. Rather than spoil the rest of my story, I am not going to ask you to make your decision on the validity of my statement just yet and reserve your decision and base your opinion on the culture on what I've present throughout the course entire book.

Examples of member tattoos from various outlaw motorcycle clubs

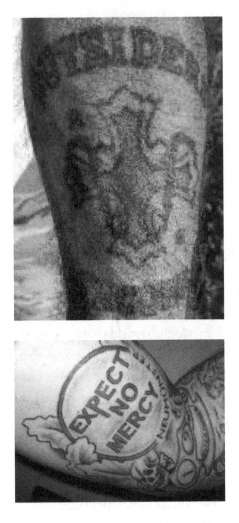

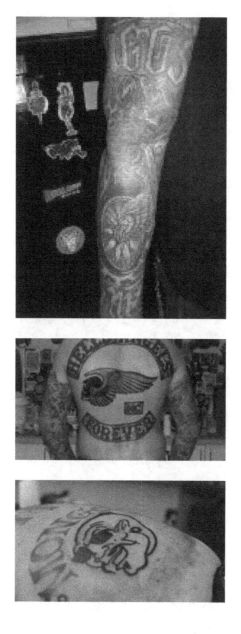

I had several tattoos which were not club controlled tattoos but were directly associated to the club, or something club related and included the Tacoma T on my right arm intended to show my pride in being a member of the Tacoma chapter of the Outsiders Motorcycle Club. I had the letters O.F.F.O (Outsiders Forever, Forever Outsiders) on several of the tombstones in the cemetery on my right shoulder as a memorial to the fallen Outsiders, the devil gunner wearing my serape on my right forearm to symbolize my role as a protector and enforcer for the club, the giant safety pin my sponsor Spanky gave me on my right arm, a one-percent diamond with Tacoma-T on my left arm, and an exact replica of my Tacoma bottom rocker tattooed on my right side.

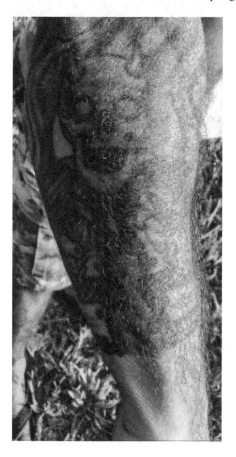

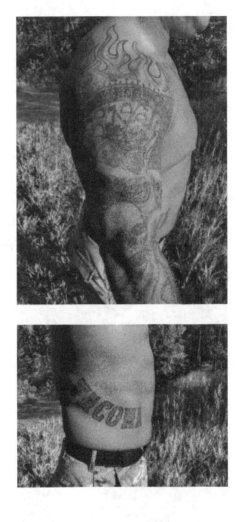

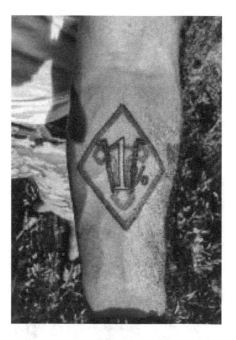

In addition, I had several tattoos related to my time in the outlaw motorcycle club world that Rod had given me when I was running around with the Hells Angels and includes a large demon warrior and Viking battle scene on my right calf in which there are several one-percenter related symbols like a 1% diamond to show my pride in being a one-percenter, SS bolts to show that I had taken care of business and committed acts of bravery, Facta Non Verba (Deeds Not Words) across my collar bone, and the phrase "Snitches are a dying breed." on my leg in the battle scene.

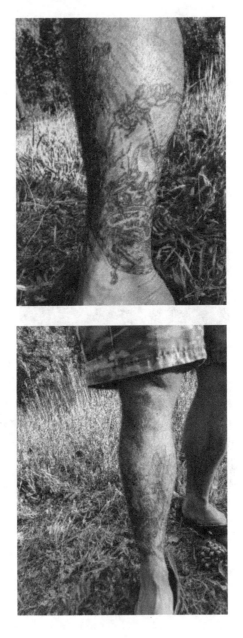

I did not just go slapping on tattoos like a lot of guys do these days. I had earned my respect in the club and the community by living by the one-percenter code, living my life dedicated to loyalty, honor, respect, and brotherhood, and by adhering to that self-imposed moral code of deeds not words. I was not just a member of an outlaw motorcycle club; it was my religion, and it was influencing if not dominating every aspect of my being. So, when I got my tattoos, they made sense to the community. I was not just a painted pony like so many of the guys these days, all my tattoos had stories behind them, many had stories about getting them, most were given to me by respected one-percenters from other prominent one percent outlaw motorcycle clubs, and all of them were earned.

Regardless of the club, most outlaw motorcycle clubs view member's tattoos and club related tattoos as property of the club. The rules may vary slightly from club to club, but generally if a member leaves in good-standing they are allowed to keep their tattoos although some clubs may require that they out-date them, which means to add the date they quit the club to their primary or any club related tattoos. It is a different story if the member leaves in bad-standing, in which case they may have their tattoos forcibly "X"d out, blacked-out, scrubbed off with a rigid steel wire brush, sanded off with a belt sander, burnt off with a stream iron, or cut off with a knife. While I have never personally seen or heard of the Sons of Anarchy burn it off with a torch method being used, it is not a stretch to think that some sick son of a bitch out there has tried that method of tattoo removal at one point over the years. The 1960's and 70's were a volatile crazy time in the outlaw motorcycle club world due to methamphetamine and un-diagnosed and untreated P.T.S.D. in the guys coming home from Viet Nam. How the member's tattoos were handled all depended on what the member did to the club to deserve to be kicked out bad.

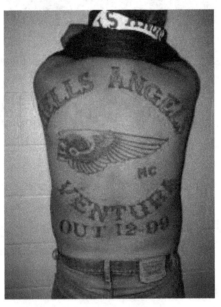

Out in "Good standing"

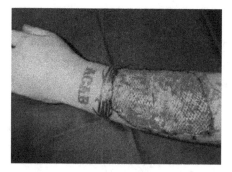

Out in "Bad standing"

The way I looked at it, I knew the rules and consequences when I got my tattoos, I understood my level of commitment, and I felt like if should I ever do something to deserve to be kicked out, I would gladly accept the consequences because they would no longer be badges of honor, I was worthy of wearing. Basically, if you get club tattoos, earn them, live up to them, and be a man and accept the consequences like a man if you fuck up. That said, taking club tattoos or even forcibly blacking them out anymore is getting increasingly rare and clubs have proactively begun to discontinue the process anticipating it would be twisted into some sort of kidnapping and torture R.I.C.O. indictments by the feds which it now has. Instead in many cases these days' former members are simply given a specific amount of time in which they must cover their tattoos or face the consequences. This practice has proven moderately effective, but I know of several former one-percenters who were thrown out of their clubs for being legitimate shit-bags and given a time limit to get them covered, they ignored it and are still running around with their tattoos.

Like I said, the motorcycle club world is changing and somehow, I went from repossessing tattoos, to being told to stand down and forced to watch lames that stole the clubs honor run around with my flag after they have disrespected the entire club. I wasn't alone and I know several other one-percenters from different clubs that had lived through the wars and that transitional period in the club culture, and this new millennial, huggy, give them a chance, avoid conflict at all cost one-percent world that was emerging was totally foreign to us, and we could see important pieces of the culture, foundational beliefs and traditions, being done away with and the effect it was having on motorcycle club culture and club life was not one we liked.

27

OUTSIDERS AND ALOHA

Double D and I had built a strong national buzz in the motorcycle club community, the unification of the Washington motorcycle club community and the motorcycle profiling movement, and we were asked to speak at the Western Regional N.C.O.M. convention in Honolulu, Hawaii in January. Lucky Les from the Bandidos MC, Irish McKinney from the A.D.G. MC, and Jim Gibbons from Christ's Disciples MC were going to represent the Washington C.O.C., and we decided that since it was in Hawaii and the threat level was low, we would bring some of our brothers and their ol'ladies, so Single D, and Pecker Paul from the Portland chapter joined us with their ol'ladies, along with our ol'ladies.

I cannot remember why but for some reason Double D could not fly out with the group and had to take a separate flight. I didn't like him flying by himself but there was nothing we could do, so that left me, Single D, Pecker Paul and our ol' ladies flying out ahead of Double D, and then he and his wife would meet us. We had an early 5:00am flight and as we were checking in at the airport, I noticed that we had both uniformed and plain-clothes surveillance on us. As we moved through the airport the plain-clothes guys stayed with us and the uniformed guys disappeared when we got into line for our security check. Our brother Pecker Paul was in a wheelchair and a friendly T.S.A. agent ended up pulling us all out of line unexpectedly and told us that we could all bypass the line because Paul was in a wheelchair. Once on the other side we took the train to the concourse and then grabbed a quick breakfast, during which I noticed that our surveillance had rejoined us. I joked to the group that they were not fucking with us because I am with the group and they do not want to end up on YouTube and said if we had Double D, they would not even think about fucking with us because he'd drop an "Article 1, Section 7" on them. A reference to one of Double D's favorite quotes about unlawful search and seizure from the Washington State Constitution. After breakfast we headed to the gate, but we were still early and the gate which sat at the end of a long concourse was empty.

With time to spare, Candace and I decided to go get a coffee at Starbucks back down at the concourse. We did not pass anybody on the way down to Starbucks and I was standing in the doorway watching who was going up towards the gate since the fellas were up there, and I did not observe any threats. As Double D and my status elevated in the motorcycle club community and the profiling movement continued to gain momentum, the amount of law enforcement surveillance we received increased, and Candace had started to notice it and make her own jokes about them. She did not like the surveillance and I always felt bad she had to endure it, but like me knowing what I got myself into when I went prospect for the club, Candace knew what she got herself into when she went on that first date with me, and she was committed so she just shrugged it off as best she could. As we waited for our coffee Candace joked about our surveillance and said that they probably waited until she and I came down to get coffee before they vamped on the fellas to fuck with them since they did not have Double Jesus' or Twitch's protection. "Double Jesus" was a nickname I came up with for Double D and the fellas adopted to help keep his head in check after he spoke on the steps on the Oregon capitol during one of their motorcycle rights rallies, and we happened to get a perfectly timed photo of him with rays of sun beaming down into his hands off the golden statue on the top of the capitol building. As an ol'lady it is totally unacceptable to disrespect a one-percenter president, but Candace had earned a lot of respect from the club over the years and she and Double D were very good friends, so occasionally she would drop some great Double D comments knowing she could get away with it, and it would crack us all up. This was another one of those instances and she was good enough to test it with me in private first before dropping her first Double Jesus in front of the fellas.

As Candace and I walked back, we rounded a slight bend in the concourse and saw a group of several Port of Seattle Police officers surrounding the fellas. When the officer facing me made eye contact with me, he said something, and all the officers left and exited out of an unmarked door between me and the group. The fellas told me that as soon as I had left them, the cops came out of nowhere and started questioning them about me, Double D, where we were going, what our plans were, etc. The fellas said they did not say shit and as soon as they saw me, one cop told the others, let's go and they left. We were on our way to speak at a motorcycle rights convention and have a vacation in Hawaii, there was nothing nefarious going on, nothing that warranted surveillance, and certainly nothing that warranted the contact and questioning, but this was a typical example of the type of profiling that all motorcycle club members endure. Additionally, it was clear that Candace was right, they waited to fuck with the fellas until I was not around the group which means law enforcement clearly viewed me as a threat or high value target, and there were folks with a much higher pay grade working me and Double D and providing "intel". We made our flight, and it was time for some drinks and a little Hawaiian vacation with my brothers. I was stoked.

We arrived in Hawaii, got zero hassle from the cops at the airport, and took a limo to the hotel. The limo ride with Single D and his ol' Lady Puppy to the hotel was a lot of fun. They had never been on a plane before or ridden in a limo, so they were having the times of their lives and it was great to share that experience with them. I had been to several national and regional N.C.O.M. conventions and the hotels were always pretty nice, so I was shocked when our limo pulled up in front of dumpy high-rise hotel that was badly in need of renovation and about five blocks from the beach. Wow, this is the best they could do. What the fuck? The inside was as bad as the outside but if this is where the convention is this was where we would stay. We would later find out that Richard and Joey Lester and the N.C.O.M. attorney's booked in rooms at a nice resort on the water and stuck the bikers in the dump assuming that we would not be able to afford rooms at the nice resort because we were bikers. Fuck them, we were there to have a good time and we were about to.

As we were waiting to check-in, Double D and his wife arrived. We were all starving and agreed to drop our bags in our rooms and meet back in the lobby to go find lunch. Double D and I were waiting in the lobby for Single D and Pecker Paul when we noticed a huge man with long white hair, a long white beard, and wearing a Hawaiian shirt and shorts, get dropped off across the street by a taxi. Immediately we both said, "I wonder what club he's from?" As he got closer, we could see he had tattoos on his arms but could not tell what they were. Double D said, "Based on his size, I bet he's Sons of Silence." Lots of clubs have members that are huge, but the Sons of Silence MC seems to have more huge guys than any other club and Double D was right, he was in fact Sons of Silence. As he entered the lobby Double D and I walked up and introduced ourselves to the giant. He set down his bag, took Double D's hand, cracked a big smile and said "Boar, National Vice President of the Sons of Silence Motorcycle Club. Good to meet ya!" He turned and gave me the exact same introduction. Boar is a very respected old school Sons member and was J.R. Reed's bodyguard. When J.R. died, Boar stepped up and continued J.R.'s legacy with N.C.O.M. and the C.O.C. Boar is a man of honor and integrity who has gone to great lengths to protect his club and the motorcycle club culture, and while I did not know it at the time, over the years our relationship would develop to point that we considered each other brothers.

When everyone gathered in the lobby, we headed down the street towards Waikiki beach in search of a place for lunch and drinks. With it being early afternoon on Waikiki, all the restaurants were packed, and Double D has the patience of a three-year-old, so we bounced between three or four different restaurants looking for one that could seat us immediately before finally deciding to wait in line at a bar on the second floor of a building where we could sit outside overlooking the beach. It was great, we sat there enjoying each other's company, people watching and planning how we were going to spend our trip. The Hawaii Bandidos had invited us to dinner that night and we were excited to meet them and find out what a Hawaiian Bandido was like. Inevitably, the talk turned to the motorcycle profiling movement. The enthusiasm from all the motorcycle clubs, not just from Washington but on the national level, and momentum we were having with our motorcycle profiling bill was invigorating and Double D and I were constantly scheming about ways we could unify the club community nationally, educate them, and help them pass profiling bills like the one we were attempting to pass in Washington. Speaking at this regional N.C.O.M. conference was an excellent way for us to do that.

Twitch and Double D having lunch on Waikiki Beach.
Photo by Candace Burns

We went back to the hotel and had a few drinks. Bandido Lucky Les had been telling us how his Hawaiian brothers were looking forward to taking us to dinner and had some place special lined up which had us excited because we were all in the mood for some real Hawaiian food, but when the call came in on where to meet the Bandidos for dinner, it was the Old Spaghetti Factory. We had one right down the hill from the clubhouse in Tacoma. To us, Old Spaghetti Factory is a chain restaurant that serves overpriced knock-off Italian food, but to the Bandidos from Hawaii it was first rate, and it was the only one in the state, so it was special. Then came another huge cultural difference.

Over dinner the Bandidos explained they did not understand why we had come to Hawaii because they do not have a problem with motorcycle profiling since they're all pretty much family, so the cops are their brothers and sisters, some guys have been in three or four clubs, all the clubs get together once a week to BBQ, and law enforcement harassment is not an issue because the cops are their relatives. It was shockingly different from motorcycle club life on the mainland. Regardless, my dinner was good, the company was great, and we drank and laughed together for hours. The Bandidos were great hosts, offered us bikes to ride and showed us a great time while we were in Hawaii.

From left to right: Outsider Pecker Paul, Outsider Single D, Bandido
Lucky Les, three Hawaii Bandidos MC members, Outsider Double D,
and Outsider Twitch.
Photo by Candace Burns

The next day was the main portion of the N.C.O.M. conference. There were club members from Washington, California and Colorado representing the mainland but most club members in attendance were from Hawaii, and they could not have looked less interested in what we had to say about motorcycle profiling and using public records to develop a pattern of evidence. It was clear they did not have the same problems with law enforcement in Hawaii as we do on the mainland, but they listened to us and afterwards they all wanted to hangout, have drinks, and take us on the short ride around the island.

Motorcycle club members from Hawaii, Washington and California look on as N.C.O.M. board member and ABATE of Washington C.O.C. Liaison Irish McKinney addresses the room. Rest in peace brother and thanks for everything you did to protect the culture.

Members of various motorcycle clubs from the west coast and
Hawaii socialized at the N.C.O.M. convention in Honolulu, HI.

Hanging out with the other clubs after we spoke was a unique experience. The motorcycle club culture in Hawaii is similar to the culture on the mainland but at the same time it is very different. The major one percenter clubs were a relatively new phenomenon in Hawaii at this time with the Bandidos and Vagos being the first to open chapters in Hawaii, after patching over members from homegrown Hawaiian one percent clubs, and the Hells Angels only had a support club there at the time. Because all the clubs were homegrown, they did not have the history of club wars and violence like motorcycle clubs on the mainland and everyone got along. You may have fathers and sons in different motorcycle clubs, and methamphetamine was not tolerated. It was a great environment, and I am glad I got to experience the Hawaiian motorcycle club culture.

Another highlight of the trip for me was the time we spent with Lucky Les. Les is another great one-percenter and man of honor who I am proud to have called brother even though he was a respected officer in the Bandidos Motorcycle Club. Double D and I had gotten close with Les working with him as Lt. Commander in the U.S. Defenders and this trip to Hawaii with him and his ol'lady had really allowed us to bond. Irish had been appointed the A.B.A.T.E. Liaison to the Washington C.O.C. and was there in that capacity which allowed us to spend some more time with him. The brotherhood between the Washington motorcycle clubs was real at this point and spending time together representing Washington in what felt like a foreign country only strengthened that bond and became infectious to the clubs around us.

Bandido Lucky Les, Outsider Twitch, Outsider Double D, and our wives.

Hawaii gave us all a chance to do some very nontraditional biker bonding. The little bar where we had our first lunch had become our go-to spot in the evenings and we had made friends with a kick-ass Hawaiian reggae band called Natural Vibrations. We spent multiple evenings hanging out with Peni, Galen, and Wayne from the band, they showed us a great time while we were in town, and we attended several of their shows at different venues. If you like reggae, I highly recommend you check them out.

Natural Vibrations

During the days, we would spend our time doing the standard tourist activities. We hiked Diamond Head, went snorkeling at Hanauma Bay, and spent time wandering around checking out the various markets and galleries. It was a great time and just the trip we needed to recharge for our battle with the profiling bill.

Double D cruising Waikiki after stealing
Pecker Paul's scooter.

Left to right: Double D, Pecker Paul and Twitch at a Natural
Vibrations show.
Photo by Candace Burns

Double D and Twitch at the top of Diamond Head, Oahu, HI. January 2010.
Photo by Candace Burns

28

VICTORY IN WASHINGTON

We came home from Hawaii and held the annual Black Thursday event that same week. There was noticeably less law enforcement presence this year, in fact there was no visible law enforcement presence. Our motorcycle profiling bill had dozens of sponsors in both the House and Senate and there did not appear to be any legislative opposition. We had back-to-back public hearings scheduled in front of House committee on Public Safety and Emergency Preparedness, and the Senate Judiciary committee.

We had proven the U.S. Defenders was an effective tool, so we sent out a Call to Action requesting that all available motorcyclists show up to the hearing as a visible show of unity and support. The response was tremendous, and both the hearings were packed with members of all the various motorcycle clubs of Washington, leaving the room lined with aids, reporters, lobbyists, and civilians who had come to watch the hearing. It looked very us against them and was an unmistakable demonstration of unity and show of force. It was fucking beautiful! Pig Pen and I took a seat in the front row and once all the rows behind us were filled to capacity with club members, I set up a camera in the middle of the aisle to film the proceedings. Double D was going to testify on behalf of the Washington Confederation of Clubs and U.S. Defenders, and Donnie "Mr. Breeze" Landsman would be testifying on behalf of A.B.A.T.E.

Since all the legislators were familiar with the issue of motorcycle profiling from our previous hearing, Double D began this hearing by focusing on the motorcycle profiling incidents that had occurred over the last year and the cost of not implementing our motorcycle profiling bill which would have no cost associated with it. He discussed the recent $90,000 judgment against the Washington State Patrol for discrimination and profiling a motorcycle club member and reminded them that the trooper involved was the same trooper who admitted under oath to using the tactics from Basic Biker 101 regardless of an existing injunction prohibiting their use. His testimony was strong, well evidenced and made sense to everyone in the room. The only opposition who appeared to testify was the Washington Association of Sheriffs and Police Chiefs (WASPC). The Policy Director for WASPC testified that the bill would ultimately have a staggering $2.7-million-dollar fiscal impact to local governments and agencies. The committee was not persuaded and gave our bill a unanimous do-pass recommendation. When the bill passed there was a brief eruption of cheers that almost immediately stifled itself because everyone remembered we were not allowed to applaud, but our excitement was almost uncontrollable. We were doing it again, we were making history together, and we were determined to get our bill passed into law and protect our culture and the Constitution.

Once outside in the hallway it was hugs for everyone. There were over thirty motorcycle clubs in that hallway, but we were all brothers and proud American patriots. After the hugs we hopped on our bikes and rode back to Tacoma. Double D and I went to his house and spent the afternoon watching the video I had shot of the hearing repeatedly. We researched the fiscal argument that the policy director from W.A.S.P.C had made and developed a counter argument that clearly proved her argument was a total bullshit lie. Then Double D practiced his testimony for the following morning's hearing in front of Senate. The Senate Judiciary committee had never heard Double D testify before, but word of Double D and the horde of patriotic bikers had spread, and the hearings were now drawing spectators wanting to see what we were all about.

The hearing the next day was standing room only, and this time we had bikers from Oregon and Idaho in attendance as well. Double D was allowed to speak first, and the committee chair Senator Klein warned him that he would be restricted to five minutes testimony. However, Senator Klein forgot to set the timer and Double D was allowed to speak for over twelve minutes, during which time he unloaded with what he had prepared and was able to clearly outline a need for legislative relief and defeat every argument that the policy director for W.A.S.P.C. had made the day before.

The W.A.S.P.C. policy director was a cute little brunette in her late twenties that stood maybe 4'11" with her heels, and I kind of felt bad for her as the entire room watched her visibly short-circuit in her seat when Double D destroyed WASPC's one and only argument opposing our bill and prove it was lies, but she was there representing a corrupt element of law enforcement who was our enemy, so in that moment she was our enemy. She was able to compose herself enough that when Senator Klein gave her the floor she simply agreed with Double D's analysis and appeared as if she wanted to run out of the room and cry, but before she could Senator Hargrove took the opportunity to tell her that every Senator present thought W.A.S.P.C.'s fiscal analysis was "bogus". Then one of the Senators asked Double D where he went to law school. The legislature had gone from looking at us like a bunch of dumb bikers a few years ago to showing us respect and assuming Double D was an attorney. We were changing their perception of bikers and if we could do it with them, we could do it with the world. By the end of the hearing, we had received another unanimous do-pass recommendation and for the first time our bill would be headed to the floor of the Senate for a vote after a short stop in Rules. It was a fucking great outcome, and we were all elated.

Because W.A.S.P.C. had asserted there would be such a huge fiscal impact, the Public Safety and Emergency Preparedness committee sent the bill to Appropriations for analysis. We knew that W.A.S.P.C.'s bullshit fiscal report could delay or even kill our bill, so once again we used the U.S. Defenders to issue a Call to Action requesting a public hearing be scheduled for the House Appropriations committee, and once again we were successful, and a hearing was scheduled. It was becoming clear that the legislature no longer looked at us as just some bikers but as a legitimate political force with an issue of public concern that deserved attention, and that gave me a real sense that we would be successful this legislative session. Once again, Double D prepared well evidenced testimony that refuted every claim made by W.A.S.P.C.'s fiscal impact statement.

Simply put, our bill would require law enforcement agencies to integrate a policy statement and training into their current policies and procedures which would have absolutely no economic impact, and the costs of ignoring the problem of motorcycle profiling could easily amount to millions of dollars in judgments against law enforcement for civil rights violations. At the Appropriations hearing, W.A.S.P.C. sent the policy director's boss to testify in her stead, he was totally unprepared, and it appeared as if law enforcement was relying on just putting an officer with an impressive history and title in front of the legislature as being all they would need to defeat the bikers and their silly bill, but they were wrong. W.A.S.P.C.'s representative fell on his face, and it was clear to everyone in the room that their bullshit fiscal impact statement was a deliberate attempt to use their credibility as law enforcement to mislead the legislature and public because they did not support our bill and had no way to defeat the pattern of motorcycle profiling evidence we had built and our fiscal analysis. Taxes pay W.A.S.P.C staff's salaries and the fact that the Washington Association of Sheriffs and Police Chiefs would waste precious taxpayer dollars to deliberately craft and argue a false fiscal analysis in an attempt to defeat our clearly needed civil rights bill was a total corrupt misuse of public funds, a betrayal of their oath to protect and serve, and it was sickening to me. They spent citizen's money to craft a lie in an attempt to defeat a bill, so they (law enforcement) could continue to victimize us and violate our civil rights unrestrained when they swore and oath to protect and serve. Regardless, the Appropriations committee found their fiscal analysis to be bullshit and ended up giving our bill a unanimous do-pass recommendation.

As a last-ditch effort to derail our bill, W.A.S.P.C. proposed an amendment to our bill in Executive Session. Their amendment changed the fundamental definition of motorcycle profiling, eliminated critical language, and even went so far as to limit motorcycle profiling to incidents that occur only when an individual is operating a motorcycle and would offer no protection from the profiling incidents that occurred when we were not on our motorcycles. To counter W.A.S.P.C.'s move we sent out another Call to Action, this time requesting a floor amendment to correct the definition of motorcycle profiling, and we had a representative file a floor amendment correcting the definition. Law enforcement had tried to pull some sneaky shit and we effectively countered like professionals, we were bikers and the bulk of us leading the movement were one-percenters. I was so proud of us. It was awesome and we were a force to be reckoned with, but we were not out of the woods yet.

On March 5th, 2011, the Senate unanimously passed SB 5242 addressing motorcycle profiling. The bills primary sponsor Senator Hargrove offered a floor amendment Enjoined Senate Bill ESB 5242 that required law enforcement to adopt a policy condemning the practice of motorcycle profiling and integrate training into their current programs to address motorcycle profiling. It also preserved the original definition of motorcycle profiling which was modeled after the states definition of racial profiling and details a broad range of profiling incidents. The companion bill, HB 1333 sat in rules and missed the cutoff period. We were on the verge of making history but all we could do at this point is sit back and nervously wait.

While we waited, we had something to celebrate as a community, my documentary *What It's All About* was finally ready for release. What had started as dash cam footage of motorcycle profiling and some motivational videos for bikers on YouTube had evolved into a feature length guerilla style documentary that told the story of the unification of the motorcycle club community of Washington state, the formation of what would eventually become the historical national grassroots American Motorcycle Profiling movement, and it served as a how-to video for Confederations of Clubs to follow across the United States who wished to purse similar legislation. The University of Puget Sound had been so supportive of my/our project from early on that when it was time for the film to be premiered, they graciously offered to host a screening of *What It's All About* in one of their auditoriums.

On March 7th, 2011, *What It's All About* premiered to an audience of several hundred motorcycle club members and independent motorcyclists from Washington, Oregon, and Idaho, as well as many U.P.S. students. The film was incredibly well received and after the film; me, Pig Pen, Double D, Lucky Les, Mr. Breeze, Rotten and the C.O.C. attorney Marty Fox took questions from the audience. It was interesting to hear the student's thoughts on the film and motorcycle profiling. They were incredibly engaged and could not believe that motorcycle clubs were nothing like what they had learned from the media and T.V. Many expressed shock that they had been so misled about motorcycle club culture and found it heroic and inspirational that we unified as a community to stand up for ourselves, our rights, and to protect our culture. By far the panel session was my favorite part of the screening.

Promotional poster for What It's All About.

Left to right: Twitch (Outsiders MC), Pig Pen (Outsiders MC), Double
D (Outsiders MC), Mr. Breeze (A.B.A.T.E. / B.O.L.T.), Lucky Les
(Bandidos MC), Rotten (Unchained Brotherhood MC), Martin Fox
(Attorney for Washington Confederation of Clubs)
Photo by Irish McKinney

Twitch answering audience questions at the University of Puget
Sound screening of What It's All About.
Photo by Irish McKinney

Before I move on, I would like to take a moment to express my sincerest gratitude and appreciation to Rotten from the Unchained Brotherhood MC for all his help and hard work with the editing of the film.

Those hours upon hours spent drinking Monsters with you and working on this film is an experience I will always treasure; I love you brother and am always here for you if you need me.

Another brother who I could not have had the impact with this film that it has had is my brother Irish McKinney from A.D.G. MC. Irish provided many of the still photos used in the film and in this book. Irish came from the civilian world into the club world and when I first met him, he did not really understand motorcycle club protocol and almost got himself beat up a few times. Over the years, he would become a key leader in the motorcycle profiling movement, a critical link between A.B.A.T.E and the Confederation of Clubs, a respected member of A.D.G. MC, a member of the N.C.O.M. Board of Directors, and someone I would call my brother and was willing to take a bullet for just like one of my own. He rode the shit out of his motorcycle, protected motorcycling and motorcycle club culture on a national level, was respected by many, and made a fucking difference. Unfortunately, Irish was killed in a motorcycle accident and is no longer with us. I love and miss you brother.

There were too many great people who assisted us to list them individually, but I want to say thank you to all the motorcycle club members, Candace, Puppy, and all the other ol' ladies who provided footage for the film, as well as the University of Puget Sound for all their support. To be able to make this film with you all has been truly an honor and a privilege. I really appreciate all your help, trust, and support. We did something great together and I will always be proud of what we made.

With a March 25th cut-off date, when we had not heard anything by March 15th, we sent out another Call to Action requesting a public hearing. Double D and I were checking for movement on the bill multiple times a day and could not understand why nothing was happening. Were they just trying to appease us and planning on running the clock out on our bill and tell us better luck next time? It made no sense. When the responses to our Call to Action began to come back, we got our answer. Chairman Hurst explained to us that members of A.B.A.T.E. contacted his office and other committee members after ESB 5242 passed the Senate and requested that a hearing not be scheduled because the wording of the Senate's version was not in line with the goals of A.B.A.T.E. Chairman Hurst said that due to the five-day public notice requirement we would not be allowed to schedule a hearing and assured us that our bill would move through quickly next year.

We were pissed! Who the fuck would have contacted a Representative and say we didn't support the Senate's version of the bill? Mr. Breeze was doing a great job serving as the liaison between the Defenders/C.O.I.R. and A.B.A.T.E., and I knew there was no confusion in our mission and message since I had joined the Tacoma A.B.A.T.E. chapter and was regularly attending their meetings. When Double D contacted Mr. Breeze and other A.B.A.T.E. leadership they were equally outraged. It turned out some glory hound decided if he could not shine in A.B.A.T.E. and have his name out front on this bill, he would sabotage it so nobody could.

Undeterred, Double D did some research of the rules governing the House of Representatives and found an exception to the five-day notice requirement under Rule 24, which allowed the Speaker of the House to approve a hearing on issues previously heard in committee in cases that demanded it. Another Call to Action was put out via the U.S. Defenders, and letters articulating the exceptions to the five-day rule were sent to Chairman Hurst and the other Public Safety and Emergency Preparedness committee members, requesting that a hearing be scheduled in consideration of the circumstances and the Constitutional implications of motorcycle profiling legislation. Once again, we were successful and a public hearing for ESB 5242 was scheduled for the next day.

The U.S. Defenders sent out another Call to Action requesting that all the motorcycle clubs send representatives to the hearing as a show of our unity and support for the bill, and this time the room was overflowing, and many patch-holders and civilians were left standing in the hallway. Double D was ready for this one and so was the committee. His testimony was concise and focused on the bullshit fiscal impact assertions W.A.S.P.C. had made in an attempt to derail our bill, and it was clear that he had the support of the full committee. W.A.S.P.C. knew they were defeated and did not even appear to testify in opposition to our bill this time, and once again our bill received another unanimous do-pass recommendation and was on the way to the floor via the Rules committee. The U.S. Defenders issued one final Call to Action urging every representative to vote in favor of ESB 5242 and on Friday April 1st, 2011, the Washington State House of Representatives unanimously passed ESB 5242. We were thrilled and together as a community, the motorcycle clubs of Washington state had made history by passing the first law addressing motorcycle profiling in the United States. Even more exciting was that since ESB 5242 unanimously passed both the House and the Senate, the Governor could not veto our bill even if she wanted to.

Our new motorcycle profiling law would provide motorcyclists in Washington with protections that would prove to substantially reduce motorcycle profiling in Washington and gives motorcyclists the same type of constitutional protection against law enforcement discrimination and profiling granted under the state's racial profiling law. All law enforcement in Washington were required to adopt a written policy condemning motorcycle profiling and the Criminal Justice Training Commission was required to address the issue of motorcycle profiling in their required basic law enforcement training. Specifically, the new law defines motorcycle profiling as "the illegal use of the fact that a person rides a motorcycle or wears motorcycle-related paraphernalia as a factor in deciding to stop and question, take enforcement action, arrest, search a person or vehicle with or without legal basis under the United States Constitution or Washington State Constitution."

On the steps of the capitol the day of the bill signing.

On April 13th, 2011, the Governor was scheduled to sign our bill. Double D, Pig Pen, and I met Lucky Les, several Bandidos, members of other motorcycle clubs, and representatives of A.B.A.T.E. on the steps of the capitol. We had a short meeting with Representative Steve Kirby in his office before heading to the bill signing. Like always, we were all wearing our colors and the sight of all the various club members drew friendly and amused stares as we walked the halls and crossed the rotunda in the capitol building. When we arrived at the room where the bill signing was to take place, we had to wait for them to open the room and allow us in. I was surprised that there were no metal detectors or even visible law enforcement presence at the signing, and they just allow the public in with the Governor unscreened, but that's how it was at the time. Surprisingly, the cute little policy director from W.A.S.P.C.

showed up for the bill signing which I thought was a really classy and brave move on her part, and it earned my respect.

A group photo showing W.A.S.P.C.'s Policy Director standing just to my left Sleazy Senator Pam Roach is standing next to Representative Kirby wearing a white leather jacket.

When they opened the doors, we all piled in and made sure the W.A.S.P.C. policy director got put right up front. She is the pretty brunette with the bright red face next to me and Pig Pen in the photo. Senator Hargrove showed up for the signing wearing leather chaps, a leather vest, and a do-rag. And for some reason even though she did everything she could to trick bag us and help law enforcement kill our bill, corrupt Senator Pam Roach took it upon herself to photo-bomb our bill signing. She would later ask for the C.O.C.'s support with her reelection and we would tell her to go fuck herself.

The Governor sat in a large high-back chair at the end of one of the longest conference tables I have ever seen. At the other end was a half dozen photographers. The Governor read the bill and then signed it as we all looked on and the photographers snapped away. Double D had made a big deal about how he wanted the ceremonial pen that the bill was signed with, so as soon as the pen left the Governors hand, PigPen reached in and swiped the pen. Then we all posed for a group pic with the Governor, and it was over. ESB 5242 became R.C.W. 43.101.419, it was officially the first law in American history that addressed the problem of motorcycle profiling by law enforcement, and it was the product of a grassroots rights movement that was spearheaded by the motorcycle clubs of Washington State.

Double D, Lucky Les and I had wanted to see if we could get our photo with the Governor. We knew she had to take a group photo with us during the bill signing but figured she would bow out of a photo with one-percenters who were the founders of what would become one of the most effective grassroots rights movement in American history. Turns out we were wrong, and she graciously agreed to pose for a photo with us. While I may not have agreed with her politically, I personally believe she treated us with respect both when we were in the room that day and with this next part of the story, and for that she has my respect.

From left to right: Lucky Les, Washington Governor Christine
Gregoire, Double D, and Twitch.
Photo by Irish McKinney

Law Enforcement uses the media as their tool to spread their propaganda about motorcycle clubs, destroy the motorcycle club's reputations, and even try and manipulate the political climate of the club
world and incite violence amongst the clubs. The situation with our
motorcycle profiling law was no different and a week after the bill signing Jim Camden published a photo in the Spokesman Review along
with an article about how the Governor had taken a photo with a cop
killer. In the age of Sons of Anarchy, the media snapped it up and by
the noon the photo and versions of the article talking about Governor
Gregoire taking a photo with a cop killer and outlaw motorcycle gang
members had spread around the world.

Governor Christine Gregoire immediately after signing our bill into law. This photo and identifying those of us in it would become the focus organized crime investigators throughout the state.
Photo by Jim Camden, The Spokesman-Review

At our weekly club meeting the Outsiders decided it was time to speak up. Outlaw motorcycle clubs had rarely spoke to the media previously, but our brother PigPen was being misrepresented and his honor tarnished, so we decided it was time to set the record straight about what happened December 12th, 1979. Double D prepared the following press release that was then approved by the entire club and the Washington C.O.C. before release.

Press Release: Confederation of Clubs of Washington State
Re: Controversy surrounding motorcycle profiling bill signing on April 13, 2011.

In the days following Governor Gregoire signing ESB 5242, a bill addressing motorcycle profiling, there has been controversy surrounding the fact that the Governor took a picture of the signing with a "cop killer" The Confederation of Clubs serves as the official voice of motorcycle club members present at the bill signing and would like to address this controversy.

Describing Robert Christopher as a "cop killer" instead of a victim of the most notorious law enforcement scandal in the history of Portland, is biased and unjust. On the night of December 12, 1979, members of the Portland police department and narcotics squad illegally raided the Outsider Motorcycle Club clubhouse in Portland and Officer David Crowther was shot and killed by Robert Christopher. Officers were knowingly attempting to serve an illegal warrant obtained through perjured statements about a nonexistent informant.

Narcotics officers Scott Deppe and Neil Gearhart, both present during the raid, corroborated this indisputable fact and furthermore revealed that the narcotics squad officers had come with drugs ready to plant in and around the clubhouse. In fact, it was discovered that police had planted amphetamine tablets during the raid. Narcotics officers also admitted that drugs were removed from David Crowther's pockets at the hospital after he was shot.

These are incontrovertible facts. The entire basis for law enforcement's presence at the Outsiders clubhouse that night was to serve an illegal warrant and plant drugs. Robert Christopher was released after serving 14 months in prison because of the egregious conduct of the narcotics squad was uncovered.

Robert Christopher maintains that the police did not announce themselves and that his only choice to avoid being killed was to defend himself. It was later proven that police witnesses lied at trial when they testified that they had knocked and announced themselves. Although his death was a tragedy, David Crowther and the officers on the narcotics squad were corrupt and 58 tainted convictions were overturned before the scandal was over. Robert Christopher was defending his home and his life against an illegal intrusion and criminal conspiracy perpetrated by Portland narcotics officers.

Robert Christopher's presence at the bill signing on April 13th was understandable and appropriate. As a victim of police abuse and discrimination, Robert Christopher has put his energy into fighting for the rights and freedoms of motorcyclists because he understands firsthand the impact of law enforcement discrimination and abuse. Washington's law condemning motorcycle profiling is the first of its kind in America. Robert Christopher was vindicated and is now a free and voting citizen and had as much business as anybody in the Governor's office on April 13, 2011.

David Devereaux
Spokesperson
Confederation of Clubs
Washington State

(All claims made in this statement are based on publicly available and previously published material readily available. For example, The Oregonian, April 21, 1981, "Retrial of Christopher for killing appears doubtful." The Times-News, May 29, 1981, p5, "Narcotics trade triggers police misconduct.")

National Public Radio reached out to us hoping to interview Pig-Pen. The reporting ended up being fair, balanced, and told the truth about the incident. Governor Gregoire did a televised address siding with us and saying that it would have violated the bill she was signing into law to exclude us from our own bill signing. With that, all the negative publicity stopped. Because it did not involve us murdering anyone or trafficking drugs, and the truth involved dirty cops, the mainstream media turned a blind eye to the fact that a bunch of outlaw bikers helped unite the Washington motorcycle club community and then passed a law condemning motorcycle profiling by law enforcement, but Double

D and I did several interviews for various domestic and international biker radio shows and media outlets. I have got to say, it felt pretty cool reading an article about what we had done and my documentary in the September 2011 issue of Easyriders magazine, but the hands down the coolest thing was what happened at the Mountain Jam Motorcycle Expo.

The Mountain Jam is an annual motorcycle show that takes place over three days at a large convention center just on the Washington side of the border with Oregon and draws motorcyclists from all over the northwest. With the media coverage of the bill passing and the documentary, the organizers of Mountain Jam had asked me to come down and make an appearance at the show. One of the positive articles that was written about us passing the bill had been picked up by the A.P., was run across the country and got a brief story on C.N.N. which mentioned that I would be appearing at the Mountain Jam Motorcycle Expo that weekend. The Mountain Jam was a cool experience for me. The show had given me a booth and I screened a copy of my documentary *What It's All About* and fielded questions from the public about motorcycle clubs and the motorcycle profiling movement. Since it was right on the border, several of our Portland brothers and the Oregon motorcycle clubs attended the show and that made it a lot of fun. The Oregon clubs were excited to talk to me about the profiling law and really wanted Double D and I to help them try and pass a profiling bill of their own. There was also interest in starting to hold joint Washington/Oregon C.O.C. meetings throughout the year to help keep us all on the same page since most of the Oregon one percent clubs also had chapters in Washington.

Twitch speaking to motorcyclists at Mountain Jam 2011.
Photo by Candace Burns

It was just before lunch on Saturday when I noticed an older, nicely dressed woman and a man approximately her age walking towards my booth with purpose. Neither looked like they had ever ridden a motorcycle which really piqued my curiosity. When she got to the booth, I was busy talking to some people and as I finished my conversation with them, she watched my documentary *What It's All About* that was playing and grabbed copies of the literature I had about the movie and motorcycle profiling. As soon as the people I had been speaking with walked away, the woman began speaking to me about profiling and motorcycle clubs. She had a level of confidence and professionalism that I was not used to seeing in the women who spent time around the motorcycle world, and she was so comfortable with how she addressed me that it made me feel like she felt like I should know who she is.

After several minutes of speaking about motorcycle profiling, law enforcement harassment and motorcycle club culture, I had to stop mid conversation and ask. Excuse me, should I know who you are? "Oh, I apologize, I'm former U.S. Congresswoman Linda Smith and I haven't had a day off in twenty-eight days, but I heard about what you guys did and I wanted to come down and meet you, introduce myself, and tell you that I think what you all did is the most American thing I have ever seen. I am proud you are from Washington and if there is ever anything that I can do for you all please let me know."

Former U.S. Congresswoman Linda Smith (R) and Twitch at
Mountain Jam 2011.
Photo by Candace Burns

It was like I got kicked in the balls and my eyes began to tear up because it was one of greatest compliments I have ever been given, and when you're an outlaw motorcycle club member there are never compliments from the mainstream let alone from people in positions of respect, you expect the world to look at you unfairly as a gang member and a criminal, so for a former U.S. Congresswoman to use her first day off in twenty eight days to come to tell me that what we did was the most American thing she's ever seen, it absolutely floored me. We spent almost forty-five minutes talking, she told me all about her non-profit Shared Hope International that helps rescue girls and women from sex-trafficking, and she gave me a copy of her book *Renting Lacy: A Story of America's Prostituted Children*, which explores the traumas endured by young girls who are forced into the commercial sex industry. It was truly an honor to meet Ms. Smith and I commend her on her noble work.

As a result of the new motorcycle profiling law, incidents of motorcycle profiling in Washington were reduced by 85%-90% and law enforcement surveillance of motorcycle club runs, and events is not near the problem now that it was.

The fallout that resulted from our success passing the profiling bill into law and the photo with the governor extended to me personally and professionally almost immediately. Even though I had done nothing wrong and only helped unify the motorcycle club community, start a successful grassroots rights movement, followed the processes laid out in the U.S. and Washington Constitutions, and helped pass a bill into law intended to protect American citizens and their Constitutional rights from the abuse they had been suffering at the hands of law enforcement for almost fifty years.

For approximately the last six months of our legislative push I had been working an investigation against members of a Mexican drug trafficking organization that was operating in western Washington. As part of that investigation, a week prior to the bill signing we had executed search warrants on multiple targets during which we not only seized a large of amount of narcotics and cash, but also seized their cell phones, computers, and other electronic devices. At the time, the backlog for computer analysis and forensics with the state's crime lab was over a year which would have caused all sorts of problems for my investigation and the solid case I had built and ultimately referred to the Attorney General for prosecution of over seventy major felony charges against multiple defendants. To avoid this delay, we got approval to send the electronic devices to the Washington State Gambling Commission Organized Crime Unit for forensic analysis since they had a Special Agent in-house who was trained and certified to conduct the computer forensics work and would be able to complete the work in a month or less, allowing us to maintain the integrity and timeliness of my investigation.

The week after our profiling bill was signed into law, I got a call from the Special Agent who was handling the forensic analysis and he advised me the work was complete and I could come down and take possession of the devices and results from the analysis. We set an appointment for me to meet him at his office in Olympia to take possession of the devices and review the results. Up until this time, I had never worn any clothing or jewelry during my work hours that would identify me as a member of a motorcycle club, and I deliberately wore long sleeves to keep my club tattoos covered, even during the hottest days of summer. The office the Special Agent worked out of was similar to the offices a lot of us who work undercover use, and it was located in a building with no other law enforcement agencies in it, in a non-descript office that did not identify it as belonging to the agency or unit and was on a secured floor, so the Special Agent had to come down and see me up. When I arrived at his office, I called up to the Special Agent to let him know I had arrived, and he was waiting for me when I walked into the lobby of the building.

The building was an older building with one of those slow, noisy elevators from the late 70's and as we waited for the elevator to arrive, I noticed the Special Agent looking me up and down, clearly checking me out for some reason. Since I worked undercover every day I was dressed for the part and was wearing a plaid long sleeve shirt, Dickies jeans and my black Georgia boots. The wallet I used had a chain attached to it like a lot of biker wallets, but this chain was a little thicker and was made as a gift for me by a member of another motorcycle club. While I was clearly dressed and carried myself like a biker, I had no visible club indicia, but this Special Agent was clearly checking me out and since I knew he was with the Organized Crime Unit, I knew he was not telling me something and I wanted to see if I could get the canary to sing. "What's up man, are you thinking about asking me out, you want a kiss? What's your deal?" The special agent stammered "Ahhh, Ahhhh, Ahhh, the chain. I recognize your chain from the photo with the Governor. Every gang unit and organized crime unit in the state has been studying that photo since the day you guys took it trying to identify you guys. "You're Twitch!" His tone was excited like I was a Hollywood celebrity, and I could not tell if it was because he had identified me and connected the dots when others could not, or in awe because I was the very first top tier outlaw biker that he had ever met, and I also happened to be an undercover investigator. "What are you talking about? I don't know what you're talking about." I said, playing dumb and sticking to the outlaw biker code that we do not give any information to the cops. "You have to be him, it's the same chain and you're the guy wearing it standing right next to the governor in the photo", he said. I have no idea what you are talking about I said, as the elevator hit the ground floor and the doors opened. A flood of people came out of the elevator, and I was really expecting him to say he could not bring me up to his office, but instead he said nothing, and we boarded the elevator. As we rode the elevator we proceeded to engage in small talk, and he tried to ask me questions about the one-percenter world to which I continued to play dumb. When we reached his office, we both took a seat and we proceeded to review his findings and he showed me how to access and interpret the results so that I would be prepared to discuss them with the assistant Attorney General and provide court testimony should that be needed.

As I reviewed some of the photos and text messages recovered from the phones the Special Agent was working on his computer, when suddenly the Special Agent exclaimed, "I knew I was right!" and spun his computer monitor around to show me the screen which had the photo of all of us with the Governor at the bill signing. I stuck to my initial story and refused to acknowledge it was me even though it clearly was and asked the special agent what the men in the photo did wrong. They are gang members, and they just passed a law to protect their criminal activity from us and they got into the same room as the Governor. No man, that is not what I see in the photo. I see a group of Americans who were suffering abuse from a corrupt element of law enforcement simply because of who they choose to associate with and how they dress, that stood up for themselves, acted like Americans and patriots in their situation are supposed to, and used the legislative process to try and obtain relief from the abuse they were suffering. I don't see anything criminal there and certainly nothing that would warrant the time and resources you guys have been spending on trying to identify everyone in that photo when they've done nothing illegal." They have all got criminal records and PigPen murdered a cop! He exclaimed. "Nah man, you know that isn't true and you know it because I guarantee that in the time since we've been in your office you've run me and know I don't have any criminal record, so if that is me in the photo you just deliberately lied to me to try and evidence your bullshit claim." Come-on he said, we know you guys passed that law to protect your criminal enterprises and PigPen killed a cop. "No, from what I've know about it, PigPen shot a dirty cop in self-defense, a dirty cop who came to Pig-Pen's house with an illegal warrant and other dirty cops to assault and kill members of the Outsiders M.C. and plant drugs to frame them, and the legislature passed the law because cops with bullshit prejudices like you were totally abusing their civil rights for no reason, assaulting them, even murdering them and getting away with it because they know bikers don't cooperate with cops, even if it's against dirty cop's."

Ahhhhhhhh, fuck. Is that really true? He asked inquisitively. "You've known me professionally for quite some time and you know I have no criminal history, if that is me in the photo, what makes more sense to you, that I'm an organized crime member who busted my ass to help the motorcycle clubs get along and start a national grassroots rights movement to protect my criminal enterprise but I have no criminal history, carry a badge like you, and don't display any other personal indicators that I'm involved in organized crime other than because law enforcement says so, or does my version that these are good men who simply love riding motorcycle and brotherhood that passed a law to protect themselves from decades of law enforcement persecution for those beliefs and associations?", I asked. The cop took a long pause and then responded, well if you guys did it for the reasons you say you did, that is really cool. Thanks for your help with my case, I said as I stood up and shook the Special Agents hand and then grabbed my box of evidence, had him sign the chain of custody form and left for the long drive back to my office, assuming my boss would be receiving a call from him about his discovery before I could get back. To my surprise, either he did not call my boss, or my boss simply did not care when he did call because I never heard anything from my boss about my motorcycle club membership. However, shortly after this contact my agency held a special meeting to discuss my motorcycle club membership and how they could terminate me for being a "gang member." When they ran my termination up the pole to the Attorney General, they were informed that it was not illegal to be a gang member and with consistently excellent performance reviews and no criminal history, the A.G. told them they could only fire me if I broke the law and committed a crime.

Determined on trying to fire me, my agency launched two different bullshit internal investigations against me, the first alleging that I had sexually harassed a five-foot tall, 350-pound, illegal Mexican who was one of the suspects and a senior member of the drug trafficking organization I had been investigating. The second investigation alleged that I used my state credit card to steal one gallon of gasoline once every month when I would fill my undercover vehicle. I was not worried about either investigation since I had both video and audio taped the interview with Princess Short-Round from the cartel, and I knew I never stole any gas, so I figured the investigations would be closed almost as soon as they started, however after completing interviews about the allegations with two different internal investigators who were so outmatched when it came to their interview and interrogation skills that I found the interviews amusing, especially the second one during which the investigator hammered me for stealing gas and treated me like a criminal, but when I demanded to see the credit card bills that evidenced me stealing gas and she allowed me to review the bills and demanded that I explain the charges, it was a simple explanation that destroyed their case. The charges showed that once every month I would fill my gas tank and then immediately after the fueling charge there would be a second fuel charge for around six dollars. This type of charge always occurred at the same gas station where I would wash my undercover vehicle once a month, and it was clear that when I was buying a car wash via the pump when I fueled up, the charge for the car wash was identified on the bill as a fuel charge rather than a car wash. There was no evidence I was involved in any criminal activity but in the State's frenzy to frame me for a crime so they could fire me for being Twitch, this was the only thing they could grab onto and try and attempt to either frame me or cause me to get pissed off enough that I quit and solve their dilemma for them.

Their game was clear, and I was pissed but I knew it would piss them off even more if I maintained my cool and stayed on the job just to spite them. Plus the four day a week gig worked great with the club life and I really didn't want to give that up, so I decided to use my extensive interview and interrogation training and experience to have a little fun with the investigator and beat her down with logic about the allegations, her attempt to frame me in order to fire me, the Constitution, and her undeniable corruption, to the point where she was visibly purple faced, sweating, shaking, tearful, and my boss had to step in and stop the interview before I totally broke her mentally. It was so much fun and incredibly satisfying.

As we walked out of the interview my totally ineffective idiot of a union rep turned to me a said "I've never seen anything like that. You didn't need me in there, I think you did great." I knew I had fun with the corrupt bitch and felt some personal satisfaction from being able to fight back without exposing myself to being terminated and knowing they would never have her interview me again, but I knew this was not the last of the willful and unconstitutional abuse I would suffer at the hands of my own government and employer. In fact, even though the video and audio of the interrogation of Princess Short-Round totally exonerated me from the sexual harassment allegation, they had nothing to disprove my explanation of the fuel charges, and I had no further contact from Internal Investigations regarding the allegations, but they kept those two internal investigations open against me with no findings for over two and a half years, until late in 2015 when my then boss stood up for me and confronted our Chief and the Director and told them that they had been running investigations against me for over two and a half years with no findings of wrong doing while I continued to received excellent performance eval's, they were violating my employee rights and opening not only the agency and administration up to a lawsuit by me but also himself, and he didn't want to become a defendant. A few weeks after he confronted them, they finally closed both investigations against me with no findings of any wrongdoing.

This was the kind of stuff I have dealt with my entire adult life because I chose to be part of the outlaw motorcycle club world, but I knew what I was getting into and it was the life I chose, so I didn't complain and just continued to focus on working with Double D and the leaders of the other major one percent motorcycle clubs to use our success to motivate the rest of the country to unify and try for their own legislative success. Little did I know that my story was just getting started and passing the motorcycle profiling bill in Washington would lead to some of the greatest and most dangerous adventures of my life, I would go on to become one of the most respected and influential outlaw motorcycle club members in American history, and what should have been a story about riding motorcycles and brotherhood, became a complex spy story full of dirty cops, violence, intimidation, betrayal and murder, which you can read all about in my next book in the *Patriot Gangster* trilogy; *Patriot Gangster: Volume 2, The Enforcer.* The best is yet to come!

ABOUT THE AUTHOR

Jeff "Twitch" Burns, CDEP, CMAS

Without exception, Jeff "Twitch" Burns is the most authoritative Subject Matter Expert on Outlaw Motorcycle Clubs (OMC's) and Outlaw Motorcycle Gang (OMG) Investigations in the world, and his unique experience and expertise allows him to translate seemingly impenetrable outlaw motorcycle club realities and share insight and perspective at a level far beyond any other expert. When it comes to his life in the outlaw motorcycle club world, Jeff was mentored by notorious Hells Angels enforcer's "Mouldy Marvin" Gilbert and Josh Binder. Jeff spent over twenty-two years as a prominent member of the outlaw motorcycle club world, and was a well-known and respected one-percenter (1%er) in arguably one of the most influential outlaw motorcycle clubs in the U.S. Proving himself to be fiercely loyal to his motorcycle club and the culture, he epitomized the roles of brother, bodyguard, enforcer, and freedom-fighter, and his actions helped shape modern outlaw motorcycle club culture. Unlike any other expert on the subject, Jeff has been involved in numerous closed-door meetings with the highest-ranking leadership in the 1% outlaw motorcycle club world from all the most powerful Outlaw Motorcycle Clubs in the country, as well as been a guest in their clubhouses, homes, and businesses, giving him an unequaled base of knowledge on the subject. Additionally, Jeff helped unify the motorcycle club community on the national level for the purposes of fighting law enforcement harassment and helped pass the first two laws addressing Motorcycle Profiling by law enforcement in the United States (Washington & Maryland). Jeff produced the award-winning guerrilla documentary *What It's All About*, which chronicles the unification of the Washington state motorcycle clubs and the birth of the American Motorcycle Profiling Movement, and in 2014, he was nominated for induction into the American Motorcycle Hall of Fame in two categories: Leadership and Motorcycle Rights.

Professionally, Jeff is nationally and internationally recognized as an elite counter-terrorism expert and covert operator. He has over twenty-five years of international high-threat protective services and covert operations experience in both the government and private sectors, which includes ten years of law enforcement experience conducting complex undercover operations. Jeff has completed over 8,500 hours of advanced level special operations and law enforcement training, he is board-certified in Dignitary and Executive Protection (CDEP), a board-Certified Master Anti-Terrorism Specialist (CMAS), U.S. Department of State Worldwide Protective Services 2 (WPS2) qualified and holds numerous advanced special operations and firearms instructor certifications. Jeff is now retired and continues to serve as a Counterterrorism and Outlaw Motorcycle Club Subject Matter Expert (SME), Director of the non-profit Burns Group International Counterterrorism Training Center, Technical Advisor to the film, television and gaming industries, Adventure Travel Expedition Leader, and Public Speaker.